MW01273495

FOUR YEARS
IN
BRITISH COLUMBIA

VANCOUVER ISLAND.

AN ACCOUNT OF THEIR FORESTS, RIVERS, COASTS, GOLD FIELDS, AND RESOURCES FOR COLONISATION.

By COMMANDER R. C. MAYNE, R.N., F.R.G.S.

Indian Family migrating

WITH MAP AND ILLUSTRATIONS.

LONDON:

JOHN MURRAY, ALBEMARLE STREET.

1862.

BRITISH AND UNITED STATES BOUNDARY LINE—YAHK RIVER.

FRONTISPIECE.

TO

CAPTAIN GEORGE H. RICHARDS, R.N.,

OF H.M. SURVEYING SHIP 'HECATE,'

UNDER WHOM I HAD THE HAPPINESS TO SERVE DURING

THE TIME I WAS IN THE COLONIES I HAVE

ATTEMPTED TO DESCRIBE,

THIS BOOK IS DEDICATED, BY HIS SINCERE FRIEND,

THE AUTHOR.

PREFACE.

So little is yet known about British Columbia and Vancouver Island that the Author hopes his experience of four years, spent in the survey and exploration of both these Colonies, may be found of interest.

To Dr. Wood, R.N., of H.M.S. 'Hecate,' to the several travellers from whom information has been obtained and whose names occur in the book, as well as to the others— too many to enumerate—who have assisted him in various ways, the Author begs to return his thanks.

To Mr. E. P. Bedwell, R.N., Dr. Lyall, and Dr. Lindley, for the sketches which enliven the text, his thanks are also gratefully tendered ; and last, but by no means least, to Mr. William J. Stewart—without whose aid these pages would probably never have seen the light — he gives his most cordial thanks.

For any errors which may occur in the latter part of the book the author claims the reader's indulgence, as the revision of it has been carried on in great haste amid the bustle of fitting out a ship for foreign service.

H.M.S. 'Eclipse,' October, 1862.

CONTENTS.

CHAPTER I.

CHAPTER VIII.

CHAPTER IX.

CHAPTER X.

CHAPTER XI.

CHAPTER XII.

CHAPTER XIII.

CHAPTER XIV.

APPENDIX.

(xi)

LIST OF ILLUSTRATIONS.

FOUR YEARS

IN

BRITISH COLUMBIA AND VANCOUVER ISLAND.

CHAPTER I.

Appointment to H.M.S. 'Plumper' — Historical Sketch of the British
Possessions in North-West America.

In February, 1857, I received my appointment as Lieutenant
to H.M.S. 'Plumper,' then at Portsmouth, fitting out for
service at Vancouver Island.

This distant possession, and the adjacent mainland of
British North America, were then little known and still less
heeded. What little was known of them, from the chance
visits of explorers, and their more recent occupation by the
Hudson Bay Company for the purposes of their great fur-
trade, may be very briefly stated.

The Spaniards were the first Europeans who set eyes
upon the coasts of the Pacific. During the earlier half of
the sixteenth century they busied themselves at intervals in
exploring it. At that time Spain and Portugal were the two
great maritime powers of Europe, and there had been
concluded between them a treaty, which the Pope was
expected to confirm; by which, while the latter nation was
to enjoy all rights of discovery and possession eastward of a
meridian line passing 370 leagues west of the Cape Verd

B

Islands, to Spain were to pertain all seas and lands west of that line.

There was another maritime power in Europe, however, which, although of little importance then, was destined one day to eclipse theirs totally. The rising navy of England was little disposed to consider itself bound by an arrangement that closed so many seas and shores against it. Nor was the English people, flushed with its recent repudiation of the Papal power, inclined to submit without a struggle to the partition of the unknown world by the Court of Rome. Elizabeth did not understand, it was explained to the Spanish ambassador, "why her subjects should be debarred from traffic in the Indies. As she did not acknowledge the Spaniards to have any title by donation of the Bishop of Rome, so she knew no right they had to any places other than those they were in actual possession of. As to their having touched here and there upon a coast, and given names to a few rivers and capes, these were such insignificant acts as could in no way entitle them to a proprietary farther than in the parts where they settled and continued to inhabit."

The adventurous mariners of that time were ready enough to act in the spirit of Elizabeth's protest, and entered upon the career of discovery in the West energetically. It must be confessed that they sometimes went beyond it, and the Gulf of Mexico—and later the southern shores of the Pacific—were haunted by free-traders and freebooters, who, carrying their defiance of Papal authority and Spanish prohibitions to an extent somewhat unjustifiable, plundered the Spanish settlements of the coast, and took and sacked their trading vessels. For a time it seems that their dread of the passage of the Straits of Magellan kept them from the Pacific; but at length the reports which reached England of the wealth that lay there mastered their fears, and Drake in his first voyage round the world came there in 1578. A year later, when he started to return, gorged with the spoil of the coast, being anxious to avoid the passage of the Straits of Magellan, where he might be intercepted by the Spaniards, he sailed west and north-west, thinking to reach home by that way. He is supposed to have got as far north as the 42nd—by some it is asserted the 48th—parallel of latitude, when, meeting adverse winds, and the wintry, foggy weather telling seriously upon his crew enervated by their stay in the sunny south, he was forced to return.

In his wake came, among others, Cavendish, to the same shores upon the same errand.   In the year 1587, he captured a galleon near Cape St. Lucas, the southern extremity of California.   Setting fire to the vessel he landed the Spanish crew upon the friendless, desolate shore, where they were like to perish of exposure and starvation.   Fortunately, however, a storm blew their deserted vessel ashore in their immediate vicinity; and repairing it as well as they could, they set sail and in time reached Europe.   Among them there happened to be a Greek sailor, named properly Apostolos Valerianos, but more commonly known by the designation used by his fellows —Juan de Fuca, of whom we shall have to say more hereafter.

About this time that search began, which our own days have seen concluded, for a northern passage of communication between the Atlantic and Pacific Oceans.   The English and the Dutch had already prosecuted it eagerly, and vague reports were rife in the maritime world of its having been at one time or other really made.

Among them the following narrative was current.   It will be found related at full length in an historical and geographical collection called 'The Pilgrim,' published by Samuel Purchas, in 1625, under the title of 'A Note made by Michael Lock the elder, touching the Strait of Sea commonly called Fretum Arrianum, in the South Sea, through the North-west Passage of Meta Incognita.'   The following is a summary of Mr. Lock's narrative.

That being at Venice in the year 1596, upon business connected with the Levant trade in which he (Mr. Lock) was concerned, he came across an old man, aged 60, called Juan de Fuca, but named properly Apostolos Valerianos, a Greek mariner, an ancient pilot of ships. The account which he gave of himself was that he had come from Spain to Florence, whence, finding one John Douglas, an Englishman, a famous mariner, ready coming to Venice, he had accompanied him thither. This John Douglas, to whom the Greek seems to have been communicative, being acquainted with Mr. Lock, gave him knowledge of the old pilot, and brought them together that his brother Englishman might in his turn listen to his passenger's yarns; and so we are informed that, in many long talks and conferences, the following story came out.

Apostolos Valerianos, by his then name of Juan de Fuca, professed to have been in the West Indies of Spain for forty years, and had sailed to and fro many places in the service of that power. He happened to be in the Spanish ship which, in returning from the Philippine Islands, was taken off Cape California by Captain Cavendish; upon the occasion of that capture, losing 60,000 ducats of his own goods.

Subsequently to this event he had been in the service of the Viceroy of Mexico, and on one occasion had been sent with a small caravel and a pinnace up the shores of California, now called North America. He reached the latitude of 47°; and there finding that the land trended north and north-east, with a broad inlet of sea between the 47th and 48th parallels, he entered the same, sailing therein more than twenty days,—still finding land, trending sometimes north-west, and north-east, and north, and also east and south-eastward, with much broader sea, islands, &c. So he sailed until he came to the North Sea, finding it wide enough everywhere, and then, being unarmed, and the native people being savage, he returned, and was not rewarded for his services. Having thus a grievance with Spain, he was willing to serve England, by whom he hoped to be recompensed for his loss, by Captain Cavendish, who by this time was dead. And if His Majesty would but give him a ship of 40 tons' burden, he undertook on his part to perform the North-West passage in thirty days.

Upon this Mr. Lock wrote to Lord Treasurer Cecil, Sir Walter Raleigh, and Master Richard Hakluyt, the famous cosmographer, and prayed them to disburse him 100*l.*, to bring the pilot to England, his purse not stretching so wide. To his request came an answer, that the action was well liked and greatly desired by his correspondents in England, but no money; and the Greek pilot sailed for Cephalonia, his native place. Mr. Lock, it further appears, at a later period corresponded with him there, and he wrote in reply, stating that he was ready to come with twenty companions and fulfil his promise, but that money was indispensable, for he had been utterly undone in the ship 'Santa Anna,' taken by Captain Cavendish. No money, however, was forthcoming until much later, when Apostolos Valerianos, being then an old man, at the point of death, could not take advantage of it.

This story of the old Greek pilot's was long current in England, and, although it was considered legendary by some, it generally met with credit. There were not many, however, who had the courage or the fortune to test its accuracy. As late as the year.1769,—although we know that long before that time the shores of the Atlantic as high as the 74th parallel of latitude, had, in the search for the long-desired North-West Passage, been explored and taken possession of by the Hudson Bay Company,—little, if anything, of the Pacific above the 43rd parallel north was known. About that time, however, the Spaniards sailing north came upon the mouth of the Columbia River, while the Russians began to push down from their far-away settlements at Kamschatka. But it was not until the year 1776 that the British Government, having thirty years before offered a reward of 20,000l. to whoever should make the passage between the Atlantic and Pacific from either sea, commissioned Captain James Cook to examine the shores of the latter ocean. His instructions were to sail for the 45th degree of latitude north. Having reached it he was to make his way northward to the 65th, searching in his course for rivers or inlets pointing towards Hudson or Baffin Bays; taking possession, by the way, of the new lands he might discover, in the name of his master, King George.

In March of the year 1778, Cook sighted the coast at 44°, sailing thence up to 48°, where he named the projecting point of the shore Cape Flattery. Southward of Cape Flattery, Cook examined the coast with minute care, having it in his mind to decide for ever upon the truth or falsity of the story of Juan de Fuca's discovery, which had so long been current. The old pilot, in his account, had put it between the 47th and 48th parallels of latitude. Examining this extent of the shore carefully, and with no success, Cook authoritatively pronounced the Greek's story a fiction, and sailed on past the wide strait that now bears Fuca's name, stopping at Friendly Cove and Nootka Sound, which he took to be part of the main shore. It was not, indeed, until ten years later that Captain Berkeley, an English seaman in charge of a merchant-vessel, found that a passage of some sort existed, immediately north of Cape Flattery. He did not explore it, but a year later an English naval officer on half-pay, Captain Meares, coming upon it, named it the Strait of Juan de Fuca, and sailed up it in a boat some thirty leagues, until, attacked by the natives on the northern shore, he was forced to return.

A few years later there were matters of difference between the Governments of Spain and Great Britain relative to the north-west coast of America and the navigation of the Pacific; and in the year 1792, Captain Vancouver, an officer in the English navy—and not, as has been often erroneously supposed, a Dutchman—was despatched to Nootka, to settle, with the Spanish Commission, named for the like purpose, what lands, buildings, and vessels seized there by Spain should be restored to England, and the amount of indemnification that should be paid her.

In addition to the official business upon which he was despatched, Vancouver was directed to explore the coast of the Pacific, from the 35th to the 60th parallels of north latitude, and to look out for any water passage, which it was still thought might be found connecting the two oceans; particularly the Strait of Juan de Fuca, reported as recently rediscovered. On Vancouver's reaching Nootka, he found the Spanish Commissioner had not arrived, and proceeded to survey the Strait of Fuca, Admiralty Inlet, and thence northward. On the 22nd June, 1792, as he was returning to his ship from Jervis Inlet, he met the 'Sutil' and 'Mexicana,' two men-of-war, commanded by Signors D. Galiano and C. Valdes, and forming part of the Spanish exploring expedition. These officers exchanged information in the most friendly way. Then separating, Vancouver, after long and difficult navigation, forced his way between the islands of the Gulf of Georgia and through the strait named by him Johnstone, coming at length into the Pacific, at Queen Charlotte Sound, 100 miles north of Nootka. The island thus discovered it was decided should bear both their names, and will be found designated in all but quite recent maps, Quadra and Vancouver Island.

Let us now inquire what was known of these regions from the eastern side of the great American continent. The first to reach them, crossing the Rocky Mountains from Canada— the first at least who left the impress of his name there—was Mr. Simon Fraser, an employé of the North-West Company, an association formed in Canada to rival the Hudson Bay fur-trade. Mr. Fraser, penetrating the range of mountains from Fort Chipewyan, in 1806, formed a trading establishment upon a lake bearing his name, situate on the 54th parallel of latitude. Later, rival American fur companies were formed, and in 1810 the most important of them, the Pacific Fur Company, having at its head Mr. Astor, a German merchant of New York, founded the well-known, unsuccessful settlement bearing his name at the entrance of the Columbia River.

Before this time, the shores of the Pacific, the theatre of these comparatively unimportant events, attracted little if any attention from the Governments, who were yet prepared to lay claim to their exclusive possession, whenever their occupation should appear valuable. About this period, however, the attention of the American Congress was directed to the districts through which the Columbia flowed; and the subject being referred to a Committee of the Senate, a report was made by it, that all the territory in question, from the 41st to the 53rd, if not to the 60th degree, belonged to the United States. Their claim to its possession was grounded upon the purchase of Louisiana from France in the year 1808, and the acquisition of what titles of discovery and occupation might be possessed by Spain, by the Florida Treaty of 1818; together with the rights conferred by the settlement of American citizens there. No active steps, however, ·to enforce these pretensions were taken until 1823, when President Monroe, in his Address to Congress, asserted that the American continent was henceforth not to be considered as subject for colonisation by any European Powers.

There were but two Powers with any pretensions to oppose the claim of the United States to the exclusive possession of the shore of the Pacific, viz., Russia and Great Britain. The former had for many years been settled in some force at Sitka and the neighbourhood. Both by Great Britain and the States of America, the right of Russia to the districts which she had in some measure colonised was readily conceded. In 1824 a convention was entered into between that Power and America, by which Russia bound herself not to encroach south of a line drawn at 54° 40′, and in the following year Great Britain entered into a similar treaty; both nations thus confirming the claims of Russia, but careful in no way to compromise their own, to the country south of the line of boundary thus laid down.

It can serve no purpose to rake up the yet live embers of the irritating and difficult boundary dispute between this country and the United States, relative to the possession of that portion of the shore of the Pacific which has since proved so valuable. It is sufficient to say, that by conventions renewed at intervals, the territories and waters claimed by either Power west of the Rocky Mountains were declared to be free and open to the vessels, citizens, and subjects of both; until, urged by their growing importance, and the impatience of settlers east of the Rocky Mountains to colonise them, the boundary question assumed the importance of a great political crisis, more than once threatening to result in war. Happily this was averted, and in 1844, by a treaty, the details of which were settled at Washington by Mr. Richard Pakenham on behalf of the British Government, the line of boundary from the Rocky Mountains to the sea was declared to be the 49th parallel of north latitude. The course which the line should take upon reaching the sea—fertile as it has been and may still be in difficulties and misunderstandings— was thus declared to continue to "the centre of the Gulf of Georgia, and thence southward, through the channel which separates the continent from Vancouver Island, to the Straits of Juan de Fuca." It was subsequently found that there were three separate channels existing between the island and the mainshore, and contention arose as to the construction of the treaty in respect to them.

In the year 1856 the American Government appointed a commission to settle this disputed line of boundary after it reached the sea-coast, as well as to determine the course which the parallel of 49° took across the continent.

The English Government in their turn appointed Commissioners for the like purpose. Captain Prevost was the first
selected, and in the autumn of 1856 was ordered to commission H.M.S. 'Satellite' and proceed to Vancouver Island. It
was then discovered that no accurate chart of the channels in
dispute between the island and the mainshore existed; that
the position and extent of the group of islands among them
were very imperfectly known; while the relative value of the
channels themselves could only be arrived at from such
meagre information as the masters of two or three Hudson
Bay Company's trading vessels were able to give. It was
therefore determined that a surveying vessel should also be
despatched—in the first place to make a complete survey of
the disputed waters, and afterwards to continue it along the
coasts of Vancouver Island and the mainland of the British
territory. For this purpose Captain George Henry Richards
was selected, and commissioned H.M.S. 'Plumper.'

The 'Plumper' is what is called in the navy an auxiliary
steam-sloop, barque rigged, of 60-horse power, and armed
with two long 32-pounders and ten short ones, of a pattern
which has now nearly gone out of date. She had been paid
off from a long cruise on the West Coast of Africa the day
before Captain Richards commissioned her, and it was not
to be wondered at that when she came to be " overhauled "
in the dock she was found very rotten in some parts. It was
discovered also that she would be very inefficient for the surveying work unless a chart-room were built on deck, and
accordingly this had to be done. Owing to these causes her
preparation for sea was greatly prolonged, and we were not
ready for a start till the middle of March.

Captain Richards was well known both as a surveyor and
an Arctic explorer, he having been the Commander of Sir E.
Belcher's ship the ' Assistance,' in the search for the remains
of the Franklin expedition, and having while there made one of
the longest and most harassing sledge-journeys upon record.

He had previously assisted in the surveys of the Falkland Islands, New Zealand, Australia, &c.   Besides the command of this survey, Captain Richards received an appointment as Second Commissioner for the settlement of the boundary, in conjunction with Captain Prevost.   Of the other officers, Mr. Bull, the master, was the principal surveyor, and with him were Messrs. Pender and Bedwell, then second masters, now masters.   These three, with the captain, made the whole of the surveying staff at starting.   Of course in five years several changes have taken place.   On Mr. Bull's death Mr. Pender became the senior assistant-surveyor, and other junior officers have learnt the work and have been added to the strength of the survey.   The surgeon, at that time Dr. Forbes, undertook the Natural History and Botanical departments; but he was likewise changed.   He was invalided when the ship arrived at Valparaiso, and relieved by Dr. Lyall.   Subsequently when the Land Boundary Commission, under Colonel Hawkins, arrived at Vancouver Island, Dr. Lyall was detached from the ship to them, and his place taken on board by Dr. Wood.

The repairs which were found necessary before the 'Plumper' could start for so long a voyage, kept us in Portsmouth Harbour till the 11th of March, on which day we made our trial trip on the measured mile in Stokes Bay. The average speed obtained was six knots (nautical miles of 2000 yards each) per hour, which, although as much as we expected from the horse-power of the vessel, we afterwards found by no means adequate to the rushing currents in the inner waters between Vancouver Island and British Columbia.

Recurring to my description of our destination, I may remark that the manner in which the northern shores of the Pacific are parcelled out is simply thus.   From the Mexican boundary, as far north as the 49th degree of latitude, the Americans hold possession; a few colonists at long intervals being thinly scattered over the states of Oregon and Washington. Vancouver Island had in the year 1843 first been occupied by the Hudson Bay Company, a party of whose employés, landing at Victoria, had settled there, building a fort and laying the foundation of what became an important trading station. In 1849 a grant of the island to the same Company was made by the Home Government, upon condition that within five years steps should be taken by the lessees for its perfect colonisation. What steps were taken, however, proved unsuccessful; and at this time, beyond a somewhat prosperous station and farm at Victoria, a fort at Rupert, in the north of the island, and a small settlement at Nanaimo, no use of Vancouver Island was made by the English. Of the mainland, secured to Great Britain by the boundary treaty of 1844, and known then as New Caledonia, the same Company also held possession under a similar grant. It was used by them exclusively for the purposes of their fur-trade, a few forts at distant intervals sheltering them from the Indians and serving as trading stations.

North of the British possessions the Russians were busy, too, in the pursuit of furs, which they exported to China and their own country. The mainland of their possessions was utterly valueless for any other purpose, the islands only being available for agriculture. They, too, possessed their forts and factories, but in greater number and strength than the English, having taken further trouble to colonise the country. The aboriginal inhabitants pay formal allegiance to the Russian-American Trading Company, in the service of which they are bound to enter, if required; while from the more distant tribes tribute of furs is enforced. Moreover the Company possess twenty-eight establishments south of Behring Straits; and on Baranof Island, at Sitka, or New Archangel, the capital of Russian-America, a fortified town will be found, with arsenals, shipyard, foundry, hospital, a church, splendidly adorned shops, schools, library, museum, and laboratory.

Such, briefly, was the condition of the neglected and unknown land for which the 'Plumper' was bound. This much was known of it: and that its area, exclusive of Vancouver Island, itself half the size of Ireland, was about three times as large as Great Britain, with a coast-line of 500 miles, made up of lake and mountain, forest, marsh, and prairie.

CHAPTER II.

———•◦•———

ON the 12th of March we left Portsmouth for Plymouth, getting away from England finally on the 26th of the same month. During our passage out we met with several accidents, which had the effect of delaying our arrival at our destination for a considerable while, but which would be of little if any interest to the reader. I may say shortly, then, that after springing a leak in the Bay of Biscay, which compelled us to run in to Lisbon, and breaking the screw-shaft a few days later, which left us for some time without the aid of steam, we reached Rio Janeiro on the 25th of May. We were detained here until the necessary repairs could be effected, leaving it on the 9th of July. After meeting with nothing more remarkable than a heavy gale off the River Plate, we entered the Straits of Magellan on the 29th of July, and were detained there by stress of weather for three weeks. On the 19th of August, however, we passed out, and picking up a fair wind, reached Valparaiso on the 28th of the same month. Starting thence on the 8th of September, we arrived, after a pleasant passage, at Honolulu, Sandwich Islands, on the 16th of October.

Although our stay at Honolulu was short, opportunity was given us to see a great deal of the place and neighbourhood. Of late years, from being a mere Indian village, it has become an important harbour for the ships engaged in whale-fishing in the North Pacific. This is conducted principally by vessels of the United States; and the white population of Honolulu,

therefore, is almost exclusively American. It is no secret, I
believe, that great efforts have been made by these settlers
and their Government for the annexation of the Sandwich
Islands. In this they have been baffled by their own unpopu-
larity, and the strenuous counter-exertions of the advisers of
King Kame-hame-ha II., who have been hitherto selected
from the few English and Scotch residents in his dominions.
Kame-hame-ha, indeed, is essentially English in his habits,
dress, the fashion of his residence, and in his system of government, which is enlightened and progressive. He has for his
chief adviser a very worthy old Scotch gentleman, by name
Wylie; and his queen is the daughter of an Irish settler in
his dominions, and a very pleasant, sensible woman.

Personally this monarch with the unpronounceable name
is a well-educated, gentlemanly man, who speaks English
and French fluently, and who has travelled a good deal both
in Europe and America. It is said that, when travelling in
the States, he was not allowed at some place to join the
table d'hôte, on account of his having black blood in his veins,
although he is really little, if at all, darker than a sunburnt
Englishman. Considering the many temptations incidental to
his position, and that his royal father was, I believe, almost a
savage, Kame-hame-ha II. may, in extenuation of his evil
habits, offer pleas which have before now excused the much
more glaring excesses of enlightened European monarchs
and gentlemen. Unfortunately, King Kame-hame-ha is not
without many social faults; but though addicted, as there is
no doubt he is, to the pleasures of the table and conviviality
generally, I believe him to be anything but the drunkard
and debauchee that I have heard him called by some of his
guests and critics.

Something—much, I think—should be conceded to the
influences of his childhood, and the difficulties of his maturer
years. Son of a father who, although wild and uncultivated
as any North American Indian, had seen enough of the ad-

vantages of education to desire them for his son, he was put
under competent masters, and afterwards sent to travel; thus
European habits, tastes, and manners were engrafted upon
his semi-wild nature. Of course these placed a barrier for
ever between him and his native subjects. He could no
longer associate with them, and he naturally joined the only
society that was in the least suited to him—viz., that of the
American residents. Among these he had offered him the
choice of the American missionaries or merchants. The
former, though most exemplary and useful men, who have done
a great deal of good among the natives and the crews of the
whaling ships, led lives far too austere and ascetic to please
the young monarch. The others, however ineligible asso-
ciates for a young man with strong passions, had at least the
merit of being pleasant companions. It is therefore, perhaps,
little to be wondered at that he should have preferred their
society.

The King may frequently be met at the houses of his
foreign subjects, at their balls, dinners, and supper parties;
and although always treated with a certain amount of defer-
ence, and placed in the seat of honour, it sounds strange to
hear a man say across the table, " King, a glass of wine with
you !" or, " Do you feel like brandy-and-water this morning,
King?" I believe in his heart, Kame-hame-ha is thoroughly
sick of his present life; but the task of reformation is no
easy one, and he has no one to help him in it. He has lately
expressed a great desire that England should assist him
socially and morally, as she has done politically. He has
long desired the establishment of the Church of England in
his dominions. So anxious is he for this, that he has post-
poned the christening of his child in the hope of being able
to have that ceremony performed by an English bishop. He
endeavoured to enlist the sympathies and obtain the services
of the Bishop of British Columbia for this purpose; and
failing that, Queen Emma actually at one time contemplated

making the voyage to England with her child, with the double object of having him baptised by episcopal hands, and of inducing our gracious Queen to become his sponsor.*

During our stay at Honolulu, the King's brother, Prince Lot, acceded to our request to show us a native dance, or Hula-hula, such as we had read of in the voyages of the old explorers. It was common enough in the days of Cook and Vancouver, but has gone out of fashion since quadrilles and champagne have been introduced at Honolulu. Probably the missionaries have had much to do with its abolition, and indeed no objection they may entertain to it can be considered unreasonable.

A Hula is a festive entertainment which I find it somewhat difficult to describe. The one we saw was held near a village some ten or twelve miles from Honolulu, to which we all rode on the horses which are so good and plentiful in this island. Some 200 or 300 natives were present. Almost all the dancers were women dressed in a costume somewhat similar to that of our European ballet-girl. The music was played by some half-dozen men seated on their haunches at the far end of the room behind the dancers, who sang a wild chant, accompanied by perpetual rapping on small drums. Some of the dancers carried large shields made of feathers bound up with very bright-coloured cloth—a gourd, fixed on to the centre at the back, forming the handle. The gourds were filled with pebbles, and were rattled with extraordinary vehemence as the dancers became excited. The contortions into which they put themselves are quite beyond my powers of description. There was, however, a certain wild grace in all their movements, and they kept admirable time with each other and to the music. The chants have a peculiar signifi-

* Since writing the above, the King's wishes have been acceded to. The newly-appointed Bishop of Honolulu has recently left England for his diocese, and he carries with him the assent of her Majesty to be sponsor to King Kame-hame-ha's heir.

officers—for whom a separate table is kept—eight dollars, for
their board and lodging.

23rd October, 1857.—Sailed from Honolulu this day, and
on the 9th of November entered the Strait of Juan de Fuca,
which divides Vancouver Island from the mainland of the
American continent. In making the Strait of Fuca, should
the weather be clear enough for the navigator to see the
Flattery Rocks, he will at once know his position. These
rocks, which lie twelve miles south of Cape Flattery and
extend some three miles off shore, have a considerable
elevation, and are sufficiently peculiar in their aspect to be
readily identified. In fair weather the entrance to the
Strait is plainly visible from them; and as they are passed,
the lighthouse upon Tatoosh, off Cape Flattery, opens in
view.

All high northern latitudes are peculiarly liable to sudden
changes of weather, and in entering the Strait of Fuca all
the knowledge and experience of which the navigator is
master will often be called into requisition. The currents at
the entrance of the Strait are not very strong, varying from
one to four knots; but their set is uncertain, although when
once fairly in the Strait the flood-stream will be found to
run in, and the ebb out. Captain Trivett, of the Hudson
Bay Company's service, who has made many voyages to
Victoria, recommends * that the south coast of Vancouver
Island should be avoided in light winds, as, should it fall
calm, the ship would be at the mercy of a heavy swell that
almost always sets in on the shore, and renders it at times
difficult to get off the coast. My subsequent experience,
however, would incline me, on the contrary, to hug the
island-coast, as, although the swell sets on to the island, the
current appears almost invariably to set to the southward.
This southerly set nearly caused the loss of H.M.S. ' Hecate,'

* ' Mercantile Journal ' for 1861, p. 196.

c 2

in 1861, when, during a fog, she was drifted on to the rocks inside Tatoosh Island, when we thought we were still well north of it. Captain Stamp, an old seaman who, living at Barclay Sound, is in the habit frequently of taking small schooners to and from Victoria, also told me that he almost always experienced a southerly set at the entrance of the Straits.

Off the shore of Vancouver Island a large bank, some fifteen miles in breadth, extends the whole length of the island. It is, therefore, advisable, as Captain Trivett in another place remarks, to be to the northward rather than the southward in making the Strait. The edge of this bank has been very accurately defined by the soundings of H.M.S. 'Hecate,' which have since been published; and as the depth of water changes suddenly from 100 or 200 fathoms to no more than 40 or 50, the soundings will serve as a capital guide for the approach.

The breadth of the Strait of Juan de Fuca, at its entrance between Cape Flattery, its southern point upon American territory, and Bonilla Point in Vancouver Island, is thirteen miles. It narrows soon, however, to eleven miles, carrying this breadth in an east and north-east direction some fifty miles to the Race Islands. The coasts are remarkably free from danger, and may, as a rule, be approached closely. Upon either side there are several convenient anchorages, which I shall shortly describe, and which may be taken advantage of by vessels inward or outward bound. They are well lighted, too, by both the countries interested in their navigation; although, in this respect, the United States may be said to carry off the palm. They have a small staff of officers whose duty it is to attend to the lighthouses on the coast; and until the recent home exigencies of the United States, a steamer, the 'Shubrick,' was especially detailed for this service.

To return, however, to a description of the Strait of Juan

de Fuca. Upon the northern side, from the shore of the island, densely-wooded hills rise gradually to a considerable height; while on the southern, or American shore, the rugged outline of the Olympian range of snow-clad mountains, varying in elevation from four to seven thousand feet, and in breaks of which peeps of beautiful country may be seen, extend for many miles. As the Strait is ascended the tides and currents, which at its junction with the Pacific are of comparatively little strength, become embarrassing, and often dangerous, to the navigator. In the neighbourhood of the Race Islands, where the Strait takes an east-north-east direction and meets the first rush of the waters of the Gulf of Georgia, which have been pent-up and harassed by the labyrinth of islands choking its southern entrance, the tidal irregularities become so great and perplexing as to baffle all attempts at framing laws calculated to guide the mariner. Fortunately, the course of the winds can be ascertained with greater accuracy. At all seasons they blow up or down the Strait of Fuca. During the summer the prevailing breezes from north-west or south-west take a westerly direction within the Strait; while the south-east gales of winter blow fairly out. The mariner, however, running out of the Strait with a south-east gale, must be prepared for a shift to the southward immediately he opens Cape Flattery. This generally occurs, and it is of the first importance to be ready for it; as, of course, the southerly wind catching a ship unprepared drives her on to the dead lee-shore of the island, off which it is no easy job to work. Upon her last voyage home the Hudson Bay Company's bark 'Princess Royal,' under the command of the Captain Trivett I have before alluded to, was placed in great jeopardy for a whole night from this cause.

At the Race Islands the Strait may be said to terminate, as it there opens out into a large expanse of water, which forms a playground for the tides and currents, hitherto pent up

among the islands in the comparatively narrow limits of the
Gulf of Georgia, to frolic in. Between Port San Juan, which
is the first anchorage on the north side of the Strait just
inside the entrance, and the Race Islands two good anchorages
occur. Sooke Inlet, the more westward of these, lies some
nine miles from the Race Islands, and forms a splendid basin
a mile and a half square, and perfectly land-locked. The
entrance, however, is so narrow and tortuous, as to make
Sooke Harbour of little practical value. Some farms have,
however, been established there, and what land there is in its
neighbourhood available for cultivation has been found to be
good and fertile.

Becher Bay lies between Sooke and the Race Islands, some
four miles from the latter. The depth of water at its
entrance varies from twenty to fifty fathoms, with a rocky
and irregular bottom ; and it cannot be recommended as an
anchorage, being too open to winds from the south and west.

On the south side of the Strait is Neah Bay, four miles
east-north-east from Tatoosh Island, offering a safe and
convenient anchorage to vessels meeting south-west or
south-east gales at the entrance of the Strait. Indeed, it is
very fairly sheltered from all but north-west winds, and if
threatened by them a vessel will generally be able to run out
of the bay inside the adjacent island of Wyadda, which is
protected on the north-east side. It was in Neah Bay, however, that the Hudson Bay Company's brig 'Una' was lost in
1857. She had come down from Queen Charlotte Island,
whither she had been sent to examine into some reported gold
discoveries, and was lying here when a heavy north-west wind
set in. Most of the crew were on shore at the Indian village,
and the 'Una' was anchored in deep water. The anchor
could not be weighed, and before they could get sail on ready
for cutting the cable, she had drifted so much that, when they
tried to run through between the island and the main, they
grounded on the point. The brig was totally lost, but the

crew were saved and treated kindly by the Indians, who muster here in large numbers, owing to the quantity of cod, halibut, and other fish, upon the bank which I have before referred to as running out from the shore of the island. This fishery will no doubt, at some future time, prove a source of considerable profit to the colony. It was for some time doubted by the Governor and others, whether the true cod was to be caught upon this bank; but some years later, when we were here with the 'Hecate,' we settled this in the affirmative beyond a doubt. The halibut runs here to an enormous size; it is a large flat fish, and I have seen specimens caught that were six or seven feet long, by three or four feet wide and six or eight inches thick. Fish of this size are very coarse; but a small halibut is good eating. The Indians catch them with the hook, their lines being made usually of the fibres of the cypress-tree, or of the long kelp which abounds in these waters. They now very generally use hooks purchased of the Hudson Bay Company, but the native implement made of wood backed with bone may still be seen. The canoes of these fishermen may always be met with off the entrance of the Strait, tossing about in the chopping sea, with a coil of some fifty or sixty fathoms of line wound round their bows. Their method of killing large fish is particularly ingenious; they carry in their canoes a number of bags of seal-skin made air-tight, to each of which is attached a small harpoon barbed with iron, fishbone, or shell. A short line connects the harpoon with the bag, and the handle being withdrawn after the fish is struck he is allowed to play it out. He is often strong enough to carry one or more of the seal-skin bags under the water, but in time he comes to the surface, and is harpooned again and again, until worn out he is towed to the shore.

Between Neah Bay and Admiralty Inlet, there are several anchorages more or less to be recommended. The rugged coast is quite unfit, however, for settlement; although behind the rocks that line the shore lies much rich and fertile land, which, however, can only be reached from Admiralty Inlet and Puget Sound.

Eight miles north of the Race Islands is the harbour of Esquimalt,* and three miles northward of that lies Victoria, the capital of Vancouver Island, and the present seat of government for both that colony and British Columbia. As a harbour, Esquimalt is by far the best in the southern part of the island or mainland. It offers a safe anchorage for ships of any size, and although the entrance is perhaps somewhat narrow for a large vessel to beat in or out of with a dead foul wind, it may usually be entered easily and freely. It is moreover admirably adapted to become a maritime stronghold, and might be made almost impregnable. Its average depth is from five to seven fathoms, and in Constance Cove, on the right-hand side as the harbour is entered, there is room for as large a number of ships as we are ever likely to have in these waters to take refuge in if necessary. As yet the want of fresh water in the summer time is felt as an inconvenience; but there are several large lakes a little up the country, at a level considerably above that of the harbour, and from them, when the resources of the colony are developed, water can easily be brought down to the ships.

Each new admiral that is appointed to the North Pacific station appears to be more and more impressed with the evident value and importance of Esquimalt as a naval station. It is to be regretted, indeed, that more land in the neighbourhood of the harbour has not been reserved by the Government, and that steps were not long ago taken to develop its resources. Had, for instance, a floating dock been built here in 1858, it would by this time have more

* The second syllable of Esquimalt is pronounced long. Its Indian name is Isch-oy-malt, and it was so written in the early letters of the Governor to the Hudson Bay Company.

than paid for its construction; and we should not be depen-
dent, as we are now, upon the American dock at Mare
Island, San Francisco, for the repair of our ships of war.
During the four years of my service on this station, such a
dock would have been used on five occasions by Her Majesty's
ships, and at least a dozen times by merchant-vessels, who,
as it was, were put to great inconvenience and even danger.
For instance, when H.M.S. 'Hecate' ran ashore in the
autumn of 1861, we were a fortnight at Esquimalt patching
her up, before we ventured to take her to San Francisco,
whither after all we had to be convoyed by another man-of-
war. This occurred too, as it may be remembered, at a time
when war with the United States seemed imminent. Had
it broken out, the 'Hecate' must have been trapped, and
the services of a powerful steamer would have been lost to
the country.

Esquimalt has seen, and is still likely to see, many startling changes. I found it altered very much from the time
when as a midshipman, I first made its acquaintance in 1849.
In that year, when we spent some weeks in Esquimalt
Harbour on board H.M.S. 'Inconstant,' there was not a house
to be seen on its shores; we used to fire shot and shell as we
liked about the harbour, and might send parties ashore and
cut as much wood as we needed without the least chance of
interruption. Now, as we entered, I was surprised to catch
sight of a row of respectable, well-kept buildings on the south-
east point of the harbour's mouth, with pleasant gardens in front
of them, from which a party of the crew of the 'Satellite,'
who had been expecting us for some time, received us with
a round of hearty cheers. This was, we found, a Naval
Hospital erected in 1854, when we were at war with Russia,
to receive the wounded from Petropaulovski, and since that
time continued in use. Opposite the hospital, our attention
was directed to a very comfortable and, standing where it
did, a rather imposing residence, which was the house of

Mr. Cameron, Chief Justice of Vancouver Island, and in which I have since spent many a pleasant hour. At the head of Constance Cove, at the east end of the harbour, might be seen through the trees the buildings of Constance farm, in the occupation of the Puget Sound Company; and as we held on beyond the hospital, we came in view of the site of the present town of Esquimalt, whose growth is of a more recent date than that of which I am now writing.

Nor were other signs of the already growing importance of Esquimalt wanting. It must be remembered that as yet gold, although known by some to exist both upon the island and mainland, had attracted no notice; but the colony was growing slowly yet surely without its stimulating aid. Further up the harbour stood another building, named Thetis Cottage, and at the north entrance of Constance Cove the new bailiff of the Puget Sound Company was building a house. So, everywhere ashore, there were changes and improvement visible. Nine years back, we had to scramble from the ship's boat on to the most convenient rock: now Jones's landing-place received us; and in the stead of forcing a path over the rocks and through the bush to the Victoria Inlet, whence, if a native should happen to be lounging about in the Indian village of the Songhies, and should see us or hear our shouts and bring a canoe over, we might hope to reach Victoria, a broad carriage-road, not of the best, perhaps, and a serviceable bridge, were found connecting Esquimalt Harbour with Victoria.

Victoria, too, was altering for the better, though slowly. The Hudson Bay Company's fort was still the most imposing building in the town, and its officers the chief people there; but it had grown into a more important station of the great Fur Company than of yore, and Mr. Finlayson, whom we had left chief in command nine years before, we now found Mr. Douglas's lieutenant.

As the capital of the island, Victoria undoubtedly owes its

pre-eminence to Mr. Douglas, the present governor. As far
back as 1843, when it was considered desirable by the Company to establish a station in the island, Victoria had been
selected by him for that purpose; and later, when the Oregon
boundary question was settled, and the mouth of the River
Columbia, on which Fort Vancouver, the principal station of
the Company in Western America, stood, fell into the hands
of the United States, it was to Victoria that their head-quarters
were transferred by Mr. Douglas, who was then, and had been
for some time, their chief agent in the countries west of the
Rocky Mountains. Mr. Douglas was guided in his selection
of Victoria simply by its possessing qualities which met the
requirements of the Company he represented. No one ever
dreamt then of the mineral wealth of the valleys that sloped
from the Rocky Mountains to the sea; or that in a few
years cities (I should say, perhaps, their promise) would
spring up upon shores almost unknown to the civilised world.
But, long before the present rush of immigrants to these
regions, Victoria, as a port, had been virtually superseded by
the adjacent harbour of Esquimalt. The entrance to Victoria
is narrow, shoal, and intricate; and with certain winds a
heavy sea sets on the coast, which renders the anchorage
outside unsafe, while vessels of burden cannot run inside for
shelter unless at or near high water. Vessels drawing 14
or 15 feet may, under ordinary circumstances, enter at high
water, and ships drawing 17 feet have done so, although only
at the top of spring-tides. But it is necessary always to take
a pilot, and the channel is so confined and tortuous that a
long ship has considerable difficulty in getting in. With
every care, a large proportion of vessels entering the port run
aground. No doubt steps might be taken to improve the
harbour of Victoria, but it is highly problematical whether it
can ever be made a safe and convenient port of entry for
vessels even of moderate tonnage at all times of the tide and
weather. Under the most favourable circumstances, accidents

happen constantly. Last year, and again this spring, the
' Princess Royal,' a vessel of but 600 tons' burden, which goes
from London to Vancouver Island every year, in the service
of the Hudson Bay Company, grounded in entering Victoria,
although she was commanded by a very able man, thoroughly
acquainted with the place, and was towed at the time by a
steamer which plied in and out of the harbour two or three
times at least every week. Nor when she was brought into
the harbour was there sufficient depth of water to allow her
to get alongside the wharf, and her cargo had to be discharged
into lighters. Under these circumstances, therefore, although
Victoria is, no doubt, quite well adapted for the vessels
trading up the Fraser River, and the many small craft that
will be required among the islands and ports of the coast,
ships of larger tonnage must always prefer Esquimalt. I
cannot imagine any sensible master of an ocean ship endeavouring to wriggle his vessel into Victoria with the larger
and safer harbour of Esquimalt handy.

Very possibly, could the future have been foreseen, Victoria
would not have been selected as the chief commercial port of
Vancouver Island. But the selection has been made, the
town is built or building, the commerce already attracted.
The fact must be regarded as accomplished beyond the possibility of change; and the only thing that can now be done is
to connect it with the harbour of Esquimalt, towards which
task the natural formation of the country lends itself admirably.

In the way of this, however, stand several obstacles, and
chief among them, perhaps, is the jealousy of the landholders
of Victoria, who, believing that the elevation of Esquimalt
into *the* harbour of the colony would lower the value of their
property, have persistently opposed such a project. Nor
have the landholders of Esquimalt been altogether free from
blame. Irritated by the opposition of Victoria, and convinced
that in the end their demands must be conceded, they have

OUTSIDE VIEW OF VICTORIA.

Page 29.

placed a value upon their land which is quite exorbitant. Many of the merchants of Victoria would, I believe, long ago have been glad to transfer their wharves to Esquimalt, could they have obtained the necessary land at anything like a fair price.

Some efforts had, however, been made to connect the two places. As I have before said, in 1849 the country between them was impassable, and the only communication possible was by creeping round by the shore and crossing the head of the inlet in a canoe; but now we found a broad road carried from Victoria to the Naval Hospital, passing through what has since become the site of Esquimalt town, with branch ways to several important points of the harbour. At that time this road fulfilled its purpose moderately well; but later, when the rush to British Columbia commenced, it broke down miserably, and it was, in the autumn of 1861, when I left, a disgrace to the colony. In the winter it was practically almost useless, and the waggons had to take to the grass by the side, with what result may easily be imagined; and when the mails were expected, the express-men and waggon-drivers had to go over the ground the day before and patch it up sufficiently to enable them to get to Victoria at all.

Very few words need be given to the description of Victoria. Reaching it by the road just mentioned, the traveller passes the Hospital, supported by voluntary contributions, and first established by the Rev. E. Cridge, who was the Hudson Bay Company's .chaplain at Victoria for some years, and did much good in many unobtrusive ways before the arrival of the present bishop. Beyond, situated upon a point of land that juts out between the first and second bridges, has since been built a foundry, about which, in the winter season, may generally be seen miners busy building flat-bottomed boats, raising the gunwales of old canoes, and in other ways making preparations for crossing the Gulf of Georgia and ascending the Fraser River early in the spring. Further on, across the first bridge, the road ascends a little hill, on the summit of which lies the Indian village of the Songhies, once the sole inhabitants of this place. The close contiguity of these Indians to Victoria is seriously inconvenient, and various plans for removing them to a distance have been discussed both in and out of the colonial legislature. In consequence of their intercourse with the whites—chiefly, of course, for evil—this tribe has become the most degraded in the whole island, having lost what few virtues the savage in his natural state possesses, and contracted the worst vices of the settlers. It is scarcely possible to walk along the road by which their village lies without stumbling upon half-a-dozen or more, lying dead-drunk upon the ground; and it is no uncommon thing at night to hear a ball whizz past your head, fired, not at the traveller, but from a hut on one side of the road to one on the other in some drunken squabble. Altogether, what with the drunkenness and the gambling—for Indians are great gamblers, and numbers may be seen squatted on their haunches by the roadside playing for whatever they have earned or stolen—this village of the Songhies presents one of the most squalid pictures of dirt and misery it is possible to conceive. To the right of these, and stretching far along the northern side of the harbour, are the tents of the tribes who come down several hundred miles from the northernmost part of our West American possessions to barter furs, buy whisky, and see the white men.

The Company's fort, long the chief feature of the place, is situated on the north-east side of the harbour. Upon my first visit to Victoria in 1849, a small dairy at the head of James Bay was the only building standing outside the fort pickets, which are now demolished. But shortly after, upon Mr. Douglas's arrival, he built himself a house on the south side of James Bay; and Mr. Work, another chief factor of the Company, arriving a little later, erected another in Rock Bay, above the bridge. These formed the nucleus of a little group

of buildings, which rose about and between them so slowly
that even in 1857 there was but one small wharf on the
harbour's edge. Still, the least experienced eye could see
the capabilities of the site of Victoria for a town, and that
it was capable, should the occasion ever arise, of springing
into importance as Melbourne or San Francisco had done·
As it was, the place was very pleasant, and society—
as it is generally in a young colony—frank and agreeable.
No ceremony was known in those pleasant times. All the
half-dozen houses that made up the town were open to us.
In fine weather, riding-parties of the gentlemen and ladies of
the place were formed, and we returned generally to a high
tea, or tea-dinner, at Mr. Douglas's or Mr. Work's, winding
up the pleasant evening with dance and song. We thought
nothing then of starting off to Victoria in sea-boots, carrying
others in our pockets, just to enjoy a pleasant evening by a
good log-fire. And we cared as little for the weary tramp
homeward to Esquimalt in the dark, although it happened
sometimes that men lost their way, and had to sleep in the
bush all night.

CHAPTER III.

Semiahmoo Bay — Gulf of Georgia — Visit Nanaimo — Coal — The Haro
Archipelago — Discovery of Gold — Consequent Excitement — Growth of
Victoria — Arrival of H.M.S. 'Havannah' — Threatened disturbance at
Victoria — Arrival of Colonel Moody — Abatement of the Gold Fever.

THE first duty which devolved upon Captain Richards on the
'Plumper' reaching these waters was the determination of
the exact spot where the parallel of 49° north latitude
met the sea. This was known approximately, but it was
necessary now to determine it accurately as a starting-point
for the Commission which was to carry the line across the
continent, and also for the purposes of the Naval Commission
to which Captain Richards belonged, and whose business it
was to determine the channel by which it was intended, by
the Treaty of 1844, that the boundary-line should pass to
the Strait of Fuca.

Accordingly, after a short stay in Esquimalt Harbour,
Captain Richards decided to accomplish this part of his
mission at once. The Commissioners of the United States
had already made their observations, and, having encamped
upon a spot of the mainland near the computed line of
parallel, awaited the 'Plumper's' coming to confirm them.
So on the 18th of November we steamed up the Haro Strait
and across the Gulf of Georgia, to Semiahmoo Bay.

It would be unjust to the scenery of these channels
to describe it as we then saw it in the depth of winter.
Although the weather was open, and there was hardly any
snow upon the ground, both the shores of Vancouver and
the numerous other islands that we passed wore that dull,
sombre hue common to northern countries at such a season.

CAIRN, ETC., ON THE BOUNDARY LINE, AT EAST KOOTENAY.

Page 32.

At all times, indeed, the scenery of these islands, with that of the shores of the mainland, is little attractive, covered as they are with pine-trees to the water's edge, through which knobs of trap show in places, but in winter it is peculiarly uninviting.

Semiahmoo or Boundary Bay, is an extensive sheet of water, some eight miles wide, flowing inland towards the Fraser River, from the south bank of which it is only divided by a flat and narrow delta three miles across.

As the parallel of 49° north latitude meets the sea in this bay, it will be well to give a slight description of it. It lies between Birch Bay, one of Vancouver's anchorages, on the east, and Point Roberts on the west, the tip of which latter point falls south of 49°. The distance between the east and west points is 8 miles, and the length of the bay northerly is 7 miles, though at low water it dries off from the head for 3 miles.

There is anchorage in 7 to 15 fathoms nearly all over the bay, though the western and southern parts of it are exposed to southerly winds, which send in a considerable sea. In the eastern part there is good anchorage, except with a south-west gale.

The south bluff terminates at its east end in a long, low spit, more than a mile long, covered with grass, drift-timber, and a few pines. This spit was afterwards, for a short time in the summer of 1858, the site of "Semiahmoo City," and it forms a small but snug nook called Drayton Harbour, which affords shelter from the south-west gales when the outer anchorage is not safe.

Here we stayed until the 16th December, making the necessary observations, when, on Captain Richards proceeding to mark the spot where he considered the parallel met the sea, it was found to differ only eight feet from that fixed upon by the American Commissioners. Whilst here, of course, we were thrown a good deal in the way of the officers of the American Boundary Commission. Their party consisted

D

of Mr. Campbell, the Commissioner ; Lieutenant Parke, of the United States' Topographical Engineers, astronomer ; two or three assistant astronomers, a doctor, naturalist, botanist, and a captain and subaltern in command of the military escort, which consisted of about 70 men. They had been here nearly a year, and were able to form some idea of the work that lay before them. Some of the party were veterans at the work, having been engaged upon the Mexican Boundary Commission. Their instruments were admirably packed for travelling, and of very superior make and workmanship. Until recently, the Americans were obliged to come to our English manufacturers for their scientific instruments ; and I think it was with some natural gratification on their part that our attention was drawn to the fact that these were made by Mr. Wordeman, an American, at Washington, who began life as a repairer of Troughton's instruments.

Their estimate of the probable expense of settling this boundary question rather surprised us, and showed us at once that the cost of a clearing on this side of the continent could not be calculated by the expense of a similar undertaking east of the Rocky Mountains. Colonel Estcourt, whose opinion was asked, and formed upon his experience of cutting a line thirty feet wide from Lake Superior to the Lake of Woods, had estimated the whole expense of continuing it on this side to the sea at 32,000*l.* ; but Mr. Campbell, the American Commissioner, told us that he had asked for an annual appropriation of 45,000*l.* for three years. Although he did not get this, it was much nearer the requisite sum than the other, and the issue proved the correctness of his judgment.

Our work over at Semiahmoo, it was decided to return to Esquimalt until the weather should be fine enough to enable us to commence our surveying work. Before making that harbour, however, we visited Nanaimo, a settlement 75 miles north of Victoria, for the purpose of coaling.

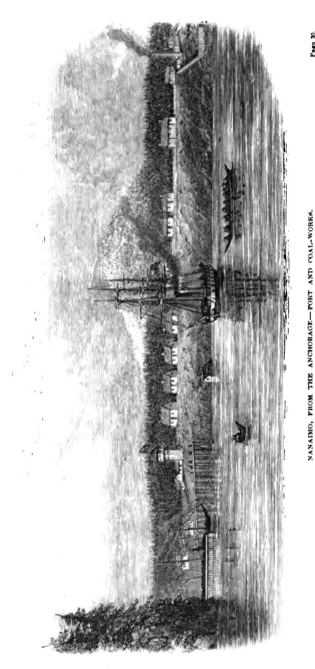

NANAIMO, FROM THE ANCHORAGE.—PORT AND COAL-WORKS.

Page 35.

Nanaimo is the only spot in the island where the coal is worked, although it appears in several other places. The harbour is good, and there is no difficulty in making it. A small island lies off the entrance, which is admirably adapted for a lighthouse when the harbour becomes of more importance. The town, such as it is, stands upon a singular promontory, which seems to have been severed from the mainland by some violent volcanic eruption which twisted the strata of which it is composed most curiously. Along the shore are the colliery buildings, and about a dozen remarkably sooty houses, inhabited by the miners and the few Hudson Bay Company's officers here. There is a resident doctor in the place, who inhabits one of these houses, and to the left of them stands the Company's old bastion, on which are mounted the four or five honeycombed 12-pounders, with which the great Fur Company have been wont to awe the neighbouring Indians into becoming respect and submission.

The coal obtained at Nanaimo, although it burns rapidly, and is excessively dirty, answers sufficiently well for steaming purposes, and is not likely to be soon exhausted. It has been found at several other places besides this promontory of Nanaimo. On Newcastle Island which, with Protection Island, form the shelter of the harbour, coal has been worked to a considerable extent, and found good. It has also been discovered cropping out on the Chase River, a few miles up the country, and further inland at a spot known as Pemberton's Camp. As yet the resources of Nanaimo and its neighbourhood have not been fairly developed. The appliances for delivering the coal, for instance, were so faulty that a ship had to lie there often for three or four weeks before she could take in a load. There can be no doubt that with a more liberal outlay of capital, under judicious and enterprising management, Nanaimo might drive a very flourishing trade at home and with California, where coal might be delivered at 12 to 15 dollars a ton, which would be almost as desirable as the Welsh coal, which is seldom below 20, and sometimes fetches as much as 30 dollars a ton. For domestic consumption, and for use in the factories, I believe the coal of Nanaimo to be almost equal to that brought at such an immense expense and labour from the Welsh mines. Indeed, when I happened to be at San Francisco, I was informed by one of the leading iron-manufacturers there, that they preferred mixing Nanaimo with Welsh coal when they were able to obtain it.*

One decided drawback to Nanaimo as a harbour is the existence there of a species of augur-worm (*Teredo navalis*). It is remarkable that, although this insect infests Nanaimo to such an extent that a new pier, built there shortly before our first visit, has since given way to its ravages, we never found it elsewhere on the coasts of the island or mainland. Of course there are many inlets and harbours still so little known that no positive opinion on the subject can be entertained, but Esquimalt and Victoria, among many others, are certainly free from it.

January 1st, 1858.—A novel feature in marine merry-making was introduced by the ' Satellite's ' crew, who invited our men to a dinner on board their ship. I do not imagine that such an entertainment was ever witnessed before. It was capitally managed, and the crews of both ships behaved remarkably well. The upper deck of the ' Satellite ' was covered in with flags, under which tables were laid down the whole length of the port side, at which about sixty of our men dined with the ' Satellite's.' Of course we all went to look on. The sergeant of the ' Satellite's ' marines took the chair, proposing the toasts with introductory speeches that none of us need have been ashamed of.

February 10.—After spending six weeks in Esquimalt

---

* Since writing the above, I have been informed that by the company which has lately purchased these mines a new wharf has been built and increased facilities for shipping coal provided.

VANCOUVER'S ISLAND SURVEY DETACHED SERVICE—GRIFFIN BAY—ST. JUAN ISLE.

Page 37.

Harbour, we sailed this day to Port Townsend for the mails, Victoria at that time being too insignificant a place for the American mail-steamers running between San Francisco and the Sound to put in at. Indeed, just then the letters of the 'Satellite' and 'Plumper' formed nearly the whole contents of the English mail-bags. Upon our way a party was dropped at San Juan Island to commence surveying operations. Here we—for I formed one of them—remained until the 27th, when we returned to Esquimalt. The weather we experienced convinced us that the middle or end of March was quite early enough to commence work with any hope of success. Out of the seventeen days we spent there six only could be called fine, and at the best the cold was so severe and the fogs so frequent as to render boat-work extremely dangerous, particularly in channels so full of tide-rips and over-falls. Upon one occasion, during our stay, the 'Shark'—as the 'Plumper's' pinnace after being raised and half-decked had been christened—was a subject of great anxiety to us. In crossing from San Juan to Esquimalt she missed her port, and having drifted during the night past the Race Rocks—it might just as well have been upon them—picked herself up in Sooke Inlet, twenty miles below Esquimalt. Upon another occasion, the 'Shark' was caught in a storm of wind and snow, of the violence of which the accompanying sketch may enable the reader to form some idea. She is there depicted dragging her anchor and drifting on shore, the men on board of her signalling to us for assistance that we were utterly unable to give them. I may mention in connection with this sketch that the hill on which we were standing watching the 'Shark's' danger was that upon which the Americans afterwards, upon taking possession of the island, planted their battery, and near which, although the battery has disappeared, their camp now stands.

The few weeks of mid-winter which we had spent in Esquimalt had been of necessity somewhat idle. How-

ever, as the colony was new to us, time did not hang at all
heavy on our hands. Directly the weather would permit, it
was intended to commence surveying operations. The plan of
our campaign was to spend the summer at this work, returning to Esquimalt as winter set in again. With some inter-
ruptions, this plan was adhered to, and the winter months
of each year were spent ashore at our office, making up the
past and preparing for the future summer's work.

March 16.—We left Esquimalt to commence in earnest our
surveying work. I have said that Captain Richard's first duty
on arrival was to determine exactly where the parallel of
of 49° N. met the sea. This was done in the winter, and
we now commenced that part of our work next in importance, *viz.* to make an accurate chart of all the disputed
islands and channels. As the whole summer of 1858 was
taken up with this work, I will here give a description of
these islands; the name of one at least of which—San Juan
—has since become familiar to every one.

The American territory which joins British Columbia on the
south is called "Washington Territory," and between this
and the south-east shore of Vancouver Island lie the group of
islands I am about to describe, all of which are included in
the Haro Archipelago.

In the first chapter I have said that Captains Prevost and
Richards were sent out to endeavour to adjust the rival
claims of our Government and that of the United States to
the possession of these islands; the wording of the treaty of
1844 being so vague as to leave the right to them in doubt.

The treaty appears to have been made under the impression that there was only one channel between Vancouver
Island and the continent, and in ignorance that any islands
existed there at all. Practically at that time there was only
one channel, for the eastern, or Canal de Rosario, was the only
one about which anything was known, and had been used
by all the navigators who had entered the Gulf of Georgia.

WEST ORCAS SOUND, FROM SHIP PEAK.

Page 39.

The Canal de Haro had, it is true, been marked on the maps by the Spaniards, but it was only when the Hudson Bay Company established their head-quarters at Victoria that this passage became used, and even then their vessels generally went up the Rosario Strait, which, being more familiar with, they preferred.

Of the rights and wrongs of this question, which is as unsettled now as it was then, my official position in the survey prevents my entering into a discussion, and obliges me to refrain from anything like a detailed account of the "San Juan difficulty," which, in the year following that of which I am now writing, caused so much excitement both in the colony and in England.

To return to the islands: the distance between the two above-named channels is about twenty miles, and their length the same, thus making a space of four hundred square miles full of islands, varying in size from ten or twelve miles long to a mere heap of trap with two or three pines on them. The group consists of the three important islands of San Juan, Orcas, and Lopez, and about thirty smaller ones. Of these Orcas, the most northern, is the largest, and contains the finest harbours. It is mountainous, and in most parts thickly wooded, although in the valleys there is much land available for farming. On the east side of the island Mount Constitution rises nearly five thousand feet, and is a very conspicuous object from all parts of the Gulf of Georgia. Deer abound more in Orcas than in any other of the islands. During our stay of about a fortnight in East Orcas Sound, upwards of thirty were shot.

San Juan, the best known by name, and in size the second of these islands, is eleven miles long, by an average of three miles wide. There is more land available for agriculture here than on any other of the group; and of this the Hudson Bay Company took advantage some years ago, and established a sheep-farm upon it. This farm has ever since its establishment been in charge of Mr. Griffin, a gentleman whose kindness and hospitality render him every one's friend. It is situated on a beautiful prairie at the south-east end of the island, which, rising 140 feet above the water, looks most attractive to the emigrant passing onward towards the Fraser. I have never seen wild flowers elsewhere grow with the beauty and luxuriance they possess here. Perhaps I cannot illustrate the attractions of San Juan better, than by saying that it was the spot selected by his Excellency the Governor's daughter and niece in which to spend their honeymoon.

At one time I believe the Company had as many as 3000 sheep on the island, distributed at various stations, all under Mr. Griffin's charge. His house, which is very pleasantly situated, looks out on the Strait of Fuca, and commands a magnificent view up Admiralty Inlet. Directly in front of it lies a bank, which is a very favourite fishing-station of the Indians, where they catch a large number of salmon and halibut. This spot was, in 1859, the scene of a double murder, which excited no little speculation that will never be satisfied in this world.

Mr. Griffin told the story thus. He was sitting in his balcony one summer afternoon, watching a vessel working her way up the Strait, when he saw two boats, each containing one man, pull past in the direction of Victoria. He was rather surprised at seeing them thus single-handed, but at that time, when the gold-fever was raging fiercely, every sort of boat was employed to cross the Strait, and he concluded that they were two Americans, making their way from Bellingham Bay to Victoria. They had hardly rounded the point, just beyond the farm, and passed out of his sight, when a small canoe with a single Indian shot past in the same direction. There was nothing in all this to attract particular notice, and Mr. Griffin was surprised when, an hour or so later, two boats, which he at once recognised as those that had so lately passed, drifted into view, floating back, to all appearance, empty. A canoe was at once sent out to them, when one was found empty, and in the other lay the body of a white man, shot, but not pillaged,—even the provisions that were in his boat being untouched. Who shall say who his murderer was? Had his white companion shot him, landed, and pushed off his boat?—for, except in the boat in which the murdered man lay, not a drop of blood could be seen. Or had the Indian killed him, and had his companion, on seeing the fatal shot fired, leapt overboard, and been drowned? If so, it was in revenge, for nothing was taken from the boats; perhaps in performance of that duty which is still considered "sacred"—if one may use the word—among the Indians—of taking a life for a life.

Lopez Island is lower and more swampy than the others. It forms the south-east end of the group, and is nine miles long by three wide. The other islets are, as I have said, mere masses of rock covered with pines, and too insignificant to claim especial notice.

Thus of the whole group San Juan is the only island worth anything for purposes of colonisation, while it only contains a few thousand acres of good land. To allege, therefore, that an island of such paltry extent is of any real value in this respect, either to a country possessing the adjacent island of Vancouver and territory of British Columbia,—or still more to one possessing the hundreds of miles of fertile prairie contained in Washington Territory, Oregon, and California,—is manifestly absurd. A study of the chart—which we were then preparing—however, will show quite clearly why the country that holds Vancouver Island and British Columbia must also hold San Juan Island, or give up the right of way to her own possessions. It will be seen at once that the party that holds this island commands the Canal de Haro. The narrowest part of the channel from shore to shore is five miles. This distance from San Juan can certainly be kept by steamers, but they must be thoroughly acquainted with the navigation to do so, as they must pass inside several reefs, and west of Sydney Island. To go up the centre of the channel—as big ships should do—San Juan must be passed at two miles' distance ; as must Henry and Stuart Islands also, both of which would belong to the nation holding the east side of the Canal de Haro.

San Juan can be of no use to any country but Great Britain, except for *offensive* purposes; and, on the other hand, it cannot be of any use to her but for *defensive* purposes, as *its* eastern shore in no way controls or affects the Rosario Strait, from the western side of which it is eight miles distant at the nearest point, with Lopez Island between.

The same argument might be used against our holding possession of the islands which form the western side of the Rosario Strait, but here Nature befriends us; for during our survey we found there was a middle channel passing eastward of San Juan and a small island north of it, called "Waldron Island," which channel, though not so wide as either of the others, is quite safe for steam navigation. A boundary-line, therefore, passing down the middle channel would give to the nations on either side a road to their dominions perfectly free of interruption, and well out of shot of each other, for some years to come at least; and this certainly appears the simplest and best solution of the difficulty.

I will not weary the reader by describing all the lesser channels, inlets, and harbours which were discovered and surveyed, and of which the accompanying map is too small to give an adequate idea. Any one who feels an interest in such matters should obtain the large charts now published, which show the extraordinary shape of the outline of this coast and its islands: deep channels and inlets, with more shallow bays and harbours running in every possible direction, sometimes between huge crags, and elsewhere through or into low level land ; the whole forming islands, promontories, and peninsulas of most grotesque shape, and bearing more plainly

than I have seen in any other country the evidence of volcanic action. Two features, and two only, are constant everywhere—the everlasting pine-trees and the igneous rocks.

We remained among these islands till the 16th of May,
when we returned to Esquimalt, to find that during our
absence that most infectious of all maladies—a gold-fever—
had broken out, and had seized every man, woman, and child
there and in Victoria. The existence of gold on the mainland of British Columbia, had been proved incontestably;
and everyone whom a few weeks ago we had left engaged
steadily in pursuits from which they were reaping a slow
sure profit, seemed to have gone gold-mad.

The story of the discovery of the precious metal in British
Columbia should have taken no one by surprise; the only
wonder was that years before, its existence in quantities large
enough to attract gold-seekers had not been discovered. Its
existence had been known, indeed, to a few people for many
years, but it was only quite recently that attention had been
called to the subject, and that Mr. Douglas, who had a very
accurate prescience of what was likely to happen, had drawn
the attention of the Home Government to this fact. Common
report says, however, that the Hudson Bay Company had
been in the habit of getting it from the Indians for years;
and if this be so, Mr. Douglas's prescience was not very
remarkable.

Mr. Anderson, a chief factor in the service of the Hudson
Bay Company, and a well-known explorer, had some time since
been despatched to the mainland, with instructions to examine
into its resources generally. His expedition proved of value, re-
sulting as it did in the discovery of the Harrison-Lilloett route,
by which, as I shall have occasion to show, the worst obstacles
of the ascent of the Fraser River have been overcome; but he
threw little, if any, light upon the main object of his search.
The Company's brig 'Una' had also been despatched to Queen

Charlotte Island, and succeeded in blasting gold in quartz, at a place called Gold Harbour. But owing in part to the fierceness of the natives, and still more, perhaps, to the mechanical difficulties attending the working of the blasts, the Company shortly gave up this as an unprofitable speculation.

Now, however, time had brought to notice what the little search made had failed to find, and the excitement of Victoria was indescribable. To any one who had known San Francisco or Melbourne under similar circumstances, the condition of Victoria was not surprising; but to those hitherto unacquainted with the earliest febrile symptoms attending the discovery of gold, the change in its aspect and prospects might well seem magical. The value of land was raised immensely, and the impulse given to its sale was, of course, very great, although the fluctuations in its price, as contradictory reports came down from the mines, made dealing with it a somewhat hazardous speculation. All the available Government lands had been snapped up by far-seeing speculators when the first drops of the golden shower descended. Lots in Victoria and Esquimalt, that a few months ago had gone begging at their upset price of 1*l.* an acre, sold now for 100*l.* an acre, and soon for more. Merchants' stores were rising in every direction. On the shore of the harbour, wharves were being planted; and, as if there were something magnetic in the demand that at once attracted a supply, sailing-ships, laden with every description of articles which a migratory population could, and in many cases could not, want, flowed into the harbour. Victoria appeared to have leapt at once from the site of a promising settlement into a full-grown town. Its future had not, previous to this, looked by any means bright; and we had been in the habit of regarding the map of the town of Victoria, kept in the land-office, as an amusing effort of

A STREET IN VICTORIA.

the surveyor's imagination. But now the promise seemed
likely of fulfilment. Here was actually a street, and there
were not wanting indications the most palpable that in a
short time there would be two, even three erected. Several
of the old settlers had already made enough by the sudden
rise in the value of their lands to be thinking how they
might spend the rest of their lives easily, even luxuriously.
Expectation was written in every face, which before had
been placid, even stolid; for with occasional visits from
Her Majesty's ships of war, the great event of Victoria had
been the advent of the 'Princess Royal' once a year, with
the latest fashions of the Old World and fresh supplies,
human and material, for the Honourable Company's service.
Now, with vessels arriving and leaving constantly, with
thousands pouring into the port, and "sensation" news
from the Fraser daily, a new mind seemed to have taken
possession of Victoria; and whether the 'Princess Royal'
arrived or foundered on her way, was one and the same thing
to the excited people, who had hitherto looked upon her
coming as the one event of the otherwise uneventful year.

   That road, too, from Esquimalt to Victoria, about which
so much has since been said in and out of the Colonial
Assembly, was changed, with the rest, almost beyond recognition. Only a few months before, we used to flounder
through the mud without meeting a single soul; now it was
covered with pedestrians toiling along, with the step and air of
men whose minds are occupied with thoughts of business;
crowded with well-laden carts and vans, with Wells Fargo's,
or Freeman's " Expresses," and with strangers of every tongue
and country, in every variety of attire. Day after day on they
came to Victoria, on their way to the Fraser; the greater part
of them with no property but the bundle they carried, and with
"dollars, dollars, dollars!" stamped on every face. Miners,
indeed are always ready for change. However good the prospects of to-day may be, the idea of better will tempt them to

exchange them without a moment's hesitation. The merest whisper of a new find is enough to unsettle a whole neighbourhood, and send hundreds into the wilds "prospecting." It frequently occurs at San Francisco that individuals who happen to possess land speculate for a rise by setting afloat some cleverly-planned rumour that a great find has been made in their locality. The greedy miners and speculators, whose experience has taught them to discredit no account however wild, hasten to buy the land in question at fabulous prices. I remember when I happened to be in San Francisco in 1860 that a place in the Washoe country was reported to have been found full of silver,—a rumour which was confirmed by some very rich specimens of that metal which were exhibited as having been found there. Upon the strength of this, Washoe land was being bought by feet, and even inches, and nothing else was talked about at the dinner-tables or in the streets of San Francisco from morning until night.

The excitement in Victoria reached its climax, I think, in July. On the 27th of the previous month, the 'Republic' steamed into Esquimalt harbour from San Francisco with 800 passengers; on the 1st of July, the 'Sierra Nevada' landed 1900 more; on the 8th of the same month, the 'Orizaba' and the 'Cortez' together brought 2800; and they all reported that thousands waited to follow. The sufferings of the passengers upon this voyage, short as it is, must have been great, for the steamers carried at least double their complement of passengers. Of course Victoria could not shelter this incursion of immigrants, although great efforts were made, and soon a large town of tents sprung up along the harbour side. Wherever time and material were handy for building, a wooden house was erected, and in this respect Victoria had greatly the advantage of San Francisco under similar circumstances, from the ease and comparative cheapness with which building timber and planks could be obtained from the American saw-mills in Puget Sound. Of course these buildings were run up without much regard to the previous architectural arrangement of the town. But this was of little consequence. Wooden houses in a new settlement in America are always built with an eye to their removal, if necessary, the side supports being morticed into the flooring; so that, should the surveyor run a new, or determine to carry out the design of an old, street through them, their owners make no demur, but mounting them on wheels transport them to their proper position. It is by no means unusual to see a family residence moved from one street to another, a distance, perhaps, of a quarter of a mile, in this way. It happens not unfrequently that a lot which was bought by the settler upon his arrival, and upon which he has built himself a house, becomes in course of time the Bond or Regent Street of the place. Some speculator then offers him a handsome price, not for his little house, which would be useless to him, but for its site, on which he intends building some handsome store. The bargain struck, the house is forthwith mounted upon rollers, and wheeled into some back street, whence perhaps in time it may be called upon to move again; and this plan was carried out in Victoria.

In the mean time the gold-seekers had, as they arrived in Victoria, provided themselves with such necessaries as they required for their adventure; and, by every means of conveyance at their disposal—by steamer, sailing-vessel, canoe, and boat—were making their way across the Strait of Georgia to the mouth of the Fraser River. For this passage steamers had already been brought up from the Sacramento River at great expense and trouble. Too frail to bear an ocean passage, it was necessary to construct an enormous skow or lighter for each steamer. The lighter was decked over and fitted with pumps, like a caisson. It was then sunk under the steamer in shoal water, built up at the bow and stern, so as to completely cover her hull, and pumped out, a mast being stepped through the deck and bottom of the steamer on to the lighter's kelson. The whole was then taken in tow by an ocean steamship, some sort of sail being fitted to the mast above-mentioned, so that, if she should break adrift from the consort, or it should be found necessary from stress of weather to cast her off, the two or three men who made the voyage in her should not be left altogether at the mercy of the waves.

A good story, illustrative of that American " cuteness" about which so much has been heard, was told me by one of them-selves, relative to a steamer that had been bought to ply upon the Fraser. She had been purchased of an American company, which had secured the monopoly of the Sacramento River steam-navigation, by the process of buying up all the vessels started to oppose them. These they sold occasionally for use on other rivers, with the one stipulation that they should never be brought back to the Sacramento. The Fraser River season being over, the stipulation stood very much in the way of the Yankee owners of one of these boats, who were prevented from making the only profitable use of it that was then open to them. A way, however, to keep the letter, if not the spirit, of the bond they had entered into, was found. They exchanged their steamer for another that was then plying on the Fraser, and, putting her on the lighter that had brought the other up, took her to San Francisco, where the monopolising company had to buy her off at the owners' own price.

The most glowing accounts of the successes of the miners reached Victoria, and, stripped of the exaggeration natural to the subject, enough remained to prove that the mineral resources of the country had not been over-estimated by those who were most likely to be acquainted with them. The miners had, during the first few months after their arrival at the mouth of the Fraser, pushed far up it, finding gold still more and more abundant. I shall have in due time, and of my own experience, to speak of this route through a wild and rocky country to the valleys indenting the minor ranges that rib the country west of the Rocky Mountains, although, travelling with the aid of men and means that the miners first in the field could not command, my difficulties were not to be compared to the dangers of life and limb that beset them. The voyage alone across the gulf from Victoria to the mouth of the Fraser was fraught with peril to many who, too impatient or too poor to wait until they could take passage in the ordinary steamer or sailing-vessel, fitted up a crazy boat or old canoe, and committed themselves to the mercy of one of the swiftest and most capricious channels in the world. Several, no doubt, of whom no record was taken or left lost their lives in this adventure; more, perhaps, in the perils of the Fraser, or from exposure, want, and hard living at the mines. But these were few in comparison to the hundreds lost in trying to cross the continent to California in 1849, whose bones are now bleaching in the Sierra Nevada.

Those who were then disposed to blame Governor Douglas for many of the calamities that occurred, could scarcely have reflected upon, or made due allowance for, the difficulties of his position. Roads to the interior there were none, if I except that most dangerous path from Fort Hope across Manson Mountain, in which the Hudson Bay Company's brigade, experienced as they were, yearly lost a number of horses. The "freshets" had commenced; as the snow melted, the river rose so that its navigation above Yale was impossible, as several found to the cost of their lives. Added to this, the only vessels upon the river were two belonging to the Company, the 'Otter' and 'Beaver,' whose draught of water prevented their going above Langley, whence the journey to Yale had to be made in boats and

E

rafts extemporised on the spot, or in canoes navigated by
Indians. Half despising, and more than half fearing these
Indian auxiliaries, as the miners do, they frequently treated
them with a degree of cowardly cruelty that in many cases cost
them dear. The only way to travel safely with Indians is to
trust them, or affect to do so, implicitly, and, above all, to
show no fear. I have frequently travelled alone with them,
and slept alone among them, and had the greatest care taken
of my life and property, whereas when travelling in a party
nothing is safe from their thievish hands.

It must be remembered also that as yet the colony had no
revenue to work with. Except the small amount realised by
the sale of lands, the sole source of revenue then existing
was the licence of five dollars from every miner ascending
the Fraser. However, despite these difficulties, the Governor
determined to make an effort to open up a route to the
upper country, by which the miners might journey with
comparative safety, and supplies be conveyed to them; and a
body of about 600 men was organised to cut a way from lake
to lake along the route explored and recommended by Mr.
Anderson, and since known as the Harrison-Lilloett trail.
The difficulties of this work can scarcely be estimated by any
one who has not seen British Columbian bush. Some idea
may be formed of it, if I state that I have travelled for days
in this country where we scarcely advanced at the rate of one
mile an hour.

By the middle of the summer, however, the Fraser had
been taken possession of unmistakeably. The banks between
Forts Hope and Yale were being worked productively, and
some of the miners had forced their way as far up as Lilloett,
or Cayoush as it was first called, about 220 miles from the
mouth of the river. A few had settled at the forks of the
Thompson and Fraser Rivers, 160 miles from the mouth of
the latter, and their group of huts had been dignified with
the name of the then Colonial Secretary—" Lytton."

When the rush to the river began, it was resolved, as I
have said, that a gold licence of five dollars should be charged
to every man ascending the river.   Of course considerable
difficulty was found in enforcing this tax, and numbers evaded
it.   Even now, I believe, the cost of its collection is so great
in the out-of-the-way places, that the Colonial Exchequer is
little, if at all, benefited by its imposition.   Captain Prevost
was at this time requested by the Governor to undertake the
enforcement of this tax, by placing the 'Satellite' at the
river's mouth, and stopping all miners who refused payment.
This was done, and she remained there until the middle of
the summer, when a small schooner named the 'Recovery,'
formerly belonging to the Hudson Bay Company, was bought,
armed, and stationed in the Fraser River for this purpose.

12th July. — H. M. S. 'Havannah' arrived this day at
Esquimalt, bringing from Panama a commission under
Major (now Colonel) Hawkins, R.E., who had been appointed
to determine and mark the 49th parallel in conjunction with
the United States Commission, of which I have before spoken,
from the coast at Semiahmoo Bay to the Rocky Mountains.
It was then thought probable also that this commission would
cross the Rocky Mountains and carry on their observations to
the west side of the Lake of the Woods, to the east of which
it had already been completed by the late General Estcourt.
This was not carried out, however, and the party have now
returned from the westward, having gone as far as the summit
of the Rocky Mountains.

This party was composed much as the American Commission with which it had to work in concert was, and consisted of Captain Haig, R.A., astronomer, and two officers of
Engineers, Lieutenants Dahrer and Wilson, with a naturalist,
geologist, and botanist; the latter office being undertaken,
as I have before said, by Dr. Lyall of the 'Plumper.'

Upon his arrival, Major Hawkins was naturally anxious to
commence work, and accordingly the 'Plumper' took him to

E 2

Semiahmoo Bay for a few days, that he might see the nature
of the task that lay before him and meet the American
Commission. We found that the spirit of emulation had
seized upon Semiahmoo and Point Roberts. Since our last
visit the greater part of the spits and all the level land
at the extreme of Point Roberts had been "Pre-empted,"
half-a-dozen wooden huts had been built on each, and called
respectively Semiahmoo and Roberts "City." My English
readers who know only the "cities" of the Old World should
be informed that, in such a rapidly progressing country as
America, any spot whereon a liquor-store and a post-office,
with two or three huts about them, are built, is immediately named a "city." All over the country these "Bogus"
cities, as the more staid Americans call them, are to be found.
Many, of course, to use their own phrase, "cave in," and this
was the fate of Roberts and Semiahmoo Cities, for in less than
six months they were deserted.

A few days after our return from Semiahmoo, on the 29th
July, the quiet tenor of our life in Esquimalt Harbour was
disturbed by a messenger from the Governor, with a requisition
that an armed force should be at once despatched to Victoria
to quell an imminent disturbance in that city of wood and
canvas. Steam was with all haste got up, and embarking
the engineers of the Boundary party, we started for Victoria.
Things had for some time been critical there, and it had been
thought more than once that it would be necessary for the
Governor to make an exhibition of force at least, that should
effectually tame the more unruly of the strange, heterogeneous
population that had placed themselves under his rule. The
new-found mineral wealth of British Columbia had attracted
from California some of the most reckless rascals that gold
has ever given birth to. Strolling about the canvas streets
of Victoria might be seen men whose names were in the
black book of the Vigilance Committee of San Francisco, and
whose necks would not, if they ventured them in that city,

have been worth an hour's purchase. Aware of this, and that the police force had only just been established, and consisted of some dozen untrained men, while it was well known that no naval or military auxiliaries were nearer at hand than Esquimalt, it may easily be conceived that we were not much surprised to receive the Governor's message, and while we steamed round to Victoria thought it advisable to prepare ourselves for what might possibly be a grave encounter with the lawless spirits of California. Many a subsequent laugh have the recollections of that night's work excited. Upon the quarter-deck, small-arm companies were having ammunition served out to them; forward, the ship's blacksmith was casting bullets by the score; while our doctor was spreading out his cold, shining instruments upon the ward-room table, and making arrangements for the most painful surgical operations with that grave, business *sang-froid*, which is no doubt caused by a benevolent desire to show the fighting men what is in the opposite scale to honour and glory.

Directly the ship anchored outside the harbour, we were landed and marched into the Fort square, where we were left under arms, while Captain Richards waited upon the Governor. Whatever disturbance there had been had now evidently ceased, and his Excellency was found going or gone to bed. However, upon being informed of our arrival, he turned out, thanked and dismissed the troops, and our evening, begun so fiercely, wound up with a supper in the fort. The fact proved to be that the police, in endeavouring to arrest a drunken rioter, had been prevented by some of his companions, by whose aid he had been got on board a schooner lying in the harbour. Under the escort of one of our boats, the police now felt themselves strong enough to effect his capture; and the schooner in question being boarded, a harmless, sleepy, drunken miner was dragged out of the hold and lugged ashore, where on the morrow, no doubt, he was soundly rated and fined. And so ended the first and only difficulty which has ever threatened the peace of Victoria from its white population.

Few men could perhaps have been selected better adapted for dealing with the strange, heterogeneous population of Victoria than Mr. Douglas. Many stories are rife in Victoria of his coolness and readiness, when without these valuable qualities dangerous consequences might have ensued. I remember one, which, however, loses much of its point to those who are not familiar with the man, and his slow, deliberate action and utterance. Many years ago, when white men were fewer in these regions, and Indians less cowed than they have now become, Mr. Douglas was in command of one of the Company's trading stations. His subordinate officer was alarmed upon one occasion by the Indians, who had for some time past showed symptoms of insubordination, becoming more violent than usual, and forcing their way in large, unruly numbers into the Fort square. Rushing to Mr. Douglas in an excited tone and manner, he reported that the Indians were in possession of the Fort, and desired to know whether he should turn the men out and man the bastion, &c. He was not a little surprised to hear his senior say in his measured, deliberate fashion of utterance, " Give them a little bread and treacle, Mr. ——; give them a little bread and treacle." And indeed the specific completely soothed the excited multitude, which probably no force they could command would have done. Another annecdote of the same kind occurred while we were out there. A blustering Yankee went to the Governor apparently with the notion of bullying him, and began by asking permission for a number of citizens of the United States to settle on some particular spots of land. They would be required, he was informed, to take the oaths of allegiance.

"Well," said he, " but suppose we came there and squatted ?"

" You would be turned off."

"But if several hundred came prepared to resist, what would you do?"

"We should cut them to mince-meat, Mr. —— ; we should cut them to mince-meat."

From this time until the 8th October, we were engaged at intervals among the islands of the Haro Archipelago surveying. On that day ended our outdoor work for 1858.

27th November.—Work over for the year, we proceeded to Nanaimo, where the 'Plumper' was beached in Commercial Creek, for the purpose of repairing the mischief she had done herself by running ashore. And a very moist, unpleasant business it was.

The low water was at night between the hours of 9 P.M. and 1 A.M.; it froze all the while, and the mud on which the ship lay was so soft that half the working time was taken up in keeping the trench, which had to be dug under her, open, so that the injured false keel and forefoot could be got at. At last, however, the carpenters got their work done, and on the 9th December we returned to Esquimalt for the winter.

On Christmas-day the packet arrived, bringing Colonel Moody, R.E., the Chief Commissioner of Lands and Works; Mrs. Moody; Captain Gosset, R.E., Treasurer of British Columbia, and his wife; and the Rev. B. Crickener, now chaplain at Yale. The arrival of any officials from England was welcomed as a sort of connecting link with home, and a practical acknowledgment of the colony's existence.

By this time the gold-fever had subsided, and something very like a reaction had set in. Many declared that British Columbia was a bubble that would soon burst, if, indeed, it had not burst already. Victoria now was full of miners, who had come down the Fraser, and were as eager to get back to San Francisco as they had been to leave it in the spring. And although they all spoke well of the bars, brought much gold with them, and talked confidently of returning directly the winter was over, Victoria was uneasy at their departure, and would not believe in their return. The exodus, indeed, was startling, but not without a cause. To winter at the mines was scarcely suited to the tastes of men the majority of whom, accustomed to the climate of California, where snow is never seen, were ill adapted to endure the severity of a British Columbian winter. Such of the miners, principally Canadians and Englishmen, who passed the winter season up the river, suffered severely. The weather, which, with the ordinary comforts of civilization, might be easily borne, told heavily upon men poorly clad and housed, and obliged, from the exorbitant price of provisions, to live hardly. Indeed, more than once no little fear was felt lest, from the difficulty of getting supplies up the country to them, the inland population might be starved outright. At that time, and subsequently, a great number of the Indians who, in the hunt for gold had neglected to store fish and roots, and otherwise to prepare for the winter's coming, did die of sheer starvation.

The task of transporting provisions to the bars high up the river was, indeed, great. The Harrison-Lilloett trail had, it is true, been cut, but as yet it was impassable for mule-trains, so that the only way of transporting things from lake to lake was by Indian packing. The snow, too, had blocked up many of the trails, the navigation of the Fraser itself was impeded by ice, so that it cannot be wondered at that such of the miners as had the hardihood to pass the winter near their claims were paying as much as 6s. a lb. for flour, and 3s. for bacon.

The old miners of California and Australia, men whose lives had made them impatient of hardship, except in the immediate pursuit of their darling object, and whose rapid gains provoked and permitted the utmost licence and extravagance, were little likely to remain up-country, with the comforts and vices of Victoria and San Francisco within their reach. But the people of Victoria did not then understand this; and when they saw their friends and customers of the summer depart southward, and heard accounts of the gold-bars being comparatively deserted, it required more faith than they possessed to enable them to believe that the tide of immigration would ever reflow, and that it was better for the country that these dubious Californians should leave and be replaced by a more steady and plodding population.

CHAPTER IV.

JANUARY 10th, 1859.—The rumour of another outbreak, not at Victoria, but at Yale, up the Fraser River, arrived to disturb, not altogether unpleasantly, the monotony of our winter life in Esquimalt Harbour. Intelligence had been sent down the river to Victoria that some miners had made a disturbance at Yale, and that Colonel Moody had, immediately upon being informed of it, started from Langley for the scene of action with the Engineers stationed there, which, numbering 25 men, had just arrived in the colony. The Governor considered it desirable at once to strengthen his hands. Fort Yale, ninety miles up the Fraser, was one of the stations to which some of those miners who were anxious to remain near their claims on the upper bars, so as to commence work directly the season opened,—or to whom, for sundry delicate private reasons, the delights of San Francisco were not obtainable,—flocked to pass the winter. The climate at Yale was milder than that of the Upper Fraser, which induced a great number of the men having claims north of it to come down and pass some months there, while others working on the bars near Yale were wont to spend their Sundays and holidays in the town. Among them, pre-eminent for certain social qualities which had rendered him generally obnoxious to the laws of whatever country he had favoured with his presence, was a certain Edward M'Gowan. This individual had spent some time in California, where he had become

very notorious, and had been honoured with the especial
enmity of the "Vigilance Committee" of San Francisco. Nor
without good cause. He had, I believe, had the misfortune
to kill several of his comrades in those little personal encounters which one sees reported so frequently in the
American newspapers under the head of "shooting" or
"cutting affairs." The act for which the Vigilance Committee of San Francisco doomed him to the gallows was
killing a man in cold blood in the streets of that city who
knew too much of his antecedents. M'Gowan of course denied
this, and always asserted that he had shot his foe in self-
defence: but there is little doubt that the view which the
Vigilance Committee took of the matter was the correct one.
As an instance of the working of universal suffrage, it may
be mentioned that this man at one time filled the office of a
judge in California; and quite recently, when, after shooting
at a man at Hill's Bar, whom, luckily, he missed, he escaped
across the frontier into American territory, he has been
elected to the House of Representatives of one of the border
states that lie east of the Rocky Mountains. This worthy
has given his adventures to the world in the shape of an auto-
biography, published some five years since, and written with
considerable spirit. The story told in it of his hairbreadth
escape from the clutches of the Vigilance Committee is
extremely exciting. Its agents pursued him with such
rancour that, after with the greatest difficulty he had escaped
to a steamer starting for Victoria, he was recognized, fired at,
and a bullet sent through the lappel of his coat.

That such a man as this was known to be at Hill's Bar,
some two miles below Yale, where he had a very rich claim,
and to have with him, and under his influence, a strong party
of followers bold and lawless as himself, might well give the
authorities serious concern. Upon the news, therefore, being
sent down of M'Gowan's having created a disturbance, the
Governor requested Capt. Prevost to send a party to aid the

Colonel. The 'Plumper' was the only vessel available for this service, and accordingly we embarked a party of marines and blue-jackets, under Lieutenant Gooch, from the 'Satellite,' and started at once for the scene of action.

Upon arriving at Langley we found that Colonel Moody had taken the 'Enterprise,' the only steamer then on the river capable of going further up it than Langley, and had pushed on to Yale with twenty-five of the Engineers under the command of Captain Grant, R.E. As the field-piece we had brought with us must have been parted with had the men been sent on, there being no other way of despatching them except in canoes, it was considered advisable to keep them on board the 'Plumper' at Langley, and that a messenger should at once follow and overtake Colonel Moody. This service devolved upon me, and I received orders to proceed up the river with despatches from Captain Richards informing the Colonel of the presence of the force at Langley, and to bring back his instructions.

Mr. Yale, the Hudson Bay Compay's officer at Fort Langley, undertook to provide a canoe and crew for the journey, and my own preparations were soon made—a blanket, frock and trowsers, a couple of rugs, two or three pipes, plenty of tobacco, tea, coffee, some meat and bread, a frying-pan and saucepan, completing my outfit. At this time canoe-travelling was quite new to me, and, familiar as it has since become, I quite well remember the curious sensations with which this my first journey of the kind was commenced. It was midwinter, the snow lay several inches thick upon the ground; the latest reports from up the river spoke of much ice about and below Fort Hope, so that I was by no means sorry to avail myself of the offer of Mr. Lewis, of the Hudson Bay Company, who had accompanied the 'Plumper' to Langley as pilot, to be my companion. Mr. Yale had selected a good canoe and nine stout paddlers, four half-breeds and five Indians, and when I landed from the ship a few minutes before eleven they were waiting on the beach, dressed in their best blankets, with large streamers of bright red, blue, and yellow ribbons, in which they delight so much, flying from their caps. Mr. Yale had previously harangued them, and presented them with these streamers by way of impressing them with the importance of the service in which they were engaged. Seating ourselves in the canoe as comfortably as we could, away we started, the frail bark flying over the smooth water, and the crew singing at the top of their wild, shrill voices, their parti-coloured decorations streaming in the bitter winter wind.

The North American Indians, and, indeed, the Canadians as well, paddle much more steadily when they sing. They keep splendid time, and, by way of accompaniment, bring the handle of their paddles sharply against the gunwale of the canoe. In singing their custom is—and the greatest stickler for etiquette among us will find himself outdone by the Indian's respect for whatever habit or fashion may have dictated—for the steersman to sing, the crew taking up the chorus. Although I have frequently tried to induce one of the others to start a song, with the view of testing the strength of their social habit in this respect, I have never succeeded unless supported in my request by the steersman. This post of honour is usually conferred upon the senior of the party, unless the owner of the canoe happens to form one of the crew, when he takes the seat by virtue of his interest in it. Next in position and importance to the steersman are the pair of paddlers who sit immediately behind the passengers; then come the two forward hands, who have a great deal to do with the management of the canoe in keeping it clear of blocks of floating ice, or the snags which often appear suddenly under its bows, and preventing the current from spinning it round and swamping it, which, but for the keen look-out they keep and their dexterity in the use of the paddles, would often happen in such swift and treacherous currents as those of North American rivers.

We paddled along quickly until five o'clock, when we stopped for supper, and, landing, made tea. This meal over, we started again and held on steadily all night. If the journey by day was strange and somewhat exciting, how much more so did it become when night set in! Wet, cold, and tired, we rolled ourselves up in the rugs, and in time fell into a broken sleep, lulled by the monotonous rap of the paddles upon the gunwale of the canoe, the rippling sound of the water against its sides, the song of the men now rising loud and shrill, now sinking into a low, drowsy hum. Ever and anon roused by a louder shout from the paddlers in the bow, we started up to find the canoe sweeping by some boat moored to the shore, or a miner's watch-fire, from which an indistinct figure would rise, gaze at us wonderingly as we passed howling by, and sometimes shout to us loudly in reply. We might well startle such of the miners as saw or heard us. Whenever we passed a fire, or a boat drawn up ashore, or moored to the trees by the beach, in which miners might be sleeping, the Indians would commence singing at the top of their voices; and we often saw sleepers start up, in wonder no doubt, who could be travelling on the river at night at such a season,—and in some fear perhaps, for several murders had lately been committed, which were attributed rightly or wrongly to Indian agency. And, indeed, as we swept by a watch-fire near enough for its glare to light up the dark figures straining at their hard work, and their wild, swarthy faces, with the long, bright ribbons streaming behind them,—we might well give a shock to some wearied sleeper roused abruptly from dreams of home, or some rich claim which was to make his fortune, by the wild Indian boat-chant.

Most of our journey lay close along the shore, where, of course, the current was less rapid and advantage could be taken of the numerous eddies that set in near the banks. Our chief man was quite well acquainted with the river's navigation, having been for years in the Hudson Bay Company's employ.

When we came to a rapid, or it was necessary to cross the river from one bank to the other, by one consent the singing would cease, the paddlers' breath be husbanded to better purpose, and every muscle strained to force the canoe over the present difficulty. At such times when any greater exertion was necessary, or a more formidable obstacle than usual seemed on the point of being mastered, the Indians would give a loud prolonged shout terminating in a shriller key, and dash their paddles into the boiling water with still fiercer vehemence. There can be few stranger sensations than that which we felt many times that night, when after paddling so steadily alongshore that we had fallen fast asleep, we were awoke suddenly by a heavy lurch of the canoe, and found the water rushing in over the gunwale, and the boat almost swamped by the fierce exertions of the paddlers, and tearing broadside down rather than across the rapid river, until with a shout it was run ashore on the opposite bank, and the excited rowers rested a few minutes to regain their breath before again paddling up the quieter water by the shore.

Next morning, about four o'clock, we landed for a short spell of rest, and, clearing away the snow, lit a fire and lay round it for a couple of hours. At the end of that time we picked ourselves up, stiff with cold, and breakfasted, and by half-past seven were under weigh again and paddling up the river, the Indians, to all appearance, as lively and unwearied as if they had slept the whole night through. I cannot say the same for their passengers. It was very cold, a sensation which we both tried in vain to get rid of by taking an occasional turn at the paddles; and the few snatches of short, disturbed sleep we had managed to obtain had left us very much fatigued. The novelty of the situation, too, in my case had worn away, and I confess that the second night of my journey was one of unmitigated discomfort and weariness. Upon the second morning we rested a little longer by our watchfire, Myhu-pu-pu, the head man of the party, assuring us that we had plenty of time to reach Hope before nightfall. But Myhu-pu-pu was wrong: night fell while we were still some miles below the fort. About three in the afternoon we had boarded the 'Enterprise' and learnt that she had been three days in the ice, had only got out of it indeed the previous morning, and that Colonel Moody had not, therefore, been able to reach Hope until that day. We had reason to congratulate ourselves upon our good fortune, as we had only met some floating ice and been nowhere in very serious danger from it, although once or twice we had narrowly escaped being swamped by floating blocks. But as we proceeded we found the river more and more swollen, the ice thicker and in greater quantities, and despite all the efforts of the crew, darkness set in while we were yet some miles short of our destination. On we pushed, however, and I had fallen asleep, when I was suddenly awakened by a sharp crack almost under my head. The canoe had struck a rock in crossing a rapid in the river, at a spot now known as Cornish Bar, but then called Murderer's Bar, from a murder that had taken place there, and she was stove in unmistakeably.

Thanks to the courage and skill of the elder of the crew, we were extricated from our perilous predicament. Leaping on to the rock, against which the full force of the current was driving the canoe, they lifted her off without a moment's hesitation, and the other rowers shooting her ashore, we all jumped out and ran her up upon the snow. Of course everything was wet, ourselves included; but we were too grateful for our narrow escape to heed this trifling inconvenience. Meanwhile the men, whose courage and readiness had preserved us, were still upon the rock, the current sweeping by up to their knees and threatening to carry them away. The canoe being hastily repaired and veered down to them by a rope, they too were brought safely ashore. Then arose the question, how were we to be got to Fort Hope that night? It was a serious one, not admitting of a very easy solution.

To get the canoe afloat again was soon found impossible, as she was split fore and aft, and it was ultimately determined to leave two of the Indians in charge of it while the rest of us tried to make the trail, which was known to pass near this spot to the Fort. I have since that night walked that trail, when it was as pretty and pleasant a summer evening's stroll as any one would wish to enjoy; but on this occasion, with two or three feet of snow upon it, and three or four feet more ready to receive us on either side if a false step was made, that three-mile walk to Hope was very hard work while it lasted. It was worse for my companion (Mr. Lewis), for in crossing a river by a fallen tree, which served as a bridge, his foot gave way and he slipped in, drenching his frozen clothes and limbs afresh. Fortunately, however, it was not very deep, and he was fished out, and we reached the Fort without further accident.

Since the time of which I am now writing the old Hudson Bay Fort has been pulled down, and a more commodious one erected in its stead. Then the officer in charge of it had only one chamber to serve for both sitting and bed room; and late at night into this and the presence of Colonel Moody, Captain Grant, Mr. Begbie, and the Hudson Bay Company's officers, gathered round the fire, we made our way, looking, I dare say, pitiable objects enough. With the ready kindness which I never failed to meet with from the Company's officers in British Columbia, Mr. Ogilvy soon equipped both of us in suits of dry clothes, and seated us before a hot supper.

In a subsequent chapter I shall have occasion to speak more fully of " bars ;" but as the word will occur frequently in this book, I may here say that all those places where gold is found and worked on a river's bank are called by that name. This term has become the recognised one, and is not mere miner's slang; all proclamations referring to gold-extracting, &c., being addressed to the " mining bars " of such and such a district.

F

Bars are formed simply by a deposit of heaps of detritus at various bends of a river flowing through accumulations of irrupted rock, and between mountains whose sides have been broken down by former great convulsions. The rushing river tears away mass after mass of this rock and gravel, and, carrying on a natural combination of the "sluicing" and "crushing" processes, deposits the gold, with its ever-accompanying black metallic sand and a certain quantity of common earth, at intervals along its banks, carrying most of the lighter sand, &c., out to its mouth, there to form sandbanks and flats. It will be easily understood, therefore, that these bars are formed at every place where there is or has been anything to catch the drift as it comes down. But what is somewhat curious is the very different value of the deposit at various bars, or even parts of the same bar, some being very rich, others very poor, even where they are close together; and this happens not in the vertical section, which would be to some extent intelligible, but at an equal distance under the surface. One part of a bar may "give out," while another part will be worth working 20 feet deeper.

Thus all bars are formed in the same way, even although the rivers which deposited some of them have long since ceased to flow, or been diverted into other channels, causing what are termed "dry diggings," of which I shall speak hereafter. Very rich bars are often covered with sand, mud, &c., for, in some instances, several hundred feet. In California some of the richest diggings now worked are the beds of old rivers, quite dry, often running in very different directions to those of the present streams, and occurring from 100 to 300 feet below what is now the surface of the earth.

The Commissioner was, when I reported myself, rather surprised at the promptitude with which his requisition for troops had been met by the Governor, and perhaps a little embarrassed. His impression now was that the reports which had reached him at Yale and hurried him hither had been greatly exaggerated, and from the accounts which had since reached him he had the best reason to believe that the feeling of the mining population at Yale and elsewhere had been grossly misrepresented. However, he said that he had decided on proceeding next day to Yale with Mr. Begbie only, leaving Captain Grant and his party of Engineers at Hope; and he desired me to accompany him, so that if, upon his arrival at Yale, the presence of troops should be found necessary, I might return to Hope with orders to that effect; and it was also determined that Mr. Lewis should take the canoe back to Langley as soon as it was repaired, and tell Captain Richards of my arrival and detention.

Next morning, therefore, we started, and reached Yale at three. The town was perfectly quiet, and the Colonel was received upon his entrance with the most vociferous cheering and every sign of respect and loyalty. Upon the way up we stopped at several of the bars, and made inquiries which satisfied us that the miners were doing very well, although they complained that the snow had for some days past kept them from working. The river-scenery between these two ports was beautiful, even at this season of the year. The distance is only fifteen miles, but the strength of the current is so great that in the winter five or six hours are consumed in the journey, and in the summer—when the stream is swollen by the melting snow—double that time is often taken. The only streams of any size that feed the Fraser for this distance are the Swal-lach-Coom, which flows into it some five miles below Yale, and the Que-que-alla, which runs into it two miles above Hope. The Que-que-alla is a considerable stream, dividing into two branches further in, and contains numbers of trout. The mountains on either side are from three to four thousand feet high, and are composed almost entirely of plutonic rocks, and at their base is found the "drift" in which the gold is contained.

As I have already said, Fort Yale presented the most peace-

F 2

ful aspect imaginable. The day after our arrival happening
to be Sunday, Colonel Moody performed service in the court-
house. It was the first time this had ever happened in
Yale, and the thirty or forty miners who attended formed a
most orderly and attentive congregation. After church, the
difficulty which had brought us here was investigated, and
the magistrate at Hill's Bar, the principal bar on this part
of the river, lying a mile below Yale, was suspended from
his functions. A very few words will suffice to explain
it. At Hill's Bar there was a resident magistrate, who was
one of the miners, though superior to most of them in position and acquirements; and at Yale two others—one who
was shortly afterwards proved guilty of some rascality and
discharged; the other, an honest man enough, but altogether
unfit, from temperament and social position, for the discharge
of his duties. These three dignitaries were not upon the
best terms with one another, and two of them claimed a
certain case and prisoner as belonging each to his own district, and disputed the right of adjudicating upon them to
such a degree that, one having possession of the culprit's
body, and refusing to give it up to his colleague, the other
went to the length of swearing in special constables to his
aid, and removing the prisoner by force of arms to his
jurisdiction at Hill's Bar. Among these special constables,
and very possibly among the instigators of the squabble,
Mr. Edward McGowan figured conspicuously; and it was the
outraged magistrate's report, that this worthy had been
prison-breaking in his district, that gave it to the authorities at Langley and Victoria so serious an aspect. However, upon investigating the matter, he was found to have
acted, if with indiscreet zeal, yet not illegally, and no charge
was preferred against him on that account. But the same
afternoon, while Colonel Moody, representing the majesty of
the law, was still at Yale, Mr. McGowan outraged it unmis-
takably by committing an unprovoked assault. This, coupled

with sundry other suspicious circumstances, caused Colonel Moody to think that McGowan's friends and admirers would, if provoked, break into serious insubordination; and he at once instructed me to drop down the river to Hope and Langley, and order up the Engineers, Marines, and blue-jackets left at those places.

The utmost precaution was taken about my journey.   Mr. Allard, the Hudson Bay Company's officer at Yale, was instructed to have a small canoe launched unseen by the miners, who, it was thought, might endeavour to stop me, as they no doubt easily could have done.   The darkness was waited for, and, the canoe being launched and dropped about half a mile down the river, Mr. Allard came to the house for me, and led me to it along the river's bank.   As we dropped down the stream I was afraid even to light a pipe lest we should be stopped at Hill's Bar.   Absurd as all this now seems—especially as I heard on my return that the miners knew perfectly well of my starting—it was not without its use at the time.   The promptitude with which Captain Grant appeared on the spot with the Engineers at daylight next morning astonished the miners a good deal, and it need not be assumed that, because they apologised and paid their fines, they would have done so equally had coercion not been threatened.

Reaching Hope at half-past eight that night, I very much astonished Captain Grant by telling him that he was to start for Yale at once, and, landing his men below Hill's Bar on the opposite side of the river, to march thence into Yale.   Having given these instructions, I embarked in the canoe again, and about midnight—spinning down the Fraser being a very different matter to struggling up against its current—reached the 'Enterprise,' which was to convey me to Langley, and bring the men there up.   Here a slight delay took place, as the steamer could not be got ready to start until day-break; but away we went the instant dawn broke, and

reached Langley in the afternoon of the following day, where,
the 'Enterprise' having wooded, every one was got aboard,
and we were struggling up against the current by six P.M.,
reaching Smess River by nine or ten that night, and Cornish
Bar by 8·30 the following night.

There the 'Enterprise's' further progress was effectually
barred, and, taking a canoe again, I made my way to Hope,
where I found that further instructions had come from the
Colonel to the effect that the blue-jackets were to remain
there, and only the Marines to go on to Yale. So things
were looking less martial, and I was not surprised, on pushing
forward to Yale next morning, to find that the short campaign was at an end, and the peace, which had hardly been
disturbed, restored. Mr. McGowan, after enjoying the sensation he had caused, paid the Commissioner a formal visit,
and, after making a very gentlemanlike apology for the hasty
blow which had disturbed the peace of British Columbia,
and entering into an elaborate and, I believe, successful
defence of his previous conduct in the squabble of the rival
judges, committed himself frankly into the hands of justice.
What could be done with such a frank, entertaining rascal?
Justice herself could not press hardly for her dues in such a
case. He was fined for the assault, exonerated from all previous misdemeanours, and next day, upon Hill's Bar being
visited by Mr. Begbie (the Chief Justice) and myself, he conducted us over the diggings, washed some "dirt" to show us
the process, and invited us to a collation in his hut, where
we drank champagne with some twelve or fifteen of his Californian mining friends. And, whatever opinion the Vigilance
Committee of San Francisco might entertain of these gentlemen, I, speaking as I found them, can only say that, all
things considered, I have rarely lunched with a better-spoken,
pleasanter party. The word "miner" to many unacquainted
with the gold-fields conveys an impression similar, perhaps,
to that of "navvy." But among them may often be found

men who, by birth and education, are well qualified to hold their own in the most civilised community of Europe. Here, for instance, I was entertained in the hut of a man who—by virtue of his rascality, no doubt—had been selected to fill the office of judge among his fellows in California; while one of my neighbours had taken his degree at an American University, and may since, for aught I know, have edited a Greek play and been made a bishop. I remember afterwards travelling with two men, who, meeting casually, recognised one another as old schoolfellows and class-men. Neither was in the least surprised at the other's condition, although one was a well-to-do surgeon with a very remunerative practice, and the other was an "express" man, penniless, and carrying letters some 130 or 140 miles for a subsistence.

As I have several times mentioned "expresses" and "express-men," I may here explain that all over California and British Columbia letters or parcels are carried with perfect safety, and, all things considered, very cheaply, by means of them. The organisation of some of these companies is most elaborate. The principal one there is Wells Fargo's, which has agencies all over the world. Their office at Victoria is one of the finest buildings there; and their house in San Francisco is as large as our General Post-office. I have never known a letter sent by them miscarry. The charge for sending anywhere in California is only 10 cents (5d.), and so great is my faith in them that I would trust anything, in even that most insecure country, in an envelope bearing the stamp of Wells Fargo and Co.'s Express. There are several minor expresses in different parts of the country—Ballou's Fraser River Express, Jeffray's Express, Freeman's Express—all of which appear to flourish; and so great is the trust reposed in them, and the speed with which they travel, that the miners, as yet, prefer sending their dust by them to the Government escort.

A few days later we dropped down the river to Hope,

where the blue-jackets were paraded, and our one field-piece
fired the first salute ever heard at Fort Hope in honour of
the Colonel. The men were then got safely on board the
'Plumper' again, which proceeded to examine the river
and its north bank a few miles below Langley, and report
whether it would do for the site of the capital of British
Columbia—it having been decided that Derby, or New
Langley, the spot first selected, was not desirable. The site
of New Westminster—or Queenborough, as it was first called
—is, so far as its geographical position is concerned, very
good indeed, as it is also in a strategical point of view;
but the bush there was very thick, while at Derby there was
a large space of clear ground. The work of clearing the
bush has been the great drawback to the progress of New
Westminster. Dr. Campbell and I went to examine a part
a little north of where the town stands, and so thick was the
bush that it took us two hours to force our way in rather
less than a mile and a-half. Where we penetrated it was
composed of very thick willow and alder, intertwined so
closely that every step of the way had to be broken through,
while the ground was cumbered with fallen timber of a larger
growth. During this scramble I stumbled upon a large bear,
which seemed to be as much surprised to see me as I was at
sight of him, and I dare say equally discomposed. At any
rate, he showed no disposition to cultivate my acquaintance;
and, as I was some way ahead of my companion and had
only one barrel of my gun loaded with small shot, I was not
sorry to find that our ways seemed to lie in opposite directions.

The site hit upon by Colonel Moody was a little below
this thick bush, where the ground was somewhat clearer.
Regarded both in a military and commercial light, it was
infinitely preferable to the spot which had previously been
fixed upon for this purpose higher up and on the opposite
side of the river. New Westminster has many natural

advantages in which Derby is wanting, not the least being
sufficient depth of water to allow the largest class of vessels
capable of passing the sand-heads at the Fraser mouth to
moor alongside of its wharves. I shall have occasion at a
future time to speak at greater length of this and the other
settlements upon the Fraser River.

Our time for some weeks after this was employed in
cruising among the islands, creeks, and inlets, upon surveying work, which, however valuable to the future settlers
and navigators of British Columbia, is but little likely to
interest the general reader.

March, 1859.—Upon our return to Victoria a difficulty
which had been felt for some time, arising from the growing
immigration of Northern Indians, who came down from
Queen Charlotte Island, Fort Simpson, and the inlets north
of Vancouver Island, to see and trade with the white men,
had reached such a pitch that it was necessary for the
Government to take some steps in the matter. Numbers of
these, with their families, came down Johnstone Strait in large
canoes, carrying furs and skins which they expected to sell
for fabulous prices. They were scarcely pleasant visitors—
not likely to be welcomed by a young community with a
newly-formed and small police, as, although quiet enough
when sober, they got drunk as often as they had a chance,
and then became quite unmanageable.

These Indians of the northern coast tribes of British
Columbia and Vancouver Island are much finer and fiercer
men than the Songhies, the tribe living at and in the neighbourhood of Victoria, or indeed than any of the southern
tribes. They are constantly at war with one another, and
were as likely as not to bring their feuds south with them,
and could be as little trusted to keep from blows, if they
met in Victoria, as the rival Highland clans in old times
when they came into collision in the streets of Edinburgh.
They all travelled armed; for in their journey to Victoria

they had to pass the neighbourhood of several hostile tribes, by whom they were certain to be attacked if caught unprepared. One tribe especially, living at Cape Mudge, the south point of Valdez Island, and known as the U-cle-ta, ar: the Ishmaelites of the country, whose hands are literally against every man, and every man's against them. There was a great fight between these and the men of a northern tribe coming south in 1858, in which a good many were killed on either side; and they are always on the lookout for any one passing by their neighbourhood, and of course suffer in their turn whenever they are caught at a disadvantage. Upon one occasion, when I was camped for the Sunday in a pleasant little cove, just southward of Point Chatham, in Johnstone's Strait, it happened that a party of some hundred Haida Indians from Queen Charlotte Island came past on their way to Victoria. On seeing our boats, they came alongside, as Indians always do, and began, after their fashion, chattering and exhibiting their furs and specimens of the gold they had collected in Queen Charlotte Island. In the middle of our talk the canoes which had been keeping watch outside in the strait while the rest were with us raised an alarm. Two small canoes of another tribe, that had been near us all the morning fishing, just then hove in sight again, and immediately our companions pulled out and examined the muskets that lay under cover ready to their grasp. Although we were not in sufficient force to interfere between them, I have no doubt whatever that the poor fellows in the canoes, who had slept at our camp the night previously, would have been murdered or taken into slavery but for our presence.

Efforts have been made to put down this cruel system of predatory warfare, and occasionally a grand peace-making of the hostile tribes is held, at which eternal friendship is vowed. But it is not long before some fresh depredation is committed, or some solitary Indian is caught by a party of another tribe, and the temptation to murder or take him prisoner being too strong to be resisted, war breaks out again. The U-cle-ta are great offenders in this way. In the summer of 1860 a lesson was administered to them, which, it is to be hoped, may do them some good. A party of them had attacked and robbed some Chinamen, and escaped to their village at Cape Mudge, which, being stockaded for protection against the other tribes, they no doubt thought would be equally efficacious against white men. H.M. gunboat 'Forward' was sent there to demand restitution; and, on approaching the village, she was fired upon from the stockade with loud shouts of defiance. The gunboat first fired a shell or two over; but, Indian-like, they mistook this leniency for inability to hit them, and coming out in front of the stockade fired several volleys at her, which fortunately, however, fell harmless against her rifle-plates. She then opened fire upon their canoes on the beach, and lastly upon the stockade; and it was not till several men were killed that they came to terms, and restored the stolen property.

One of the most fertile sources of quarrel among all the tribes on this coast with whom I am at all acquainted arises from the intrigues of the Indians with the squaws of neighbouring tribes. Indeed the breach of the Seventh Commandment is as fashionable in this out-of-the-way part of the world as it has been at times among European communities. A code of reprisals and compensation has been adopted among them which certainly has the merit of simplicity. The aggrieved husband whose wife has been misled troubles his head very little about her; and when she comes back to him, which she does very soon, shows no inclination to visit her offence at all hardly upon her. But although he receives her again, he to a certain extent discards her, and, if he can afford it, adds another wife to his establishment. Should number two go astray, as is very probable, he takes a third wife; but he keeps the sinners, penitent or not, with him still, and they all live together to all appearance contentedly enough. Meanwhile he is busy making reprisals upon his enemy; and the result, when they happen to be chiefs, is probably a war between two tribes, in which the members of both join with the greatest interest and zeal.

It is in such social habits that the missionaries find their greatest difficulties when working for the reformation of these people, more particularly as the white trader generally confirms by his practice all that the red man is warned against. If nothing else pleads for the introduction of Englishwomen into British Columbia, this fact surely does. In reference to the Indian disregard of marital obligations, I remember a noted Chief, named St. Paul, in the interior of the country —of whom I shall have more to say hereafter—telling me that the Roman Catholic priests had often remonstrated with him upon his life ; and, among other social reformations that seemed to them desirable, had urged him to go through the marriage ceremony with his present wife. " To what avail ? " argued St. Paul. " So long as she remains true to me, I will hold to her; but if she fails me—married or not—I shall discard her for another."

I have said that it was partly curiosity to see the white man, and still more the hope of making larger sums for their furs than the Hudson Bay Company's agents would give them, that led the Indians to make the journey to Victoria. In the latter hope they were often disappointed ; but it must not, therefore, be inferred that the Indians are bad traders. On the contrary, they are some of the best hands at a bargain or deal I have ever met with; the squaws, as may be usual with their sex, having the most to say upon the matter, and being the harder to persuade. In buying of Indians, if the squaw be present, it is always advisable to win her favour. The man never concludes a bargain without consulting her; and I have frequently seen her put a veto upon some commercial arrangement that I had imagined settled, simply because she happened to be annoyed, and was

sulky at something that had transpired while the bargain was
being made. So, when the matter is settled, the shirts,
blankets, or other articles taken in exchange are always
passed to the woman for her inspection and approval; and
she claims the right of declaring the deal at an end, even at
the eleventh moment, if she disapproves of their make or material. It is, therefore, always advisable to win her to your
side, if possible, when buying anything; and this can generally be done by a judicious present of beads, or perhaps a
pair of gorgeous earrings.

The presence of these people in large and increasing
numbers was felt as a serious inconvenience, and possible
danger to Victoria. Several plans for checking their immigration were proposed, and at last it was determined—not,
I think, with the judgment that ordinarily characterised the
dealing of the Government with the Indians—to send them
back to their own country. The impolicy of such a measure
soon became apparent, to say nothing of the impossibility of
carrying it into effect. No one who knew anything of the
Indian character would believe that sending a few hundreds
back would have the effect of deterring others from attempting the voyage down. Besides which, how could it be
expected that men whom we had driven away or kept back
forcibly from our towns would permit whites to "prospect" for
gold or settle in their country? An endeavour was, however,
made to carry out this resolution; and upon their making
the excuse that they were afraid of encountering the hostile
Indians of Nanaimo and other places on their return, H.M.S.
'Tribune' was called upon to convoy them as far north as
Cape Mudge. But, even while on their way, they met many
others coming down; and it was evident that nothing but
violent measures of repression, backed by a strong military
and naval force, were likely to stem the tide of savage life
that was setting southward. So at last it was considered
useless to try; and Mr. Duncan, the missionary, having for-

tunately arrived from the North, his advice was sought upon
the subject, and it was decided to take measures to settle
them upon their arrival in camps of their own, near Victoria,
and to take away their muskets from them while they remained there. This latter measure was of the first importance, as for a long time past it had become positively unsafe
to take the Esquimalt road after dark at night from the
number of drunken Indians lying about, who were wont to
discharge their muskets upon the slightest provocation; and
as they occupied huts on either side of the road, they often
fired across from one to the other, to the great inconvenience,
to say no more, of the passer by.

The ordinance with respect to disarming the Indians was
not so well carried out as it might have been. The Indians
complained, and with some reason, that they rarely if ever
received their own guns back again. It was not to be expected, of course, that the police of Victoria should return to
each man his own musket; but care might have been taken
to keep the weapons of each party distinct, so that they could
select their own.

The presence and influence of Mr. Duncan, of whom I
shall have to speak at length hereafter, were, however, of
much value in keeping these Northern Indians in order; a
school was built for them, which was well attended, and they
passed the summer quietly enough.

CHAPTER V.

———◦◦◦———

MARCH 31ST, 1859.—From this time until the 7th of April, the 'Plumper' was busy surveying the Harbour of Victoria. On the 10th we sailed for Nanaimo, and then across the Straits to Fraser River, where we met the 'Satellite,' and embarked from her the Marines who had come over in the 'Tribune,' and twenty Engineers, whom we had orders to land at New Westminster, which place had since our last visit become the head-quarters of what military force was stationed in British Columbia.

Shortly before leaving Esquimalt upon this mission, the Governor had requested Captain Richards to send one of the Officers of the 'Plumper' up the Fraser River, to make a running survey of those parts of it then occupied by miners, and to report upon it generally; and I was ordered to undertake this task, Dr. Campbell, assistant-surgeon of the ship, accompanying me. The programme which was sketched out for me by his Excellency was, to ascend the Fraser as far as Cayoosh (now Lilloett), returning thence by the Harrison and Lilloett trail. Discretion, however, was given me to modify this route, if it should appear to be desirable.

From Victoria to the entrance of the Fraser, the distance by water is ninety miles. At present I will only speak of the western passage by the Canal de Haro, as it is generally if not always used. Starting from Victoria, a ship rounds

Discovery Island, the smaller river-steamers passing inside, and then turning up the Canal or Strait of Haro. This island was called by Vancouver after his ship; indeed, almost all these places were named before our arrival there. It is very easy to distinguish between the parts named by Vancouver or by the Spanish explorers Galiano and Valdes. Thus, although the eastern channel through the islands was called Canal del nostra Senora de Rosario, the presence of the English at the same time is obvious, from the fact that we find spots in it bearing such names as Cypress Island, Strawberry Bay, &c. So the earliest passage of the Spanish ships up the Strait of Haro is evident from the islands and bays bearing names such as San Juan, Cordova, and Saturna. Again, we need not ask the nationality of the voyager who named Admiralty Inlet; and we know that Puget Sound, now in American territory, owes its appellation to one of Vancouver's officers of that name.

Should the day be clear, the traveller rounding Discovery Island obtains a magnificent view of the mainland, with the snow-capped peaks of Mounts Baker and Rainier towering in the distance. Under such favourable circumstances, the view of Vancouver Island is exceedingly attractive, the otherwise barren shore being pleasantly diversified with the houses and buildings of the few farmers who have settled here, and brought the land into cultivation. Upon the Island of San Juan also, which is passed in crossing to the Fraser, may be seen the buildings of the Hudson Bay farm rising in the midst of the green prairie that forms the southeast end of that island. Leaving San Juan, the steamer's course passes through a pretty little group of islands which lie on the west of the strait, up Plumper Sound, through Active Passage, a narrow passage between Galiano and Mayne Islands, by taking which a considerable saving of time and distance is effected, and so out into the Gulf of Georgia opposite Point Roberts.

When the first rush to the diggings commenced, Point Roberts, upon or near which there was no house nor any symptom of one being built, was at once fixed upon as the site of an important " city ; " and half-a-dozen buildings sprang up on the flat in front of the bluff, where, while the stream of boats and canoes was pouring up the river, they drove a brisk and flourishing trade in whisky especially. But when the rush subsided, and steamers took the place of the boats and canoes in which the earliest miners had made their hazardous passage from Victoria, Roberts found its occupation gone, and nothing but the remains of two or three log-huts marks the site of the departed city.

In crossing the Gulf of Georgia, there may frequently be seen, as the Fraser is neared, the line of the fresh and salt waters very clearly defined. And this, indeed, is almost the only sign that a river is being approached. From Point Roberts to Burrard Inlet, a distance of 28 miles, the coast is low and swampy, the trees appearing to form so thick and unbroken a line, when looked at from the Gulf of Georgia, that Vancouver, carefully as he examined this coast for all inland waters, penetrating every inlet under the impression that some day he should hit upon the one that should conduct him into Hudson Bay, sailed past the mouth of the Fraser without the least suspicion of having passed a river at all.

The sand-bank at the entrance of the Fraser is called the Sturgeon Bank, from the number of those fish caught by the Indians upon it. It extends from Point Grey, the southern entrance to Burrard Inlet, to Point Roberts, but does not join the latter, leaving thus a small space available for anchorage on its west side. This bank, and the entrance to the Fraser river generally, have been most unfairly compared to the Columbia. But there is really no point of resemblance between them. The Columbia is one of the most dangerous bar-rivers in the world, and one upon

G

which vessels are constantly lost. The captains of the
mail-packets consider the passage of this bar the only real
danger in the voyage from San Francisco; they always
batten down everything on going in or out, and are accustomed to wait three or four days, and sometimes even longer,
for fine weather before they will come out of the river. Nor
is this at all surprising when it is considered that it has the
whole drift of the Pacific upon it; while, upon the other hand,
the Fraser is perfectly sheltered from the sea by Vancouver
Island. Indeed it is not uncommon to hear a settler of
British Columbia, between which and Vancouver Island
much rivalry exists, make the, assertion that the sole use
evidently intended by Nature for that island was to form a
breakwater for the Fraser River and the other inlets of the
mainland. This is in fact so true, that although there is no
little risk of a vessel grounding in going in or out of the
river, there is little, if any, further risk ; and if she touches
at low, or at anything but high water, as the 'Plumper' did
several times, the greatest hardship is a few hours' delay
until the rising tide floats her off. Vessels ground constantly,
sometimes from bad pilotage, and very often from the buoys
having shifted with the sands, but they rarely if ever receive
any damage; while, on the Columbia, if a sailing vessel
grounds she is almost certain to be lost; and even a steamer
touching is liable to be caught by the heavy sea and pooped,
and very likely to be lost.

A petition has been presented to the Governor by those
interested in the navigation of the Fraser, to cause a buoy
and light-vessel to be placed at the sand-head. When this
is done, there will be no difficulty in entering the river; but
at present the most careful and experienced master of a ship
is liable to be deceived by the buoys which get drifted from
their places, either by the sands shifting or by the large trees
which are constantly being borne down the river. The bad
character which, owing to these causes, has attached to the

entrance of the Fraser has been most detrimental to the interests of British Columbia. The underwriters affix as high a rate of insurance upon ships clearing for New Westminster as they do upon those bound up the Columbia. Having assisted in making the surveys of this coast, I have no hesitation whatever in saying that I would as soon take a vessel over the Fraser Bar to New Westminster, as I would into Victoria, as far as risk of loss is concerned.

Before describing those parts of the Fraser which I visited in detail, it will be well, perhaps, to give a general idea of this river and the country adjacent.

The Fraser River rises in the Rocky Mountains, a little to the northward of the Athabasca Pass, and in a straight line less than 300 miles from its meeting with the waters of the Pacific in the Gulf of Georgia. From its source it takes a north-westerly direction for about 160 miles, when it is turned southward by a spur of the Rocky Mountains, which runs east and west nearly to Stuart Lake, where it turns northward and assumes the name of the Peak Mountains. On the other side of this spur rises the Peace River, which from this point runs northward 130 or 140 miles till it meets the Finlay River, and thence flows eastward through the Rocky Mountains. I have called the reader's attention particularly to the Peace River, as it is towards it that the gold is now leading the miners, and in it and its tributaries that many expect the richest diggings will be found. This mountain-spur, as I have said, turns the Fraser sharply round to the south, and it then forces its way in torrents and rapids through the several great parallel valleys that intersect this region in a direction a little east of south for 300 miles, till it reaches Hope, from whence it runs nearly east and west for about 80 miles to its mouth.

About 45 miles below the upper turn of the river is Fort St. George. I said *about* 45 miles, for in this country the positions are as yet very roughly ascertained, and I take this

G 2

opportunity of saying that all the distances I mention on the river are only approximate.

Fort St. George, a Hudson Bay post, is situated on the west bank of the Fraser River at its junction with the Stuart River, which latter flows in a like direction from Stuart Lake, which is the southern post of a chain of three or four lakes which stretch northward 100 miles to the head-waters of the Bear River, at the foot of the Peak Mountains. At the head of the upper of these lakes stands Fort Connolly.

Lying north-west from the head of Stuart Lake, and divided from it by a narrow ridge, is Babine Lake, on which there is another Hudson Bay Company's post, and from which rises the Simpson or Babine River which thence flows westerly, running into the sea just above Fort Simpson, and as nearly as possible on our northern boundary on the coast. Forty miles up the Stuart River it is met by a stream coming from Fraser Lake, which is a small lake thirty miles south-ward of Stuart Lake, and on which is situated Fraser Fort. The stream between the Fraser Lake and Stuart River, which I believe has no English name, receives on its course the waters of the Natchuten Lakes and some others. I shall have again to speak of all these lakes and posts, and will now, therefore, pass on without further noticing them.

Five-and-forty miles below St. George is the West-road River, of no particular note at this time; but better known to geographers than the other streams, from the fact of Sir Alexander McKenzie having in the end of the last century gone by it to the coast.

Another distance of 45 miles brings us to Fort Alexandria, the head-quarters of the district for the Hudson Bay Company, and better known than the other posts to the miners as being the nearest one to the Quesnelle and Cariboo diggings. What is now called the Cariboo country, so named from a species of deer found there in large numbers,* lies between the parallels of Alexandria and Fort St. George, and east of the Fraser River.

Cariboo Lake is 30 miles north-east of Alexandria, and from that point up to near Fort St. George, in the north, stretch the Cariboo diggings, with their various local names of Williams Creek, Antler Creek, Cañon Creek, &c.

Nearly in the same latitude as Alexandria, and 30 miles east of it, are the Quesnelle Lakes, where gold was found and worked in considerable quantities in 1859. There are two of these lakes, one running southward, the other east for some distance, and then north-east until it nearly meets the head-waters of Canoe River. The first of these lakes is estimated by those who have traversed them at 70 miles in length, the latter at 100.

Thirty miles below Alexandria, on the east side of the Fraser, is a stream running in a south-westerly direction from several lakes, of which the principal are Williams Lake, Lac la Hâche, Horse Lake, Lac Tranquille, &c. Twenty miles below this again, and consequently 50 from Alexandria, is the Chilcotin River, which runs in a north-east-by-east direction to the lake of the same name, at the south end of which stand the remains of an abandoned Hudson Bay Company's fort.

Sixty miles below the mouth of the Chilcotin we come to the Pavillon, situated on the opposite or east bank of the river.

From this point downwards I am enabled to describe the river from personal experience. At Hope, it assumes the character of a navigable stream, steamers of light draught reaching this point, and even Yale, 15 miles further up.

In June, July, and August, the melting of the snow causes the river to rise so rapidly and makes the current so strong that it requires a very powerful steamer to stem it. It is

---

* The name of this animal is properly Cerfbœuf, but the country is now always called and written Cariboo.

during these months that numbers of large trees are brought down from its flooded banks, offering a serious obstruction to navigation, many of them ultimately fixing themselves in the stream and becoming "snags." Between Hope and Langley —the latter 30 miles from the river's mouth—there is always a current ranging from four to seven knots; but at Langley the river becomes a broad, deep, and placid stream, and except during the three summer months (June, July, and August) the influence of the flood-stream is felt there. The current is not more than three knots and the depth of water ten fathoms, so that vessels of any draught may conveniently anchor.

Vessels of from eighteen to twenty feet draught may enter the Fraser and proceed as high as Langley, or even a few miles above it, provided they have steam-power.

The river is at its lowest stage during the months of January, February, and March. In April the snow commences to melt and the river to rise, which it does perhaps two feet in this month at Langley, the flood-stream at New Westminster being still strong enough to swing a ship.

In May the waters rise rapidly, and continue to do so till the end of June, when they have reached their highest point. They remain so until the middle of August, with perhaps slight fluctuations. During these six weeks, the banks being overflowed, the meadows at the entrance, and the extensive plains on the banks of the Pitt River above Langley, are covered for several miles, and the strength of the stream becomes four to seven knots, and in some places even more.

The ordinary rise of the river at Langley is 14 feet; but when we were there Mr. Yale, who had been in charge of the post for 30 years without intermission, said he had known it rise 25 feet. Higher up the river, of course, the rise is much greater. In 1859, when I was at Pavillon, the river rose 18 feet in one night.

After the middle of August the water begins to subside,

MOUNT BAKER, FROM THE FRASER RIVER.

and in September the stream is not inconveniently strong.
September, October, and November are the most favourable
months for the navigation of the river, as the water is then
high enough to enable the steamers to reach Hope, and
the current not very strong. Sometimes the steamers get to
Hope as late as December, between which month and April
the navigation of the river to Hope is almost closed on account
of the snow and ice and the shallowness of the stream;
but the lightest draught vessels occasionally get up, though
with considerable difficulty.

At Westminster the freshets raise the level of the river
about six feet, but, as the banks are high, no inconvenience
is felt. The strength of the stream there is rarely five knots,
and in winter from two to three.

The rise and fall due to tidal causes is from eight to ten
feet, at the springs, between the Sandheads and Point Garry,
the entrance of the river proper. At New Westminster it is
six feet, and at Langley scarcely perceptible. The Sandheads
are five miles south-south-west of Point Garry; the south one
uncovers, the north does not.

The banks of the Fraser, for some 70 miles from its
mouth, are, as I have before said, in places low, and liable to
being flooded in the spring and summer. They are, however, very fertile, and a great deal of fine hay grows
naturally here, and is sent to Victoria for forage. At
New Westminster, the present capital of British Columbia,
the bank of the river rises and forms an admirable position for the future town. Mary Hill, upon which it is
proposed some day to plant the citadel which shall defend
New Westminster, rises some three or four hundred feet;
and the camp, which lies at the distance of a mile east
from the town itself, stands upon rising land fifty to a
hundred feet above the river. As regards its position,
therefore, there is no fault to be found with New Westminster; but the forest is so dense, and the trees of which

it is composed so large, that its growth is likely for some years to be very slow. Indeed, had it not been for Colonel Moody's determination to make a beginning, and for the labours of the Engineers in clearing the site of their camp, New Westminster would have made little, if any perceptible progress. As it is, if, as seems most probable, the tide of colonization continues to flow northward, and a route to the mines should be discovered up and from the head of one of the numerous inlets north of the Fraser, New Westminster may never repay the labour that has already been spent upon it. Of the severity of that labour, no one unacquainted with the difficulty of clearing bush as it exists in British Columbia can form any accurate conception. Felling the trees forms but a small part of it. When they are down, they are, of course, with the scanty resources at the settlers' command, too large to be removed, and they have to be sawn and cut up into blocks handy for removal or burning. That done, the hardest work yet remains. In forests such as these the roots of the giant trees have been spreading underground for ages, forming a close and perfect network some eight or ten feet beneath the surface. To dig this mass of interlaced roots up would defy the strength and patience of ordinary men ; and it is only the wonderful dexterity of the Canadian —and, indeed, of the American generally—in handling his axe, that enables him to enter upon, far less accomplish, so difficult a task. Their dexterity is indeed remarkable. I have seen three men—one of whom, by the way, had lost his right arm—fell a tree four feet in diameter in three-quarters of an hour. This may at first sight appear no very formidable feat ; but, after a few days' trial, the difficulties of such an undertaking will begin to loom upon the amateur backwoodsman. I remember, upon one occasion, that an officer of Marines quartered at Westminster, who thought himself, and who really was, no contemptible axeman, under-dertook for a wager to fell a certain tree, some three feet in

CHURCH AT NEW WESTMINSTER.

Page 49.

diameter, in a week. He made certain of winning, and commenced work in the most sanguine spirits. But the end of
three days found his hands blistered painfully, and the tree
upright and almost uninjured as before. At the expiration
of the stipulated time another week was given him, and still
the monarch of the wood held his head erect. The story
goes—this was, of course, after the bet was lost—that he was
found one night turning out some of his men to take a sly
chop at the tree after dark.

Despite all these drawbacks, however, New Westminster
has an unmistakeably thriving aspect. A church has been
built, together with a treasury and a court-house. Its
streets boast also of two or three very fair restaurants, some
good wharves and stores, and several private houses. In the
camp, the Engineers, who for some time lived under canvas,
are all housed; and commanding a very beautiful view up
the river stands a very comfortable house, the residence of
their commanding-officer, Colonel Moody. The view of the
Fraser from the camp is very pleasing. On the left, over Pitt
Lake, rise the beautiful peaks known as the Golden Ears;
to the right of these, the valley of the Fraser can be traced
almost as far as Fort Hope; while in the foreground, looking
over the buildings of the rising town, level land stretches
away into American territory beyond the boundary-line, as
far almost as Admiralty Inlet and Puget Sound.

Three miles below the town of Westminster, a fork of the
Fraser, unnavigable except for canoes and boats of light
draught, diverges from the main channel and meets the sea
some 6 or 7 miles above the main entrance of the river;
and about the same distance above the town the Pitt River
flows into the Fraser. This river runs from a lake of the
same name. Its banks are low, and a considerable quantity
of good land well adapted for agricultural purposes lies
on either side. Above, some 15 miles from Westminster,

Langley is reached. Here the steamers from Victoria are stopped by the shallowness of the river, and their cargoes, human and material, transferred to the stern-wheel steamers, boats, and canoes which from this point do battle with the swift, uncertain stream.

Stern-wheel steamers are peculiarly American. They are propelled by a large wheel protruding beyond the stern, the rudders—for there are generally two or three—being placed between it and the vessel's stern. They are admirably adapted to pass between snags and close to bluffs, where a side-wheel would be knocked away, and are affixed to flat-bottomed vessels drawing no more than eighteen to twenty-four inches of water.

American steamboat travelling has frequently been described, and its peculiar characteristics and perils are doubtless familiar to most of my readers. There is something very exciting about it, certainly; struggling up the river against the stream, the greatest risk comes from the overcharged boilers giving way; but tearing down the current at some twelve or fourteen knots an hour, bumping over shoals, striking against snags, and shooting rapids, is far more animated work. Snags, which form the most dangerous impediment to the navigation of rivers like the Fraser, are, as may be known to most of my readers, large trees which, having been carried down the steam to a shallow spot, become firmly embedded there. As a rule, they float down the river heavy end first, so that when they stick the upper part of the trunk opposes the stream and is worn by it to a sharp point, in many cases sufficiently below the surface to be hidden from the steersman's eye.

Going up against the current, therefore, at a comparatively slow pace, the steamer can afford to disregard the snags; for if she strikes on one, it is easy to shut off the steam and drift back from it. But spinning down the current, it is a very serious matter for one of these large unwieldy boats to become transfixed upon a well-rooted, obstinate snag. In some spots of the Fraser an awkward snag may equally impede the navigation of a steamer up or down the stream. One, known as the Umatilla Snag, from a steamer of that name having first struck upon it, lies in a very narrow and rapid bend of the river, at which, from the swiftness of the current, the steamer is very liable to be caught and drifted back upon it, after, as she imagined, having safely passed it. Upon one occasion, when I was going up the river in the 'Enterprise,' no less than three times after we had struggled past the snag the strong current caught and swung us broadside across the stream; and it was only by running the vessel's bow into the muddy bank without a moment's hesitation, and holding her there by the nose, as it were, until she recovered breath to make another effort, that we escaped impalement. There was something very exciting in this struggle between the forces of steam and water. Each time, as we hung by the bank, the engineer might be heard below freshening his fires, and getting up as much steam as the boilers could, or might not, bear for the next effort. The wheel-house in these vessels is situated forward, so that there is almost direct communication between it and the engine-room. By the helm stands the captain. " Ho! Frank," he hails down the tube, " how much steam have you?" " So many pounds," is Frank's reply. " Guess you must give her ten pounds more, or we shan't get past that infernal snag." And then more stoking is heard below, and the unpleasant feeling comes over the listener that the boilers lie just beneath his feet, and that, if anything should happen to them, there can be no doubt about his fate. But, presently, Frank's voice sounds again. " All ready, Cap'en: can't give her any more!" The skipper loses no time; " Stand by, then!" is his response. Then, to the men forward, who have made a rope fast to some stump on the bank to keep the boat from dropping off, "Let go!" and she falls off for a second or two; her bow cants out a little: "ting! ting! ting!" goes the engine-room bell, the signal for full speed ahead; every timber of the lightly-built vessel trembles. We watch the trees on the bank eagerly to see if she moves ahead. Presently she drops a little, but her head is still kept up; then the stream catches her on one bow. "Stand by with the trip-pole!" is heard, and, as she swings round, "Trip!" is shouted from the wheel-house. Into the swift shallow water the heavy pole plunges, and perhaps she is brought up by it and run into the bank again; or, as probably, if the bottom should be hard and rocky, or the water deeper than was thought, away she flies down the river until she is brought up against the bank or across the snag.

The perseverance of the Yankee skipper in overcoming these difficulties is certainly remarkable. Upon one occasion, after making four unsuccessful efforts to steam past this "Umatilla Snag," all the men had to be landed and track her past the dangerous spot. So further up it was found necessary to resort to the same tedious process, and the united strength of crew and passengers with difficulty got her over a few hundred yards in the space of two hours, "Frank" below in his engine-room cramming on all the steam he could to help us. Nor is the composure with which the captain meets and remedies an accident less remarkable. A supply of tarred blankets is always kept handy for service, and if a hole is stove in the steamer's bottom, the captain coolly runs her ashore on the nearest convenient shoal, jams as many blankets into the crevice as seem necessary, nails down a few boards over them, and continues his journey composedly. He is often reduced to very serious straits, no doubt, and is not at all particular in the use of means to master a difficulty. I was assured by a passenger in the 'Enterprise' to Hope in 1859, that he saw the contents of a cask of bacon turned on to the fires when additional steam to pass a troublesome rapid was necessary.

A little above Langley the Smess River discharges its contents into the Fraser, and five or six miles onward it is fed by another stream of similar dimensions, called the Chilwayhook, on the southern bank of which are the remains of an old fishing-station of the Hudson Bay Company, now · unused. Both these rivers flow from lakes bearing their names, and are in the summer-time, when swollen by the snow-freshets from the mountains, deep enough for good-sized boats to navigate them, but in the winter are almost impassable even for canoes. Three miles above Chilwayhook River Fargo Bar is reached. This, the spot on the Fraser where gold was first washed, has long since been deserted for the richer diggings higher up the river. All along this part of the Fraser the banks are low, and sandbanks occur constantly. In the winter the channel is confined to one single swift stream, but in the summer-time, when the waters are out, the navigator may well be bewildered by the numerous channels which sweep over and between the banks and islands.

At a distance of 65 miles from the mouth of the Fraser the Harrison River is reached, up which runs the Harrison-Lilloett route, which has now become the principal road to the inland settlements. I have spoken of the difficulties which lay in the way of making this route practicable. A glance at the map will show that it consisted of a chain of lakes, some a considerable distance apart, between which a way had to be cut. The existence of this route had been known to the officers of the Hudson Bay Company for years; but no effort had been made to render it available until 1858, when the rush of gold-seekers to the upper country made the opening of some way such an absolute necessity that the work was at once commenced. The scheme, which was by the time of my visit nearly accomplished, was to go by steamer up the Harrison River and Lake, a distance

of about 45 miles, to Port Douglas, and from that place to
cut a road to Port Lilloett, a station at the south end of the
Lilloett Lake, and distant from Douglas some 32 miles.
Along this part of the route, or " portage," as these trails
are designated, over which material has to be transported
from one sheet of water to another, the Lilloett River, which
·runs by or near it, is found of considerable use.   In the summer
it is too rapid and dangerous even for canoe navigation ; but
in the winter-time, when the waters have subsided, the Indians
make their way up it, charging just one-third of the price
required by the land-packers.   From Lilloett the lake carried
them as far as Pemberton, from which place another portage
of some 22 miles brought them to the south-west end of
Lake Anderson, which is almost connected with Seton, a lake
of similar size, from the upper end of which the route to
Lilloett, upon the Fraser, is only three or four miles, and
comparatively easy.   By this trail the dangers of the passage
of the Fraser above Yale are avoided, and a distance of
some 120 miles of the most perilous travelling saved.   At the
worst, when everything had to be carried from one piece
of water to the other by Indians, with immense labour and
at most extravagant rates of charge, it was far preferable to
the river route.   And now that a broad waggon-road has been
laid between Douglas and Lilloett, which by the end of the
year will be continued from Pemberton and Anderson, the
task of getting up to the mines from the seacoast is rendered
comparatively easy.

The main engineering difficulties in constructing the Harrison-Lilloett route lay at its commencement.   The Harrison
River, which flows for about five miles into the lake of the
same name, is in one spot so shallow, that the steamers, when
the water is low, have to land their cargoes on the bank, and
boats inside the bar re-ship them for Port Douglas.   Many
plans were suggested to obviate this difficulty.   Among others
it was proposed to cut through the valley from the lake to

the Fraser, thus making no use of the Harrison River whatever. It was at last, however, decided to make a canal through the flat, deepening it and walling it up with large baulks of timber. This task gave Captain Grant and a party of Engineers very moist occupation for two summers, and still I believe baffles their labours.

Above the Harrison River the banks of the Fraser rise somewhat, and the stream sweeps more swiftly between clay cliffs, from 10 to 30 feet high. The navigation here becomes more and more difficult for steamers, and at times, when the river is swollen by the snow-freshets from the hills, they are altogether baffled. Between Hope and Yale they are at present stopped by some rocks, which almost meet in the channel: were these blasted away, steamers might reach the latter place; but at that point, 85 miles from its mouth, the river, tearing between high, in some cases perpendicular banks, becomes impassable even for canoes. Steamers have occasionally reached Yale, but it is seldom attempted, and still more rarely accomplished.

Hope is perhaps the prettiest town on the Fraser. Indeed until Cayoosh, or as it is now called Lilloett, is reached, there is no other settlement that will bear comparison with it. Behind it Ogilvie Peak rises abruptly to a height of 5000 feet: to the right stretches the valley of the Que-que-alla, through which the trail to the new gold districts in the Semilkameen country is cut; while in the front the river glides, its channel divided by a beautiful little green island, the hills upon its opposite bank rising gradually to a considerable height, and forming a charming background to the prospect. High expectations are .entertained of Hope by its settlers; and indeed, since the discovery of gold in Rock Creek and the Semilkameen Valley, for both which districts Hope must serve as the emporium, there is a probability that they may be, in some degree at least, realised, though at present, all traffic being directed to Cariboo, it is not thriving.

Yale, 15 miles above Fort Hope, lies at the entrance of the Lower or Little Cañon, and is consequently the head of canoe or boat, as Hope is of steam, navigation. As I have before said, the only obstacle presented to steam-navigation between these two stations lies in some rocks, which almost meet in the channel of the river off Strawberry Island, some six or eight miles below Yale. There would be no great difficulty in removing these, and I believe that at one time the Governor did invite tenders for the work ; but the scheme was wisely, and I should hope for some time to come, if not finally, given up. The only benefit which would accrue to the colony would be shifting at a great expense the head of steam-navigation some 15 miles higher up the river, and thereby supplying provisions to the bars between Yale and Lilloett a few cents cheaper than at present.

There is nothing calling for any notice in Yale. It was selected by the Hudson Bay Company as a convenient resting-place before commencing the arduous ascent of the Cañons, and where, having come down, they might dry the furs and skins that had got wet in the passage. It is chiefly useful now as a port for shipping and unloading materials from and to the mines, and is besides enriched by the diggers from Hill's and other bars in its vicinity, who come hither on Sundays and holidays and spend a great deal of their money. The site of the town is itself auriferous, and all the front part of it has been washed.

At Yale my work in reality commenced, and several days were passed discussing with those who were most likely to be well informed upon the subject the best route I should take, and making preparations for it. These were at last completed, and on the afternoon of the 2nd of May we—that is, Dr. Campbell and myself, with a party of nine Indians—were ready to start to ascend the banks of the Fraser to Lytton. While talking the matter over, several highly cheering accounts of the perils of the way had been volunteered by some officials, who had been there recently collecting the licence-fees. They agreed in describing the dangers of the Cañons and Jackass Pass, through which our route lay, as really great, and one of them, who had not been up, said quite seriously that he should hesitate to undertake the journey for a thousand pounds. These cañons, of which there are two between Yale and Lytton, are narrow passes, through which the river forces its way between steep, in some cases perpendicular, banks, from three or four hundred to a thousand feet high.

The journey between Yale and Lytton occupied five days; but as I think it scarcely possessed sufficient interest to carry the reader over it step by step, it will be better perhaps to give him a general idea of our mode of travelling and the country through which we passed. It had been intended at Yale that I should be supplied with a white man who knew the country, as interpreter; but upon its being proposed to him, he declined to accompany me, having mining plans of his own, and I was therefore obliged to be content with an Indian who spoke French, not, of course, of the purest. It is by no means uncommon to find natives in the interior of the country possessing a useful knowledge of French. It was the language spoken by far the larger number of the Canadian voyageurs who first came across the mountains in the service of the Hudson Bay Company, and indeed their trade at their inland posts is mostly carried on in French.

An Indian has a great objection to travelling without a companion of his own tribe, and consequently after Mr. Ogilvy, the Hudson Bay Company's officer at Fort Hope, had succeeded in obtaining for me the services of Tom (by which name my interpreter was known), I found myself compelled to engage a friend to accompany him. The inconvenience of this arrangement was subsequently felt to be very great; for Tom falling ill at Fort Kamloops, his friend, who by that time had become valuable to us, persistently declined to leave him, although of course I in my turn refused to pay him if

H

he remained. A few words here as to our personal equipment may be permitted. For trips such as these I always wore a shooting-jacket with as many pockets as possible; strong corduroy trowsers, tied under the knee after the fashion of English navvies, to take the drag off it when they are wet; and an old uniform cap, which I always found had a capital effect upon Indians, inspiring them with an idea of the wearer's exalted position as a "Hyas Tyee," or great chief. Slung over my shoulder I carried an aneroid, which, with a spy-glass, completed my equipment. Dr. Campbell carried the gun on this occasion, as I had a chronometer in my pocket, which it was of the greatest importance not to disturb, and I therefore did not shoot. My spare things, packed in a small valise, consisted of a clean flannel shirt, six or eight pairs of socks, a Hudson's Bay capot (a sort of blue frock-coat, made with a hood to it)—upon the cuffs of which a lieutenant's gold lace was put to add to the effect, and which was worn before the natives upon all particularly important occasions—and a coat and trousers made of blue blanket, which I put on as soon as we camped at night, and in which I always slept. As to provisions, all we ever carried was a side or two of bacon, four or five bags of flour—the quantity depending upon the time that was likely to elapse before fresh stores could be reached—plenty of tea and coffee, and a bottle of brandy in case of accidents. Our fare upon occasions like this consisted almost exclusively of bacon and dampers, with tea and coffee. Now and then we might be lucky enough to shoot a grouse; but this happened rarely, as when you are travelling with an object, time cannot be given to going out of the way to hunt up game. Dampers, although well known to colonists in new countries, are, I may explain for the benefit of my English readers, cakes of dough rolled out to the size of a plate, and one or two inches thick. They are cooked either by being baked in the wood-ashes of the fire, or fried in the pan with bacon fat.

Besides the things already enumerated, I had to carry a sextant and an artificial horizon for getting observations for latitude and longitude. Upon these things being packed, they were found to amount to so considerable a weight and bulk, that nine Indians were required to carry them. These were engaged at two dollars (or 8s. 4d.) a-day, which, with their food, was the lowest price at which the Indians would work in those parts. The things were then divided into bundles or packs, as they are called, of as even weight as possible, giving some 50 or 60 lbs. to each man. Arranging these packs is a matter of no little difficulty, for the Indian has a great objection to altering his load after he has once started, so that you have to give the men carrying the provisions, which grow lighter daily, a heavier load at starting than those who have the canteen or the tent to carry. The majority of these Indian porters have now adopted the dress of Europeans, and turn out for the journey in trowsers and shirt, usually carrying an old coat of some sort, which they are careful to put on upon nearing a town. I have known them to be absurdly particular about this ceremony. I once journeyed with half-a-dozen Indians, each one of whom positively carried a suit of clothes in a bundle on his back for more than three weeks, to have the gratification of wearing them at Port Douglas. When we were within a mile or so of the place the party halted, untied their bundles, donned their clothes, and painting their faces bright red, filed into the town with dignified gravity. · Shoes are the one article of European attire which they do not take kindly to wearing, although they always ask for a pair at starting, which, too, they carry in the pack upon their backs. They either travel barefoot or in mocassins, which are not the pretty things embroidered with beads which one sees in pictures, but a plain piece of deerskin, laced round the foot with a strip of the same material. I have known occasions when an elk has been killed by me, and within a quarter of an hour after its death all the meat has been slung at their backs and its skin been laced upon their feet.

Previous to beginning a journey with Indians, they always look for a present. Indeed it would be difficult, if not impossible, to get them to start without this ceremony being gone through. It is not a very serious tax, all that is expected being that you should give them a " cultus-patalatch " (literally, a useless present).* Tobacco is often selected for this purpose, and it is generally advisable, if their squaws are present, to remember them, as this will do more than anything else towards starting them. The Indians, too, are always pleased at having a clay pipe given to each on starting, even if it is never used. Smoking, by the way, has a curious effect upon them. As a rule, although they soon learn to smoke as we do, they begin by inhaling it, swallowing enough in a few minutes thoroughly to intoxicate them. I have seen one pipe passed from one to the other of the party suffice to bring them all into this condition. The effect does not last long, and in a quarter of an hour they wake up from their drunken dose, looking and no doubt feeling very much the worse for it.

The daily routine of life upon the march varies little. About five in the morning we rose and got under way as quickly as possible. I used to indulge in a cup of coffee before starting, but experience soon taught me that it was better to make only two good meals a-day; between ten o'clock and noon, therefore, we halted for breakfast. For this meal we only unloaded what was absolutely necessary, and did not pitch the tent. A likely spot was selected near a stream and if possible under some shady trees, a fire was lit, and the cooks were soon busy kneading the dampers and boiling the tea. While this was going on—for after the first day we were glad to leave the cooking with the Indians—I used to get

* " Cultus-patalatch " means more correctly a present for which nothing is expected in return.

out my sextant to be ready for the meridian altitude of the
sun at noon, and, if our halt were sufficiently early, get a set of
A.M. sights first.   By the time I had done this, breakfast was
ready, and our appetites being freshened with a six hours'
walk, dampers of the consistency of saddle-leather disappeared
as if they had been puff-paste.   After breakfast we would
start again, holding on steadily until evening, when the most
convenient camping-place was selected for the night's rest.
The Indians in walking are accustomed to stop for some five
minutes' rest every half-hour, and this they do with surprising
regularity.   They generally squat down near a ledge of rock,
on which they can rest their burdens without removing them.
They carry everything in the same way, viz., with a band
over the forehead, the pack resting on their shoulder-blades,
or a little below.

When a halt was called for the night, the Indians divided
the labours of camping.   The cook, who was sometimes the
same throughout the journey, collected small wood, and made
the fire; upon his way he had very likely picked up pieces of
charred wood, to assist him in this operation; another cut
larger logs, for use during the night; the head man pitched
our tent, while another gathered a quantity of fir-boughs, on
which we should sleep; others fetched water; and if any deer-
tracks had been seen, or it was thought game might be found
in the neighbourhood, one took a musket, and went in search of
it, generally, I must say, with little success.   As a rule, Indians
make very bad shots.   They never think of shooting a bird on
the wing, and only bring down deer by hiding near a river,
to which they know the animals will come at nightfall to
water.   When these preparations have been effected, and
while the dampers are cooking, the Indians are, perhaps,
making themselves drunk upon tobacco, which does not,
however, at all affect their appetite, or are busy making
spoons for their repast.   It is not at all uncommon for them,
if they have leisure, to spend it in making a set of bark

spoons for supper. This they do in a very ingenious manner,
cutting a strip of bark some three or four inches, and splitting
it half-way down; then bending back the slit portion at right
angles to the other, and tying them with fibres of the same
material. It is an operation that must be seen to be thoroughly understood, but they do it with considerable dexterity, and the task of allotting the spoons when made among
the party, according to the size of each mouth, leads to very
great merriment. Stolid as Indians appear in their villages,
upon a cruise of this sort I have always found them in high
spirits, and they would discuss the adventures and mishaps of
the day's journey with great animation, frequently referring
to me to settle any vexed question that might arise. They are
very quick, too, at noticing any breach of their own code of
manners, and are unsparing in their raillery of the offender.
Gluttony particularly excites their ridicule. I remember on
one occasion an individual of my party happened to be a
great eater, and the others scarcely gave him any rest whatever, explaining to me that he deserved it, being "carqua
cushon" (like a pig). Another of their comrades happened
to be a very good-looking fellow, and, although I believe he
was secretly respected for it, he had to endure a great deal of
raillery upon his reported successes with the fair sex. Indians
appreciate nothing more highly than physical prowess; and a
good warrior or hunter needs no other recommendation to be
admired and envied — the words are synonymous there as
elsewhere—by both the men and women of his tribe; and
these qualities my friend the lady-killer possessed in such
a marked degree, as to make his companions' raillery so sub-
dued in its tone as to be almost flattering. In travelling
with Indians, should the Englishman be anything of a
sportsman, he will find it easy to secure the respect of his
guides and packers. Shooting a bird or two on the wing, or
bringing down a deer running, will raise him high in their
estimation; and he may secure it beyond a doubt by walking

them well off their legs on the first day's journey. They will
not bear him the least ill-will, and they respect him ever
after.

Now that I am on the subject of Indian manners, I
may mention a strange vanity of their young men who aim
at gaining reputation as great hunters or warriors. This is
their fashion of scoring their legs, under the impression that
it gives them strength and endurance, and renders them
impervious to cold. The limb is deeply cut in circular
fashion, from the hip to the knee, making it look not unlike
fish crimped for cooking. These indentations are very deep,
and can, of course, only be made gradually, one wound having
to heal before another is inflicted, so that a man is generally
twenty-five or twenty-six years old before the process is completed. Some such fashion is not uncommon among other
savage tribes. The natives of Moreton Bay, in Queensland,
for instance, are in the habit of cutting their bodies deeply
round from the shoulder to the waist, filling up the gash with
dirt, so that, when it heals, the scar projects like a large rope
or wheal tied round their bodies.

I have strayed, however, from our camp-fire, although
not so far, perhaps, as our thoughts wander sitting by it,
with night closing in. While the Indians laugh and talk,
or busy themselves mending their garments and patching
their mocassins, turning and twisting them about in every
direction to find a sound part to serve as a sole to protect the
foot for the next day's journey over the rocky trails, a pipe is
smoked, the notes of the day discussed and transferred to the
field-book, to-morrow's work talked over, and then to bed—
my companion and myself in the tent, the Indians grouped
about the fire. I have said that I always slept in a blanket
suit, and I recommend this precaution to travellers emphati-
cally. However hot the day may have been, the night in
British Columbia, even in the months of summer, is always
fresh and cold. Cold as it may be, however, the Indian

invariably strips to sleep, and lies with his blanket wrapped about him, feet in towards the fire. Even when camped in snow, I have observed they always take off their clothes.

Fort Yale is situated on the left bank of the Fraser, at the entrance to the Little Cañon. The banks of the cañon are so perpendicular that the traveller is obliged to leave the river's side to pass it, unless the water is very low indeed, when there is a narrow trail at the bottom of the cliff. The trail commonly used, and which is now made into what would be a very fair mule-road, save for the snow, which blocks it up for seven or eight months of every year, leads up a considerable height, and through a gorge between two mountains, coming down on the river again between the two cañons, about five or six miles above Yale. As we did not start until after noon, it took us till camping-time to pass the cañon, and we pitched our first camp when we came again upon the river. Next day we passed the Upper, or Big Cañon, which is six or eight miles long. Before entering we had a magnificent view up it, and very striking and wonderful it was.

These cañons, pronounced by all the miners *canyons*, are narrow passes, where the steep, almost perpendicular mountains, close in upon the stream. Overhead the rocks near each other, in some places almost meeting; so that from below a mere irregular thread of light is seen. The surface of the river is uneven, and the fall so great, that here and there cascades are formed, over which the stream rolls with fearful rapidity. In the summer time it sometimes tears along at the rate of 20 miles an hour, and when I was there it was flowing 15 or 16, as I ascertained by experiment. In winter, when the stream is at its lowest, they are navigable for canoes and boats, but this is always attended with considerable danger, and many lives have been lost in them. Miners, however, dare anything; and when Governor Douglas was at Fort Yale, in 1859, he saw a man who had actually

come down through the cañons lashed on to a large log of
timber!

As I have said, the view before entering the Upper Cañon
is grand. Looking up between the precipitous cliffs, the
water is seen rushing through them at fearful speed. I
hardly know which was more grand, the view from this spot
or that further on, as we got well into the cañon, in
which in some places the trail led up crags so steep that
we had to clamber up them with our hands and feet,
until we arrived breathless at the top of a projecting ledge,
on which we were glad to halt a few minutes, to draw
breath and gaze with wonder on the scene. Before and
behind, peak after peak rose 1000 or more feet above us,
although we were probably 600 or 800 feet above the river,
each more rugged, bold, and grand than the other; while beneath, the river, white with foam, whirled along, gurgling and
eddying, its wild reverberations continued in endless echoes.
Grand as the scene was, watching it, my brain grew dizzy,
and I was glad to turn away and continue my journey, fearful
lest, if I looked longer, that strange desire which creeps over
you to spring into the boiling torrent should become too
strong for further resistance. At the present day the trail—
which is the name given in the country for any sort of path—is
so improved that I believe mules travel by it without difficulty
when the snow is not on the ground. I should be very sorry,
therefore, to say anything disheartening to the intending
settler, although I may add that anyone who would be dis-
couraged by difficulties such as these had better not visit
British Columbia. At the time I speak of there were three
trails, though they were not entirely separate. The first of
these, the Mule-trail, was completely blocked up by snow; it
is hardly ever open till June. The others were known as the
" Lower " and " Upper " Cañon trails. The lower trail could
only be passed when the water was low, at which time there is
a ledge of boulders along the bottom of the cliff, over which

a rough path was carried. The upper trail passed along from ledge to ledge, at a height ranging from 50 to 800 feet above the river. We went partly along each of these trails. When we could we kept the lower, but constantly, on coming to some bluff of rock jutting out into the river, we had to scramble up into the upper trail to pass it. The mode of rounding these cliffs, which literally overhang the river, is peculiar, and makes one's nerves twitch a little at first. There are two or three of them, the trail coming up to them on one side, and continuing again on the other. The difficulty, of course, was to pass the intervening space. This was managed by the Indians thus: they suspended three poles by native rope, made of deer-hide and fibre, from the top of the cliff, the inner end of the first and third resting on the trail, and the middle one crossing them on the front of the bluff. Of course there was nothing to lay hold of, and the only way was for the traveller to stretch out his arms and clasp the rock as much as possible, keeping his face close against it; if he got dizzy, or made a false step, the pole would, of course, swing away, and he would topple over into the torrent, which rolled hundreds of feet beneath. The land-slips in the mountain crevices are also very dangerous. Several times we had to make an ascent of about 200 feet up a land-slip, at an angle of quite 35°, in loose sand, and with nothing to check our downward progress if the sand should slip quicker than we could scramble over. The most dangerous of these, which we did not pass till the third day, but which I may as well mention while upon the subject, is called the Jackass Mountain. Several people have lost their lives in crossing this, and on one occasion a mule, which some miners tried to get across it, was, I believe, with his driver, precipitated into the river; which circumstance may, perhaps, account for the name of the mountain.

This mountain rises abruptly out of the river, and the old trail leads across the face of it. To pass it several land-slips,

of twenty or thirty yards wide, and at an angle of about 50°,
had to be crossed. To do this the traveller had to make
a bolt from the rocky ledge on one side to that on the other;
and if he chanced to get dizzy, or the land slipped away with
him, he must inevitably be lost. My companion had here
a most merciful escape. He got dizzy, and slipped, but had
got so far across that he was just able to grasp a root above
his head, and thus save his life. I had just crossed, and was
watching him, when I saw him turn pale and slip. It was
all the work of a second, however, and before I could move
he was hanging on to the root.

The following extract from the Journal of the Bishop of
Columbia, when travelling over the same ground, will prove
that my description is not exaggerated :—" We continued
the ascent for some distance. Impassable, indeed, much of
it was for horses and mules, and even for man not without
danger. We must have been at the height of 2500 or 3000
feet; our pathway lay along the edge of a perpendicular fall
of such a height, sometimes along beds of loose rock, and
most warily must the feet step from stone to stone; a slip
would either precipitate to the abyss below, or cast you
among the rocks, where a limb might easily be broken. At
other times in the descent the path was *nil*, the projections
for the foot not an inch; it seemed like the crawling of a fly
upon the perpendicular wall. This sort of work lasted for
hours. It was, however, so absorbing, and required the
utmost constant stretch of attention for self-preservation,
that the time passed more rapidly than one would have
thought. At the time the critical character of this operation
was such that, though near together, no one spoke; there
was a solemnity, as if we realised hanging between life and
death. Frequently we had to crawl upon hands and knees.
It was quite wonderful to see the Indians, with their heavy
loads, pass along; one of ours did fall, however, once. We
came occasionally to mountain torrents, bringing down the

cool water from the snowy height. At one time we slaked
our thirst from the snow itself. At length we had gone over
the worst of the Lake Mountain; the Fraser was again spread
out before us; the smoke in the distance pointed out the
dwellings upon Boston Bar."

Fifteen miles above Yale is Spuzzum, an Indian village,
where there is a ferry, and here the mule-trail leads across
to the east bank of the river, which from this point runs
nearly north and south. The foot trail, the best in winter,
keeps along the west bank to Island Bar, which is opposite
to Boston Bar, and forty miles above Yale. Boston Bar is
at the mouth of the Anderson or Cŏqūiŏme River, and it is
to this Bar that the people of Fort Hope wish to have a direct
road made, which, I believe, has since been begun, cutting
off the small elbow which the river makes, and avoiding Yale
and the cañons altogether. This will very likely become a
valuable route for the Lytton and Thompson River country,
but not for that which is attracting the greatest notice now—
viz. the Cariboo. The Anderson River is a considerable one,
and, after running in a short distance, it divides into two
branches, one trending northward till it nearly meets one of
the tributaries of Nicola River, and the other running southward and almost joining the north branch of the Que-que-alla
coming up from Hope. It is along the banks of these
streams that the Hope and Boston Bar trail passes.

At Boston Bar the Fraser Valley opens out a little, and
between it and Lytton several flats occur, which will some
day, no doubt, be converted into pretty little farms. The
largest of these, which is five miles above Boston Bar, was
already fenced in when I was there, and had a hut built on it.
These flats, or benches as they are called in this country,
are found generally at the bends of the river, and are
raised some fifty or sixty feet above it. They occur much
more frequently on the Thompson and Nicola Rivers, and
higher up the Fraser, than here. They are all covered

with the long sweet grass of which cattle and horses are
so fond, and which has so wonderful an effect in fattening
them. I have seen horses on Vancouver Island, where the
same grass grows, which have been turned out in the autumn,
brought in in April in splendid condition, and as fresh as if
they had been most carefully treated all the time. This is,
indeed, the common custom with the island horses, and I
remember one of the oldest and best farmers there saying
that the only horses he had ever lost were killed by being
taken too much care of, and kept in all the winter. Jackass
Mountain is ten or twelve miles above Boston Bar, and when
it was crossed all dangers were past, and we trudged on
easily, reaching Lytton two days after we passed Boston
Bar, and five days from the time we left Yale.

The whole way from Yale to Lytton, which is 60 miles,
the geological formation of the country is the same, and we
passed between steep trappean and granitic mountains 2000
to 3000 feet high, the distance across the river from peak to
peak not averaging more than a mile. There is very little
land fit for cultivation, except, as I have said, on some of those
benches which are found on all the rivers of this country,
and which point out the higher level their streams once occupied, and the subsequent upheaval of the whole country.

Lytton, at the time I saw it, consisted of an irregular row
of some dozen wooden huts, a drinking saloon, an express
office, a large court-house—as yet unfinished—and two little
buildings near the river, which had once belonged to the
Hudson Bay Company, but which were now inhabited by
the district magistrate. This gentleman happened to be
absent from Lytton, but I found his constable, and at once
took up my quarters in the courthouse. Next day, thinking
we should find it preferable, we pitched our tent without;
but the clouds of dust which swept over Lytton continuously
soon made us glad to seek its shelter again.

Whilst here I determined, instead of making our way

direct to Lilloett, to diverge by the way of the Nicola River
and Lake to Fort Kamloops or Thompson, situate some 90 miles
up the Thompson River. Seven of our Indian escort, when they
heard of my purpose, refused to accompany us to Kamloops,
unless I would promise them to return from that place direct
—a programme I had no intention of following. Tom and
his friend, however, stuck to us; and I found an Indian who
owned two horses, and who undertook the transport of our
packages, by this time, of course, considerably reduced in
weight and bulk. As it proved, we were most fortunate in
this arrangement, for without horses we should have found it
impossible to ford the Nicola, and must inevitably have been
turned back on reaching that river. Pleased enough to leave
the dust and wind of Lytton, our little party started for
Kamloops.

CHAPTER VI.

———◦❖◦———

Journey continued — Kamloops — Life of the Hudson Bay Employés — Indian
Chief, St. Paul — Pavillon — The Harrison-Lilloett Route.

FOR about nine miles our course lay along the south bank
of the Thompson, close by the water's edge. The scenery of
the river resembled that of such parts of the Fraser where
the trail lay along its shore—a shelving bank of large
boulders, covered in the summer with water. Coming to
the Nicowameen River,—where, it is said, gold was first found
in British Columbia by an Indian who, stooping to drink, saw
a rich nugget glittering in the water, which he carried to Mr.
McLean, the officer in charge of Fort Kamloops,—we turned
off, and, crossing a mountain on our right, found ourselves in
a long, narrow valley, in which I saw the first land I had
as yet found that seemed unmistakeably fit for agricultural
purposes. From this time all the way to Kamloops the
aspect of the country had completely changed from that of
the Fraser below Lytton; and we passed through a succession
of valleys sufficiently clear of timber to make settling easy,
yet with enough for building purposes, well watered, and
covered with a long, sweet grass. There are no prairies in
British Columbia, but it consists of what is called rolling
country—that is, long valleys from one to three or four
miles wide, divided one from the other by mountain ridges.
Through the centre of these runs usually a river, and in some
cases may be seen a chain of small lakes. In summer, when
the water is high, streams and lakes meet, and the valleys
become sheets of water, dotted with large islands. At such
a time it is very curious to see the same river flowing diverse

ways, as you may at almost all the watersheds or turning-
points of the water.

After passing along the first of these valleys, in which
many trees had been felled, and two log-huts erected, most
probably for the sake of claiming pre-emption, we passed
through a gorge of the mountains, and came out in view of
the Nicola River, flowing some 600 or 800 feet below us.
The view from this spot was one of the most lovely I ever
saw in British Columbia. It was a fine, clear May day.
The sun shone brightly, giving a warmth and freshness
to the hill-side, which sloped to the water's edge, not
in craggy, precipitous masses like those of the cañons on
the Fraser River, but clothed with long, soft grass, and
bright with the numberless wild flowers which grow so
luxuriantly in this country. Unlike them, too, instead of
terminating abruptly at the water's edge, they sloped down
to it in plateaux a mile or so in breadth, terminating sometimes in steep, perpendicular banks, but as often sweeping
down gradually to a neutral ground of reeds and swamp, yet
always vying with the hill-sides in fertility and luxuriance.
Between these banks the Nicola coursed with great rapidity,
leaping over the many rocks which check its progress, and
sweeping round the numerous small islets that dot its
surface.

It is very difficult to impress the reader with the
beauty of the view on which we stood gazing, unwilling to
tear ourselves from it. As yet we had seen nothing at all
equal to it in British Columbia. The shores of the coast
are lined with dense, almost impenetrable forests, while the
Fraser cuts its way through steep and rugged mountains.
It is true that between Forts Langley and Hope there is
some level land on either side of the river, but even there you
see a mountain barrier rise in the near horizon, and feel sure
that it must be scaled before rich fertile land like this can
be reached.

It was about three in the afternoon when we reached the
Nicola River. Coming to where it should be forded, we found
that we had to pay a heavy price for the sunny weather that
had seemed so welcome, but which had melted so much snow
among the mountains, as to swell the river and make it nearly
impassable. However, it must be crossed somehow; and now
we found the advantage of having horses with us. Removing their loads, two of the Indians swam the horses across.
So swift was the swollen stream, that, although it could
not have been more than 100 yards wide, they were swept
at least half-a-mile down the river before they could gain
a footing on the opposite shore. Next we crossed, only
getting over one at a time, as the other had to swim the
horses back; and lastly the baggage was taken over. It was
rather a lengthy process, and by the time it was all done night
was setting in, and it was time to camp.

Next morning we followed the course of the Nicola River,
until, during the second day, we came up with the Lake.
Here for the first time I saw mounted Indians of the interior.
They were as yet uncontaminated by intercourse with white
men: indeed all they had ever seen were the people of the
Hudson Bay Company stationed at Fort Kamloops. When
we camped overnight, I had no idea that we were in the
close proximity of Indians, and upon waking in the morning
I was not a little surprised to see an old Indian on horseback
looking into the tent. Tom at once introduced him as Nō-
ăs-ĭs-ticun, the chief of the Skowtous tribe, and a connection
of his own, and very soon a large number came riding up to
our encampment, all fairly mounted on light yet fleet horses.
My new friend with the long name was very friendly and
sent one of his men to his hut for a grouse, which he presented to us for breakfast, and which Dr. Campbell and
I ate with no little relish. It was one of the willow-grouse,
which is found commonly both in Vancouver Island and on
the mainland.

I

Coming out of the tent—(it was quite dark when we had
camped the night before)—I found that we were upon rising
ground, with a river flowing beneath us, and that beyond a
wide valley of undulating land extended for several miles,
which was dotted with Indian villages, the smoke of whose
fires was rising into the clear air, while over it we could see
Indian horsemen galloping about in various directions. The
old chief informed me that these were the homes of his tribe,
the Skowtous, and that his domain extended as far as the
Thompson River, which divided him from the Shuswap Indians.

Upon my telling him whither I was going, the chief at once
expressed a desire to accompany us through his territory, and
offered us horses for the journey. These, for several reasons,
we declined; but we accepted the offer of his company, and in
a little while he joined us with a staff of eight or ten of his
tribe, all well mounted. Passing through another fine valley
about ten o'clock, we came to the Nicola Lake. This lake
is about fourteen miles long by one to two wide, and lies
nearly north and south. Its Indian name is " Smee-hāat-
loo," but it has long been called the Nicola, after an old chief
of the Shuswap Indians. Its banks are low, except in one
place on the west side, where a perpendicular granitic cliff
barred our progress and compelled the horsemen of our party
to take a considerable detour to avoid it. Upon the west
side of the lake the mountains approach it closely; but on
the east, northward of a mountain about 2000 feet high,
called by the natives Whā-hăt-chāllōo (Otter) Mountain, two
rivers run into it from large valleys, in which there appears
to be, and according to my native friend there is, some very
good land. These rivers are called respectively M'Donald
and Bodinion.

A small chain of lakes or ponds stretches eastward from
the Nicola in an almost unbroken line to the Thompson
River. Passing these, we ascended the side of a mountain
called by the natives Skȳe-tă-kĕn, upon the summit of which

we were, as nearly as I could estimate, 3600 feet above
the sea. The view from hence was very extensive and
beautiful, ranging as far as the Semilkameen Valley and the
Shuswap Lake, and disclosing a fine tract of grass land which
will some day become a noble grazing country. Descending the mountain-side, we crossed a succession of low grassy
hills, coming in time to the Thompson River.

It was about 8 o'clock in the morning when we came
here, and found ourselves in sight of Kamloops. The view
from where we stood was very beautiful. A hundred feet
below us the Thompson, some 300 yards in width, flowed
leisurely past us. Opposite, running directly towards us and.
meeting the larger river nearly at right angles, was the North
River, at its junction with the Thompson wider even than
that stream; and between them stretched a wide delta or
alluvial plain, which was continued some eight or ten miles
until the mountains closed in upon the river so nearly as
only just to leave a narrow pathway by the water's edge. At
this fork and on the west side stood Fort Kamloops, enclosed
within pickets; and opposite it was the village of the Shuswap
Indians. Both the plain and mountains were covered with
grass and early spring wild flowers.

We descended to the river-side, and our Indian companions
shouted until a canoe was sent across, in which we embarked and paddled over to the Fort. Kamloops differed
in no respect from other forts of the Hudson Bay Company
that I had seen—being a mere stockade enclosing six or eight
buildings, with a gateway at each end. Introducing ourselves
to Mr. M'Lean, the Company's officer in charge of the fort
and district, we were most cordially received, and, with the
hospitality common to these gentlemen, invited to stay in his
quarters for the few days we must remain here.

At this time the only other officer at the Fort was
Mr. Manson. With them, however, was staying a Roman
Catholic priest, who, having got into some trouble with the

I 2

Indians of the Okanagan country, had thought it prudent to leave that district and take up his abode for a time at Kamloops. The life which these gentlemen of the great Fur Company lead at their inland stations must necessarily be somewhat dull and uneventful; but they have their wives and families with them, and grow, I believe, so attached to this mode of existence as rarely to care to exchange it for another. As it happened we visited them just as the one stirring event of the season was expected—the arrival of the great Fur Brigade from the north.

It may be well if I pause here to describe, in as few words as possible, the position of the Hudson Bay Company in these districts, of which until lately, they formed the sole white population. Those who have seen the "fur traders" only at their seaports, can form but a very inadequate idea of the men of the inland stations.

Inland you find men who, having gone from England, or more frequently Scotland, as boys of fourteen or sixteen, have lived ever since in the wilds, never seeing any of their white fellow-creatures, but the two or three stationed with them, except when the annual "Fur Brigade" called at their posts. They are almost all married and have large families, their wives being generally half-breed children of the older servants of the Company. Marriage has always been encouraged amongst them to the utmost, as it effectually attaches a man to the country, and tends to prevent any glaring immoralities among the subordinates, which if not checked would soon lead to an unsafe familiarity with the neighbouring Indians, and render the maintenance of the post very difficult, if not impossible.

In the Company's service there are three grades of officers —the "Clerk," "Chief Trader," and "Chief Factor." The clerk is paid a regular salary of 100l. to 150l. per annum, and he has his mess found him, which is estimated by the Company to be worth another 100l. a-year. In this grade they

BLOCK-HOUSE FORT OF HUDSON BAY COMPANY.

Page 117.

are usually kept 14 or 15 years, though interest with the directors or great efficiency sometimes enables a man to get his promotion in 10 or 12 years.   He then becomes a chief trader, and, instead of being a salaried servant, is a shareholder, his pay varying with the value of the year's furs from 400*l.* to as high as 700*l.* or 800*l.* The mode in which he receives his share is somewhat peculiar.   The accounts of the Company are made up at intervals of four years, and no pay is given to the higher servants—*i. e.* the shareholders—until this is done.   Thus a man who is made a chief trader in 1862, will get no pay till 1866, when the dividends for the former year are declared.   Of course in the long run this is the same thing; as, if a man retires in 1862, he keeps on his full pay till 1866, when he is paid his dividend for 1862; and no real inconvenience is felt, as the Company always lends whatever moneys are required, within certain limits, and indeed prefers its officers being in its debt.   The posts of chief factors are filled up as vacancies occur, the number being limited.   A man is generally a chief trader for 15 to 20 years before he reaches this—the highest step in the service. The chief factor's share varies from 800*l.* to 1500*l.* per annum.   Every station is, as a rule, in charge of a chief trader, chief factors having the control of several posts, or a district, as it is called, or being stationed at head-quarters.

As all Hudson Bay posts are much alike, I will here describe them generally.   They are built usually in the form of a square, or nearly so, of about 100 yards.   This space is picketed in with logs of timber, driven into the ground, and rising 15 to 20 feet above it.   In two of the corners is usually reared a wooden bastion, sufficiently high to enable the garrison to see a considerable distance over the country.   In the gallery of the bastion five or six small guns—six or twelve pounders—are mounted, covered in, and used with regular ports like those of a ship; while the ground-floor serves for the magazine.   Inside the pickets are six or eight houses: one containing the mess-room for the officers at the post, and their dwelling-house, where the number of them is small; two or three others—the number of course depending on the strength of the post,—which seldom exceeds a dozen men—being devoted to the trappers, voyageurs, &c. Another serves for the Indian trading-store, and one for the furs, which, as will be-hereafter explained, remain in store at the inland posts during the greater part of the year.

Some of these forts have seen some hard fighting, and have often been as gallantly defended against Indians and the rival traders of the old North-Western Company as military posts for the defence of which great glory has been gained.

The day after our arrival at Kamloops we went across North River to the Indian village, to pay a visit to the chief of the Shuswap tribe, who was described to us as being somewhat of a notability. Here was the site of the old fort of the Company, which some twelve years back, after the murder of Mr. Black, the officer in charge of it, by the Indians, had been removed by his successor to the opposite side of the river. No doubt the old site was preferable to the new, which is subject to the summer floods. Only the year before our visit, indeed, all the floors had been started by the water, and the occupants of the fort buildings had to move about in canoes.

We found the Shuswap chief located in a good substantial hut. The Indian constructs but two kinds of abodes anywhere: one a permanent hut, in his village; the other a temporary one, to shelter himself when he is moving about from place to place, fishing or collecting clams. In their permanent houses the architectural peculiarity that strikes the observer with most surprise is the solidity and size of the cross-beams. They erect ten or twelve upright supports, according to the size of the hut, the tops of which are notched to receive the beams; and it is a great object with them to have as large a beam as possible, because, as it must be raised by sheer strength and numbers, its size is supposed to testify to the number and cordiality of the builders' friends. The ends of these huge beams—some of those I have seen being 40 to 50 feet long, by two to three feet in diameter—are usually ornamented with the head of some fish or animal, which, projecting beyond the wall, shows the crest or distinguishing mark of the house. The sides of the building are formed of large planks, wonderfully smooth considering that the Indians use no plane, and until lately, indeed, had no axes. The interior of the hut is divided into compartments, and, upon entering, you may see a fire burning in each, with six or eight individuals huddled about it, their dusky forms scarcely distinguishable in the cloud of white blinding smoke, which has no other outlet than the door, or sometimes a hole in the roof. Their temporary hut is constructed lightly of thin poles covered with mats; but these, as I have said, are generally used only in the summer, and upon their fishing-expeditions and travels. It is not, however, unusual for the Indian to have a permanent residence in two or three villages, in which case he usually makes one set of planks useful for all, carrying them with him from place to place, and leaving only the upright posts and beams stationary. They have been known, however, from some superstitious reason, or because of sickness breaking out in a place, to leave their villages with everything standing, and never to return to them.

The building into which we were introduced was more like a regular wooden house than an Indian hut. In the centre room, lying at length upon a mattrass stretched upon the floor, was the chief of the Shuswap Indians. His face was a very fine one, although sickness and pain had worn it away terribly. His eyes were black, piercing, and restless; his cheek-bones high, and the lips, naturally thin and close, had that white, compressed look which tells so surely of constant suffering. Such was St. Paul, as the Hudson Bay Company

called him, or Jean Baptiste Lolo, as he had been named by
the Roman Catholic priests who were in this district many years
before.   Behind him stood his wife, and presently he summoned two handsome-looking Indian girls, whom he introduced to us as his daughters.   St. Paul received us lying
upon his mattrass, and apologized in French for not having
risen at our entrance.   He asked Mr. M'Lean to explain that
he was a cripple.   Many years back it appeared St. Paul
became convinced there was something wrong with his knee.
Having no faith in the medicine-men of his tribe, and there
being no white doctor near, the poor savage actually commenced cutting a way to the bone, under the impression that
it needed cleansing.   In time, at the cost of course of great
personal suffering, he succeeded in boring a hole through the
bone, which he keeps open by constantly syringing water
through it.   Mr. M'Lean described him as a man of very
determined character, who had been upon many occasions
most useful to him and his predecessors at the fort.   Although
obliged to lie in his bed sometimes for days together, his
sway over his tribe is perfect, and, weak as he is, he rules
them more by fear than love.   Upon my remarking casually
that I wondered he was not sometimes afraid of some or other
of his people taking advantage of his comparatively helpless
condition, he heard me with a grim smile, and for answer
turned back his pillow, where a loaded gun and a naked
sword lay ready to his hand.   Upon our rising to leave
Mr. M'Lean whispered that our host would take it ill if
he were not asked to accompany us ; and this being done,
to my surprise St. Paul at once assented.   Being assisted to
rise, he hobbled to the door on crutches, and, having been
with considerable difficulty got into the saddle, rode about all
the day with us.

The mountain up which Mr. M'Lean guided us was one of
two standing side by side opposite the fort, and about a mile
from it.   Its companion had been named Roches des Femmes,

from the fact that, in summer, many Indian women were to be seen scattered about its sides gathering berries and moss. From its summit, at a height of some 1500 feet, we had a very fine view of the land along the banks of the Thompson and North Rivers. It appeared to be very good, and in this opinion we were confirmed by Mr. M'Lean, who further informed us that the land at the head of the Thompson River, and southward of that point to the Semilkameen Valley, was equally fertile and valuable. Descending the mountain, which we christened Mount St. Paul, in honour of the old chief, we lunched with him, returning to the fort for a tea-dinner. Tea is a beverage drunk usually at this and other meals. Indeed, Mr. M'Lean informed us that he took nothing else. Nor had total abstinence disagreed with him. A finer or more handsome man I think I never saw, with long beard and moustaches, and hair hanging in ringlets down his shoulders. The Indians, we heard, had given him the sobriquet of the Bearded Chief.

On the following day we went out to see the bands of horses driven in, and those that were past work selected for food. There were some two or three hundred horses, of all sorts and ages, at the station. Just outside the Fort were two pens, or corrals as they called them, and into these the horses were driven. A few colts were chosen for breaking in, and then the old mares, whose breeding-time was past, were selected and—for it was upon horse-flesh principally that the Fort people lived—driven out to be killed, skinned, and salted down.

It was curious to note the close discipline in which the stud-horses of each band kept their mares. There are generally three studs in each band, and while they were in the corral they might be seen galloping about, administering a kick here and a bite there. For a few minutes, perhaps, one would stand still and look about him, then suddenly, without the least perceptible cause or provocation, he would make a rush at some unfortunate mare, and bite or kick her severely.

The mountain-sides in the neighbourhood of Kamloops are covered with a bright yellow moss, called by the Indians Quillmarcar. It is much used by them as a dye, and when boiled gives them that yellow which is so familiar to those who have travelled among them in their dog-hair mats and other native work. There is also a kind of lichen which grows here, called by them "Whyelkine," and which is one of their most important articles of food.* In its natural state it somewhat resembles horse-hair, and being boiled it is pressed into cakes, three or four inches thick, looking not unlike our gingerbread. Its taste is very earthy and rather bitter. Our companion, St. Paul, gave us this, which they call "Wheela," with milk, upon our return to his hut, but two or three mouthfuls were all we cared to take.

While at the Fort I learned that the rivers between Kamloops and Pavillon on the Fraser, for which place I had determined to start, were likely to be so swollen with the late thaw that we should not be able to cross them without horses. Accordingly it became necessary to make arrangements for mounting our party. We discovered that the best way of effecting this would be to seek the aid of St. Paul, who happened to be the possessor of a score or more horses. Willing as Mr. M'Lean was to render us every assistance, he could himself spare us no horses, a message having been received from the officer in charge of the Fur Brigade, which was expected to arrive daily, saying that he should require all they could supply him with. Terms were accordingly made with St. Paul, and upon their completion, to my surprise, the old chief said that he should like to accompany us. We were very glad of this, if for two reasons only. In the first place, Tom, my interpreter, had fallen ill, and, as I have before said, his friend steadily refused to leave him, so that we were without a guide, and the information we had lately received convinced us that, without the aid of some

* L. jubatus.

one well acquainted with the fords, it would be difficult, if not altogether impossible, to cross the rivers that lay in our path. Secondly, St. Paul possessed considerable influence with the Indian tribes through which we had to pass, and we might feel pretty sure that he would, if he lived through the journey, conduct us safely to its end.

On the morning of the 14th May, then, into the Fort rode St. Paul, with an escort of eight men mounted, and with led horses for Dr. Campbell and myself. Four of these men were to have charge of our packages; the rest formed his own body-guards, two being the old chief's sons. We were soon ready to start, and, following the course of the Thompson for about twelve miles, came to the river Tranquille. Here Mr. M'Lean, who had ridden so far, was compelled to part company with us, regretting that the hourly expected arrival of the Fur Brigade prevented his leaving Kamloops for any length of time.

The plains that lay along the course of the Thompson seemed rather light and sandy, but in spots good land was observable. Crossing the Tranquille close to its mouth without any difficulty, the water being little above our horses' knees, and turning to the right, we mounted a somewhat steep gorge leading to a long, narrow valley running nearly parallel to the Thompson River, but quite out of sight of it. Emerging from this pass, we descended to Lake Kamloops, along the side of which we held until night, camping at a spot called the Coppermine, where the Indians said they had found perfectly pure specimens of that metal. We made a very careful examination of the place, and although there were unmistakeable signs of the presence of copper, we saw nothing to cause us to doubt that the Indian's story was not, as usual, very much overcharged.

At this spot the trail by which the Fur Brigade would travel to Fort Kamloops met that along which we were

journeying, and St. Paul was very anxious that we should
deposit a note for the officer in command of it, expressive of
his, the chief's, good wishes.   I was rather puzzled what to
say, but St. Paul was so urgent that I should, as he expressed
it, " *Bon jour* Mr. Peter," that I scrawled a few hurried lines;
and when a year later in Victoria I chanced to meet Mr.
Peter Ogden, the officer who had been in charge of the
Brigade, I learnt that upon his arrival at Coppermine he had
found my note.   It was not without regret that I missed
seeing the Fur Brigade.   It is one of those old institutions of
this wild and beautiful country, which must give way before
the approach of civilisation.   The time will come—soon,
perhaps—when such a sight as a train of some 200 horses,
laden with fur-packages, winding their way through the rough
mountain-passes of British Columbia, will be unfamiliar as
that of a canoe upon its rivers.   No doubt the change will
be for the better, but it is sometimes hard to believe it.
Of course it is much more practical to ascend the Fraser in a
river steamboat than to make the journey in an Indian canoe;
and perhaps, taking the chances of an explosion into consideration, equally exciting; but it will be long before I
should prefer the former method of locomotion to the latter
when the weather is fine.   With all its many inconveniences,
there is something marvellously pleasant in canoe travelling,
with its tranquil, gliding motion, the regular, splashless dip,
dip of the paddles, the wild chant of the Indian crew, or better
still the songs of the Canadian voyageurs, keeping time to the
pleasant chorus of " Ma belle Rosa " or " Le beau Soldat."

   Miss the Fur Brigade we did, however, and next morning
we pursued our way along the shore of the Kamloops Lake.
The scenery here was very pretty, and the lake was, we found,
perfectly navigable for steamers.   Indeed it has since been
proposed to start steamers here, and run them past Kamloops
for some miles up the North and Thompson Rivers, from the
latter of which a small portage would connect them with

another line of steamers to be stationed on the Okanagan Lakes.

About half-way along the north side of Kamloops Lake the trail passes round a very steep and dangerous cliff, overhanging the deep water below. A ledge barely wide enough to give the horses footing is the only pathway. This pass, known as the Mauvais Rocher, was one of the most unpleasant places I had ever ridden over; and I was not at all surprised to hear that several horses had, with their riders, been precipitated into the lake below. St. Paul told us that he had discovered a way along a narrow gorge in the rear, by which this might be avoided, but that it required some labour to clear it before it could be used. There is also a trail upon the other side of the lake by which the passage of the Mauvais Rocher might be avoided; and a horse-ferry had just been established at its west end, which was very generally used by the American packers from Walla-Walla. But travelling northward as we were, had we followed this trail we should have had to cross the Thompson twice.

A little below Shuswap Lake the Buonaparte River joins the Thompson. This river is said to have its rise in Loon Lake, some 40 or 50 miles north of the Thompson. At this point we left the Thompson and camped for the night, by the side of the Rivière de la Cache, a small stream flowing into the Buonaparte.

Next morning's work commenced with fording the Buonaparte. It cost us some time to find a suitable spot, the floods having made the ordinary ford impassable; but at last we managed to cross, the horses being now and then swept off their legs into deep water, and having to swim for it. *En passant,* I would remark that it is by no means so easy to swim a horse across a rapid stream as it may seem to a horseman who has not tried it; the rolling motion given to the animal by the swift current making the rider very apt to lose his balance.

The Buonaparte, however, was not the most difficult river we had to cross on this day's journey. For at the Rivière Defant the water was found to be so deep as to make it necessary to swim the horses all the way across, without the chance of their gaining a footing from shore to shore. We were particularly anxious to avoid this necessity on account of the instruments, which would infallibly be damaged, and after a long search we came upon the trunk of a tree by which Indians were evidently accustomed to cross. To our annoyance, however, the river had risen so high that this rough bridge was at least two feet under the water, which tore over it with the rapidity of a mill-stream ; so that, unless a rope could be carried over and fastened at the other side to form a balustrade, it seemed quite impossible to get ourselves and the luggage across safely. However, St. Paul seemed determined that this should be done, and several of his men stripping to the work endeavoured gallantly to cross the river. As often, however, as they managed to get to the middle of the primitive bridge, the elasticity of the tree, together with the velocity of the current, sent them spinning off, and they were swept down the stream, having to swim vigorously for their lives. After many successive failures, we had almost made up our minds that we should have to loiter by the river's side for a day or so, until its waters should have subsided—for there were no trees handy large enough to frame a bridge with—when St. Paul, whose anger had risen at the ill-success of each fresh attempt, to our astonishment leapt up—we were all lying on the ground watching the baffled Indians—and throwing off his clothes ran forward to their aid. In his weak and exhausted condition, we made sure that the effort and excitement of such an attempt would act most injuriously if not fatally upon him, and did our best to dissuade him from making it, Nor were we altogether unselfish in this, perhaps, since we knew that, if the old chief lost his life in our service, it would not only be most painful to us, but that we should lose all the Indians, who would infallibly return to Kamloops with his corpse, to take part in his wake. However, the spirit of the old man was roused, and breaking from us he was soon standing mid-stream, the rope in his hand, yelling to his men, and swearing in a French jargon peculiar to himself, with a zeal and originality that would have inspired the members of Captain Shandy's troop in the Low Countries with admiring envy. Very much to our relief, as may be supposed, St. Paul succeeded in scrambling over the fragile bridge with the agility of a monkey, and, the rope being made fast to the other side, we crossed with comparative ease. Not, however, without getting thoroughly wet and spoiling one of the instruments about which I felt so anxious. With all my care, when I came to look at my sextant, I found that it had been under water, and that the pieces of wood that kept it in its place in the case had been loosened and were floating about. Fortunately, however, I had a pocket one with me, so that its loss was not so important as otherwise it would have been. All now fairly over, we halted for breakfast. I had found before leaving Kamloops that when travelling with the officers of the Hudson Bay Company, St. Paul was always admitted to their mess, and upon starting I had of course invited him to join ours. The Indian is so quick at observing and imitating the manners of those with whom he is brought into contact, that the old chief had learnt to conduct himself with perfect composure and decorum, and the beef with which he had provided himself on starting, proved a welcome addition to our bacon.

Following the course of the Buonaparte until its junction with the Chapeau, we turned up the valley through which that river flows. There is much good land along the Buonaparte; the whole being clothed with long grass, of which the horses seemed very fond. We carried no fodder with us on this expedition, turning the horses loose at night to graze.

They never strayed far. One of course was hobbled, and at daybreak an Indian caught and mounted him, driving in the others.

We followed the course of the Chapeau until it opened into a large valley running southward, in which the river rises, and through which also another small river runs to join the Fraser, some 20 miles above Lytton. Through this valley the Indians told us there was a trail by which Lytton might be reached in two days.* Taking a northerly direction, we passed a small lake called Lake Crown, and soon came to the Pavillon Lake. The mountains here are of limestone and rise abruptly from the lake's edge, causing the trail to be somewhat narrow and dangerous. But this place and the Mauvais Rocher on the Shuswap Lake were the only spots upon the whole of our route from Kamloops to Pavillon, along which waggons might not have travelled with ease.
 · Of course in saying this I suppose the rivers bridged.

Lake Pavillon is six miles long by one wide. On its south bank there is a mountain some 3000 or 4000 feet high, which is topped with a very remarkable peak, not at all unlike a watch-tower built there to keep a look-out over the Fraser. The Indians call this Skillipaalock, which being interpreted means a finger or joint.

Just beyond the Pavillon Lake we passed a log hut, near which a farmer was ploughing—it was the first time I had seen such an implement in use in British Columbia—very diligently with two horses. This farm, of which I shall have occasion to speak hereafter, had, we found, been occupied by a couple of Americans for more than a year. They described their land as good, and spoke well of their prospects. Their principal occupation at present consisted in growing vegetables, &c., for the miners. The Pavillon River ran close by their hut, giving them a plentiful supply of

* Lately this valley has become the high road from Lytton to Cariboo.

water. It is a small stream flowing from the lake, and discharging itself into the Fraser at Pavillon.

Altogether we were five days making the journey from Kamloops to Pavillon, although the distance is a little under 100 miles. We had been much impeded, however, by the swollen state of the rivers, and had ridden very leisurely, constantly stopping to take bearings and make observations generally. Pavillon stands upon a terrace very similar to that upon which Lytton is situated, but some 100 feet or so higher. It consisted at that time of a score or so of miners' huts, and had gained its name from the fact of an Indian chief having been buried here, over whose grave, after the fashion of this people, a large white flag had been kept flying. It has since become a much more important place, forming a sort of head-quarters for the miners and the mule-trains, who from Pavillon, branch north and south to the diggings at Alexandria, Cariboo, and Kamloops.

We wished much to have pushed on from Pavillon to Alexandria, although at that time the diggings at Cariboo and Quesnelle were unthought of, and Alexandria was only known as a more distant station of the Hudson Bay Company. But poor St. Paul was knocked up by the efforts he had already made, and in such suffering that it was quite impossible to expect him to accompany us further. Almost all the way, indeed, he had been obliged to ride his horse in side-saddle fashion, and his exertions at the Defant River had used up what little strength he had, besides aggravating the pain he always suffered from his wounded knee. Accordingly, these considerations, coupled with the expense of preparing a new party for the trip, and the fact that we had already done more and gone farther than had been marked out for me in the Governor's programme of instructions, determined us to return by the Harrison-Lilloett route to the mouth of the Fraser. After staying three days at Pavillon, during which time the wind blew and the dust tormented us

K

much as it had done at Lytton, we bade St. Paul and his party adieu, starting for Cayoosh, or as it is now called Lilloett.

I may say here that while at Pavillon we experienced the only trouble with Indians I have ever had while travelling. A half-breed who was journeying with us, although not of our party, having a bullock to sell, disposed of it for 200 or 300 dollars, purchasing with part of its price a keg of whisky. Upon the contents of this he very soon got drunk, and must needs reduce the rest of our party to the same plight; so that in the dead of the night I was roused by the sound of scuffling going on outside the tent, and became aware of what all who have had any experience in camping will agree with me in calling a very disagreeable sensation, caused by a number of men tumbling over the tent-ropes. Going out, we found that St. Paul and one of his sons were the only sober men of our escort. Fortunately my gun was the only one belonging to the party, and most of the knives were in St. Paul's tent, or the consequences might have been serious. As it was, the offending half-breed was driven away, two or three of the more refractory Indians knocked down, and peace re-established, in a way we, without St. Paul, would have found it very difficult to accomplish.

It may be interesting to note that when I was at Pavillon, flour was selling at 35 cents (1s. 5½d.) the pound, and bacon at 75 cents (3s.). A few months earlier in the winter these high prices had been more than double. The charges for the carriage of goods were also very high, as much as 25 cents per lb., being paid from Pavillon to Kamloops, while to Big Bar, a place only 18 miles distant, the rate was 8 cents, or 4d.

We were now left without any attendants, but as we knew that there were regular mule-trains on the Harrison-Lilloett route, we determined only to engage two horses to take our baggage as far as Lilloett, and thence to accompany a train down to Port Douglas.

We started on the morning of the 23rd May, and proceeded towards Fountain, keeping the left bank of the Fraser, and passing along a fair trail over very good land; our party consisting of our two selves, a couple of horses, and one man, who served as guide, driver, and packer.

Fountain is a flat at a sharp turn in the river 12 miles below Pavillon, and derives its name from a small natural fountain spouting up in the middle of it. It is a much prettier site than Pavillon, and the river-bend shelters it from the gusty north and south winds which I have mentioned as being so very uncomfortable both at Lytton and Pavillon.

About three miles below Fountain, and on the opposite side, the Bridge River (or Hoystien, as the Indians call it) joins the Fraser. This river takes its English name from the fact of the Indians having made a bridge across its mouth, which was afterwards pulled down by two enterprising citizens, who constructed another one, for crossing which they charge the miners twenty-five cents. Bridge River rises in some lakes 50 or 60 miles from its mouth. I have never visited them, but from information obtained at various times from Indians, I believe that the Bridge, Lilloett, Squaw-misht, and Clahoose Rivers, all of which will be mentioned hereafter, take their rise in these same lakes, which, so far as I could ascertain, lie very high up in a mountain-basin, nearly north of Desolation Sound.

The Bridge River also runs through two lakes about 40 miles from its junction with the Fraser. I once met a miner who told me he had visited these lakes, and thought the land round them very good and well adapted for agriculture. A man at Pavillon also told me he had travelled from Chilcotin Fort to these lakes by a valley parallel to the Fraser, and had then descended the river. I am inclined, however, to doubt whether these lakes lie so far as 40 miles up the river, as I have found that travellers almost always overestimate distances when going *up* a rapid river.

K 2

Just before coming to the Bridge River our guide pointed to a deserted bar opposite, and said, "Last summer I and two others made 600 dollars (200*l.*) each in a week there." "Why did you leave it?" I asked. "Oh, we thought we had done enough," was the reply ; "and went to Victoria and spent it all in two or three weeks : and when I came up the river again I hadn't a cent, and so I took to packing." This is the story nearly every miner has to tell. If you question him, you will find that at some time or other he was worth several thousand dollars. Hè may still, perhaps, have a gold watch, or a large brooch stuck in the front of his mining-shirt, as a memento of that time, but all the rest has gone.

About a mile and a half below the Bridge River, at a place called French Bar, is a ferry, which we crossed. After crossing we came upon a fine flat, lightly timbered with small trees, which continued to Lilloett, which is about two miles from the ferry.

Lilloett is a very pretty site, on the whole decidedly the best I saw on the Fraser River. It stands upon a plateau some hundred feet above the river. On the opposite side of the Fraser is another large plateau on which the Hudson Bay Company were building a fort when I was there, which was to be named Fort Berens, after one of their directors.

Lilloett has now grown into a somewhat important town, situated as it is at the north end of the Harrison-Lilloett route, at its junction with the Fraser.

The Inkumtch River runs in at the south end of the flat on which the town stands. It is a rapid stream, 40 or 50 yards wide at its mouth, and not fordable in summer.

At Lilloett we found that the pack-trains came up to Port Anderson at the south end of the lake of that name, and that we must take boat across it and Lake Seton. We procured two or three Indians to carry our baggage and instruments to Lake Seton, which was about four miles off; but

finding upon calculation that the expense of conveying our
cooking-utensils, &c., would be considerably more than their
original cost, we determined to leave them behind for the
benefit of any travellers who might pass that way. We knew
we could not starve, as there were several "restaurants" on
the trail down; still we took some bread with us in case of
accidents. It is very awkward at first when you have to make
any purchases at these places, getting your change in gold-
dust. There is little or no coin in use among the miners,
and they pay and transact all business in gold-dust. For a
purse every one carries a chamois-leather bag containing the
dust. If you offer coin, they take out their scales and weigh
you off your change. I have mentioned the fact of there
being "restaurants" all along the Lilloett portages, and I
should have mentioned their existence in the cañons of the
Fraser also. All such places in this country are called
"restaurants," although they are simply huts, where the
traveller can obtain a meal of bacon, beans, bread, salt butter,
and tea or coffee, for a dollar; while, if he has no tent with
him, he can select the softest plank in the floor to sleep on.
Of course these places vary with their situation. At those
on the Lower Fraser meals can now, I believe, be had for
half-a-dollar, and sometimes eggs, beef, and vegetables can
be got. On the other hand, at those far up the river I paid a
dollar and a half for the bare miner's fare of bacon, beans, and
bread. Miners suffer a great deal from inflamed mouths,
which is very generally attributed to their constant diet of
bacon. By some, however, it is attributed to the water of
the river.

We started for Lake Seton on the afternoon of the same
day that we reached Lilloett, and, turning off from the
Fraser River, followed the Inkumtch, up a deep narrow
valley between two magnificent mountains some 5000 feet
high. About half-way to Lake Seton we found that the
river divided; one branch coming from the lake and the

other down a gorge on the left. This branch is said to take its rise in a lake some miles below Lilloett, and between the lake of that name and the Fraser River.

After walking about four miles we emerged from the mountain-pass and came out on Lake Seton. Here we had to get a canoe to cross the river, as the boatmen's huts were on the other side of it. We crossed, and, as it was late, pitched our tent and made arrangements for a boat with four men to take us over the lake in the morning.

In the morning accordingly we started, and had a most tedious cold pull of four hours' duration. On this lake, and, indeed, on all the chain of lakes, it blows almost incessantly from the southward during the day, the wind commencing at nine or ten and dying away at four or five, leaving the mornings and evenings calm. Lake Seton and Lake Anderson are very like each other, although the latter trends much more to the southward than the former. Both are very deep, and bounded by mountains of 3000 to 5000 feet, which rise so abruptly from the water as to leave no room for a road even along their banks without a good deal of blasting and levelling. These mountains are densely wooded, like those along the coast. The two lakes are each 14 or 15 miles long, and are separated by a neck of land a mile and a half in extent, with a stream of 20 or 30 yards wide running through it. There is a small restaurant at the south end of Lake Seton, and another larger one at the south end of Lake Anderson, for the entertainment of the muleteers, &c., who sleep there after coming from Port Pemberton; returning on the following day.

We were lucky enough to find a mule-train starting next morning, and arranged to accompany it. At this time the charge was eight cents (4½d.) per pound for packing goods along this portage, the length of which is about 25 miles. This portage, which extends from Port Anderson to Port Pemberton on the Lilloett Lake, was at first called the

Birkenhead Portage, but since has acquired the much more appropriate name of Mosquito Portage. When I passed along it the trail was on the whole good, though in some parts very indifferent. But this summer will probably see a waggon-road constructed from one end to the other. The valley through which the road lies averages about 1500 yards in width. At Port Anderson, however, where it is widest, it is about two miles broad. There is a stream running the whole way along it, having a watershed at the Summit Lake about nine miles from Port Anderson. From this lake, when the water is high, the rivers run either way, one into Lake Anderson and the other into the Lilloett River, just above Port Pemberton. When the waters are out the north branch only runs from the lake, the true source of the south branch being a few yards from it. The Summit Lake is, as nearly as I could estimate it, 800 feet above Lake Anderson and 1800 above the sea. The banks of the river are low and covered with willows, &c., and there are a number of small streams running into it at intervals all the way along. There are only two of these of any size, which come down rather large valleys. The mountains on either side range from 1000 to 5000 feet high, and are generally very steep. All the level spots are covered with wild peas, vetches, lettuce, and several sorts of berries. The mosquitoes along the portage were more troublesome than I had ever found them (at that time) elsewhere.

Five or six miles before reaching Port Pemberton the valley opens out, and there are several miles of splendid grass-land on the right, through which the Lilloett River runs into the lake of the same name. On this occasion I had not much opportunity for observing these Lilloett meadows, as they are called, but upon my next visit I came upon them by the Lilloett Valley, and walked all over them. Several agricultural settlers were already there, and it is a lovely spot for settlement. The river here divides into several small streams, which run through the plain in all directions, cutting it up into fine fields, and greatly adding to its beauty.

Port Pemberton is at the north end of Lilloett Lake, and consists of a couple of restaurants and half-a-dozen huts, occupied by muleteers and boatmen. The great objection to its site is that there is a large flat off it, which in winter dries the whole way across the lake, so that even boats cannot get to the town, and all goods have to be landed a quarter of a mile below it. This is, however, quite unavoidable, as there is no place further down the lake on which to build a town, the mountains rising nearly perpendicularly from the water. When the road was in contemplation Captain Grant, R.E., who had command of the men at work upon it, examined the meadows with a view of seeing if it would answer better to take the road from the other side of the lake, but he decided against it. This lake is in appearance much like the others I have described.

We got across the Lilloett Lake the same afternoon, sleeping that night at Port Lilloett. Early next morning we again set out. It rained the whole night while we were at Port Lilloett, and we were informed that this was the first rain that had fallen since the beginning of the year. This illustrates the partiality of the rain in this region, where January, February, March, and April had passed without a shower, while at Victoria it had rained almost incessantly for the first half of that period.

Next morning we started for Port Douglas. At the time I first went along this—which I have before said is called the Douglas Portage—there was only the trail which had been cut by the party who had volunteered for the purpose. Having no engineer with them, they gave themselves a vast deal more trouble than there was any occasion for, by making the

trail pass over all sorts of ridges which might have been
avoided. Eight miles from Port Lilloett the traveller comes
to a very curious hot spring, called St. Agnes' Well, so
named from one of the Governor's daughters. It runs in a
small stream out of a mass of conglomerate into a natural
basin at its foot, overflowing which it finds its way into the
Lilloett River. Here have been built a restaurant and bath-
house. On my first visit I stopped to bathe, and found the
water in the basin hotter than I could bear. Unfortunately
my thermometer was only marked to 120°, up to which the
mercury flew instantly. I believe its temperature has since
been ascertained to be 180° Fahr.

I have said that the Lilloett River runs down nearly to
Port Douglas. When I passed down no canoes were able to
ascend, though some went down the stream. In winter, however, a good deal of traffic is carried on by the river, at a
cost less than the land-carriage. This river varies greatly
in width, ranging from 50 to 150 yards. About nine miles
below Port Lilloett a large stream, called by the Indians
the Amockwa, joins it; and about the same distance above
Port Douglas another river, called the Zōālklūn, runs into
it, coming, it is said, from a lake called Zōālklūck. Two
large hills have to be crossed on this portage, which have
been named Sevastopol and Gibraltar; the latter rises just
before entering Port Douglas, and on its south side are the
finest cedars * I saw in the whole country. There is a stream
running down a gorge in this hill, and a large water-mill
has been erected about half-a-mile from the town, so that
I dare say considerable havoc has been made among the
cedars by this time.

The scenery on the Harrison Lake is much finer than on
the upper ones. It is also much longer, being 45 miles in

* Juniperus occidentalis?   I believe there is no true cedar in British
Columbia.

length, and four or five broad. There are several islands
upon it, and some large and apparently fertile valleys
running into it. In some of these silver has been found, and
one or more companies have been started to work it.

During our journey we found the change of temperature
very great and sudden. I have seen the thermometer 31°
in the shade in the morning, 95° at noon, and 40° again the
same evening.

On the 19th June we rejoined the ‘Plumper’ at Esquimalt.

SKETCH MAP OF HARO ARCHIPELAGO, SHOWING THE THREE CHANNELS.

- - - - - - - - - - - LINE CLAIMED BY THE UNITED STATES.
·· · ·· ··········· LINE CLAIMED BY GREAT BRITAIN.
- - - - - - - - - - - PROPOSED MIDDLE CHANNEL.

Page 130.

CHAPTER VII.

———◇———

American occupation of San Juan Island — Arrival of the Flagship, H.M.S. 'Ganges' — Inlets of the Coast of British Columbia — Autumn Survey between Nanaimo and Victoria — The 'Plumper' leaves for San Francisco — Our stay there.

July, 1859. — The Boundary Commissioners had been all this while working to little effect. The treaty concluded in 1844 between the English and American Governments was, as I have before said, somewhat vague. It set forth clearly enough that the boundary-line should follow the parallel of 49° north latitude, to the centre of the Gulf of Georgia; but it was at this point, as the reader may remember, that the difficulties attending its interpretation began. Thence the treaty stipulated that the line should pass southward through the channel which separates the continent from Vancouver Island to the Strait of Juan de Fuca. *The* channel. But there were three. Were the most eastward of these meant, such a construction would give possession of all the islands of the Gulf to Great Britain. On the other hand, should the line, as the American Commissioners contended, be taken to pass down the Haro Strait, these islands would pertain to them. Reasons, which I have previously given, exist which prevent my making any remarks upon the merits of the matters in dispute between the Commissioners of Great Britain and the United States, or the results which followed them. I may only say, that it was at this time, while the question had been referred by the Commissioners to their respective Governments, that General Harney, who had lately been appointed to the command of the United States troops in the territories of Oregon and

Washington, without any notice, landed soldiers upon the island of San Juna, who still remain there.

The same reasons which keep me silent upon this proceeding of the American General prevent my doing more than allude to the angry excitement which it caused in the colonies and at home. The events of that period will still be fresh in their memory of my readers. It will, therefore, be remembered how nearly war between the two countries was approached, and by what judicious and timely arrangements it was averted. I will merely remark, in conclusion, that, during the present domestic troubles of the American people, this dispute is temporarily shelved. San Juan is at present held by equal bodies of troops of Great Britain and America,* and the question remains open for settlement at some future period.

August 5th.—The flagship arrived, with divers on board, who, upon examining the 'Plumper,' found that she had received so much damage that it was determined, so soon as the coming winter-work was finished, to proceed to San Francisco, where the necessary repairs could be made.

August 19th.—A report reaching the Governor of some settlers in Burrard Inlet having been seized and detained by the Indians, we were despatched thither to investigate this matter, but, upon our arrival, we found the report untrue.

I will take the present opportunity of giving a short and general description of the more important of those long arms of the sea, or inlets, which, as a glance at the map will show the reader, stretch at comparatively small intervals inland along the coast of British Columbia. Some of these were not surveyed until a period considerably later than the time of which I am now writing, while others are still unexplored. It must be many years before these shores can be of any value to the new colony; and it is mainly with the hope

* About 100 men of each nation.

of discovering, from the head of one of them, a more
direct route or routes to the gold-fields on the Upper Fraser
than that afforded by the river, that exploring parties have
been, and still are, busy examining them.

All these inlets possess certain general characteristics.
They run up between steep mountains three or four
thousand feet in height; the water is deep, and anchorages
far from plentiful; while they terminate, almost without
exception, in valleys,—occasionally large and wide, at other
times mere gorges,—through which one or more rivers struggle
into the sea.   They may be said, indeed, to resemble large
fissures in the coast more than anything else.   In the days
of Vancouver these arms of the sea were diligently searched in
the hope of discovering through one of them the long looked-
for passage that should connect the Pacific and Atlantic Oceans.
It was not indeed until after many successive disappoint-
ments that Vancouver seems to have relinquished this hope;
and although of course some inaccuracies have been found
in his charts of these parts, their general correctness, together
with the amount of labour they must have cost him, and the
patience and perseverance with which he forced his vessels
through intricate passages difficult and dangerous even to
steamers, deserve more credit than he ever obtained.

The southernmost, and as yet the most important, of the
inlets of British Columbia was named, by Vancouver, "Burrard," after a friend of that name in the Royal Navy.
This inlet differs from most of the others in possessing
several good anchorages.   It is divided into three distinct
harbours, which are separated from each other by narrows,
through which the tide rushes with such velocity as to render
them impassable by any but powerful steamers except, at
slack-water or with the tide.

The entrance of Burrard Inlet lies 14 miles from the
sand-heads of the Fraser River.   English Bay is the anchorage immediately inside the entrance on the south side

and is of considerable importance to vessels entering at
night, or when the tide is running out through the narrows,
affording them an anchorage where they can wait comfortably
until morning or turn of tide, instead of drifting about the
place. Two miles inside the first narrows is Coal Harbour,
where coal has been found in considerable quantities and
of good quality, although the demand is not yet sufficient to
induce speculators to work it in opposition to the already
established mines at Nanaimo. Six miles above Coal Harbour, the inlet divides again into two arms; one of which runs
inland about ten miles, the other opening into Port Moody,
which forms the head of the southern arm. Port Moody is a
very snug harbour, three miles long, and averaging half-a-
mile wide, though only 400 yards across at the entrance. It is
the possession of this port, with its proximity by land to New
Westminster upon the Fraser River, from which place it is
distant but five miles, which gives to Burrard Inlet its present importance. During the winter the Lower Fraser is
sometimes frozen up, and the only access to British Columbia
then open is by the way of Burrard Inlet and Port Moody.
Hither the steamers have to take their passengers, mails, and
cargo; whence, by a short, good road, they are conveyed to
New Westminster. During last winter (1861-62), which was
unusually severe, the Fraser was entirely blocked up; and
this way, and an out-of-the-way, inconvenient trail of seven
miles from Mud Bay, inside Point Roberts, were the only
routes by which the interior of British Columbia could for
some considerable time be reached.

Immediately north of Burrard Inlet is Howe Sound, the
north point of the former forming the south shore of the latter.
This sound runs inland for about 20 miles, and is wider
than the other inlets, having a breadth at its entrance of six
miles. At its head is a wide, extensive valley, the soil of
which is very good, and through which several rivers run into
the inlet: the largest of these, the Squawmisht, is navigable

for 20 miles for canoes. From this point, which, however—so tortuous is the river—is only distant ten miles
from the head of the sound, a road might, with no great difficulty, be cut to Port Pemberton, on the north end of the
Lilloett Lake, the distance being only 40 or 50 miles. I
examined this route in 1860, and found it perfectly practicable; but as a road between Port Douglas, at the head of
Harrison Lake, and the south end of the Lilloett Lake had
already been constructed, it was not thought advisable to
make another so near it. Had this route met the Fraser
above instead of below Cayoosh, it would have been worth
cutting at any expense; but coming out where it does, its
construction would not have been of sufficient benefit to the
colony to have justified the great outlay which must have
been incurred in making it.

Next to Howe Sound is Jervis Inlet, a narrow arm running inland 45 miles. Vancouver appears to have thought
this the most promising of all the inlets he had explored for
the great object of his search; and experienced great disappointment when, after sailing up it for several days, he
reached its head. It seems strange that such an experienced
explorer should have expected that so narrow a passage—its
greatest breadth after the first ten miles being but two—
would be found to divide the American continent from shore
to shore.

It was for some time thought that a highway to British
Columbia would be found to exist up this inlet; and, with the
view of ascertaining its practicability, I was instructed to
start from the head of Jervis Inlet, and make my way to the
Fraser River. An account of this journey and its unsuccessful issue will follow in its place. Whilst making it, I
constantly interrogated the Indians who accompanied me as
to the probability of a way existing from the head of Toba or
Bute Inlets, which run up from Desolation Sound, and are
the two next inlets northward of Jervis. From their answers,

I was for some time under the impression that Bute Inlet
was the place whence a start might be made for the Fraser
with every prospect of success.   But upon returning to Victoria, and submitting the accounts of my informants to the
scrutiny of an interpreter, and making them map out in their
own way the route that they suggested, I came to the conclusion that the route they spoke of led, not to the Fraser
River, but to Lake Anderson.

It may seem strange that Indians living at Jervis Inlet
should know the country about Desolation Sound so well,
seeing that the two arms of the sea are distant from
each other 60 miles, and that the inhabitants of each inlet
are constantly at war.   The tribe, however, to which my
guides belonged, although in the summer dwelling by the
coast, were settled really at Lake Anderson, from which
neighbourhood they migrated to Howe Sound, Jervis, Bute,
and Toba Inlets, to fish, and were, therefore, likely to be well
acquainted with the country through which at such times
they must pass on their way to the coast.   They were called
Loquilts, the proper Indians of Jervis Inlet being named
Sechelts.

From these Indians I ascertained that the Bridge River,
one—the north—branch of the Lilloett, together with the
Squawmisht and the Clahoose Rivers, which empty into
Desolation Sound, all take their rise in three or four small
lakes lying in a mountain basin some 50 or 60 miles from
the coast due north of Jervis Inlet.   Mr. Downie, when
exploring Bute Inlet with a view to a way from the coast
inland, went four or five miles up the Clahoose River, which
he described as large and broad, running in a north-east
direction.   "The Indians," he wrote, "told me it would take
five days to get to the head of it.   Judging from the way a
canoe goes up such rivers, the distance would be about sixty
miles, and it must be a long way above the Quamish (Squawmisht), and not far from the Lilloett.   The Indians have

gone this route to the head of Bridge River, and it may prove
to be the best route to try.   It is very evident there is a pass
in the coast-range here that will make it preferable to Jarvis
Inlet or Howe Sound.   If a route can be got through, it will
lead direct to Bridge River."

It is now three years since Mr. Downie made the above
statement; and I think it is probable that he has long since
changed the opinion he then expressed as to the route to the
Bridge River being the most practicable and best of those
proposed to the Upper Fraser.   So little, however, is known
of this valley—and that little comes from Indian information
—that the route advocated by Mr. Downie may yet be found
to equal his expectations of it.   Since my return from the
colony it has been again examined and adopted by a company, who propose at once to open it up.   It is asserted
by them that this way is nearly twenty miles shorter than
the Bentinck Arm route to Alexandria, and that no serious
obstacles intervene to prevent striking the Fraser at a point
where steamers can be put on to ply on the Upper River.
The right to construct this route, and to collect tolls on
the pack-trail for five years, at 1½ cents per lb., and 50
cents for animals—with, should a waggon-road be constructed,
5 cents per lb. toll—has been conceded to them.   In their
prospectus the distance of the route proposed is set down as
241 miles, of which 83 miles are river and lake navigation,
and 158 land-carriage, offering an advantage over the rival
route by Bentinck Arm, which has a longer land-carriage.
Before this summer is out, the question of superiority will
in all probability be settled.

The next inlet, north of Bute, is Loughborough.   Beyond
are Knight Inlet and Fife Sound, of which comparatively
little is known.   In 1861 Mr. Downie went up Knight Inlet
and discovered plumbago, which, when tested, did not prove
to be so rich as he at first sight thought it.

The entrance to Fife Sound is marked by a magnificent

L

mountain on its north side, which Vancouver named "Stephens," after the then First Lord of the Admiralty.

Above this point up to our coast boundary, in 54° 40′ north latitude, is a succession of inlets known only to the Indians who inhabit them, and some of the Hudson Bay Company's employés. One of these, through which it is thought by many that the much-desired road to the interior of the country will be found to lie, "Deans Canal," has recently attracted considerable notice. The entrance to this inlet is about 80 miles from the north end of Vancouver Island; it runs inland some 50 miles, under the name of Burke Channel, and then divides into three arms: one, Deans Canal, running nearly north for 25 miles; the others, called the North and South Bentinck Arms, pursuing north-easterly and south-easterly directions. By one or other of these channels it is pretty confidently expected that a good available route to the interior will be found to exist. No doubt attention was drawn to this spot not a little from the fact, that years ago Sir Alexander McKenzie did actually penetrate from the interior to the sea here. Subsequently it was known that a Mr. McDonald had found his way from Fort Fraser to the coast, coming out at Deans Canal, and, it was said, making the journey with ease and expedition; while later, letters were conveyed more than once by some such route, by Indian messengers, from the Hudson Bay Company's steamer 'Beaver,' lying in the Bentinck Arm, to the officer in charge of Fort Alexandria, high up the Fraser River.

When Sir Alexander McKenzie explored this part of the country, he appears to have ascended the West-road River from the Fraser, and then, crossing the ridge forming the watershed, to have descended to the sea. His route has never been exactly followed; but in 1860 Mr. Colin McKenzie crossed from Alexandria to the same place on the coast, viz., Rascals' Village, or Bell-houla Bay,* in thirteen days by way

* This is sometimes spelt Bell-whoula.

of Chilcotin Lake. His party travelled the greater portion of the way on horseback: Mr. McKenzie told me that they might have taken their animals all the way by changing the route a little. On their way back, indeed, they did so. The ascent to the watershed was, he said, so gradual, that they only knew they had passed the summit by finding that the streams ran west, instead of east. Since that time another gentleman, Mr. Barnston, has travelled by much the same route. His journey is described in a letter which he wrote to Mr. P. Nind, Gold Commissioner at Cariboo, in July, 1861, and which, as illustrating the character of the country and the obstacles met with in the construction of trails, I am enabled, by the kind permission of that gentleman, to give to the reader:—

" We left Alexandria on the 24th May last, and after the loss of several days from accidental causes, such as missing trail, &c., arrived at Lake Anawhim on the 8th June. We left this place on the 10th. On the 12th we camped in the Coast Range. On the 13th we descended into the valley of Atanaioh, or Bell-houla River, and camped a few miles down. Here we left our horses with Pearson and Ritchie. On the evening of the 17th McDonald and I, accompanied by Tomkins, started on foot for the coast. We arrived at the Bell-houla village, Nout-chaoff, early on the morning of the 19th. Here we obtained a canoe and descended to Kougotis, the head of the Bell-houla (North Bentinck Arm), in six hours. The cause of our horses being left behind was the swollen state of the mountain-torrents running into the Bell-houla River. These streams are, however, quite small and narrow, and could be bridged at little expense. On the 24th we left Kougotis to return in the same canoe, and arrived at Nout-chaoff on the 25th. The trail between the two villages is good. From Nout-chaoff to camp it took us two days, a distance usually travelled by Indians with packs in one. On the 30th we broke up camp on Bell-houla River, and arrived

L 2

in Alexandria on the 10th, travelling moderately with packed animals. The Bell-houla River could be made navigable for light-draught steamers as far up as Nout-chaoff, and perhaps above. From thence pack-trains could make Alexandria, or the mouth of Canal River,* if a trail were made there, easily in 14 or 15 days. The trail to Canal River would probably have to diverge from the Alexandria trail at Chisikut Lake about 75 miles from Alexandria. The trail runs the whole distance from Alexandria to Coast Range on a kind of table-land, which is studded in every direction with lakes and meadows : feed is plentiful. The streams are numerous, but small and shallow; in fact, mere creeks. There are some swamps, which require corduroying. There is plenty of fallen timber; but it is light and could easily be cleared. There is also a kind of red earth, which is in places very miry; the cause of this is I think, want of drainage. This miry ground and the swamps are the greatest objections that can be urged against the road. The swamps, however, have one advantage over such places generally,—that is, in their foundation, which is rocky and strong. The trail might be shortened in some places, but not a great deal. We made the distance from our camp on Bell-houla River to Alexandria easily enough in 11 days with packed horses. The trail is, with the exception of the descent of the Coast Range, comparatively level, and could easily be made a good practicable road. The descent on to the Bell-houla River is not by any means steep, with the exception of a slide, down which we, however, took our horses. This slide might be avoided, or could be easily overcome by a zigzag trail. The trail would have to be considerably improved before pack-trains could pass over it. When the Coast Range is passed there is no perceptible ascent.

"From the place where you first strike the Bell-houla River in the Coast Range, the trail runs along its bank through a

* Probably Quesnelle River.

deep gorge or pass in the mountains the whole way to the coast. There is, however, another road from Lake Anawhim, which strikes the river at Nout-chaoff, which the Indians informed us was the better road. They also told us that if we had taken this road we could have reached Nout-chaoff with our horses, as we should have thereby avoided the worst part of the other road and the torrents. Kougotis, the head of the inlet, would be the head of navigation for sea-going vessels.

"We think that if a road were made from the Bell-houla Inlet, to strike the Fraser somewhere about the mouth of the Quesnelle River, and from thence into the Cariboo, &c., a considerable saving in the cost of transportation would be effected. We can hardly make an approximate estimate even of what it would cost to make the trail passable; but it would not cost much considering the distance and style of country, and could easily be made available for next summer's operations."

If the reader will follow on the map the line between the Bentinck Arm (Bell-houla) and Alexandria, he will see that it runs straight east and west between the two places for 160 miles. This is the route to the gold-fields, south of that taken by Sir A. McKenzie, which is proposed to be adopted, and to open up which another company, in opposition to the Bute Inlet scheme, has been organised. It is affirmed that the road becomes open and practicable for animals in the beginning of April, and that the snow at Bell-houla and the main plateau above it disappears early in the year. At present and for some time to come no accommodation for travellers can be expected along this route; but in reply to this objection it is urged that the journey is comparatively short, and may be walked without a pack in seven days; and that the Indians of the various tribes through which it will be necessary to pass are not only friendly but seem anxious for white settlers to come, inquiring constantly when the Boston and King George men may be expected, and looking forward to remunerative employment in packing to the mines.

The following account of this route has also been given by one of its projectors, who assumes to speak from personal experience :—" My suggestion would be, let a man take up sufficient provisions for the road ; or if he wishes to avoid the heavy outlay which a poor miner must experience before he has struck a claim, let him take sufficient to last him three or four weeks, and pack one, two, or three Indians, as the case may be.   I assure him he will find no difficulty in procuring Indians.   Nootlioch (an Indian lodge) is 30 miles up the river; for 15 miles above this goods can be taken in small canoes.   Narcoontloon is 30 miles; a good road with the exception of one bad hill.   Here there is another Indian lodge, from which it is 50 miles to Chilcotin; good trail, perfectly level.   From there it is 60 miles to Alexandria, or about 70 to the mouth of Quesnelle River.   The trail from the top of the Nootlioch hill is for foot-passengers as good the whole way as any part of the Brigade Trail, with the exception of one or two places, where there is a little fallen timber.   The trail follows a chain of lakes, and could consequently, if taken straight, be made much shorter, and also avoid much soft ground.   Game and fish are abundant on the road : I caught several trout with a string and a small hook and a grasshopper on my way down.   The Aunghim and Chilcotin Indians have a good many horses, which might be turned to use for packing."

Alexandria, however, which is the proposed terminus in this route from Bell-houla, is some 50 or 60 miles south of those diggings, which are now the most profitable in the country, and which, under the general name of the Cariboo gold-fields, extend from the lake of that name to Bear River, and are likely to extend still farther north, should the opinion of many of the miners that the richest diggings still remain to be found on the Peace River, northward of that spur of the Rocky Mountains, which turns the course of the Fraser southward, prove correct.   It seems, therefore, likely

that the line of route proposed by other adventurers, running
from Dean's Canal, in a north-easterly direction, to the
Nachuten Lakes, and along the river of the same name to
Fort Fraser, may bear off the palm, particularly if, as is very
probable, Stuart River be found navigable for steamers from
that place to Fort George, where it meets the Fraser.

In the summer of 1859 Mr. Downie explored a still more
northward route from Fort Essington, by a river called by him
the Skena, but which must be the same as that known inland
as the Simpson or Babine, and which flows from Lake Babine.
This route is less direct than any of the others, and is so far
north as to be unavailable for the greater part of the year.
Mr. Downie's interesting account of this journey will be
found in the Appendix. It will be seen that he reports the
country through which he travelled to be auriferous, that he
found evidence of most extensive deposits of coal of a quality
superior to any specimen of that mineral which he had previously seen in British Columbia and Vancouver Island, and
that the land generally seemed excellent and well adapted for
agricultural purposes.

Forty miles north of Port Essington, and 240 from the
north end of Vancouver Island, Fort Simpson is reached,
which is situated as nearly as possible upon the line of boundary between Great Britain and Russia. This post has been
established for many years, and is surrounded somewhat thickly
by Indians, among whom Mr. Duncan; the missionary teacher,
of whose self-denying life and valuable labours I shall hereafter have occasion to speak at greater length, works with
such singular success.

From the 25th August to the 30th September we were
employed among the inner channels between Nanaimo and
Victoria, and in putting down a set of buoys on the sands at
the entrance of the Fraser River. On the islands in these
inner channels there are now several agricultural settlements,
the principal one being on Admiral Island, an island fourteen

miles long by four or five wide, having two or three excellent harbours, and containing much good land. On this island there are saltsprings.

Admiral Island is next to Vancouver, from which it is separated by a narrow strait, called Sausum Narrows, which at its narrowest part is little more than half-a-mile wide.

Four miles west of the south part of Admiral Island, Cape Keppel, is Cowitchin Harbour. As a harbour this is not worth much; but it will be of importance when the Cowitchin Valley, which runs back from it, becomes settled. This valley is the most extensive yet discovered on the island, and is reported by the colonial officers who surveyed it to contain 30,000 or 40,000 acres of good land. It is peopled by the Cowitchin tribe of Indians, who, as I have mentioned,. are considered a badly-disposed set, and have shown no favour to those settlers who have visited their valley. Although it has been surveyed it cannot yet be settled, as the Indians are unwilling to sell, still less to be ousted from their land. Through this valley runs the Cowitchin River, which comes from a large lake of the same name, and 24 miles inland, and empties itself into the head of Cowitchin Harbour. It is navigable for several miles for canoes. Between Cowitchin and Nanaimo there is a considerable quantity of good land, which has been surveyed and is called the Chemanos district.

Immediately south of Cowitchin Harbour is the Saanich Inlet, a deep indentation running 14 miles in a south-south-east direction, carrying deep water to its head, and terminating in a narrow creek within four miles of Esquimalt Harbour. This inlet forms a peninsula of the south-east portion of Vancouver Island of about 20 miles in a north-north-west and south-south-east direction, and varying in breadth from eight miles at its southern part to three at its northern. On the southern coast of this peninsula are the harbours of Esquimalt and Victoria, in the neighbourhood of which for some five miles the country is pretty thickly wooded—its prevailing features lake and mountain—with, however, some considerable tracts of clear and fertile land. The northern portion for about ten miles contains some of the best agricultural land in Vancouver Island. The coast here, as everywhere else, is fringed with pine; but in the centre it is clear prairie or oak-land, most of it now under cultivation. Seams of coal have also been found here. On the eastern or peninsular side of the inlet are some good anchorages, the centre being for the most part deep. A mile and a half from the head of the inlet is a large lake, called Langford Lake, which is very likely to be called into requisition some day to supply the ships in Esquimalt Harbour, from which it is two miles and a half distant, with water. Outside the Saanich peninsula is Cordova Channel, extending to Discovery Island, seven miles from Victoria. Like all these inner passages, this one is quite safe for steamers, but, from the varying currents, dangerous for sailing vessels. As several farms have been established along the shore of the island here, looking out on the Haro Strait, and the land is much more clear than usual, this is one of the prettiest parts of the island.

On the 30th September the Admiral (Sir R. L. Baynes, K.C.B.), came on board, and we took him to Nanaimo and Burrard Inlet, returning to Esquimalt on the 4th October. From this time until the 28th we continued working northward from Nanaimo, when, having been drenched to the skin nearly every day for a month, the captain determined to close the season's operations, and we made for Nanaimo. Here we found—what was not unfrequently the case—that the Indians were all more or less drunk, owing to a grand feast which had been given by the chief of the tribe a few days before, and that they would not get the coal out of the pit for us: we had, therefore, to help ourselves.

On the 10th of February, 1860, having brought our winter duties to an end, we started for San Francisco, and anchored

that night in Neah Bay, of which I have spoken in describing
the Strait of Fuca. Next morning we proceeded out of the
Strait, passing several vessels on their way in. The sight of
these vessels could scarcely fail to remind us of the colony
which had sprung into existence since we had rounded Cape
Flattery and entered that Strait three years before, when we
might have steamed up and down it for a week without meeting more than a few vessels, and those bound to American
ports. In the passage between San Francisco and Vancouver
Island there is nothing worthy of particular notice, except
the change from the everlasting pine-trees which fringe all
our shore, to the almost treeless coast of California. One
cannot help feeling that Nature has been unfair in its distribution of timber in these regions. California, comparatively
speaking, may be said to have none, all their plank being
supplied from the saw-mills before spoken of as being at
work in Puget Sound and Admiralty Inlet. It was with
considerable difficulty and at great expense that they managed
to get sufficient wood to build a small steamer, ordered by the
Federal Government to be constructed at Mare Island, the
dockyard of San Francisco. The coast all the way down is
well lighted, but there are no good harbours; San Francisco, indeed, is the only good one between the Strait of Fuca
and Acapulco, which is 1500 miles below it, on the coast of
Mexico, although there are several open anchorages. The
distance from Cape Flattery to the Golden Gate, as the
entrance of San Francisco harbour is called, is 700 miles,
and the mail-steamers make the passage generally in three
days and a half to five days. We, however, were under sail
much of our time, and did not make it until seven days
after leaving Esquimalt. On the morning of the 17th we
sighted the noble head, the name of which has been changed
from "Punta de Los Reyes"—the grand name the old
Spaniards had given it—to "Point Reyes"—and crossing
the bar, entered the harbour at four in the afternoon.

Nothing can be finer than the entrance to this magnificent harbour; and, considering also the country of which it is the only port, its name of "Golden Gate" is very appropriate, although the name was given to it long before the discovery of gold in California. It had reference, no doubt, to the beauty of the country generally, and to the golden appearance it wears in spring, before the parching summer sun has scorched its verdure.

Fifteen miles off the harbour is a group of rocky islands, called the Farrallones, on the southern of which is a lighthouse. Off the entrance of the harbour is the "Bar," on which the surf is generally rough. This bar, however, serves to let the mariner know he is off the entrance if he is trying to make the harbour in a fog; which, as they prevail constantly from May till October, he is very likely to do. The current in the entrance varies from two to five knots. There are two lighthouses at the mouth of the harbour, and on the hill above, on each side, is a telegraph-station. The constant fogs make this of little use, as ships are always slipping in and out without their arrival or departure being known. When we went in H.M.S. 'Hecate,' in October, 1861, nobody knew anything of our arrival till some of the officers appeared at the club. Generally speaking, however, vessels arriving are seen as they pass Alcatraz Island, which lies in the middle of the harbour, and is a military station. Although some attempt has been made to fortify San Francisco, it is still very imperfect in this respect. The only defensive works as yet existing are, a brick fort on the south side of the entrance, intended to carry 140 guns, in three tiers of casemates, and one tier *en barbette.* A battery, intended to mount eleven heavy guns, is being constructed on the hill above this fort. Alcatraz Island, in the middle of the harbour, is partially fortified; and as the guns on this island are 150 feet above the sea, it would be an awkward place to attack with ships. This island is about three miles and a half from Fort Point; it is a small place, about 550 yards long, by 150 yards wide. Their guns are all *en barbette*, and number about 100. There is no water on the island, and they have to supply it from Saucelito Bay, five or six miles distant, and keep it in a large tank, said to hold 50,000 gallons.

I had last visited San Francisco in 1849, when the gold-fever was at its height, and there were only a dozen houses in the place, the 5000 or 6000 inhabitants being scattered about in tents. At that time the site of the present magnificent city was a bare sand-hill. In those days the harbour was filled with merchant-ships, as now; but although they entered in great numbers, few went out, both officers and men deserting the ships for the diggings as soon as the anchors were let go, and leaving their cargoes to be unloaded by others. Where these vessels used then to be anchored fine streets have been erected, for all the lower part of San Francisco is built out over the harbour. Many accidents are constantly occurring from the insecure way in which these streets are left. It is dangerous to go down to the wharves after dark, from the large holes left exposed, through which many poor fellows have fallen and been killed. Constant actions are being brought against the Town Council on this account. Greenhow, the American historian, was killed by falling through one of these places, and his widow brought an action against the Town Council, recovering the sum of 10,000 dollars for her loss.

San Francisco has been twice burnt down in the twelve years during which it has been in existence. These fires have been most beneficial to the town, as most of the wooden buildings which were destroyed have been replaced by very fine brick ones. Montgomery Street, the principal thoroughfare in the town, is now almost as fine a street as any European capital can boast of; equal, indeed, in the size of the buildings and magnificence of the shops, to the best thoroughfares of London. No city in the world has, I imagine, a history so short and wonderful as San Francisco. In February, 1849, the population was about 2000: in the middle of the same year it had risen to 5000; while it is stated that from April, 1849, to January, 1850, nearly 40,000 emigrants arrived, of which only 1500 were women. By the year 1860, the population had risen to 66,000. In addition to these, thousands went to the mines direct, many crossing the continent and the Sierra Nevada, where hundreds left their bones to bleach among the mountains.

Among the thousands who hurried to California from every part of the world, it may be imagined there were many of the very dregs of society. Convicted felons from our penal colonies—every one, indeed, whose own country was too hot for him, hastened hither. Murders, incendiarisms, and every kind of crime were being daily perpetrated; no decent man dared to walk the streets after dark, and no property was safe. Law there was not; and where two-thirds of the population were scoundrels, it may be imagined what class of public officials would be elected under the system of universal suffrage. What, therefore, between the weakness or partiality of the judges, the technicalities of the law, the dishonesty of the juries, and the dread of witnesses to tender their evidence, San Francisco, in 1851, was suffering from anarchy unparalleled in modern history. It was this social condition of the city that caused the organisation of that most remarkable society, the "Vigilance Committee," to which I have had occasion to allude in a former chapter.

This association was formed in June, 1851, "for the protection of the lives and property of citizens resident in the city of San Francisco." A council was appointed and a place of meeting fixed, while the tolling of the bell of the Monumental Fire Engine Company was the signal for assembly. Although the "Vigilance Committee" has for several years now allowed the law of the land to take its course, it still exists, and is ready to assemble whenever the signal may be given. " What has become of your Vigilance Committee," I asked one of them when I was in San Francisco in October last. " Toll the bell, Sir, and you will see," was the reply. " Oh, then you are still under orders ? " " Always ready at the signal, Sir. If it were now given, you would see thousands at the meeting-place before the bell had ceased to sound.".

There is no doubt that this strange organisation exercised, and still exercises, a most wholesome restraint over a society that, but a few years since, elected a miner to be chief judge of the State, and whose two principal judges now go by the significant sobriquets of " Mammon " and " Gammon." The first proceeding of the committee in the summer of 1851 was to arrest, try, and hang four men, three of whom confessed their crimes, while the fourth was, I believe, undoubtedly guilty. The moral effect of this proceeding was wonderful. All the other towns, which were rising all over the State, formed Vigilance Committees of their own. Many known ruffians, whose crimes could not be brought home to them, were ordered to leave the State; while others were kept in surveillance, and reported from Committee to Committee as they traversed the country. For years after this California was almost free of crime. Although by the greater number of the people the Vigilance Committee was held in favour, the officials and some others denounced it, and to this day stigmatise its existence as a disgrace to California. These termed themselves the " Law and Order " party; but upon many occasions their weakness to restrain the mixed and dangerous population of San Francisco was made apparent.

I have entered more fully into the history of San Francisco than I otherwise should have done, since I think a valuable and fair comparison may be drawn between these scenes and the peaceable course of British Columbia since the

UNITED STATES DOCKYARD, MARE ISLAND, SAN FRANCISCO.

Page 156.

discovery of gold there five years ago. The reader unacquainted with the past history of California, would scarcely credit the fearful scenes through which she has reached her present growth.

If San Francisco were the only city in California, its dimensions would not, perhaps, be so surprising; but it is only one of many, almost as large and equally beautiful, in the State. Sacramento, the seat of government, Stockton, and others, vie with it in size, while Marysville, Benicia, Los Angelos, &c., are far more beautifully situated.

After a few days' stay off San Francisco, we proceeded to Mare Island, where the Government dockyard is established. Mare Island is 23 miles from San Francisco, across San Pablo Bay, and at the mouth of the Sacramento. Here we were received by the American naval officers, and immediately put on the dock.

It may be interesting to some of my readers if I here say something of a Sectional Dock, such as that we were now placed upon, and which, though generally used in America, is very little known, and still less liked, in this country. In a new country where there is plenty of timber, this kind of dock has one great advantage, in its cheapness and facility of construction, compared with the ordinary stone docks. But in California, where, as I have before said, there is very little timber, a stone dock might have been constructed almost as cheaply. The dock of which I am speaking had to be built at Pensacola, and then taken to pieces, and sent out to California at an expense, I was there told, of about 70,000 dollars (15,000l.)

The Sectional Dock is composed of a series of sections, or iron tanks, each being fitted with a complete pumping-apparatus, elevated on a framework 60 or 80 feet above the top of the tank. These tanks are fitted with gates, like the caissons used in English docks, so that they can be filled, sunk, or again pumped out at pleasure. A number of these sections, varying according to the weight and length of the ship to be lifted, are securely chained together, and the whole is moored in water sufficiently deep to allow of their being sunk beneath the vessel's keel. They are generally kept level with the water's edge; but when a vessel is to be docked, they are sunk low enough to allow her to come over the blocks which are placed along the centre. The vessel is then hauled over the blocks, the pumps started, and, as she rises, shores from the sides of the tanks, and from the frames of the pump-houses, are placed under her and against her sides, and she is gradually raised till her keel is out of the water. If proper care is taken, these docks are quite safe, but the ship must be placed cautiously on the blocks, or an accident is very likely to happen. In 1860 H.M.S. 'Termagant' was allowed to fall over in this dock, and was for some time in great danger. Her stern was allowed to rest on the edge of one of the sections, which, as her weight came upon it, rose up and turned over. This canted the ship, and she fell with her masts against the pump-houses. Fortunately she had only been raised a little way; had she been further out of the water, she would probably have broken down the pump-houses, and very likely sunk. One advantage possessed by these docks is, that the ship being, as it were, raised into the air, there is better light for working at her bottom than in a stone dock.

While at San Francisco we had, of course, many opportunities of remarking those peculiar habits of manner and phraseology indulged in by the Americans. At Victoria, peopled as it is by Americans, we had been made familiar with them; but here they were more commonly and glaringly used. Certainly, they justify anything that Mr. Dickens or other English satirists have written of them. Americans

all say—not, however, with perfect truth—that these eccen-
tricities belong only to the lower orders of society. I have
the pleasure of knowing both American gentlemen and ladies
quite free from their use; but still I have met many others,
holding good positions in society, thoroughly "Yankee" in
tone and expression. These Americanisms must lose much
of their ludicrous effect by being written, as it is impossible
to give the tone and peculiar emphasis of the speaker. Words
are often used by them to convey a sense entirely different
to that which we apply to them. Thus, "I'll *happen* in
directly" is considered rather a good expression for a contemplated visit. So, "clever" does not imply any talent in the
individual of whom it is spoken, but is said of a good-natured,
gentlemanly man generally; while "smart" answers for our
"clever." Speaking to an American naval officer, just
before leaving Victoria for San Francisco, he said, "Well,
sir, "I guess you'll have quite an *elegant* time down there.
Elegant place, sir, San Francisco." A very pretty young
lady, living in Puget Sound, and happening to be on board
the 'Plumper,' said to one of the officers: "Well, sir, if you
come over to Steilacoom, I guess you shall have a tall horseback ride;" by which form of expression she meant to imply,
not that the horse should be longer in the legs than is usual,
but that care should be taken that the ride should be more
than ordinarily agreeable. In a book on Americanisms, published last year, a Baltimore young lady is represented as
jumping up from her seat on being asked to dance, and
saying, "Yes, sirree; for I have sot, and sot, and sot, till I've
nigh tuk root!" I cannot say I have heard anything quite
equal to this; but I very well remember that at a party
given on board one of the ships at Esquimalt, a young lady
declined to dance a "fancy" dance, upon the plea, "I'd
rather not, sir; I guess I'm not *fixed up* for waltzing;"—an
expression the particular meaning of which must be left to
readers of her own sex to decide. An English young lady,

M

who was staying at one of the houses at Mare Island, when
we were there, happened one evening, when we were visiting
her friends, to be confined to her room with a headache.
Upon our arrival, the young daughter of our host—a girl of
about twelve—went up to her to try to persuade her to come
down. "Well," she said, "I'm *real* sorry you're so poorly.
You'd better come, for there are some almighty swells down
there!" A lady, speaking of the same person, said, "Her
hair, sir, took my fancy right away!" Again, several of
us were one day talking to a tall, slight young lady about the
then new-fashioned crinoline which she was wearing. After
a little banter, she said, "I guess, Captain, if you were to
take my hoops off, you might draw me through the eye of a
needle!"

Perhaps one of the most whimsical of these curiosities of
expression, combining freedom of manner with that of speech,
was made use of to Captain Richards by a master-caulker.
He had been vainly endeavouring to persuade the Captain
that the ship required caulking, and at last he said in disgust,
"You may be liberal as a private citizen, Captain, but you're
mean to an almighty pump-tack!"—in his official capacity, of
course. Again, an American gentleman on board one of our
mail packets was trying to recall to the recollection of the
mail agent a lady who had been fellow-passenger with them
on a former occasion. "She sat opposite you at table all the
voyage," he said. "Oh, I think I remember her; she ate a
great deal, did she not?" "Eat, sir!" was the reply, "she
was a perfect gastronomic filibuster!" One more example,
and I have done with a subject upon which I might enlarge
for pages. The boys at the school at Victoria were being
examined in Scripture, and the question was asked, "In
what way did Hiram assist Solomon in the building of the
Temple?" It passed two or three boys, when at last one
sharp little fellow triumphantly exclaimed, "Please, sir, he
donated him the lumber."

Hardly less remarkable than their peculiarities of language
is their habit of taking drinks with remarkable names from
morning till night.   No bargain can be made, no friendship cemented—in fact, no meeting can take place—without
"liquoring up." The morning is commenced with a brandy,
or champagne, cocktail, not unfrequently taken in bed.
This is continued, at short intervals, until bedtime again,
and no excuse will avail you unless you can say you are a
"dashaway," which is their name for a total abstainer.   This
habit, I must say, does not extend so high in the social scale
as the other ; it is, however, the great social failing of the
Western States.

The repairs of the ship were finished, and on the 9th March
we left San Francisco to return to our work; little thinking
that in scarcely more than a year we should revisit it again
with another ship in a worse state than we had brought the
' Plumper.'

CHAPTER VIII.

---◆◇◆---

Johnstone Strait — The North-East of Vancouver Island — Fort Rupert and Queen Charlotte Sound.

On the 5th of April we left Esquimalt to commence the summer work, and proceeded to Nanaimo to fill up with coal. On our way we stopped at the northern settlement on Admiral Island, as it had been reported that some Indians had been troublesome there. We found, however, that the Indians had done nothing more than tell the settlers occasionally, as Indians do everywhere, that they (the whites) had no business there except as their guests, and that all the land belonged to them. At the Ganges Harbour settlement some of the black settlers had been robbed by them. The Indians always stedfastly refused to regard black men as entitled to any of the respect claimed by and shown to the whites. They also entertain the same feeling with regard to the Chinese. I remember an Indian once asking me about them, and saying, " Wake, wake ! " (" No, no ! "), most decidedly, when I told him they were " carqua King George men " (" the same as Englishmen ").

It appeared to be most desirable here, as at other places, that the Indians should be duly paid for their land. This is not so simple as it may seem, however, even supposing the money necessary for such a purpose to be forthcoming. In New Zealand the Government spent many thousand pounds purchasing the land, appointing agents, commissioners, &c., and something of the same is no doubt as necessary here. Vancouver Island, however, has no revenue available or sufficient for such a purpose, and of course the revenue of British Columbia cannot, while the two colonies are distinct, be applied to it. Another difficulty would be found in the con-

flicting claims of the various tribes, arising from their habits
of polygamy and inheritance from the female side, together
with the absence of any documentary or satisfactory evidence ·
of title.

If, therefore, any one chief or tribe were paid for a piece
of land without the acknowledgment on the part of adjacent
tribes of the vendor's right to the land sold, five or six other
claimants would in all probability come forward asserting the
land to be theirs, and founding their title to it upon some
intermarriage of its former possessors. The difficulties arising from the Indian custom of descent from the female side
are most perplexing. Mr. Weynton, of the Hudson Bay
Company, who resided some years at Fort Rupert, told me
he had known, on the death of a chief, a man from quite
another tribe step in and take the chieftainship, without, so
far as he could ascertain, any close connection with the tribe
he claimed to rule. Admiral Island, for instance, of which
I am now speaking, would, in all probability, be claimed by
no less than four tribes, viz., the Cowitchin, the Penalikut-
son, a small tribe living among these islands, the Nanaimos,
and Saanitch Indians. On the occasion of our present visit,
the settlers, in reference to this subject, said the Indians had
never been there before, and that they had established a
village there for the sole purpose of asserting their claim to
compensation for the land. Upon our telling one of them
this, he pointed to a small stump by which we were standing, and said it marked his father's grave, where he had
buried him three years ago—long before any white settler
came to the place.

From Nanaimo we went to the Qualicome River, from
which a trail leads across the island to the head of the Alberni
Canal, which runs up from Barclay Sound on the west coast.
Between Nanaimo and Qualicome, and twenty miles from
the former, is the magnificent harbour of Nanoose. The
Nanoose district, as the neighbourhood of this harbour is

called, contains a considerable quantity of very good land.
In the course of a journey I made in the following year from
the Alberni settlement to Nanaimo, I passed over this district, and found a large quantity of land well adapted for
settlement. Some parts of it are rather light and stony, and
there are a few swamps; but the greater portion is rich black
vegetable mould, lightly timbered, and well watered by the
Nanoose River, which runs into the harbour, and by several
smaller streams. From Qualicome to Alberni the distance
in a straight line is only twelve miles, this being the narrowest part of the island, except at the very northern end,
where Quatsinough Inlet runs in from the west side to within
seven miles of Beaver harbour on the east, in which Fort
Rupert is situated.

In the year 1859 Captain Richards crossed the island from
Qualicome to Alberni, before the settlement at the latter
place was established, in company with one of the Hudson
Bay Company's agents, who goes there every year to purchase sea-otter skins, &c., from the natives of the west side.
He found that, after ascending the Qualicome River for
some four or five miles and crossing a ridge 600 or 800
feet high, they came to a lake six miles long, called
Horne Lake. This they crossed in a canoe which the
Indians kept there on purpose for Mr. Horne, the Hudson
Bay Company's agent, to make his annual trip in, and then,
ascending the ridge at its western end, they looked down on
the Alberni Canal five miles off. The ridge to the summit
of which they ascended has since been named "Steep Ridge."
It lies across the head of the Alberni, and the ascent from
Horne Lake to its summit was so steep that Captain Richards
was convinced that, however well it might answer as a trail
for foot-travellers, it could never be used as a roadway. In
the summer following that of which I am now writing, and
two years after Captain Richards had examined this route,
we happened to be engaged in surveying Barclay Sound and

the Alberni Canal. The Governor having expressed a great desire to find a way of connecting the settlement then becoming established at Alberni with Nanaimo, by crossing the mainland instead of sailing round the island, I was instructed by Captain Richards to ascertain whether a way existed across the island to Nanaimo by a valley that seemed to be more favourable for the purpose than that which he had previously traversed from Horne Lake. Although, as I have said, this journey did not take place till a year after the period of which I am now writing, it will perhaps be desirable to describe it here, since it relates to the part of the island now under consideration.

On the 29th April, 1861, therefore, having made all necessary arrangements, we left the settlement at Alberni to make our way to Nanaimo, a distance as the crow flies of about 40 miles. Our party consisted of six Somass Indians, Mr. Bamfield, the Indian agent at Barclay Sound, and one Royal Marine from H.M.S. 'Hecate." I have before spoken of the difficulty of effecting a start with Indians, and on this occasion more than ordinary trouble was experienced. It was still early spring, so that while the Indian's winter stock of provisions was exhausted, the berries upon which he relied for subsistence were not yet in season; and they were living from hand to mouth on what they could shoot and their daily haul of fish. The consequence of this was, that before I could induce any of the Indians to accompany us, I had to make arrangements for the provisioning of their wives during their absence, and to give an undertaking that Captain Stamp, the gentleman in charge of the saw-mills, would see to their being provided with food if our journey to Nanaimo and back should chance to exceed the estimated time. I refused on this occasion to recognise more than one wife to each of the Indian guides, although I was aware that some had more; but even this arrangement—which is, however, absolutely necessary—adds much to the expense and trouble of such journeys.

After everything has been settled, farewells said, and the packs distributed and arranged—always a matter of much consideration—the mere process of getting under weigh will often occupy two or three hours. First, one fellow will make the discovery that he is not provided with " scaarlux " (breeches), and that he will be torn by the bushes. His want met, another will plead the need of mocassins, and although it is pretty certain he will make no use of them, a pair of shoes has to be found for him somehow. Powder and shot will next be applied for, and matches must be served out all round. When at last stirred by the strongest expressions of which the Chinook vocabulary is capable, some sort of a start is made, the leader will find that his mocassins are imperfectly laced, or his pack not perfectly balanced, or, if he happens to have his shoes on, he decides to take them off. Down he squats, the whole party following his example, and when you overtake them, you find them a few hundred yards from the starting-place, seated in a row, talking with the utmost animation and unconcern of the journey before them. Time, of course, they set no value on, and it is a great thing to get two or three miles of a journey over in the first day, or even to camp for the night at a sufficient distance from their village. The starting over, however, and once fairly in the bush, all goes well enough.

Upon this occasion, however, our difficulties did not end with the first night's camping, for our journey lay through a country over which none of the Indians had ever travelled. After their fashion, therefore, they declared it to be impenetrable, and but for one old hunter, who supported and expressed a determination to follow me, I do not think I should have induced them to remain with me. As it was we had not proceeded far on the second day's journey when one of the Indians complained of being ill, and desired to return. He was evidently ill, but it would never have done to have allowed one of them to turn back just then, so I proceeded to abuse him to the full extent of my knowledge of Chinook, upbraiding him with being " carqua klootcluman,"—" like a woman,"— and finally dismissing him with a note of explanation to Captain Stamp, in which I said that I was sorry he should have sent a woman instead of a man with me. I took care to read this note out aloud, and it had the desired effect of making him ashamed, and the others laugh; whereupon the sick man shouldered his load and completed the journey without another word of complaint.

By noon of this day (30th) we had crossed the steep ridge which lies across the head of the canal, by a path much lower than that which Captain Richards had taken coming from Horne Lake. The ascent, indeed, was so gradual as to offer no obstacle to the construction of a road. Having descended by the other side, which was somewhat steeper, we came upon a beautiful·stream, 40 or 50 yards wide, running to the northward. Following this stream, we fell across some herds of elk (wapiti), one of which I fortunately brought down, after my head Indian had made two or three unsuccessful shots. I say fortunately, for nothing raises a stranger more in the estimation of the Indians than skill with the rifle; and as I managed next day to shoot two deer through the head, it raised their opinion of me immensely, and made them follow my instructions much more readily than they might otherwise have done. It would astonish one unacquainted with Indians on a campaign like this, to note the expedition with which an elk, larger than a cow, is reduced to a skeleton. As I have before mentioned, a quarter of an hour suffices to accomplish this result, including the process even of turning its skin into mocassins. The prime cuts—those along each side of the saddle, and affording two strips of meat five or six feet long, and four inches thick, belonging of right to me as the leader of the party—were sewn up in a piece of the elk's skin and slung on the chief Indian's pack. The rest of the deer's flesh was then divided, and its skin laced on to their feet, in the way I have before described, with extraordinary despatch.

After another hour's walk we halted under a large tree to smoke a pipe, before crossing a piece of swamp which lay just ahead of us. I had leant my gun against a tree—I carried it myself just then, in the hope of getting another shot at an elk—and was striking a match, when I saw the old hunter leap up with an abrupt ejaculation, and commence tearing the cover off his gun in great haste. Seizing mine, and looking about to see what was the matter, a large black bear jumped down from the tree under which we had been sitting, and made off with all speed into the bush. With my gun to my shoulder I swung round upon my heel after him, when Mr. Bamfield, in his eagerness to get a shot at the bear, starting up, placed his head within a few inches of the muzzle of my weapon, and nothing but a sharp instinctive jerk which I gave it upward prevented his receiving the contents of the barrel. It was a fortunate escape for him, for me, and for the bear, who, in the confusion which followed, made his escape, much to the disappointment of the Indians, who prefer bear-meat to elk at this season, and would have thrown away their stock of venison for it. Proceeding, we soon came to a small lake about three miles long, of the existence of which no one of the Indians had any idea. As we had been on low land, or through thick wood all the way, I was rather puzzled to make out whereabouts Mount Arrowsmith, the position of which was well determined in our charts, was, and somewhat inadvisedly invited a discussion of the question before the Indians. I had all along been steering by a pocket-compass, which the Indians looked upon with great awe, and which I insisted, whenever I found them wavering, showed me the way to Nanaimo. My doubts as to the whereabouts of Mount Arrowsmith were therefore an admission of ignorance which it was rash of me to make; for one curious, observant old fellow, whom we had christened Wat Tyler, from a likeness he bore

to Mr. Bamfield's ideal of that personage, immediately pro-
pounded the troublesome problem—" If the compass showed
me the way to Nanaimo, why did it not show me where the
mountain was?" I had to explain that the compass, being
bound for Nanaimo, declined to trouble itself with any other
consideration.

We walked along the beach for about half the length
of the lake, when the Indians proposed making a raft to
continue our journey on. As it was near camping-time, and
I did not know how much farther the lake extended, we
halted and commenced making the raft to proceed upon
next morning. It proved fortunate that we did so, as it
saved us a scramble over steep rocks, and round one or two
points which would have proved by no means easy or pleasant
travelling.

At the east end of the lake, which was not more than three
miles and a half long, and which we reached after a wet, cold
journey on the raft we had constructed during the night, we
found another considerable river running to the northward
through the gorge, up which a road could be carried with no
great difficulty. We did not follow this stream, but crossed
the ridge on the right of it, and descended on its north side,
the Gulf of Georgia opening before us. This was the 1st of
May, and from that till the afternoon of the 3rd, having
crossed to the east coast of the island, we passed over land
most of which would be admirably adapted for settlement,
quite equal, indeed, to the already settled Saanitch district,
although not so good, perhaps, as some other parts of the
island, particularly at Komoux, of which I shall have to speak
presently. Most of it was level, and lightly timbered; in
some parts, indeed, the soil was light and swampy, but, as a
rule, it was a dark, rich vegetable mould. It will be remembered that I am speaking now of the east coast of the island
between Qualicome and Nanoose. On the 3rd, at 1 P.M.,
we made the sea, a few miles from Nanoose Harbour, and,

skirting it, held directly for Nanaimo, which we reached next day at 5 P.M.

The Nanaimo people were very much surprised at our appearance, and delighted to hear so good a report of the way we had travelled by. We remained there till the 7th, on which day we set out on our return journey to Alberni. Three of the Indians who had accompanied me suffered so much from swollen feet and legs that I was obliged to leave them behind, finding, luckily, as many Nanaimos willing to take their place. I intended to return by an entirely different route to that which we had taken in coming, and accordingly pushed inland at once from Nanaimo, keeping behind Nanoose Harbour altogether. We found a great deal of excellent land in the valley of the Nanoose River, which flows from the southward into the head of Nanoose Harbour; so that I am able to affirm that the whole country between the Qualicome River and Nanaimo is fair, and in parts excellent. At Nanoose we nearly struck our old route, and having found that Mounts Arrowsmith and Moriarty, that lay before us, and between which I had hoped to pass, were united by a high, snow-covered ridge, held for the lake, recrossed it by means of the raft, which we found where it had been left, and reached the settlement at Alberni at ten in the morning of the 12th May.

Though the difficulties of making a road across the island were not insuperable, or even great, yet the Governor was disappointed at those which I reported to exist, he having been under the impression that there was little to prevent a waggon-road being at once laid down. This, however, will seldom be found practicable in this country. I think I am safe in asserting that road-making is the hardest and most expensive work in the colony; for when there are not hills to be scaled, there are woods and swamps to cross; and where these are wanting, rapid rivers and streams will be found that require bridging. As yet no road has been constructed

even between Victoria and Nanaimo, the main obstacle to
which is the lack of money in the colonial treasury.* When
this is done we may hope for communication across the island
to the Alberni, which I think should be carried up from that
place through the Nanoose Valley, and then along the coast,
a branch turning into Cameron Lake and Alberni, and the
main road continuing up the east side of the island to
Comax, Salmon River, Beaver Cove, and Fort Rupert—
in all of which districts there is much good land, of
which I shall presently speak. Let us now, however, return
to the 'Plumper,' and accompany her from Qualicome,
where we left her at anchor. On the 13th April we
weighed, and steamed up Baynes Sound, between Denman
Island and Vancouver, anchoring in Henry Bay, at the north
end of the former. From this place our party pushed on to
Cape Mudge, at the south end of Discovery Passage, to
prepare the way for the ship; while Dr. Wood and I
went to examine the land about the Courtenay River, which
empties itself into the head of Baynes Sound. This portion
of the island, which is known as the Komoux, or Comax
district, had been partially examined before; but although we
had been informed that there was some fine land there, the
extent and beauty of what we saw quite surprised us, and we
both agreed this was the most promising spot for an agricultural settlement we had yet seen on the island.

The Courtenay River runs into Augusta Bay, at the head
of Baynes Sound, and here we found what is of the utmost
importance in prospecting for a settlement, viz., good and
safe anchorage for ships of almost any size. At the rivers'
mouths are sands, which dry off to some considerable distance,
and in winter are covered with flocks of ducks, geese, and
other wild fowl. The stream for about a mile is perfectly

---

* Since writing the above a bill has been brought before the House of
Assembly for the construction of a road between these places; the bill was
most unwisely, rejected, and one for a mule-trail granted.

navigable for large boats at high-water, or even for small
stern-wheel steamers; although the land on the left bank
being quite clear and level from outside the river's mouth,
it is unnecessary to have steamers, or even bâteaux there.
At the point where it becomes unnavigable, the Courtenay—which as far as we examined runs nearly parallel with
the coast—is joined by a river, called by the natives the
"Puntluch," which flows from the south-west through a deep
valley, and probably takes its rise in the great central lake,
from which the Somass River runs down on the west side
of the island into the Alberni Canal. We did not go up this
stream, the Indians reporting that there was no good land
upon its banks, and that the bush was very thick. Landing
from the canoe just above the Forks of the Puntlüch and
Courtenay (or Tzo-o-oom, as the Indians call it) Rivers, and on
the left bank of the latter, we found ourselves in the middle
of a large prairie, which we discovered continued in a north-
westerly direction, or parallel with the coast, for eight or ten
miles. The Courtenay flows nearly through the centre of
this, and there are one or two smaller streams, which water
the whole abundantly. The ground slopes upwards from the
river on both sides, so as to prevent the possibility of overflow to any extent. The whole of this prairie is bounded by
dense wood, forming a sheltering coast-fringe on the east, and
affording plenty of timber on all sides (except towards the
entrance from Baynes Sound) for building, burning, &c. It
took us a day and a half to walk over this land, through
which a plough might be driven from end to end. We tried
to penetrate the forest at the northern end, in hopes of
finding some more clear land beyond, but the Indians said
they did not know of any in that direction; and as our time
was limited, we retraced our steps. I have no doubt, however, but more good land will be found to lie between this
point and the valley of the Salmon River, which is 60 miles
north of it. The Indians at Salmon River told us that they

could go by land from there to Komoux in a day and a half;
and this, if true, proves that the bush cannot be very thick.
We found the ground on the west bank of the Courtenay
nearly as good as that on the east. The soil, indeed, appeared
quite equal to it, but it is not so level. We estimated the
clear land here altogether at 7000 or 8000 acres. The
Indians told us that a great many blankets would be wanted
for the purchase of this tract, as all the neighbouring tribes
resorted there in the summer-time to collect berries, shoot
deer, catch fish, &c., all of which were found in large quantities. Indeed, they showed some reluctance at taking us
over it, feeling sure, no doubt, that we should desire to
possess it when its qualities became known. Rejoining the
ship after two days' absence, on the 20th we started for a
small harbour inside Cape Mudge, whence to commence
surveying operations up the Strait. While in Henry Bay we
witnessed the arrival of some Roman Catholic priests, which
caused the greatest excitement among the natives. They
were scattered in all directions, fishing, &c.—many on board
and around the ship—when a canoe, with two large banners
flying, appeared in sight. Immediately a shout was raised of
" Le Prêtre ! Le Prêtre ! " and they all paddled on shore as fast
as they could to meet them. There were two priests in the
canoe, and in this way they travelled, visiting in turn every
village on the coast. A fortnight afterwards, when I was in
Johnstone Strait with a boat-party, I met them again. It
was a pouring wet day, cold, and blowing hard, and they were
apparently very lightly clothed, huddling in the bottom of
their canoe, the Indians paddling laboriously against wind
and tide to reach a village by night, and the sea washing
over them, drenching them to the skin. I never saw men
look in a more pitiable plight. They had a little map
with them, and asked me to show them where they were, of
which they appeared to have a very hazy idea. One of their
men had shot a deer, which they were delighted to exchange

for some biscuit, of which they had run very short. Certainly if misery on this earth will be compensated for hereafter, those two priests were laying in a plentiful stock of happiness.

The Roman Catholic clergy located in these parts are mostly Frenchmen. They are energetic, clever men—of no very high extraction or type, perhaps—and work under the direction of M. Demers, the Roman Catholic Bishop of Victoria. They are thorough masters of Chinook, have the art of making themselves understood and feared by the Indians, and undoubtedly possess considerable influence over them.

Coming out at the north end of Baynes Sound, and rounding Cape Lazo, Cape Mudge—so named by Vancouver, after his lieutenant, the late Admiral Zachariah Mudge—appears like an island in the middle of the Gulf, presenting a high, steep face to the southward; though as it is approached, shoals will be found extending from it a long way. This part of the Gulf of Georgia forms a sort of playground for the waters, in which they frolic, utterly regardless of all tidal rules. This is caused by the collision of the streams which takes place here; the flood-stream from the south, through the Strait of Fuca, and up the Haro Archipelago, being met by that from Queen Charlotte Sound and Johnstone and Discovery Straits. The tide-rips caused by the conflict between these opponent streams are excessively dangerous to boats, and great care has to be exercised in crossing. These tide-rips exist to some extent in all parts of these inner waters, but they are certainly more dangerous here than anywhere else. A boat getting into them is almost certain to be swamped; and even a ship is so twisted and twirled about as to run considerable risk, if the passage is at all narrow, of being forced on the rocks or beach.

Fifteen miles above Cape Mudge, Seymour Narrows, at the south end of Discovery Strait, are reached. These narrows are only 900 yards wide, and as the stream turns almost

instantaneously in them, there is an incessant turmoil and
bubble going on.   On the Monday after we moved from Baynes
Sound to Quathiosky Cove, just inside Cape Mudge, Pender
and I started for these narrows.   I had to stop at them while
he was going further on for a distance of 40 or 50 miles.   We
pulled up to them with the young ebb: my boat keeping close
inshore to prevent its being carried through; Pender in the
mid-stream.   As we approached we watched his boat quicken-
ing her pace every second.   When close to the entrance we
shot into a little pool of still water, and jumping on a rock I
was just in time to see him shoot through at a tremendous
speed, laying on his oars, for they were quite useless, and
flying up the Strait.   In about an hour from the time we
parted he had reached Point Chatham, about 15 miles up.
This is very well so long as a boat is going with the stream,
but when working against it it is not so pleasant, particularly if, as frequently happens, a strong wind is blowing with
the current.   For, as the mountains are mostly very high on
each side and the Strait nowhere more than two miles wide,
the wind blows up and down it with great force.

It would be tedious both to myself and to my reader to give
a detailed description of the numerous islands and passages
between Cape Mudge and the north end of the island.   I will
therefore only speak of the few places that are or seem
likely to become of importance to the colony.   I may say
generally that the passage of the Strait is 140 miles long,
and averages one mile and a half in width: its average
depth is about 100 fathoms, and there are plenty of anchorages on both sides.   For sailing-vessels the rapid and
uncertain currents must always make the navigation somewhat dangerous, although Vancouver managed seventy years
ago to get the old ' Discovery' and 'Chatham' through.
For steamers capable of going seven or eight knots it is safe
enough, though a stranger would probably feel a little nervous

at finding his vessel twisted round and round against her helm, and apparently running full tilt at the steep trap cliffs which line it, until an opposite eddy catches and preserves her, or forces her in the same fashion on to the other shore.

Fifteen miles above Seymour Narrows is Point Chatham. Here the channel divides: the western one, Johnstone Strait, leading up to Rupert; the eastern, Nodales Channel, flowing between the islands towards Bute and Lough-borough Inlets. Five-and-twenty miles above this again is Salmon Bay and River, in the vicinity of which I believe there is some good land, and from which, as I have said, the Indians assert that they can go direct to Komoux. Ten miles above Salmon River is Port Neville, a long harbour in which is capital anchorage, and beyond the head of which we were told were some large lakes. We had a most fortunate escape of running on a pinnacle in the entrance of this harbour. The harbour had been examined carefully before we went there; but the existence of this rock was not discovered. As we went in we must have gone within a few yards of it without knowing anything about it, and on coming out we passed it so closely as to be able to see it distinctly from the deck. After a few years in a surveying ship, however, you get quite used to this sort of escape.

Five or six miles above Port Neville, on the opposite side, is Adam's River, a stream of considerable size, flowing through a large valley, which looks as though it had some good land in it. Twenty miles above Adam's River is Beaver Cove, called by the natives Quarkese. There is some beautiful land a mile or so in from the harbour, and large numbers of elk are to be found: Mr. Weynton told me that he had seen thirty or forty in a day, and shot a large number. Close above this again is the Nimpkish River, with the village of the Nimpkish Indians on its north bank. This village presents exactly the same appearance now as it did in 1792,

when Vancouver made that sketch of it which is given in his
Voyages. The river flows from a large lake in the centre of
the island. There is an Indian trail from Nimpkish to Nootka,
by which Mr. Moffat, one of the Hudson Bay Company's
officers, crossed in 1852. As Mr. Moffat is the only white
man who has ever travelled by this route, and as his explorations nearly meet those of Captain Richards and myself in
the southern part of the island, I will here introduce some
extracts from his Journal:—

Leaving the mouth of the Nimpkish River at daybreak of
July 2, 1852, in a canoe with six Indians, he reached the fishing-
village at the entrance of the lake at nine o'clock, and entered
it at ten. The Indian name of the lake is 'Tallettle; but he
afterwards called it the Nimpkish Lake, by which name it is
now generally known. "The shores on either side at this
(north-east) end," writes Mr. Moffat, "rise perpendicularly
from the water's edge to the height of some 1500 or 1600 feet,
and from 4000 to 5000 feet a little inland, and are in many
places capped with snow. The width of the lake at its
entrance is about half-a-mile, gradually widening to a mile
and a half. I endeavoured to ascertain the depth with a forty-
fathom line, but did not succeed. Our course through the
lake was about south-east, and the length I have since ascertained to be fully 25 miles. In the evening we camped at
the River Oaksey, distant about a mile from the head."

At ten next morning Mr. Moffat's party commenced the
ascent of the River Oaksey, stopping a short time to examine
the finest beaver-dam he had ever seen. "The whole of
this day was spent in working up the rapids, of which the
river is one continuation. We encamped in the evening
at Waakash, the half-way house to the second lake, a distance of 12 miles. The banks of the river are rather
low, and abounding in splendid red pine and maple * of
all sizes; but not the slightest vestige of clear land to be

* Probably *Abies Douglasii*, and *Acer machrophyllum* or *Acer rubrum*.

seen. The country a short distance inland from the river
is very high."

On the following day, after eight hours' paddling, they
reached a second village, where they got a few salmon
and trout. "The river here branches off in two different
directions: the distance from Waakash to this place is about
seven or eight miles, and the river, as yesterday, nothing but
rapids. We remained only a short time here and then started
for Lake Hanns, distant six miles." The Indians told Mr.
Moffat that this part of the river was very shallow and the
country between them and the lake clear; so he went with
some of his crew on foot, and reached the lake after a very
pleasant walk. "The country through which I passed was
clear, with occasional belts of wood and brush, and abounding
in partridges, of which I shot a good many. I also noticed a
pond of cold spring-water, of great depth, without an outlet,
similar to what are at home called blow-wells. During my
walk I was informed of a tribe of Indians living inland, having
no canoes and no connection with the coast whatever. I have
since learned that these people sometimes descend some of
the rivers for the purpose of trade with the Indians of Nootka,
and they offered to guide me to the place at any time I should
wish. The name of the tribe is Säa-käalituck; they number
about 50 or 60 men, and were only discovered a few years
back by one of the Nimpkish chiefs, while on a trapping
expedition. The following is the Indians' story of their
discovery:—Our party, while sitting round the fire on the
banks of a small rivulet, observed a beaver playing in the
water, and having followed the course of the stream in hopes
of falling in with a dam, came suddenly upon a lake, and the
first thing that struck our attention was a small village,
situated at the opposite side. Upon entering the village we
were well received by the Indians and opened a trade for
skins, of which they had an abundance, and which they used
for clothing. They informed us that Southern Indians (as we

supposed, the Saanitch) had been there on war parties, and killed a good many of them.

" This tribe are known to the Nootkas, who have a superstitious idea that they are the spirits of their dead, on account of their speaking the same language. From the time the Nimpkish say it takes to perform this journey, and from the Saanitch (or more probably the Comax) Indians having knowledge of these people, I have not the least doubt that a road might with little difficulty be discovered from here to Victoria, through the very centre of the island. After passing this lake, which is probably ten miles long, we encamped at the base of a snow-capped mountain, two very fine cascades falling several hundred feet from its summit; and the streams which they form abounding in trout of excellent quality and great size, numbers of which we caught."

Next day Mr. Moffat endeavoured to ascend the mountain mentioned, and which he called Ben Lomond, but which is probably the Conuma Peak of the old navigators. He failed from its steepness, however. " Having," he writes, "been disappointed in my walk, I returned to the camp at 9 A.M., and set out for a walk across the portage (which was a succession of mountain defiles) to the head-waters of the Nootka River. This river, during its course of three or four miles from its source, disappears three different times. Stopped at noon to dine, and, after half an hour's rest, recommenced our journey, and arrived at Nootka Sound at 7 P.M., after passing over 16 or 18 miles."

The Indians would not encamp there, however, on account of a superstitious fear of ghosts, and he had to go on farther. This was, however, the real end of the journey, so far as this route is concerned; the rest being merely down Nootka Sound in a canoe. From Nimpkish River to the Thupana arm of Nootka, occupied four days. On his arrival at

Friendly Cove, he was received with a discharge of guns from the Chief's house. "Until we were about to land," he says, "scarcely an Indian was to be seen, but at a given signal the whole tribe darted from their houses and commenced a grand dance in honour of the arrival of a white man to visit them, after which a sea-otter skin was presented to me by the Chief, and we landed amid the welcome shouts of the Nootkas. In the evening a grand fancy *dress ball* was given, and a large quantity of blankets and other property distributed." *

Ten miles beyond Nimpkish is Beaver Harbour, on the south side of which stands Fort Rupert—the only fort beside Victoria on Vancouver Island. Between the Nimpkish River and Beaver Harbour, the Straits become, comparatively speaking, very shallow; and a bank has to be crossed with not more than three fathoms of water upon it.

Beaver harbour is fine, roomy, and well sheltered. There is no extent of clear land in its vicinity, although it is pretty level. As I have before said the Quatsinough Inlet runs up from the west side of the island to within seven miles of this place, and there is a good trail connecting them. The timber here is fine—the Douglas and White pines growing very large. Three or four years ago a large number were felled, with the intention of shipping them to China and elsewhere; but from some mismanagement in the Company which had undertaken the work, they were never despatched, and are now lying about the beach in all directions. There is a considerable quantity of yellow cypress here also. This wood is not found on the south-east part of the island. Some has been cut on the west side, but it becomes more plentiful as you travel north; and in the Russian territory near Sitka it exists in large quantities. It

* Pemberton's 'Facts and Figures,' Appendix.

is very light and tough, and is by far the best wood on the coast for boat-plank. When green it emits a peculiar though not unpleasant smell, and can always be recognised in the woods by its leaf, which differs from that of the Common pine—which tree it otherwise closely resembles, being convex on both sides.

Fort Rupert is the newest and best built station of the Hudson Bay Company I have seen, and the gardens are very nicely laid out. Of course, like all the rest, it is stockaded, and has its gallery and bastions. It stands almost in the middle of the Indian village. Some idea of the number of salmon in these parts, and of the prodigality of the Hudson Bay Company under the old *régime*, may be gathered from the fact told me by one of these officers, that before he took charge of the post 3000 salmon were used annually as manure for the garden. I take it that pickling salmon here would be a very lucrative speculation. The fish can be bought for a leaf of tobacco each, and as forty of these leaves compose a pound of that herb, a fair margin of profit is left. Including the packing, they might be cured at a cost of from one and a half dollars to two dollars a barrel. The price obtained at the Sandwich Islands, where the Company at one time carried on some little trading of this sort, averaged fourteen dollars a barrel. The Hudson Bay Company, however, are shy at embarking in any but the fur trade, and perhaps they are right. Companies are proverbially unlucky in trade, and the opportunities neglected and thrown away by this one during the last few years have astonished every merchant who has visited these parts. I should add that 2000 barrels might be obtained annually at Port Rupert, and as much more at almost every inlet in the island.

It may interest the reader if I attempt some description of the profits derivable from these trading-posts of the

Hudson Bay Company on Vancouver Island and elsewhere. Fort Rupert may be accepted as a very fair specimen of its order. It is certainly not too favourable a one, as a year since the directors had some thought of abolishing it, on the ground that its profits were considered insufficient, though the figures on the next page show they are not small.

The post is manned by one officer (a clerk) and eight men. The officer is paid 100*l.* a year; the chief man, 40*l.*; and the other seven, 20*l.** The cost of provisions for the year cannot exceed 200*l.*, and perhaps firing and other small items may amount to 100*l.* more, making the total cost of the post about 600*l.* a-year. I have omitted the expense of building the fort, but this was done by the eight men whose wages I have given; and the plank, and some small sum to the Indians employed in fetching and carrying, were the only extra outlay incurred in its construction. If this were the only post along the coast, in the estimate of the cost of keeping it up would have to be included the expense of the steamer which visits it twice a-year. As it is, however, she calls there on her way to Fort Simpson and the stations on the northern coasts, whence great numbers of furs are obtained; so that but a small proportion of her cost can be charged against Fort Rupert.

Having roughly estimated the cost of this station, I will give the number and value of the furs and skins collected in the year 1859—by no means an extraordinarily productive season. The following is a list:—

---

* At this time a clerk was in charge of Rupert. A chief trader is now there, whose salary may be estimated at 500*l.* or 600*l.*

NUMBER AND VALUE OF FURS.

	Num-ber.	Price given.	Total cost.			Value of each in England.	Total Value in England.		
			£.	s.	d.		£.	s.	d.
Bear Skins	250	1 blanket each ..	81	5	0	1l. to 3l.	500	0	0
Marten ..	2000	6 for 1 blanket . ..	108	4	0	10s. to 2l.	2015	0	0
Minx	5000	30 ,, ..	54	5	0	2s. to 7s. 6d.	1250	0	0
Land Otter	250	1 blanket each ..	81	5	0	Black. 15s. to 1l. 10s. Pale. 7s.6d. to 10s.6d.	200	0	0
Beaver ..	600	2 for 1 blanket ..	97	10	0	3s. 6d. to 8s. 6d.	150	0	0
Lynx	100	3 ,, ..	10	14	0	3s. to 8s. 6d.	20	0	0
Fox	50	3 ,, ..	5	7	0	White. 3s. to 5s. Red. 6s. to 10s.	15	0	0
Sea Otter ..	50	12 blankets each ..	195	0	0	5l. to 25l.	750	0	0
Fishers ..	50	3 for 1 blanket ..	5	4	0	5s. to 1l. 10s.	42	10	0
Racoon ..	1000	12 ,, ..	4	3	0	1s. to 10s.	275	0	0
Rabbits ..	5000	1 leaf of tobacco each	2	10	0	Not sent home.			
Wolverine ..	60	3 for 1 blanket ..	6	10	0	5s. to 9s.	21	0	0
Wolf	12	3 ,, ..	1	6	0	1s. to 10s.	3	10	0
Fur Seal ..	60	2 ,, ..	8	7	0	8s. to 12s.	150	0	0
Hair Seal ..	60	{12 leaves of tobacco each .. .. }	0	9	0	1s. to 4s. 6d.	8	0	0
Musk Rat ..	100	{4 leaves of tobacco each .. .. }	0	5	0	3d. to 10d.	5	0	0
Silver Fox	..	.. ..	..			.. ..	..		
			660	4	0	.. ..	5405	0	0

If, then, we add to the cost of the furs 600l. for the
expense of the post, we have 1260l. against 5405l., showing
a profit of more than 4100l. yearly on this establishment,
which is considered by the Company as one of their least
profitable stations.

From this balance of profit has to be deducted the cost of
conveying the above articles to England, which cannot well
be estimated, as they are conveyed in the Company's own vessel,
which carries passengers and other freight. In addition to
the above list of furs, above 400 gallons of seal-oil are yearly
exported from Fort Rupert.

Between Beaver Harbour and Cape Scott, at the extreme
north of the island, there are two or three anchorages—Shu-

cartie Bay on the island, and Bull Harbour in Hope Island, on the opposite shore. Just beyond Bull Harbour a bank, called the Newittee Bar, has to be crossed, upon which, however, there is always sufficient water for ships to pass over safely. The Newittee Indians inhabit this part of the island, and coal has been found by them in considerable quantity. I should have mentioned that coal has been discovered at Beaver Harbour also, and, indeed, that measures of this mineral extend all along the northern part of the island.

Off Cape Scott, in Queen Charlotte's Sound, is a small group of islands, called the Triangles. These are high and rocky, and useless except perhaps to erect a lighthouse on at some future day.

One hundred and twenty miles north of Cape Scott are the Queen Charlotte Islands. These islands are as yet unsurveyed and unexplored. It is generally thought that the group will be found to be divided into many more islands than are at present given on the charts.

Very little is yet known of their character. The Haida Indians who inhabit them are fierce, and rather disposed to resist the encroachments of the whites. Some years ago, indeed, they fired on the boats of a man-of-war approaching their shores. These Indians have at various times brought specimens of gold in quartz to Victoria, and in 1852 the Hudson Bay Company despatched a party of men in the brig 'Una' to examine the place from whence they said it came. This party proceeded to Gold Harbour, as it is now called, on the south-west side of Moresby Island; and Mr. Mitchell, who commanded the ship, told me that they got about 1000 dollars of gold out, but that the Indians stole it from them as fast as they collected it. The miners then growing weary of their task, and quarrelling among themselves, the expedition broke up.

In July, 1859, Mr. Downie—whose name I have before
mentioned as an old Californian miner and explorer—started
with a party of twenty-seven men, provisioned for three
months, and reached Gold Harbour on the 6th of August.
They examined the place where the gold was taken out by
the 'Una's' party, and discovered a few specks in a small
quartz-seam running through slate.   They then explored
Douglas Inlet, which runs into the south of Gold Harbour,
without any success; and afterwards proceeded to Skidegate
Channel, which separates the two large islands Graham and
Moresby.   They found trap and hornblende rocks, with a
few poor seams of quartz, but no gold to the southward.   To
the northward they found talcose slate, quartz, and red
earth, but no gold; and, coming upon coal in the Skidegate
Channel, decided further search was useless, and returned to
Gold Harbour.   They had left some of the party there to
blast, and, on returning found that they too had given it up
as hopeless.   The conclusion they came to as the result of
their investigation was, that the gold found by the first party
existed in an offshoot, or, as it is technically termed, a blow,
instances of which are very common in California.   In his
report of his journey to the Governor, Mr. Downie says:
"The offshoots in question are not uncommon, as I have
often seen them in California.   On such a discovery being
made, hundreds of miners take claims in all directions near
it, and test the ground in every way; but nothing is found
except in the one spot, about seventy feet in length, running
south-east and north-west.   On being worked about fifteen
feet it gave out. . . . Before work commenced, I have blown
the sand off a vein of pure gold."   About the same time,
Captain Torrens also went with a party to prospect on Queen
Charlotte Island.   They landed at the village in the Skidegate Channel, and were very nearly being murdered there.
One of the Indians commenced haranguing the others, and

incited them to murder the party by saying they were come
to rob them of their land. One of the chiefs, however, stood
by them, and enabled them to get to their canoes, and they
escaped unhurt, though several shots were fired after them.
They crossed to Fort Simpson, and, after remaining there a
few days, were recalled to Queen Charlotte Sound by a
deputation of Indians from Gold Harbour. The part·, however, soon became discontented, and having met with as little
success in their search for gold as Mr. Downie, refused to
stay longer. Captain Torrens, in his report of the expedition,
writes: "The country north of Skiddegate Channel is low
and thickly wooded, receding, in one unbroken level, towards
a huge range of mountains about 30 miles off. Vegetation is here luxuriant, and at intervals patches of open land
occur, in which the Indians have planted crops of turnips
and potatoes." His party—originally twelve—had broken
up at Simpson: six accompanying him, three staying at
Simpson, and two going with a chief named "Edensaw" to
Copper Island and the northern islands of the Queen Charlotte group. The accounts from these latter were satisfactory,
as they brought back copper ore and quartz with sulphurets.
In a letter which I have received from Captain Torrens,
narrating the details of his journey, he says that these specimens gave, upon analysis—

1st. Copper, 96 lbs. to the ton; value about 7000 dollars
(1400*l.*) per ton.

2nd. Sulphuret of iron and gold, valued at 13,500 dollars
(2600*l.*) per ton.

As no blasting, however, was done to get these specimens,
he very justly thinks that they do not give any guide to the
real value of the spot in which they were found.

On the 17th of May the 'Plumper' reached Fort Rupert,
where we found everything quiet, on account of nearly all
the Indians being away at Shir-wattie, on the mainland,

catching "houlikin." Having been longer out than usual this time, and our coal becoming exhausted, we left Rupert on the 25th, and reached Nanaimo on the following day.

After a few days more work in the Gulf, we returned to Esquimalt on the 15th of June, where we heard that H.M.S. 'Hecate' had been ordered out to relieve the 'Plumper,' and to continue the survey of the shores of Vancouver Island and the mainland.

CHAPTER IX.

———— •◦•————

WE remained at Esquimalt till the 26th, when we went
into Victoria Harbour to assist in intimidating the Indians
from the north, who had shown symptoms of mutiny. Some
of them had raised difficulties about camping in the right
places, and a chief, called Captain John, was to be arrested,
upon which occasion it was thought likely there would be a
disturbance. Accordingly, it was decided that we should go
into Victoria, and, upon the Governor's coming on board,
fire as much blank cartridge as possible; and that all the
Marines, small-arm men, and field-pieces of the ships at
Esquimalt should be paraded ostentatiously on Beacon Hill.
The chief was to be arrested while they were all there, so
that any disturbance which might arise could be easily
quelled. The individual on whose behalf this entertainment
was provided allowed himself to be arrested quietly; but,
some time afterwards, he attempted to stab the policeman
who was conducting him into court, and was shot by him on
the spot in self-defence. We remained at Victoria over the
Coronation Day, to give the Indians the benefit of a little
more powder and noise, and started that evening (28th) for
Nanaimo. Here I prepared for the most arduous trip I made
in British Columbia, the object of which was to find a valley
along which a road might be made from the head of Jervis
Inlet to the Upper Fraser about Chilcotin.

HEAD OF JERVIS INLET.

Page 191.

We left Nanaimo on the 2nd of July, and reached the head of the Inlet the same night. Here we managed to find a spot close under the rocks, where we could anchor in twenty fathoms, and as it fortunately remained calm we were able to hold on. Next morning I managed to induce five Indians to accompany me. It came on to blow so hard that the ship could not possibly remain there, and I had to go on shore with our travelling-gear, and the five natives, Dr. Wood being again my travelling companion. As soon as we were on the beach, the ship steamed away, leaving us with water in front of us, and the thickest, most impenetrable bush I have ever had to travel through behind us. As there was no village near, however, we soon got the party off, and made our way into the bush, with the feeling, common on such occasions, of vague hope that we should come out again somewhere and somehow. The valley through which our way lay was narrow at the entrance, and the hills on each side very precipitous. After a hard walk of about five miles we halted, camping early to let things settle into their places.

Next morning, after we had travelled about a mile, we came to the Laakine River, which runs into the head of the inlet we had left. When we reached this stream, the Indians told me we should not be able to accomplish the object of our journey, as they knew from the height of the water there that we should be unable to ford the river higher up; and further, that even if we succeeded in fording this, the Squawmisht and Lilloett Rivers—both of which we should have to cross before we could reach the Fraser—would be up to our necks at the fords. Having on former occasions, however, experienced similar discouragements on the part of the natives, whose laziness and disinclination to start upon a journey I have before mentioned, we did not pay much attention to them, and pushed on. We had to cross and recross the stream three times during the

day, owing to the mountains at those places rising perpendicularly out of the water; and each time it was a task of
greater difficulty, as the stream became more rapid and
deeper as we advanced, while for a considerable distance we
had to walk along in the river up to our waists. This did not
look promising, but still we hoped it might improve, until at
4 o'clock we came to a dead stop. At this spot, if we decided to continue our journey, it was necessary for us again
to cross the river, as before us lay an impenetrable morass.
The only apparent means of crossing was on a single log,
about 120 feet long, which was two feet under water, and
over which the stream was rushing in a torrent. It was
quite evident that the packs could not be got across; and an
opinion which had grown upon us during the day, that the
gorge through which we were advancing could never be made
available as a roadway, forced itself still more powerfully upon
our minds. We were, however, unwilling as yet to return;
and set about making a better bridge by felling a tree across
the current. After some search, one was found that was long
enough for the purpose, if we could get it to fall directly
across; and we set to work upon it. An hour's hacking
and chopping brought us to the critical moment. What
ropes we had were got upon it to guide it the right way,
the last chop, upon which our fate depended, was given, and
down came the tree with a crash that for the moment
drowned the roar of the water. But it fell short of the
opposite bank, and the next moment we saw our only hope
flying down the river. The failure of this attempt, coupled
with the conviction that no perseverance on our part would
be rewarded, decided us upon retracing our steps to the
Inlet. It was too late, however, to move that night, and
I did not tell the Indians of my intention till next morning,
when I delighted them with the intelligence that we
were going back. All the arguments they had used on

the previous day to prevent our proceeding were repeated with additional emphasis now. "The water would keep on rising all the summer, as it had commenced much earlier than usual," they said; "we should never have got across the other rivers, even if we had crossed here, as this river was not to be compared with them. Our provisions would have been exhausted long before we could have reached the Fraser, if we ever did reach it; and what would be the good of exploring this way after all, when they were certain mules could never pass it?" These and many similar arguments were brought forward to confirm our purpose of returning, and justly too; for our way hitherto, when we had not been walking on the bed of the river, had been through swamp in which we sank nearly up to our knees, and where a mule would undoubtedly have gone up to his girths. I say nothing of the undergrowth of willow and wild raspberry-bushes, which formed a thick network, through which we had to force our path, but which in constructing the trail would of course be cleared away. The Indians, in their eagerness to return, had told me that they knew a way by which we could cross from Jervis Inlet to Howe Sound, and thence to Port Pemberton, and I now determined to make them take this route. Accordingly, we retraced our steps to the Inlet, and, sleeping at our first night's camping-place, reached it by nine next morning.

Having got safely out of the bush, the Indians showed the greatest reluctance to making another start, and urged all kinds of fresh and startling difficulties. Recourse to very strong expressions was found necessary; and they were threatened with the undying wrath of Mr. Douglas, whose name always acts as a talisman with them. It was vividly set forth how that gentleman would call them "cultus" (useless), if they did not go, and how they would all receive muskets, blankets, and praise if they did. These arguments, accompanied with the taunt which I have before mentioned as proving very

o

effectual with them, that they were woman-hearted, induced
them to yield and promise to go if I would consent to take
them to their village in the Arm for that night, that they
might report their safe return to their squaws and replenish
their stock.   It cost us, as I have said, no little difficulty to
persuade them to make a fresh start, and in our extremity I
remember using the powerful argument that not only would
Mr. Douglas when he heard of it exclaim that the Sechelt
and Loquilt Indians were women, but that Queen Victoria
and all the world would from the moment I reported the
circumstance, regard their tribe as unworthy of their consideration.

Much as I dislike sleeping at an Indian village, I thought
it wise to yield to their wish so far, and accordingly we
paddled down the inlet to it.   On our way we met our
pinnace, which had been left with two other boats to survey
the inlet, and I was very glad to go on board her for an hour
or so.   We slept at the village, however, as I knew if I once
lost sight of the Indians I should never get them away from
home.   Next morning, the 7th July, we started with less
trouble than I had ever experienced in leaving a village.
My chief guide I could not help pitying, as he was leaving
a young and pretty wife with a child in her arms, who cried
bitterly when we started.   He seemed very fond of her, and
constantly on the journey said he wanted to hurry back to his
" Papoose," as he called her.

We paddled down to a bay called " Deserted Bay," 15 miles
from the head of the inlet, and here met Pender, who was in
charge of the surveying party, and Gowland in the pinnace.
I spent a few hours with them, and at three we got away,
Pender and Gowland bearing us company to the edge of the
bush, and there leaving us with good wishes,—congratulating
themselves, as they afterwards told us, that their way lay no
further inland.   We camped a few miles in by the side of a
river which runs into one of the southern arms of the inlet,

and which is called by the natives the "Tzoonye." This stream, they say, flows from a lake not far north of this spot. Directly facing us was a ridge of mountains, which must be crossed on the following day. Had we then known the height of this ridge and the difficulty we should experience in making the ascent, these facts would certainly have decided us to turn back at once, as they render the pass quite unavailable for any practical purpose.

Next morning we commenced the ascent and toiled for twelve hours up it and along its summit before we could find a spot clear enough of snow to camp in. From the time we started it cost us a struggle of about nine hours up an angle of thirty to thirty-six degrees to reach its summit. Here we found the snow lying three or four feet deep, but sufficiently hard on the surface to prevent our sinking more than six or eight inches at each step. Our camp that night lay, by the barometer, 4000 feet above that of the night before, and we had ascended from a very comfortable temperature to one intensely cold. The view was certainly very fine, though it scarcely compensated for the discomforts of our situation. We were up among snow-peaks which reared their heads 1000 feet or more above us, and which we recognised as old friends seen frequently from the Gulf of Georgia. Before us lay the valley along which we must pass, and at its far end 20 or 30 miles off, on the opposite side of the Squawmisht River, was seen another range of snow-clad hills. All this when lighted up by the moon and stars, which shone out brightly as we sat by our camp-fire smoking our last pipe before turning in for the night, was very beautiful.

Next morning the way became even more difficult. It took us three days to descend the valley to the Squawmisht River, which we reached and crossed about 10 miles above the head of Howe Sound on the 12th. It will give some idea of the nature of the country to say that the distance was only about 25 miles, and that we travelled each day more than ten hours and usually twelve, making therefore an average speed of little more than three-quarters of a mile an hour. A stream, for which the Indians had no name, runs through this valley, and down to its bed the mountains, 3000 or 4000 feet high, slope at all sorts of angles. The ground on which we walked the whole way was either smooth, slippery, rocky, or swampy; while nearly everywhere the thickest growth of alder, willow, and wild raspberry I have ever seen, formed a complete network across our path. A few days of travelling such as this may well weary the strength and patience of the strongest and most enduring, and my companion, after struggling manfully against its fatigues and discomforts, was obliged at last to give in. The way before us lay through the thick bush I have described,—now over swamp in which we sank at every step, sometimes knee-deep,—then over rock covered with green slippery moss, on which a fall every few minutes was certain. Add to this the constant plague of mosquitoes, and it need not be wondered at that my companion, on reaching the Squawmisht village, said it was no use his trying to go any farther. Accordingly he arranged with the Indians to take him in a canoe down Howe Sound and up the Fraser to Westminster, which he reached the following day. Used as I am to the smell of an Indian lodge, this village of Elaawho was more than I could stand, and there was no other place to pitch the tent, except in the midst of the long rank nettles, which thrive so well in the vicinity of all Indian villages. Accordingly I said good-bye to the Doctor, and having engaged two canoes to take us about a mile up the river, started about three in the afternoon of the same day, and soon camped for the night.

The valley at the northern extremity of which this village is situated, and which lies at the head of Howe Sound, is of considerable extent, and contains much good land. Two large rivers flow through it: the one on which I was, the Squawmisht, on the west side; and the Tseearkamisht on the east. Into these rivers several smaller ones run. When I met Dr. Wood on my return to Esquimalt, he described the lower part of the Squawmisht as very winding, and the distance from the village to the head of Howe Sound as so much farther than I thought it could be, that afterwards when I came down from Fort Rupert in one of the ship's boats, I ascended it in a canoe to the village to get observations there.

I was most fortunate in finding the chief, whom I had met at Elaawho, at the mouth of the river, and he took me up in his canoe most willingly. I then found that the river had two mouths, and that through the western and larger one stern-wheel steamers might pass and ascend for several miles. How far they might be able to go is very doubtful, and cannot be determined till they are tried, as it frequently happens that those places which appear most narrow and dangerous are the easiest to pass; while in a place which appears to an explorer, walking along the bank or pushing up the stream close in-shore, perfectly clear, there is some snag or bank which forms an effectual block to steam-navigation. On returning down the river, however, we kept mid-stream, and saw nothing dangerous; and the Indians said it was all deep. The chief, who had been several times on the Fraser, frequently confirmed them, saying that "Boston steamers" could go up his river; and though we passed several banks and snags, I saw no place so bad as the Umatilla snag on the Fraser River, which I have before described, while the current did not appear more rapid than I have seen it at Sea Bird Bar and opposite Fort Hope. We saw several small villages along the river's bank, where the Indians were all engaged in salmon-fishing. The Tseearkamisht joins the Squawmisht before reaching Howe Sound; but the constant silting-up has made the mouth of the former so shallow as to be quite unnavigable. The chief said there were a great many Indians living in different parts of the valley,

and many potato-grounds; and he described the soil as being
very rich. There is no trail to his village from the Sound,
as they always use the river; but as the ground is quite level
and in many parts clear, one could be easily constructed.
The only ascent which would have to be made between this
and Port Pemberton is to the summit of a spur which separates the Tseearkamisht and Squawmisht Rivers, and which
we crossed the day after I left the village. From this summit
the whole way is by a gradual descent. There would be no
difficulty in carrying a road over this at an easy grade.
From the description of Mr. McKay, an Hudson Bay Company's officer, who traversed the other side of this spur up
the valley of the Tseearkamisht, that route would seem to
be even easier than the one I passed over.

For about 400 feet perhaps the path we took was rather
steep; but, from the general appearance of the ground, I
am confident a more easy grade could be found. We
reached the summit by noon; and for the whole of the
rest of the day our path lay through a gorge by the side
of a stream, till, about six o'clock, we passed round a small
hill, and came to a little lake, called by Mr. McKay, Daisy
Lake. Here we camped for the night. Some of the ground
over which we had passed during the day was rather rough;
but after the travelling we had experienced between Jervis
Inlet and Howe Sound, it was pleasant enough; and, as I
was by this time beginning to feel very much fatigued, the
prospect of an easy journey to Pemberton, in which I was not
disappointed, was very agreeable.

Next morning (14th) we crossed a low ridge, and immediately came upon the Tseearkamisht River, which flows
on the other side of it. This river here runs through a
large basin, which appeared as if it had been lately inun-
dated; and indeed had it not been for the dead trees still
standing in it, I should have taken it for the bed of a lake
from which the water had lately receded. Though the river

itself was here 50 yards wide, the number of dead trees, which completely blocked it up at this point, made a capital floating bridge, and enabled us to cross quite easily. We then walked along the basin, which we found to be composed of sand covered with boulders of trap and granite for two miles, when we came to that part where the river still over-flowed its banks. The appearance of the country here was most remarkable. The trees were many of them very large, and the water, though lower than it had been, still stood six or eight feet up their trunks, giving them the appearance of a forest growing in water. As we advanced, a still more curious sight presented itself, for the trees having been burned by one of those fires so common in the bush, stood up all black and charred in the flood, looking as if there had been a struggle between fire and water for the mastery, in which both might claim a victory. While speaking of fire in the bush, I may mention that in former years—for it decreases yearly as the trees are cut down—these fires were so common along the coast as to cause a smoke all over the Straits that had the effect of a fog, and made them as difficult of navi-gation as in the thickest winter weather.

From this point to our journey's end the way had been travelled previously by Mr. McKay, an officer of the Hudson Bay Company, whose name I have already mentioned. He had, however, gone the opposite way to that which I took, having started at Port Pemberton and from the Daisy Lake, following the Tseearkamisht down, while I had come up the Squawmisht. He consequently reached Howe Sound by the east side of the large valley mentioned at its head, while I went up the west; and as, on comparing notes with him, I found he thought the side he took to be as good as mine, there can be little doubt of the favourable quality of the land there.

After proceeding along the east bank of the river for six miles we came to a small cañon; and about two miles beyond this again crossed the river on dead trees, and camped. This cañon could be easily avoided by a bridge built a little below it: it is of very small extent, the river being narrow, and the bank on the opposite side low and level.

A five-mile walk next morning brought us to a lake which we found to extend, with an average breadth of one mile, about 10 miles in a north-easterly direction. Finding the Indians knew no name for it, I called it "Green Lake," from the remarkably green colour of the water. This was a very pleasant spot; and coming upon a shady tree, with good grass growing beneath it, we halted for breakfast, and waited till noon to get a latitude. We then kept along its west bank to the head where there was a small patch of swamp, and crossing this, we came upon a fine beaten trail leading through a pleasant valley, which we kept till night.

During the night we experienced one of the heaviest thunderstorms I ever heard in the bush. It was raining a little when we turned in, but there were no very threatening indications of storm, although, doubtless, had we been in the open instead of among very large trees, where we could hardly see any sky, we should have been more prepared for it. As it was, about midnight we were awakened by a crash like the falling of an immense number of large trees, although the bright flash which almost instantly shot across the door of the tent showed us its cause. My poor crew suffered badly this night. The rain fell in torrents, putting out their fire, and drenching them thoroughly; and though I soon dozed off again, their idea of supernatural agency in thunder and lightning, which I have mentioned when speaking of Indians generally, kept them awake all night; and whenever I was roused by a particularly loud clap or a brighter flash than usual, I heard their shouts of terror or excitement mingling with the thunder's reverberation. In the forest depths a storm of this kind is certainly a most awful and im-

posing spectacle. The clap of the thunder rings so much
more than in an open space, while the reverberation continues
through the forest with a succession of loud, sharp cracks
like a number of distinct reports of cannon. A storm, too,
appears so much nearer to you in the depth of a forest than
when you see it on the plain. I have often stepped suddenly
back into my tent when I have been watching it, fancying
for the moment that the fork would strike the very spot on
which I was standing, so vividly has the jagged line of light
flashed across my face. The expression of fear on the
Indians' faces on these occasions is beyond description ; they
almost grow white through the coating of dirt on their skins ;
and you can never get them to move about alone while the
storm continues.

Next day we continued our march in no very comfortable
plight, every one and every thing wet through. As the sun
rose, however, bright, clear, and warm, the past night appeared
like a dream, for, except a few freshly-fallen trees and broken
branches, no traces of the wild disturbance of the elements
were seen. Our course all this day lay along the centre of
a thickly-timbered valley with two or three small hills in it.
Ascending one of these, about nine o'clock we saw the Lilloett River four or five miles off, coming in from the westward
between very high precipitous mountains, and beyond these
appeared the snow-capped peaks, which, according to the
Indians, surround the mountain lakes, in which, as I have
said, the Lilloett, Squawmisht, Clahoose, Bridge, and other
rivers take their rise. They describe it as a basin, very high
up, containing four or five small lakes, in which rise all the
larger rivers watering this part of the country.

We soon came upon the Lilloett River, and followed its
right bank till night, when we crossed one arm of it by an
Indian bridge made over a fall of 200 or 300 feet, and there
camped. We had crossed two or three steep mountain-
shoulders during the latter part of the day, as this course

shortened the distance, and was preferable to keeping the valley on account of the density of the bush there. A traveller will find that Indians always prefer the mountain-side to traversing a valley, so that, in examining with them a line of country for a road, you hardly ever pass over the exact ground through which it would be carried. This should always be borne in mind in considering an Indian's report of any route, as, except where it crosses high mountains or rivers, his description would not convey to a road-cutter a very good idea of the work before him.

It afforded me no small gratification when we halted that night to feel that it was our last out for this trip, and that we should be at Port Pemberton in good time next day. The way, after passing the Squawmisht, was certainly much easier than before; but travelling without a white companion is always very dull work; and for the last day and a half the mosquitos had become almost intolerable, worse indeed than I had ever before known them to be even in British Columbia. Fortunately I had a small mosquito-net, which the Doctor had wisely insisted upon bringing, or I do not know what I should have done. Whenever we halted I hung this on cross sticks, and, getting inside, tucked it about me. When tea was ready, it was handed in to me under the net, watch being kept that none of the enemy entered with it. The poor Indians suffered terribly, though they coated themselves with a mixture of oil and mud. At starting they had warned us that the "quileemuck" (mosquitoes) would kill us all when we got to the Lilloett; and they certainly did their best to effect that purpose. Before we left the ship we had head-bags made of crape, and these were the only things that kept us from being devoured while we were walking. These were long veils which were fastened round the top of our straw hats, and tied in at the neck. We even went so far as to have small cane hoops inserted in them to keep them off the face. But these only answered in clear land, of which we found very little on this trip. In the bush the hoops were always catching the boughs of trees and tearing. The moment the bag touched your face you were bitten through it: the mosquitoes making nothing of any such trifling obstruction as the net of which it is composed. Indeed it was said by some of the officers engaged on the Boundary expeditions, that the mosquitoes were known to bite through two blankets! It should be said, however, that these plagues are only met with in these woods and on the Lower Fraser. The country above Fort Hope, for instance, is free, or almost free from them. And wherever the country is cleared they disappear. At Westminster, for example, they have become much less troublesome since the site of the town was cleared, although their disappearance cannot be looked for until the thick bush, which still hedges in the city closely, shall have yielded to the axes of the settlers. In Vancouver Island they are almost unknown.

An hour's walk on the following morning brought us to the top of a hill from which we looked down on the Lilloett Meadows. A small lake, at certain seasons nearly dry, lay at our feet, and before us, for some miles east and west, dotted at long intervals with log huts—the ripe corn surrounding them, and the long hay which grew all over the plain sending up a delicious perfume—lay the Lilloett Meadows. Through them flowed the river, which came from the high rugged mountains in the east, where the fertile country ended. It was lovely weather, calm and bright as July mornings always are here, and the scene was most attractive and beautiful. Our sense of its charms was not a little heightened perhaps by the few signs of civilization before us, and the sight far off of the thin white smoke which told where the huts which constitute the important city of Pemberton, whither we were bound, lay.

Descending to the little lake, we obtained a canoe from a

mountain was finished, and had been at work for some time, while the mule-trains were larger and more numerous. Except, however, as a resting-place, or point of arrival and departure, Douglas does not promise to become of much consequence, as the site is very limited, and there is little if any land adapted for agricultural purposes in the neighbourhood.

At Douglas we had to wait a day for the steamer; travelling by her to Hope, we stayed the night there, reaching New Westminster by the noon, and Esquimalt by the evening of the day following.

Rejoining Dr. Wood on board the 'Plumper,' I found that after he left me it had taken him a day and a half to reach New Westminster, and that he arrived just in time to see the 'Plumper' steaming out of the harbour. This was on the 14th July, when the ship had gone to Puget Sound to make a series of observations on the eclipse which occurred on the night of the 16th and 17th, and of which they had an excellent view. The congratulations upon the success of their mission, which they received from the American officer in charge of the troops there, were couched in very characteristic language. He remained with them while the observations were being made, standing the while at a respectful distance. When they were finished he advanced, and, taking off his hat, said, "I congratulate the world generally, and science in particular, on the result of your labours, gentlemen."

On the 12th of the month H.M.S. 'Termagant' arrived with the two gunboats, Forward and Grappler, which she had convoyed from England, and on the 30th our old companion, the 'Satellite,' left for home. She had been nearly four years in commission, three of which had been spent at this place. Her departure could scarcely fail to remind us of the change that had taken place since she had entered Esquimalt Harbour three years back. It was the first time that its waters had ever been disturbed by a steamship of such a size; and now, as she steamed out from the changed and busy port, homeward bound, she gave back the hearty cheers of two of Her Majesty's frigates, two sloops, and as many gunboats.

On the 31st we left for Burrard Inlet and Nanaimo, in company with the 'Termagant' and 'Alert.' As we steamed through the 'Plumper,' now 'Active,' Pass, the 'Termagant' met with an accident which well nigh turned out seriously for her. In rounding the point in the middle of the passage the current caught her bow, and she would not answer her helm. For a moment she appeared to be going stem on to the rocks, when she suddenly veered a little round, but not in time to clear them altogether. The rocky bank against which she grazed was, fortunately, sheer and steep, so that, although she heeled over so much that those watching her thought she must have capsized, she shot back into the middle of the stream, tearing up a tree with her foreyard, and throwing it over the yardarm, as though it had been a broomstick. Fortunately, although she leaked a good deal, she was able to go on, and we anchored in Burrard Inlet that night. Next morning we picked up the boats which had been at Jervis Inlet, and proceeded to Nanaimo. Here the damage done to the 'Termagant's' hull was found to be too low to be reached by heeling her over, and we went to Esquimalt to bring back the divers to examine her. Returning with them on the 5th, we remained at Nanaimo until the 8th, when the 'Termagant' being sufficiently repaired, we started to convoy the 'Alert' to Rupert, whence, after assisting us in quelling a reported disturbance among the Indians of that place, she was to proceed to Sitka. Anchoring the first night in Tribune Bay, Hornby Island, by the next evening we reached Knox Bay, in Johnstone Straits. Upon passing Cape Mudge this time we found that the stockaded village which, upon our previous visits had been empty, was inhabited, the Strait

being now full of fish. This habit among the Indians of
changing their places of residence, not at any particular
season, but as the fish and game shift their quarters, appears
to have misled Vancouver, who, in passing, concluded all
villages which he found uninhabited to have been deserted
altogether by their people.

Next day we went through Johnstone Strait, sounding all
the way, and reached Port Harvey at night. Weighing
anchor next morning, we got outside, when a thick fog came
on, and, as we could not see any sounding-marks, we bore up
again for the port. Here we experienced one of the curious
atmospheric phenomena which are common to these parts.
In the Strait a strong breeze was blowing from the north-
west, bringing down with it a thick fog, while inside the
harbour it was a dead calm, and perfectly clear. I have
noticed this and similar peculiarities frequently in this
Strait. The northerly wind appears always to bring the fog
down from the Russian coast, and it will remain in the Strait
until a southerly breeze springs up, while, curiously enough,
the large harbours at either side of the passage are wholly
unaffected by it.

On Monday morning we left Port Harvey, reaching Cormorant Bay at 10 A.M. Here I was left with two boats to
continue the survey, while the ships proceeded to Rupert.
Arriving there they found the Indians recovering from a debauch, consequent on their having paid a visit to Victoria,
from which place they had returned with an abundant supply
of spirits. Their conduct had, according to the report of Mr.
Weynton, the officer of the Hudson Bay Company in charge
of the station, been more furious than on any previous occasion, and as some of his men had joined in the debauch,
he became rather alarmed for the safety of the fort. The
Indian population had, it appeared, been much excited by
the murder of A-kush-ma, one of their chiefs, by a Songhies

Indian, when they were leaving Victoria, and they were now planning a campaign to the southward to avenge his death. Upon their way up they had had a brush with the Indians at Nanaimo and carried off a woman, named Hu-saw-i, whose husband had appealed to the authorities for redress. Captain Richards had visited Rupert for the purpose, among other things, of recovering her; but he saw that in their present excited state caution was necessary: so word was sent to the chiefs, who were somewhat impressed by the show of force made, that he desired to have a "war-war" (speech) with them upon several important matters next day.

Accordingly on the following morning he landed with several officers and proceeded to the fort. Judging, however, from the conduct which they would most probably pursue in such a case, the Indians, suspecting treachery, steadfastly refused to enter the gates of the fort, so the palaver was held outside in front of their lodges. In his address to them Captain Richards explained, through Mr. Hunt—who was one of the employés of the Hudson Bay Company and who spoke their language— that the time had come when it would not do for them to take the law into their own hands; that Mr. Douglas, who had been informed of their conduct, was very angry with them, and was determined to punish them if they did not behave better; that they must no longer kill in retaliation, but be satisfied that all murderers would be duly tried by law, and if found guilty, executed. At this moment the brother of the murdered chief interposed, and nearly brought the meeting to a close in some confusion by jumping up and announcing his intention of going at once with all the men he could get to revenge his brother's death. This was mere bravado, however, and he was soon pacified. At last, after a great deal of violent language and action, the chiefs said they were quite willing to give up their custom of killing and making slaves, if the other tribes of the island would amend their ways also. One old chief at this juncture was very eloquent upon the neglect of

P

his tribe by the missionaries. "Why," he asked, "was no one sent to teach their young men what was right? It was very well for us to assert that what they (the Indians) had learned from their forefathers was wrong, but why was not care taken to explain this, and to teach them better ways? They felt ashamed," he said, "before the Tsimsheans, whose young men were learning to read and write, and knew so much more than they did. Why was Mr. Duncan sent past Rupert to Fort Simpson, and no one sent to them?" He was assured that the desire of his people for instruction should be made known to Mr. Douglas, and that no doubt teachers would shortly visit them. At last, therefore, they handed one of their poles over to Captain Richards in token of the palaver having ended amicably and of their assent to his wishes, and gave their promise that they would not go on the intended foray southward.

After this followed the slave question. They had somehow got wind of our purpose, and, suspecting that she would be claimed of them, had on the previous night sent their captive across to the mainland. At first they refused to give her up for less ransom than 100 blankets, and then seeing this would not be submitted to, they asserted that she had left them and was three days' journey away. Captain Richards, therefore, gave them three days' time to bring her on board, saying that he should remain there with both ships, and use force if she were not forthcoming at the end of that period. Feeling convinced at last that it was of no use holding out longer, they said that they would send at once for her, and asked for some payment for the men who should be despatched. This was promised, and she was brought on board two days later.

Had it not been for the presence of the 'Alert,' we should probably have had great difficulty in inducing them to give up this slave. The stand they made in the presence of so much force was very significant of the attachment with which they cling to this among other habits of their restless, predatory lives. The old chief's questions, however, about Mr.

Duncan, showed a desire to learn, which the old men among
the Indians certainly feel for their children's sakes, but for
which they do not generally get credit. There is no doubt
that men of Mr. Duncan's stamp, who will in a frank, manly
spirit go among them diffusing the blessings of religion and
education, will meet with a cordial reception and an abundant
reward. But without any desire to disparage or dishearten
others, I must say that Mr. Duncan impressed us as a man of
ten thousand, possessing, with abundant energy and zeal, that
talent for acquiring the confidence and love of his fellow-
creatures, which all who came in his way, were they whites
or Indians, could not fail to acknowledge and feel subject to.

The 'Alert' proceeded on her voyage on the 17th, and on
the 18th the 'Otter' arrived with our mails, and having Mr.
Duncan on board and with him the Rev. Mr. Tugwell, who it
was intended should take his place at Fort Simpson while he
(Mr. Duncan) went to Victoria to establish schools there.
The following extract from Mr. Duncan's Journal, descriptive
of his interview with Captain Richards, who was just then
much impressed by the desire expressed by the Indians to receive European teachers, will no doubt be read with interest:—

"*Aug.* 19.—This evening we arrived at Fort Rupert and
found H.M.S. 'Plumper' in the harbour. Went on board
and was warmly greeted by Captain Richards, who astonished
me by saying he, had just been writing about me to the
Admiral. I read his despatch. It stated that he had had
some trouble with the Indians of that place, and at a large
meeting they had asked him why Mr. Duncan was not sent
to teach them, and then insisted on the injustice of my being
sent over their heads to the Tsimshean Indians. During
my conversation with Captain Richards, he said the business
he had just had with the Indians convinced him that it was
not our ships of war that were wanted up the coast, but missionaries. The Indian's ignorance of our power and strong
confidence in his own, in addition to his natural savage temper,

P 2

render him unfit to be dealt with at present by stern and
unyielding men of war, unless his destruction be contemplated, which of course is not. 'Then,' asked the captain,
' why do not more men come out, since your mission has been
so successful; or, if the missionary societies cannot afford
them, why does not Government send out fifty, and place them
up the coast at once? Surely it would not be difficult to find
fifty good men in England willing to engage in such a work?
and their expenses would be almost nothing compared with
the cost which the country must sustain to subdue the Indians
by force of arms.' Such are the earnest sentiments of one of
Her Majesty's naval captains while among the Indians."*
And such, I may add, are the sentiments of myself—in
common, I believe, with all my brother officers—after nearly
five years' constant and close intercourse with the natives of
Vancouver Island and the coast of British Columbia.

Rejoining the 'Plumper' on the 20th, I found the rescued
slave Hu-saw-i in full possession of the after cockpit. There is
no accounting for tastes, of course; but it was fortunate for
Hu-saw-i that her husband esteemed her more than we did, or
I fear she would have been left to the tender mercies of her
captors. She was one of the ugliest, dirtiest specimens of an
old squaw I have ever had the pleasure of meeting; and during
the ten days we had her on board, she excited, I fear, anything
but sympathy among us. She was turned over to the charge
of the serjeant-major, a dress being made for her of printed
calico, which, with sundry other garments, she was desired to
wear, besides being told to make herself as decent and clean as
her habits would permit. The first thing to be done was to induce her to give up possession of her filthy blanket and to take
a bath, to both of which proceedings she expressed decided re-
pugnance. The sergeant, who was a most strict-service man,
treated all men and women as stores put under his charge,

* Mr. Duncan's letters to the Church Missionary Society.

and for which he was responsible till relieved by his commanding officer.   He could not speak a word to Hu-saw-i,
and his endeavours—crowned I should add with perfect success—to get her to do what was ordered, were most amusing.
First he was told that she was to be cleaned and dressed.
Receiving the order just as he would have done one to "cane
a boy," or put any one in the Black List, he carried it out to
the letter, and then came with a military salute and reported
" Old woman cleaned, sir."   As punctiliously he took her food
to her or saw that she got it, while he used to visit her like a
prisoner three or four times a-day to make sure that she was
all right.   The poor old creature was all this while in a great
fright, and I have no doubt in her heart wished herself back
among her enemies.   All day long she would stand at the
fore end of the passage which went round our chart-room,
and every time we turned to walk aft along the quarter-deck
would begin to wave her hand and cry " Ah! Tyee, Tyee!"
(Ah! chief, chief!) in the most piteous voice imaginable, till
we were fairly driven off deck.   On the 27th, however, much
to our delight, we got rid of her, sending her in the 'Shark'
(our decked pinnace), to catch the 'Otter' on her way down
to Victoria.   The sergeant accompanied her to the last, seeing
her on board, and reporting, with the utmost gravity, " Old
woman's in the boat, sir."

This sergeant was the source of much amusement to us.
His notions of service were of the strictest and most laughable
kind.   One of his company having lost a thumb, he applied
persistently to the Captain for a certificate of the accident,
and was most uncomfortable at his refusal, regarding it in
precisely the same light as the loss of a knapsack or rifle.
He argued that the man having left the " division " with two
thumbs, he, the sergeant, was responsible for his being
returned into store with only one, and must show that its
loss was correct, and not owing to any negligence on his,
the sergeant's, part.   I remember, when the 'Plumper' was

actually heaving up her anchor, homeward bound, and we
were just leaving the ship, he came up to me, and begged me
to speak to Captain Richards about it, "as he was still without a certificate for that man's thumb, and really ought to
have one to satisfy his Colonel!"

On the 21st the ship went on to Shucartie, a bay 20 miles
northward of Fort Rupert, where we experienced very foggy
and rainy weather, which made our observations most uncertain and otherwise delayed our work. Winds from the north-
west prevailed here; with them, as I before said, comes the
fog, and, so troublesome did we find it, that not more than
one day in three was available for working purposes.

On the 27th we went on to Bull Harbour, in Hope Island,
opposite the northern extreme of Vancouver Island, where
we remained till Monday the 3rd of September, when it
was determined to make a start to the southward, the ship
going outside Vancouver Island, while I went down inside
with two boats to finish off some work and go up the Squawmisht River. The weather at this time, though still very
pleasant at Victoria, begins to be very bad at the north end
of the island; rain, fog, and strong north-westerly winds prevailing, while the nights, though usually calm and clear, are
cold. Wild-fowl also began to make their appearance in
large quantities from the northward, reminding us unpleasantly of the near approach of winter. We were not sorry,
therefore, to receive orders to move southwards.

On the morning of the 3rd, I started with the gig and
'Shark,' the latter carrying the provisions, &c., for which we
had no room in the boat. Our cruise was to extend over 350
miles, and, as there was a good deal to be done on the way,
we made preparations for a cruise of at least a month. The
ship towed us out of the harbour, and then turned northward,
while we kept down the channel to the south. Having fair
wind and tide we reached Fort Rupert by noon, where we
remained all night to wait for the 'Shark,' which had some

work to do by the way. At Rupert we laid in a great stock
of vegetables, which lasted us nearly all our cruise; and proceeding on our journey next morning, reached Beaver Cove,
in which neighbourhood we remained for two days. I have
not yet, I think, described camp-life when away with boats;
and as it differs somewhat from camp-life in the bush, I will
now attempt it. To begin with, it is much pleasanter work
than roughing it in the bush; for, instead of cutting down
everything to the smallest possible limit, you are able to
carry many comforts with you. A large bell-tent accommo-
dates the men, and, if you have a roomy boat, you will probably take a small tent for yourself also. In addition to
these, a canteen, a box, fitted for holding cups, plates, knives,
and forks; tins for tea and coffee, and bottles for grog, if you
take any, are requisite. The same stock of clothes for boat
and bush excursion is necessary, the crew washing theirs on
Sunday.   Objections are sometimes made to this work being
done on that day, and Saturday evening is recommended for
the purpose,—when the men are likely to be so tired as to
neglect the task. The bush, however, is so thick ordinarily,
that it rarely happens that the tent is pitched in a spot where
the men can get a walk on the Sunday morning; and I think
this employment before prayer-time very useful.

The daily routine of life in the boats differs, of course,
very much from that in the bush.   Instead of working
before breakfast the day begins with that meal. Breakfast
over, the boats are launched or unmoored, and operations
begun for the day at an hour depending a great deal upon
the work to be got through, and ranging generally from
6 to 8. About noon—or as near to that time as an appropriate spot for the meal was reached—we halted for dinner,
and, resting for an hour, continued our work until the
evening, taking care, however, to get our tent pitched and
boats moored before dark.   It was always necessary to keep

a watch all night, as some Indians were pretty sure to be lurking about in the neighbourhood on the look-out for a chance of thieving. When among the northern tribes, also, there was always some fear, more or less, of their attacking us. I remember, when we first began work in 1858, paying for my neglect of watch-keeping with the loss of a double-barrelled fowling-piece. We were in the American territory, on the east side of the Bellingham Channel. When we camped we had not seen any Indians near, and, having a dog with us, I did not think it worth setting a watch. We had been some time away from the ship, and, having used all my powder and shot, instead of taking my gun into the tent as usual, I left it in the boat, which was hauled up on the beach. About the middle of the night we were awakened by the dog barking violently, but, running out of the tent, could see nothing. The dog was soon quiet, and we attributed the disturbance to a deer, and went to sleep again. In the morning, the coxswain said to me, "That was a deer last night, sir; here are his tracks all round the tent." I thought no more about it, till walking down to a station close by I saw a marten, and, knowing I had one barrel of my gun still loaded, called for it. The coxswain went to the boat to fetch it, when it was found to have disappeared, and there could be no doubt that it had been taken during the night. Close behind the tent was a deep ditch, into which the thief must have jumped when the dog heard him, and so escaped.

On Saturdays we usually camped a little earlier than on other days, so that the boats might be cleaned out, &c. Sundays were always spent in camp; Church-service being read in the forenoon.

Such was our surveying life. The men generally managed to procure salmon, venison, potatoes, &c., from the natives; so that, as a rule, we did not fare badly, although sometimes we had what the seamen called very hungry cruises. On the whole, it was a happy life enough, and the time passed pleasantly and swiftly.

On Monday the 10th we proceeded down the Strait and reached Point Chatham on the 13th, the only thing we had to complain of being the weather. It rained constantly, and at such short intervals that there was no time to get our things dry between the showers. In going down Johnstone Strait we met Mr. Downie, in his schooner, on his way to Knight Inlet. He had shortly before discovered plumbago there, and was on his way for a cargo of it, which was, he hoped, to make his fortune. He gave us some newspapers and a supply of apples, which were by no means unacceptable. We passed Cape Mudge on the 15th, and reached the little island of Mittlenatch, which lies six or eight miles off it, by night, and there spent our second Sunday. The 'Shark' had not been able to reach the island, and had been obliged to seek shelter elsewhere, from which, however, she was subsequently driven by a gale that sprang up. We picked her up on Monday; and having put a mark on Savary Island, we proceeded together to Texhada Island, which we reached the same evening, remaining here all Tuesday (18th), and reaching the entrance of Howe Sound on Wednesday. Leaving the 'Shark' to take soundings about the entrance, I started for its head, being desirous, if I could get a canoe, to ascend the Squawmisht River, and reach the village which we had visited when on the way from Jervis Inlet to Port Pemberton. Reaching the mouth of the river on the morning of the 20th, we found the village there deserted by all save one old man and a little boy. I was beginning to despair of getting up the river, when to my great delight, Peter, the chief of the village I wished to go to, made his appearance. He had heard of our arrival, and had dropped down the stream from his temporary village about two miles up, where he was fishing, to see who we were. He imme-

diately recognised me and agreed to take me up on the
following day.   Accordingly, having selected a good place
to leave the boat in, I started next morning with Peter and
three other Indians up the river.   As I have spoken of this
river in the beginning of the chapter, I will only say now
that we reached the village that evening; and as it poured
with rain all night and not a star showed itself in the heavens,
I was glad to sleep in Peter's lodge and wait for the sun
next day.   Here I experienced the hospitality I have always
received from Indians when alone with them.   They cleared
everything out of one end of the large hut, and put a barrier
across, so that no children or dogs could come near me, and
kept my fire alight all night.   The children certainly were
models of quietness; for although there were no fewer than
30 or 40 in the lodge, I hardly heard a sound all night.
Altogether there were 50 or 60 men, women, and children
in the place; but, except an occasional bark by one of
the dozen dogs who slept under the same roof, and who
was probably chasing a deer in his dreams, not a sound
disturbed me.

Dropping down the river next day, and rejoining the boat
at 6 P.M. on the following morning, we started down the
Sound, and after a few days' cruise—which, with the boat-
trip altogether, would have been pleasant enough but for the
constant rain—reached Esquimalt.

Remaining some time in harbour—during which several
changes among the other vessels took place, and we hoisted
the garland * for the second time during our cruise, in honour
of the marriage of our first lieutenant—we started on the
13th for our last cruise in the old 'Plumper' to Howe
Sound.   We remained here, struggling against the rain and

---

* It is the custom on board men-of-war to hoist a garland of flowers to the
mast-head, between sunrise and sunset, when a wedding takes place among
the officers.

wind that did its best to convince us that the time had
arrived for giving up work for the winter, until the 28th,
when we went to New Westminster, where we remained
until the 1st of November. Crossing the Gulf to Nanaimo
for coal, we proceeded to Esquimalt, where we commenced
our winter chart-work and made preparations for turning
over to the 'Hecate,' which we knew had left England in
June last, and might arrive at any moment.

On the 14th we were much shocked by the sudden death
of poor Bull, our master and senior assistant-surveyor. His
death was quite unexpected, and cast a gloom over us all.
It was but ten months since he had been married, and had
built himself a house near the harbour, where he died
without the slightest warning or previous illness. On the
day previous to his death he had been working with us all
at the office.

On the 12th of December a requisition was sent by the
Governor for a vessel to go to Nootka Sound, to see what
assistance could be rendered to a Peruvian brigantine which
was on shore there, a message having been sent by the crew
that they expected hourly to be killed by the natives. As
almost invariably happens in these cases, it proved that the
white men had provoked an attack—one of them threatening
to chop an Indian down with his axe. At the same time we
heard that one or two other vessels had been lost on the coast
in the heavy gales which had prevailed since the beginning of
November. Accordingly on the 16th, the 'Forward' was
sent out to hunt up the wreck, Browning, one of our second
masters, going in her as pilot.

On the 23rd of December H.M.S. 'Hecate' made her
appearance, and it may be fancied how eagerly we all hurried
on board to see what our new home was like. We were
greatly delighted with the change, for though possessing no
external beauty, she was very roomy and comfortable

within—my new cabin alone being nearly as large as our mess-room of the 'Plumper.' It was decided that we were to take possession of the new ship on the 1st of the coming year, all of us joining her except Moriarty, the 1st Lieutenant, who was to go home with the 'Plumper.' Our fourth Christmas was spent in the usual way, finishing with a dinner at the Captain's house.

CHAPTER X,

Turn over to the 'Hecate'—Preparations for Summer's Work—Trip to West Coast to look for the 'Forward'—Visit Nootka Sound—Survey of Barclay and Clayaquot Sounds, and Remarks on West Coast of the Island—Promotion—Ship runs ashore.

WE began the year 1861 by joining our new ship, and immediately commenced such alterations as the 'Hecate's' fittings required for the work before her. We had hardly got on board, however, and had not half "shaken down," when the non-appearance of the 'Forward' caused so much anxiety that Captain Richards decided upon going out to look for her. Accordingly on the 4th we were under weigh in our new ship, and steaming out of the Strait of Fuca. The 'Forward' had at this time been absent quite a fortnight longer than she ought to have been, and as we knew that heavy gales had been prevalent outside the Straits, it was natural some anxiety should be felt for her, although most of us as yet trusted in the general luck of her commander, Robson (who, poor fellow! has since been killed), for picking himself up somewhere. Browning, too, who had accompanied the 'Forward,' knew the coast thoroughly; and we, therefore, as yet attributed her absence to some accident in her machinery. Subsequently, however, we began to feel seriously alarmed for her safety.

We reached Nootka Sound in the afternoon of the following day, and, passing Friendly Cove, steamed up to the Boca del Infierno, and anchored in a small place called Island Harbour. Here we communicated with the natives, but could only hear that a steamer had been there and left some time ago. Next day (6th) we left Island

Harbour, and went to the Tasis village, but without learning
anything more.   On our way out we despatched a boat-party
to Friendly Cove, and there found a board with a broad
arrow cut upon it, but no notice.   This we afterwards learned
had been put up by a Mr. Lennard, who was cruising about
the west coast on the look-out for furs, in his cutter, the
'Templar.'   We remained outside all night, jogging slowly
down the coast towards Barclay Sound, which we entered
next morning, and proceeded to the settlement at the
head of the Alberni Canal.   Here we remained all night,
but got no further information, and next morning steamed
to Uclulet at the north entrance of the Sound, where
we found five men of the 'Florentia,' the vessel which
the 'Forward' had been despatched to look for, and which
had been wrecked 12 miles north of this point, together with
several of the crew of the American brig 'Consort,' which had
also been lost on the coast 90 miles beyond Nootka.   From
these, whom we took on board, we learned that the 'Forward'
had arrived at Friendly Cove on the 19th of December, and
hearing there of the wreck of the 'Consort,' had gone to
rescue her crew; that she returned to Friendly Cove, having
eighteen of the 'Consort's' crew on board, and, taking the
'Florentia' in tow, had started with her for the Strait of
Fuca.   Outside Nootka Sound it appeared that they experienced a considerable swell, and twice parted the chain by
which the 'Florentia' was towed, but succeeded each time
in getting it on board again.   About 8 in the evening,
however, the 'Forward' dropped close to the 'Florentia,'
and Robson (her commander) hailed to say he could not tow
her any longer, and immediately cast her off,—or the chain
parted again,—they were not sure which.   The 'Forward'
then ran across the 'Florentia's' stem, steering for Nootka,
and was lost sight of in ten minutes, since which they had
neither seen nor heard anything of her.   The 'Florentia'
had afterwards drifted ashore again, and been totally lost.

Captain Richards, upon a consideration of these facts, came to the conclusion that if the 'Forward' had entered any of the Sounds, the Indians would have known of it, and that she had probably by this time got back to Esquimalt. We, therefore, returned thither, reaching it on the 10th, but to our surprise and alarm, we found nothing had been heard of her. It was at once determined that the 'Plumper' should start in search of her, this time examining the whole of the west coast, and communicating with Fort Rupert upon the chance of her having gone round the island. On the 11th, therefore, the 'Plumper' left, and as day after day passed without our obtaining any news of the missing gun-boat from her or any other source, we, waiting anxiously at Esquimalt, began to give up all hope.

On the afternoon of the 15th, however, when sitting in my cabin, I was told that an officer was coming alongside, and on going up the ladder, great was my surprise to find Browning standing at the top of it! I have said he had gone as pilot in the 'Forward,' and had he delayed making his appearance for a few days later, it is not unlikely that he would have found his kit sold as " dead and run men's effects." There he was, however, and he told us he had come in from the 'Forward,' which was outside the harbour, and would arrive in an hour. He explained that they had parted company with the 'Florentia,' on account of the crown of one of the furnaces coming down, and, returning to Friendly Cove, had patched this up as well as they could, and started for Esquimalt. Outside they met strong easterly gales, which blew without intermission, and so hard that they could make no head against them. After several days' struggle, Robson having 20 shipwrecked men on board in addition to his own crew, began to fear that they might fall short of provisions, and at last determined to bear up and go round the north end of the island, knowing that they could get supplies of

some sort at Rupert, which place they reached finally with
no worse mishaps on the way than running short of provisions and coal.

On the 18th the 'Plumper' returned from her search,
having learned at Rupert that the gunboat had passed down
the Strait, and on the 28th our old ship sailed for England
amid most vociferous cheering from those she left behind.
Our winter work in the office, which I have before made
mention of, went on much as usual; while, on board, the boats
were being fitted up, and other preparations made for the
coming summer. The 'Shark' which had before been only
half-decked, was now completely decked over, and turned
into a regular schooner, capable of navigating the west coast
of the island. On the 23rd of February we had official news
of Sir T. Maitland's assuming command of the station, and
changed our flag for the third admiral since we came out.

By the middle of March everything was ready for a start,
the ship caulked, chart-room fitted, our pinnace converted
into a schooner, and all the boats ready, and on the 22nd we
left Esquimalt for the Fraser River to lay down our second
set of buoys at its entrance. The 'Forward' went with us to
assist in this operation, and we both anchored that night off
Port Roberts. Next day we entered the Fraser and steamed
up to New Westminster, without any let or hindrance. This
was subject of great rejoicing to the people of Westminster,
as no steamer of the 'Hecate's' size (850 tons) had before
ascended the river, and it showed unmistakeably that it was
practicable for large vessels to do so. So delighted were the
people of Westminster, indeed, that they wanted to entertain
Captain Richards at a public banquet, a deputation of
citizens waiting on him with that object. This, however, he
steadfastly declined, representing that all he had done was
his duty, and that he had come to buoy the mouth of their
river, not to feast. So they contented themselves with pre-

senting him with a complimentary address. From the 25th to the 29th the surveying officers were employed in the 'Forward' placing the buoys. The difficulty of keeping these buoys in their places, which is very great, arises from the number of large trees which are floated off the banks of the river when the water is high, and come down the stream carrying everything before them. The buoys now put down were large spars fitted with a running chain through the heel, and moored to heavy weights in such a way that anything on a line with them would only dip them under water and pass over. The bottoms of the weights were hollowed out so that they might work themselves down into the sand, and so keep in their places. Considerable difference of opinion still exists as to whether these sands drift and change their position. My opinion is that they do, although not to the extent that some affirm. In thick weather the leading marks upon them are not of course visible, and the masters of ships losing their course and grounding are likely enough to lay their mishap to the shifting of the sands rather than to the right cause. On the 29th we crossed to Nanaimo and filled up with coal, and on the 5th April went to Esquimalt, where we found that the 'Bacchante,' with the new admiral, Sir T. Maitland, on board, had arrived, together with the 'Topaze' and 'Tartar.' The spring weather had now fairly set in, and we felt that working time had commenced. This winter (1860-1) had been by far the finest and mildest we had experienced since we came to the island, there being but a few days' frost in the month of January, while even then the thermometer sank only a few degrees below zero.* We knew, however, that the season on the west coast, to which we were going, was later than that inside the island, and so we waited until the 17th before we started.

* This has been fully compensated by the winter of 1861-2, which has been the most severe that can be remembered.

Q

We left Esquimalt on the night of the 17th, and anchored in Port San Juan on the morning of the 18th. I have before mentioned this harbour, which lies at the entrance of the Strait of Fuca on the north. Some gold had recently been found in Gordon River which runs into its head, and a party had started to work it; but although the precious mineral undoubtedly existed there, it was not found in quantities sufficiently remunerative to induce them to remain.

On the 19th we reached the head of the Alberni Canal, and anchored about a mile off the saw-mills. Although we had visited this place before in the 'Plumper,' I have as yet given no description of it. As it is already a considerable settlement, and likely to become of some importance, it claims, I think, some passing notice.

Barclay Sound, as it is now spelt, at the head of which the Alberni settlement is placed, should properly, I believe, be "Berkely," as it was named by Captain Berkely of the ship 'Imperial Eagle,' who in 1787 discovered, or rather rediscovered, the Strait of Fuca. Its eastern entrance is a little more than 30 miles north-west of Cape Flattery, and the whole length of the sound is 35 miles. The entrance, which is six or eight miles across, is filled with small islands and low rocks, many under water, over which the sea breaks with great violence during the prevalence of southerly winds, giving to the entrance a greater appearance of danger than really exists. Into this sound there are passages from the west and the east, of which the latter, although the narrower, is to be preferred, from the fact that there are no sunken rocks in the channel. It is proposed to erect a light on Cape Beale, the southern cape of Barclay Sound, which will no doubt be of great use to navigators making the Strait of Fuca. In the winter time, when the weather is so often thick and foggy, it frequently happens that observations cannot be obtained for two or three days before making the land, and the navigator does not like to keep in for Cape Flattery, for fear of getting under the American coast, where there is a perfect nest of rocks. A light on Cape Beale would enable him to make the island shore with considerably less anxiety than at present, and he could find shelter in Barclay Sound if he preferred waiting for clear weather before making the Strait, as the winds which most endanger ships here blow on to Vancouver shore, and are consequently fair into the Sound. Like all the sounds of the west coast of Vancouver Island, Barclay is subdivided into several smaller sounds or arms, running five or six, or sometimes more, miles inland. Of these the Uclulet arm is just within the west entrance, and inside this, as you coast round the west shore, is the Toquart, Effingham, Ouchucklesit, and several others, almost all containing good anchorage. In Ouchucklesit coal has been found, which will probably be of great value to the settlement. The scarcely less valuable commodity of limestone of very good quality has been discovered here. At the mills they used large quantities of it. Previously to its discovery they were entirely dependant on the clam-shells which the Indians leave in very large quantities on the beaches where they dig up the fish. Some of these arms are very curious, running in a straight line, or very nearly so, 5 or 6 miles between mountains 3000 or 4000 feet high, with a breadth in many places of not more than 50 yards, and yet 30 or 40 fathoms deep up to the head, which is invariably flat with a river running through it. Fifteen miles above the entrance, the sound narrows to half a mile, and the Alberni Canal commences. This continues at about the same width for 20 miles, where it opens out into a large harbour, on the east side of which is the Alberni Settlement. Extending north-west from the settlement is an extensive valley, which terminates in a large lake 5 or 6 miles from the head of the canal or inlet, and above this is another large lake, separated from the lower one by a mountain-ridge. These lakes were each estimated by

Q 2

Captain Stamp, who examined them, to be 30 miles long and
1 to 2 miles broad.

From the southern of these lakes runs the Somass River,
which, being joined by another river having its rise in the
upper lake, flows into the Alberni Canal. A very great
volume of water comes down by this river, so much indeed
that at the end of the ebb-tide the water alongside the ship
was quite fresh, though we lay a mile from its mouth. On
both banks of the Somass, and indeed all over the valley,
the soil is very rich, and the timber magnificent — the
Douglas pine (*Abies Douglasii*), growing to an enormous
size, and the white pine, oak, and yellow cypress also
abounding. Of these, however, more will be said when I
come to speak of the timber of the country generally. This
tract of country has been granted upon lease to the Saw-
Mill Company, who have a farm upon it under cultivation, and are commencing a brisk trade in spars and lumber.
It was here that the flagstaff which is erected in Kew
Gardens was cut. As these mills are by far the largest and
most important in the colony, a short description of them
may interest the reader.

They have been erected in a most solid fashion, and at a
heavy outlay, by English labourers, and with English machinery. They contain two gangs of saws capable of cutting
about 18,000 feet of lumber (plank) daily, and in the
best way, as is proved by the high price obtained for it at
Melbourne. Seventy white men are employed at and about
the premises, so that the place has all the appearance of a
flourishing little settlement. Two schooners and two steamers
are also employed by the Company here, the former trading
with Victoria and bringing the necessary supplies to the
place. One of the steamers, the 'Diana,' a little tug, also
trades to Victoria, and is used besides for towing vessels
up to and away from the mills. The second steamer, the
'Thames' has not yet reached the colony, but is on her way

out from England. In addition to these, several ships are employed in the spar trade between the colony and Europe, but the desire of the company is to sell on the spot.

The Alberni Mills possess several advantages over similar rival undertakings in Puget Sound, which are now beginning to be appreciated by merchants, and still more by the masters of ships. One of the chief of these lies in its accessibility, for Alberni being situated on the outside coast of the island, the navigator avoids all the journey in and out of the Straits of Juan de Fuca and Admiralty Inlet, which occupies ordinarily a week: so that a vessel bound to Alberni, making Cape Flattery at the same time with one bound for Puget Sound, would be half-loaded by the time the other reached its destination. Again, when loaded, the tug takes him to the entrance of Barclay Sound, where he can wait for a fair wind, while the other, in consequence of the more prevalent winds blowing into the Strait, has to beat for two or three days to get outside. In winter this is by no means a desirable spot to beat about in, for the squalls from the Olympian Mountains are sudden and heavy, and fogs come on very rapidly. Another consideration, which carries much weight with the skipper, is that there are no opportunities for men to desert at Albérni. Of course, when the trade becomes greater and the country more opened up, this advantage will cease to exist, but for some time to come men will be very safe there.

There are no port charges whatever at Alberni, and it is a port of entry, so that vessels can clear from the mills; whereas in Puget Sound they cannot, and have to call at Port Townshend or some other port to get their clearance. The scarcity of white pine in the American territory will probably enable the Alberni mills to compete with their Puget Sound rivals successfully even in the San Francisco market, and they are admirably placed for the supply

of America, China, and Australia, with the latter of which
countries a remunerative trade has already been opened.
Several foreign Governments have entered into contracts for
these spars, and our own has ordered two cargoes of top-
masts to be supplied. I will now, however, quit this subject,
having to speak more particularly of the qualities of the
different woods growing on this coast, when treating of the
resources of the island.

On the 29th I started by land for Nanaimo—a description
of which journey has been already given—returning on the
12th of May. I found that the 'Hecate' had gone to
Ouchucklesit, and proceeded thither in a canoe the same
afternoon, overtaking the ship at 7 P.M. The boat-surveying
parties were busily engaged by this time at the entrance of
the Sound, and the ship had moved down to Ouchucklesit on
the 9th to be nearer them. The boat parties had returned
to the ship once during my absence. Upon their next visit
on the 27th, I joined them for a week. From this time until
the 9th of June we were all hard at work about the various
inlets and islands of Barclay Sound. On the 3rd the ship
moved down to Island Harbour in the entrance, and on the
9th we went out to sound off the Straits of Fuca, leaving
two boats behind to finish Uclulet.

We spent a week running lines of soundings backwards
and forwards over an area of 400 square miles, to determine
the limits of the bank which runs off from the island shore
for upwards of 20 miles; and a most unpleasant week it was,
and very glad we were when it was over. These soundings
proved, however, of great use, as we found the edge of the
bank to be so steep that a ship may always find her approximate position by the soundings as she approaches the shore—
the depth changing quite suddenly from 200 fathoms or there-
abouts to 40 or 50. Our task being completed by the 14th,
we went right up to the head of the Alberni again for sights,

and commenced painting the ship. On Monday, the 24th, this necessary although unpleasant job was finished, and we started for Esquimalt, having in tow a main topmast for the 'Bacchante,' which Mr. Stamp sent as a present and specimen to the Admiral. We generally went about these channels with a good string of things of some kind towing after us, usually boats which were to be dropped at different places on our road; and this time was no exception to the rule, for we passed down the canal towing the topmast, with the 'Shark,' and one of the whale-boats, which we cast off at the entrance, they being bound for Clayoquot to prepare, by sounding the entrance, for our arrival there as soon as we returned from Esquimalt.

One of the whale-boats, under the charge of Mr. Browning, had been away since we started on our sounding cruise, and we now went to pick her up off Port San Juan. We usually took these opportunities for exercising at gun-drill, as when we were on surveying ground we had other fish to fry; so that on this occasion the pivot-gun was ready loaded when we opened San Juan Harbour, and saw Browning's tent comfortably pitched on the shore. There is a certain amount of pleasure, I suppose, in disturbing an unsuspecting fellow-mortal; and although we all knew, from frequent experience, the annoyance of seeing the ship gliding round some point, and hearing the boom of a signal-gun when it seemed reasonably certain that a quiet, undisturbed night might be enjoyed, it was not with much commiseration for our shipmate that we watched, through our glasses, the figures rushing out as the boom of the pivot-gun reached them, and the tent's sudden disappearance. Browning, who, with the rest of us, was pretty used by this time to decisive action in packing and shifting his quarters, lost no time; and in 20 minutes after our signal, his boat was cleared and hoisted up, and we were flying down the Strait with all sail set to a fair wind.

On the 26th the mail steamer arrived, but with no mail—
Mr. Booker, our consul at San Francisco, sending instead
the pleasant news that the Americans had refused to carry
the colonial mails without payment any longer.   We did not
think that the Company were in the least to blame, but it
was hard upon us, who had had nothing to do one way or the
other with the postal arrangements.   The American Company
had been allowed to bring and take our mails for years
without any offer of remuneration being made, and had the
colonists alone suffered, none of us would have felt disposed to
pity them.   Without any reference to politics, we could not
help wishing sincerely at the time that the Derby ministry
had remained in office, as it was understood that it was
their intention to grant a mail subsidy for the colony.   The
Company that owns the saw-mills at Alberni had made proposals for carrying the mails, and their agent told me
that a subsidy of 20,000l. for conveying them between San
Francisco and the colony had been promised them, and that
nothing but the formal confirmation of the contract was
wanting when the Government went out.

The agent also represented to me that the refusal of the
incoming authorities to ratify the contract arose from the
fact that so few letters left England addressed to British
Columbia.   The reason of this was, he said, that all men
of business at home gave instructions that their letters
should be directed under cover to their agents at San
Francisco, on account of the uncertainty of the conveyance
of the ordinary mails beyond that place.   Correspondence,
indeed, with the colony was at this time most uncertain—
the majority of letters intended for settlers there being
directed, "Post Office, Steilacoom, Washington territory."
This mode of direction used often to puzzle the post officials
and amuse us.   It was printed upon all the official envelopes,
but the cause of its origin and continuance was a mystery
which no one could explain.

Steilacoom never was the post-office of Washington territory while we.were there; and even if it had been, why letters should be directed to that place, which is 60 miles up Admiralty Inlet, when there was a post-office at Port Towns-hend, in its entrance, was most unaccountable.   To make the matter still worse, some people took to having "Oregon" printed or written also in a conspicuous place on the envelope —no doubt wholly unaware of the fact that Oregon and Washington are two distinct territories, each somewhat larger than France.

On the 2nd of July, at 9 P.M., we again left Esquimalt, having on board five-and-twenty of the pillars which had been sent out from England to mark the 49th parallel boundary-line.   We took them to Semiahmoo Bay, and landed them on the parallel; and, it being low-water when we arrived, they had to be carried about a mile across the sand.   Twenty-two only were landed at the boundary, and the other three taken to Port Roberts, where we left them the same afternoon, and proceeded to Nanaimo.   These perio-dical visits to the boundary-line gave us some idea of the rapid growth of the bush in this country, and showed us how completely futile the mere cutting down of trees to mark a boundary in such a country is.   We knew the position of the boundary-line, but could not find the stump which had been driven in to mark the spot; and when I tried to pene-trate along the line which could be distinguished from above easily enough by the gap in the larger trees which, of course, had not yet grown again, I found the undergrowth so thick as to be what people unused to that country would consider quite impenetrable.   Upon another occasion we wit-nessed a still more speedy obliteration of such a trail by the undergrowth of timber.   When we were at Port Roberts about a year after the trail had been cut, it was necessary for some purpose to pass through it.   But, although we

hunted for an hour or more among the bush, no entrance to
the trail could be found.

We remained at Nanaimo coasting until the 12th; the
'Grappler' taking the rest of the beacons to Smess River,
and there depositing them. I should have said that these
beacons or pillars were constructed of cast-iron, pyramid-
shaped, and having the words "American Boundary" on one
side, and "Treaty, 1844," on the other. They were hollow,
and fitted to screw or bolt on to a stone or block of wood, the
weight of each being about 100 lbs.

On the 13th we left Nanaimo, reaching Cormorant Bay at
nine that night; and next day we went on to Fort Rupert
(Beaver Harbour).

We occupied our time at Rupert till the 17th, getting
sights, &c., and cutting and dragging out of the bush five
trees of the yellow cypress for repairing our boats, &c., for
which and similar purposes, as I have before said, this wood
is the best I have ever seen. On the 17th we went on to
Shucartie Bay, and spent the 18th there, while the cutter and
one whaler sounded on the Newittee Bar. We tried the seine
(net) in Shucartie Bay, but only caught about thirty salmon.

On the 19th we steamed through the Goletas Channel
towards the north end of the island, but the fog came on so
thick that we anchored on the edge of the Newittee Bar. We
must have been nearer the edge indeed than we thought,
for we soon found ourselves drifting off it, and the ship
cruising about with 50 fathoms of chain hanging from her
bows. Fortunately, it cleared about this time, so we hove the
anchor up and proceeded out. At noon we reached Cape
Scott, and then went out to look at the Triangle Islands,
which lie off it, and at dark shaped our course for Woody
Point, or Cape Cook, halfway between the north end of the
island and Nootka Sound. We passed this spot next morning
at daybreak, and by three in the afternoon were off Nootka.

HEAD OF ISORIS ARM, NOOTKA SOUND.

Page 234.

We were bound, however, for Clayoquot Sound, which lies between Nootka and Barclay Sounds; so on we went, and reached the entrance at 8 P.M. It being then too dark to enter, we had to do what seamen are proverbially fond of—"stand off and on" for the night. At daybreak we found ourselves off Port Cox—so named by Meares, and described by him in terms which were calculated to lead us to suppose that, had we wanted it, safe anchorage might be found there. When, however, the spot he had thus described was surveyed, it was found that a sand-bar completely blocked up its entrance.   The whale-boat we had to take up was inside, and at six she came on board; and we went back again to the northern entrance of Clayoquot Sound, and in to an anchorage which she had found for us, where we moored, intending to remain till we had surveyed all the Sound— little thinking what was in store for us, and what mishap would befal us before we should again reach Esquimalt.

We all set to work surveying the various arms of the Sound, and the weather continuing fine our task progressed satisfactorily. We found sundry arms and passages hitherto unknown, and discovered that one previously marked upon the charts as Brazo de Topino was inaccurately described— its extent proving to be not more than half that laid down by former explorers.

On the 7th of August I returned to the ship, after a ten-days' surveying cruise, and walking as usual into the chart-room, was told that the Indians had brought a mail across from Alberni, and that my letters were in my cabin. I was going down for them, when the Captain came on deck with a service-letter in his hand, and said, "Here is something that concerns you as First Lieutenant of the ship." I instantly apprehended some question of minor punishments, and was preparing to defend my conduct, when he read out: "I have to inform you that Lieutenant R. C. Mayne has been promoted to the rank of Commander," &c. This intelli-

gence was so sudden and wholly unexpected, that it was not
until I had read the document that I fully realised it. Only
the night before my return to the ship, as I lay by my watch-
fire smoking and thinking of the future, I had come to the
conclusion that I should remain with the 'Hecate' until she
was paid off; and now I knew that this sudden change in
my prospects would lead, upon our reaching Esquimalt, to
my being ordered to return to England. As it happened,
however, my connection with the 'Hecate' did not terminate so abruptly as I then expected, and I remained with
her for three months from this date.

On the 15th August we started for Alberni, to get sights
again, reaching it the same night. On the 17th we again
left, intending to pick up Gowland, who was away on surveying service off Nootka Sound, and then going round the
north end of the island, to finish some work at Cape Scott, and
return inside the island to Nanaimo and Esquimalt. The next
morning at 10 we were off Point Estevan (Nootka Sound),
and Gowland joined us. A fresh north-wester was then
blowing, and during the afternoon it increased into a gale.
This put a stop, of course, to sounding, and as the Captain
knew that he would not be able to land on the north end of
the island for some days after a gale, he determined on
giving up work for the present, and going in by the Strait
of Fuca. At 8 P.M. we were "fixed" and steering for the
Strait, and at 10 we ran into a thick fog. This was nothing
at all unusual, and as we knew our ground, or water—indeed
I may say both—by heart, we jogged along about seven
knots, sounding every half-hour.

About 3 o'clock, as we approached the Strait, the speed
was eased to five knots, and the course altered a little; and
at 4 o'clock we got a cast of 19 fathoms. This puzzled every
one. We knew the water was much deeper than this on the
south side of the Strait, and it was agreed by all that we must
have got rather far on to the north shore. The ship was accord-

ingly kept south a mile and a half, and then up the Strait again, going four knots an hour, the fog continuing as thick as "pea-soup," to use a nautical simile. At 8.30, when I relieved the captain who had been all night on deck, he said "Three or four hours more and you will be packing up your traps," and went down to his breakfast. He had hardly reached his cabin, when he heard the orders, "Hard a port!"—"Stop her!" —"Reverse the engines!"—shouted from the bridge, and rushed on deck just in time to find the ship landed on a nest of rocks, over which the surf was sullenly breaking in that heavy, dead way which it does when it has a long drift of ocean open to it but no wind to lash it into foam. I had jumped on to the bridge, and seeing her head fly round in answer to the helm, thought we were going clear, but no such luck was in store for us, and up she went. Nothing but rocks were to be seen all around us, and we were all equally puzzled to know where we were, how we got there, and how we should get the ship off. That we were close to the shore we soon found, for high up over our foretopmast-head, as it appeared from aft, the summit of a cliff, with a few pine-trees upon it, showed itself. Fortunately for us, the noise of the steam escaping was heard by the master of a small schooner, which we afterwards found was lying close to us, and we soon saw two white men, in their usual costume of red flannel and long boots, paddling to us in a small canoe. Getting them on board we discovered that we were two miles inside Cape Flattery, that the cliff we saw was a small island close to the main, and that about 50 yards from us lay two small schooners in a little basin formed by the rocks. While this information was being gathered, both paddlebox boats had been got out, the small boats lowered, and the waist anchor placed in the paddler and laid out astern. During the time that this was being done, the ship swung broadside to the rocks and began to bump fearfully,—the masts springing like whips,—and we began to think it was all up with the

poor 'Hecate.' Presently as the tide, which was rising, came
in and then receded, she gave two tremendous crashes,
sending us all flying about in different directions. At the
second crash the chief engineer ran up from below with the
report that the cross-sleepers had started and the bottom of
the bunker fallen in, and that another such bump would send
the engines through her bottom. This was cheerful intelligence, and everything was got ready for a sudden departure
in the boats. Our friends in the schooner had previously
informed us that if she held together till the tide rose a few
inches, she could get in between the rocks to where his vessel
lay. The stern cable had been hauled on for this purpose,
but with no effect, when suddenly she slipped a little off the
rock and then forged ahead. Instantly the stern cable was
let go, and she glided quietly in between the rocks and alongside the schooner. No mortal could have put her there on
the calmest, smoothest day, but there she was, and right
thankful for our most merciful escape were we, who a few
minutes before, could see no possible chance of saving her.
We let go an anchor to hold her until the sleepers of the
engines could be cut away to enable them to move, and,
sounding the well, found she was making water at the rate
of six inches an hour. This was quite an agreeable surprise,
for, from the hammering she had received, we thought the
bottom must have been half-knocked out. Finding the
engines would soon be in working condition, it was determined to push on for Esquimalt. It was quite necessary that we should go somewhere without delay, for had
a breeze sprung up we should have been as badly off
where we now were as on the rocks. Here again the master
of the Yankee schooner, was of service. The passage by
which we must pass out was very little more than the
ship's breadth across, and lay between two sunken rocks.
He took two of our whale-boats, anchoring them over the
rocks between which our channel lay, and then, assisted by

an Indian, whom he brought with him, took us out. All this time the fog was as thick as ever, but when we got two or three miles up the Strait we passed out of the fog-bank as suddenly as we had entered it ; all ahead being perfectly clear. This fog had, the master of the schooner told us, hung at the entrance of the Strait for five days ; and he said it frequently occurred that a local fog of the sort kept about there for weeks. This man showed all the readiness and nerve of his countrymen, and was certainly of great service to us. When we were fairly outside, he said, "Now, there is plenty of water round the ship, and I'm almighty dry ! if you'll give me a chart, Captin, and a bottle of rum, I'll think of you often." I need hardly say he was abundantly supplied, and expressed himself very thankful. The Admiralty afterwards sent him a spy-glass for his services, but he, falling, I fancy, into some lawyer's hands, sent in an exorbitant claim for salvage which has not yet, I believe, been settled. We reached Esquimalt that evening without further damage or accident, the leakage continuing at the same rate,—and anchored the ship in Constance Cove, after as narrow an escape from total loss as any ship ever had. We were altogether 35 minutes beating on the rocks, and nearly an hour from the time of striking till we were quite clear again ; our fate depending upon whether the tide would rise, as it did, sufficiently to float her before she gave another bump, which would in all probability have finished her. I should perhaps have said, the ship's fate,—for calm as it was, and close to shore, we should probably have got all the men to land ; although an operation of this sort, which appears quite easy as long as you have a few planks to stand on, becomes rather difficult with a ship breaking up under you.

Next morning, Tuesday, 21st August, an examination was commenced by the diver and flag-ship's carpenter. The former after two days' examination reported about 25 sheets of copper off under the starboard wheel, and three heavy crushes in the ship's side; several sheets of copper off under the port quarter, 16 under the port wheel, and another heavy crush there; part of the fore-foot and false keel forward gone, with several other sheets of copper off in various places. Inside the carpenter reported 14 floors damaged more or less, four binding-streaks requiring shifting, one butt of binding-streak on port side leaking badly, with the first futtocks probably started. Upon this state of affairs being made known, it was decided by the Admiral that we must go to San Francisco to be docked, and that before we started the diver should patch up as well as he could, by stuffing tarred and greased oakum into the holes, nailing over that the tarred blanket or felt supplied for that purpose, and sheet lead above it. This took him six days, and most capitally he did his work: I never saw a man work so long at a time as he did, sometimes remaining down more than an hour without resting. I may here mention, for the information of nautical readers, that we found tarred blanket answer much better than the felt supplied by the service for such a purpose. The felt was too thick to suck into the cracks; and when it became saturated it swelled so much the diver could not work it, and being pressed together, and having no weft or thread through it, the action of the water separated it and wore it away while he was preparing the lead to cover it. Having a great deal of lead to put on, we found it much more convenient also to make nails for the purpose, longer than copper ($2\frac{1}{4}$ inch) and with flat heads, one inch in diameter. Where the wood was much bruised the service nails proved too short, and the heads so small that the diver could not see to hit them, and was constantly dropping them and hitting his fingers.

On Thursday (29th) the damages were so well stopped that we were only leaking one inch an hour; and we took in our coal and got ready for sea. A survey was then ordered to be held, to report whether or not it was safe for us to go to

San Francisco alone. It was decided that we ought to be attended by another ship; for although while in harbour we appeared right enough, no one could say what the 'Hecate' could or could not bear if she got into a gale of wind. Accordingly the Admiral ordered the 'Mutine' to accompany us as far as Captain Richards thought necessary.

Upon our arrival at Esquimalt, I went on board the flag-ship for my commission, expecting at the same time to be told to return home. To my surprise, however, I was informed that no orders to supersede me had been received; and that I must remain till my relief came. This did not disappoint me so much as it would have done had nothing happened to the ship, for I did not like to leave her in her present dilapidated condition, and I had determined to go to San Francisco in her even if I were ordered home.

I will pause ere I take the reader with me on this cruise, which for me, terminated in Southampton Docks, to give a slight summary of the resources and capabilities of the country, and of the habits and customs of the natives.

R

CHAPTER XI.

THE aboriginal inhabitants of the two colonies of British Columbia and Vancouver Island, of which I now propose to speak, may be divided into two classes, viz. the Coast, or, as they are generaly called, the Fish-eating Indians, and the Inland tribes. By Fish-eating Indians must be understood those who depend almost entirely upon fish for subsistence; for the Inland, as well as the Coast, tribes, live to a great extent upon salmon.

The Indians of the interior are, both physically and morally, vastly superior to the tribes of the coast. This is no doubt owing in great part to their comparatively slight intercourse with white men, as the northern and least known coast tribes of both the island and mainland are much finer men than those found in the neighbourhood of the settlements. But it is also attributable in no slight degree to the difference of their lives, the athletic pursuits and sports of the Indians of the interior tending much more to healthy physical development than the life of the Coast Indian, passed, as it is, almost entirely in his canoe, in which he sits curled up like a Turk. The upper limbs of a Coast Indian are generally so well proportioned and developed, that when sitting in his canoe he might be thought a well-grown man, but upon his stepping out it is seen that his legs are smaller than his arms. Miserable as these limbs are in size, in shape they are still more deformed, the lower

INDIAN WOMAN AND CHILD, THE LATTER WITH HEAD BOUND UP.

Page 242.

bones becoming bent to the shape of the side of the canoe, and the feet very much turned in. With the women this is worse than with the men, and when they try to walk they waddle like a parrot, crossing their feet at every step. Again, the trade in slaves, which is carried on to a great extent among all the Coast tribes, and tends undoubtedly to demoralize them, is not practised in the interior. Of course the prisoners which they make in their many fierce wars with one another are enslaved, but the practice is not made a trade of by them as by the tribes along the shore.

To begin, then, with the Coast or Fish-eating Indians. Mr. Duncan, the missionary teacher at Fort Simpson, of whose labours there I shall have occasion to speak, and upon the accuracy of whose information every reliance may be placed, estimates the Indians of the east side of Vancouver Island, of Queen Charlotte Sound, and of the coast of British Columbia, at about 40,000 in number. Among them four distinct languages are found to exist, each spoken by some 10,000 souls. One of these is shared by the Songhies, a tribe collected at and around Victoria; the Cowitchen, living in the harbour and valley of Cowitchen, about 40 miles north of Victoria; the Nanaimo and the Kwantlum Indians, gathered about the mouth of the Fraser.

In the second division are comprised the tribes situated between Nanaimo and Fort Rupert, on the north of Vancouver Island, and the mainland Indians between the same points. These are divided into several tribes, the Nanoose, Comoux, Nimpkish, Quaw-guult, &c., on the island; and the Squawmisht, Sechelt, Clahoose, Ucle-tah, Mama-lil-a-culla, &c., on the coast and among the small islands off it.

Of these the Nanoose tribe inhabit the harbour and district of that name, which lies 50 miles north of Nanaimo; the Comoux Indians being found to extend as far as Cape Mudge. The Squawmisht, Sechelts, and Clahoose live in Howe Sound,

Jervis Inlet, and Desolation Sound respectively. At and beyond Cape Mudge are found the Ucle-tahs, who hold possession of the country on both sides of Johnstone Strait until met 20 or 30 miles south of Fort Rupert by the Nimpkish and Mama-lil-a-cullas. The Quaw-guults, and two smaller tribes, live at Fort Rupert itself. Five of the first-named tribes muster at Nanaimo for trade, and, being all more or less at enmity with each other, frequent encounters between them take place there. The others assemble at Rupert, at which post there are generally as many as 2000 or 3000 Indians to be found.

Of all these Indians the Soughies at Victoria are the most debased and demoralised. The Cowitchens are rather a fine and somewhat powerful tribe, numbering between 3000 and 4000 souls. The Nanaimo Indians, who at one time were just as favourably spoken of, have fallen off much since the white settlement at that place has increased.

I have said the distinct languages spoken by the Indians are few in number, but the dialects employed by the various tribes are so many, that, although the inhabitants of any particular district have no great difficulty in communicating with each other, a white man, to make himself understood by the various tribes, would have to learn the dialects employed by all. And when it is considered that hardly any attempt has been made to investigate and define the principles which regulate their use of words, and that the common roots of the words themselves, if they possess such, are at present quite out of the student's reach, the difficulties of such a task may easily be conceived. The southern tribes, as a rule, understand the Chinook jargon, in which almost all the intercourse between Indians and whites is at present carried on. A few men may be found in almost all of the northern, and many of the inland tribes, who understand it, but its use is most common in the south. This Chinook is a strange jargon of French, English, and Indian words, of which several vocabularies have been published. It was introduced by the Hudson Bay Company for the purposes of trading, and its French element is due to the number of French Canadians in their employ.

The Comoux Indians possess a very fine tract of country inside a point called Cape Lazo, of which I shall speak hereafter. They are a large tribe, and have the reputation of being rather savage, though we always found them very peaceably disposed. They know quite well, however, the value of the 6000 or 8000 acres of clear land which they possess, and when I went over it with them, took great care to explain that the neighbouring Indians resorted there in the summer for berries, &c., and that a great many blankets would be required as purchase-money whenever we wanted it, an event which they evidently contemplated.

Next to them, as I have said, come the Ucle-tahs. The most important village of this tribe is situated at Cape Mudge, but they are spread all over Discovery Passage and the south part of Johnstone Strait. As I have before said, they may be regarded as the Ishmaelites of the coast, their hand being literally against every one's, and every one's against them. The Indians who come from the northward to Victoria in the summer, are particularly guarded when passing through their neighbourhood. Several battles have taken place at different times at or near Cape Mudge. Upon one occasion they murdered nearly all the crew of a Hudson Bay vessel which stopped there for water, one half-breed boy only, I believe, escaping. They are bold as well as blood-thirsty, and by no means disposed to yield, as Indians generally do, to the mere exhibition of force. In the year before last some of their canoes robbed two Chinamen's boats off Saltspring Island, and on the ' Forward' being sent after them, the villagers at Cape Mudge, which

is regularly stockaded, defied the gunboat and fired upon
her. The 'Forward' had to fire shot and shell among
them, and to smash all their canoes, before they gave in and
surrendered the stolen goods. Had it not been for the rifle-
plates with which the crew were protected, a good many
might have been hit, as the Indians kept up a steady
fire upon them for a considerable time. I must not be
understood to say that these Ucle-tahs are the only tribe of
Indians who have proved troublesome upon the coast, but
they are alone as yet in standing out after the appearance of
a man-of-war before their village. They also have a reputation, which may not, however, be quite deserved, of being
more treacherous than the Indians of other tribes. Many
stories are current of the cold-blooded treachery of all these
tribes one to the other, and sometimes to the white men who
have fallen into their hands. In 1858, for instance, some
members of the Cowitchen tribe made a most brutal and
treacherous attack on a body of unoffending northern Indians,
which I will detail, as it illustrates, not unfavourably, the
hardihood and endurance of the red man amid the perils
incidental to his life.

Information had been sent to the Governor of a canoe full
of people having been massacred in Ganges Harbour, and
H.M.S. 'Satellite' was sent to inquire into it. Upon her arrival
at Cowitchen it was ascertained that a northern canoe with a
dozen Indians in it was passing down the inner passage to
Victoria, when a white man, one of the settlers on the north
end of Saltspring Island, asked them to take him to Victoria,
calling at the settlement in Ganges Harbour on the way.
They were willing to take him to Victoria, but objected to
going to Ganges Harbour on account of the Cowitchens. The
settler, however, overruled their objections, and they finally
assented to his wish. When they reached the spot where
their passenger wanted to land, they found about twenty

Cowitchens camping there. These fellows came down to the canoe, and made such cordial professions of friendship to the poor northerners, that they were tempted to land. While the white man was present their manner continued to be most friendly; but unluckily the settler's house, to which he wanted to go, stood some quarter of a mile back from the shore. The moment he was out of sight the Cowitchens leaped up and fired on the others. Those who remained in the canoe shoved off, but were pursued and captured all but one, a chief of some rank among them. Six of the prisoners were slaughtered with the most barbarous, wanton cruelty; Captain Prevost of the 'Satellite' reporting that there were the marks of bullets discernible all round their hearts, and that their heads were fearfully battered in. Three women and a child were spared and kept as prisoners, all but one of whom were eventually rescued from them.

The Indian who escaped from the canoe swam to a small island at the entrance of the harbour, and his subsequent struggle for life illustrates strongly, as I have before said, the skill and endurance of his race when reduced to extremities. Although wounded in the neck, arm, and leg, he succeeded in floating upon a log from the island on which he had landed to Cowitchen Harbour, a distance of 13 miles. Here he was picked up by some other Cowitchen Indians, who, according to their own account, let him go. At any rate he escaped, and wounded and weak as he was, and with no other food than what roots and berries he could pick up, made his way through the forests and the midst of his enemies to Victoria, a distance of 45 miles, through a country entirely unknown to him. The pleasant part of the story, however, is that, on the 'Satellite's' return with the women who had been recovered from the offending tribe, a canoe of northern chiefs, among whom was this very man, knowing the errand she had been on, put out from Victoria to her. Upon his going on board the first thing he saw was his wife, who had been washed and dressed, and was no doubt looking better than he had ever seen her. Although of course each thought het other had been murdered, there was no violent manifestation of joy upon their recognition. Captain Prevost said that her face lighted up, and she started a little, but then stood quite still, while the man walked up to her without any appearance of surprise or undignified haste, kissed her once on the forehead, and turned away, taking no more notice of her whatever until he was leaving the ship, when he called her to his canoe. Kissing in token of affection is not an Indian habit, and must have been taught this man, I take it, by the Roman Catholic missionaries. I have been in their villages upon several occasions while travelling-parties were leave-taking; and although the women, while packing up the store of fish or venison for their husbands' journey have cried bitterly, and taken leave of them with every evidence of grief and affliction, I have never seen them kiss each other.

Several instances have occurred of whites being murdered by Indians in different parts of the colony, but I fear these murders have generally been the result of introducing firewater, or taking liberties with the females of the tribe; for although the Indian thinks little of selling female slaves for the vilest purposes, he sometimes avenges an insult offered to his own wives summarily. Their ideas, however, on this subject are by no means clear, for they occasionally take terrible vengeance for an insult which at another time they will not even notice. Whenever a white man takes up his residence among them, they will always supply him with a wife; and if he quits the place and leaves her there, she is not the least disgraced in the eyes of her tribe. The result of this is, that you frequently see children quite white, and looking in every respect like English children, at an Indian village, and a very distressing sight it is.

North of the district occupied by the Ucle-tahs come the Nimpkish, Mama-lil-a-cula, Matelpy, and two or three other smaller tribes. The Mama-lil-a-culas live on the mainland; the Nimpkish have their largest village at the mouth of the Nimpkish river, about 15 miles below Fort Rupert. A picture of this place is given in Vancouver's Voyages, and so little has it changed in the 70 years since his visit, that we recognised it immediately from that sketch. The Quaw-guults and other Indians at Fort Rupert possess no peculiar characteristics, but fight and drink when they can, after the fashion of Indians generally. I have previously described the 'Hecate's' palaver with them upon the occasion of their having captured an Indian woman of another tribe.* A palaver of this sort is a curious sight, and some Indians are very eloquent at them. All those present squat on crossed legs in the usual Indian fashion. The speaker, alone standing, holds a long white pole, which he sticks into the ground with great force every now and then by way of emphasis, sometimes leaving it standing for a minute or so while he goes on speaking. Then he strides to it, catches it up, and perhaps swings it over his head, or again sticks it into the ground. The exact meaning or purpose of this pole I do not know, but it has some particular office, and serves, among other things, to ratify any agreement to which they may come upon the subject discussed; for when they agreed finally to give up the slave, the chief stepped forward and handed the pole to Captain Richards.

In the third group Mr. Duncan includes all those Indians speaking the Tsimshean language, and to whom he has devoted so much care and labour. He divides these into · four parts:—

2500 at Fort Simpson, taking the Fort as the centre.

2500 on the Naas River, 80 or 100 miles to the north-east.

* Page 209 *ante.*

2500 on the Skeena River, 100 miles south-east.

2500 in the numerous islands in Millbanke Sound, &c.,
lying south-east of Fort Simpson.

These northern Indians, as I have before said, are finer
and fiercer men than the Indians of the south, or the tribes
of the west coast of Vancouver Island, and are dreaded more
or less by them. Their foreheads, as a rule, are not so much
flattened, but their countenances are decidedly plainer.

It is very difficult to give anything like a correct estimate
of Indian population anywhere in the island, but upon the
west or Pacific coast it is still harder, as no attempt whatever
at ascertaining their number, even approximately, has yet
been made. I imagine, however, that the island may contain
from ten to twelve thousand, of whom five thousand live
along the west coast. When speaking to Mr. Duncan once
of the difficulty of numbering the Indians, he gave a very
amusing account of the endeavour made to get a census
taken at Fort Simpson. After every means had, it was
supposed, been taken to prevent them from being found
in two places at once, the operator got what was thought
to be a fair start; but nothing could induce the Indians to
believe that a game of some sort was not intended, so that as
soon as the head of a house began counting heads, the younger
members of the family would dodge from one side of the
hut to the other, that they might be reckoned in again and
again.

The Indians of the west coast are divided into 24 tribes.
Some of these are almost extinct; while others number from
300 to 400 men. Among all these there are but two distinct
languages spoken, while the dialects are not so numerous as
on the other side.

All the tribes of Barclay, Clayoquot, and Nootka Sounds
speak a language intelligible to each other. The names and
approximate numbers of these tribes are as follow:—

In Barclay Sound.

Pacheenett	50
Nittinat	400
Ohiat	400
Ouchuchlisit	80
Opecluset	40
Shechart	150
Toquart	40
Ucle-tah	150
Tsomass	10
	1320

Clayoquot Sound.

Clayŏquŏt	350
Kilsămät	100
Ăhŏusĕt	250
Mănnă-wŏusŭt	10
Ishquat	100
	800

Nootka Sound.

Match-clats	40
Moachet	300
Neuchallet	70
Ehateset	70
	480

North of Nootka Sound is the largest tribe of the West coast—the Kȳcŭ-cūt—numbering 500 or 600 men; and north again of these lie the Quatsino and Koskiemo, occupying the two Sounds bearing those names.

East of Cape Scott, which is the north point of Vancouver Island, is a small tribe—the Newittees, which meet the Quaw-guults at Port Rupert. Mr. Moffatt, who was for years in charge of Fort Rupert, and had therefore the best opportunities of judging, estimates the number of Indians between Nootka and Newittee at 1500 men. This would make the number of the Koskiemos, Quatsinos, and Newittees about 500.

Between Victoria and Barclay Sound are the Soke Indians, who are few in number; while the Pacheenetts, which I have included in Barclay Sound, also inhabit Port San Juan.

All these are fish-eating Indians, though they get at times
a great deal of venison as well. The fish taken by them are
salmon, halibut, cod, rock-cod, a large pink fish, in shape
something like a rock-cod, herrings, smelt, hou-li-kun and
clams. All these are eaten fresh, and are also dried. But
although these are the fish best known to us and most commonly bought by us from them, the Indians feed upon the
whale, porpoise or sea-hog, seal, sea-lion, sea-cow or fur-seal;
sardine, cuttle-fish, squad, &c.; sea-cucumber or trepang;
crabs, muscles, cockles and clams.

For animal food they have fallow, rein, and elk deer;
mountain-goat, mountain-sheep (in British Columbia only);
beaver, bear, lynx or wild cat, badger, sea-otter.

They also eat esculent roots, sap of trees, and various oils
from the whale, seal, porpoise, and hou-li-kun; deers'-tallow,
goats'-tallow, and bears'-grease.

The following land and sea fowl are also taken by them
in large quantities:—Cranes, swans, grey or Canada goose,
white or snow goose, langley, stock-duck (like our wild duck),
widgeon, teal, black duck, surf-duck, velvet duck;* partridges, plover, sand-larks, snipe, sea-parrots, sea-hens, curlew,
oyster-catchers, dovekils, gulls. The eggs of almost all these
birds, and the spawn of fish, especially salmon and herring,
are also much eaten. The latter is collected in large quantities and spread in the sun to dry. I never saw it used
fresh.

Potatoes are now grown at almost all the villages in large
quantities.

The Indians have a favourite dish at their feasts, which
appears to answer to the carva of the South Sea Islands.
They bring canoe-loads of snow and ice, and with these
ingredients are mixed oil, and molasses if they have it:
the slaves and old women being employed to beat it up,

* There are also several other kinds of ducks. Sir J. Richardson, I believe,
collected twenty species.

which they do in large bowls, until it assumes the appearance of whipped cream, when all attack the mess with their long wooden spoons. Neither animals nor fish are eaten raw, except at certain ceremonials and festivities, which I shall presently describe. Venison, or indeed meat of any kind, is seldom dried or preserved on the coast, the quantity obtained being so small and the Indians eating so much flesh when they can get it, that it is devoured at once or sold at an adjoining settlement. Of their eating meat in large quantities, I speak from personal experience when travelling with them. When a deer or elk is killed they divide the meat pretty fairly, and, the first time they halt, cook it all in lumps three or four inches square; they then spit all the pieces on a stick and secure it on their backs, leaving one end within reach over the shoulder. As they walk along they every now and then pull a piece off the end of the stick and eat it, and in a few hours the whole is gone. In the season when bears are fat (midsummer) the Indian prefers their meat to venison.

They rely mainly upon fish for winter use. They cure it in large quantities, drying it in the sun and hanging it up in their lodges. A shell-fish, called Clam, forms a principal article of consumption: it is like a large cockle, being frequently the size of one's hand, and with a smooth shell. They are found on almost all the muddy beaches, a few inches below the surface at low water; their whereabouts being always denoted by a small hole, which they leave open as they imbed themselves in the mud when the water goes out. Through this hole they keep perpetually spouting a small jet of water, making it most unpleasant work to walk over them. The task of collecting and drying them, as indeed of preparing all food, devolves principally on the old women and slaves; and parties of twenty or thirty of them may be seen going about from beach to beach on this errand, under the charge of two or three men. They carry baskets and dig them up with their hands or a stick—the beach, dotted thickly with women in red, green, or dirty-white blankets, presenting a somewhat picturesque appearance. When a large quantity of these clams has been collected, they make a pit, eight or ten feet deep; a quantity of firewood is put in the bottom, and it is then filled up with clams; over the top is laid more firewood, and the whole is covered in with fir-branches. In this way they are boiled for a day or more, according to circumstances. When cooked, they are taken out of the shells, spitted on sticks, three or four feet long, and exposed to the sun to dry, after which they are strung on strips of the inner cypress-bark or pliable reeds, and put away for the winter store. When the Indians return to their winter villages they are strung along the beams, forming a sort of inner roof. Some Europeans profess to like them; but I confess I could never get over their smell, to say nothing of their taste.

The oil obtained from the hou-li-kun is a common article of food among the northern tribes, and one of which they are very fond. This fish is not unlike a sprat, but somewhat longer and rounder, and is so oily that when dried it will burn like a candle. They are not found at the south part of the island, but are caught in great numbers to the northward. The process of extracting the oil from them is very primitive indeed. Mr. Duncan gives in one of his letters the following description of it, as witnessed by him at Nass River:—

" In a general way," he says, " I found each house had a pit near it, about three feet deep and six or eight inches square, filled with the little fish. I found some Indians making boxes to put the grease in, others cutting firewood, and others (women and children) stringing the fish and hanging them up to dry in the sun; while others, and they the greater number, were making fish-grease. The process is as follows: make a large fire, plant four or five heaps of stones as big as your hand in it; while these are heating fill a few baskets with rather stale fish, and get a tub of water into the house. When the stones are red-hot bring a deep box, about 18 inches square (the sides of which are all one piece of wood), near the fire, and put about half a gallon of the fish into it and as much fresh water, then three or four hot stones, using wooden tongs. Repeat the doses again, then stir the whole up. Repeat them again, stir again; take out the cold stones and place them in the fire. Proceed in this way until the box is nearly full, then let the whole cool, and commence skimming off the grease. While this is cooking, prepare another boxful in the same way. In doing the third, use, instead of fresh water, the liquid from the first box. On coming to the refuse of the boiled fish in the box, which is still pretty warm, let it be put into a rough willow-basket; then let an old woman, for the purpose of squeezing the liquid from it, lay it on a wooden grate sufficiently elevated to let a wooden box stand under; then let her lay her naked chest on it and press it with all her weight. On no account must a male undertake to do this. Cast what remains in the basket anywhere near the house, but take the liquid just saved and use it over again, instead of fresh water. The refuse must be allowed to accumulate, and though it will soon become putrid and change into a heap of creeping maggots and give out a smell almost unbearable, it must not be removed. The filth contracted by those engaged in the work must not be washed off until all is over, that is, until all the fish are boiled, and this will take about two or three weeks. All these plans must be carried out without any addition or change, otherwise the fish will be ashamed, and perhaps never come again. So," concludes Mr Duncan, " think and act the poor Indians." *

The sea-cucumber, so well known in the South Seas as the Trepang or Bêche de Mer (Holothuria tubulosa) is much eaten by the natives. Captain Flinders, in his ' Voyage to Terra Australis,' says it is boiled and dried, and traded, when

* Letter to the Church Missionary Society.

thus prepared, with the Chinese. I have never seen the Red Indians dry it, nor have I ever seen it thus prepared in their huts; but I have constantly seen it boiled and eaten fresh. I once tasted some that was just cooked, and found it had much the same consistency as India rubber, but without its flavour. The Indians make some kind of cake of the berries when they are plentiful.

The lichen (L. jubatus) which grows on the pines, is also prepared for food. Twigs, bark, &c., being cleared from it, it is steeped in water till it is quite soft; it is then wrapped up in grass and leaves to prevent its being burnt, and cooked between hot stones. It takes 10 or 12 hours cooking, and when done, while still hot, it is pressed into cakes. Berries when fresh are eaten in a way we should hardly appreciate —viz., with seal-oil! I have seen the Indians land from a canoe and pick a large quantity of beautiful fresh berries, then take a small bowl and pour into it a lot of seal-oil, and, sitting round it, dip each bunch of berries into the oil, and eat them with great apparent relish. They prefer houlikun-oil for this purpose when they can get it.

They have various berries, among them the strawberry and raspberry. They are always very glad to get bread or rice, and these articles of diet are generally exchanged with them for fish. I found when travelling that neither the Coast nor the Inland Indians would ever eat pork. The invariable reply to my questions why they did not do so, being "Wake cumtax Sivash muckermuck cushom" (Indians do not understand how to eat pork).

Many of the ducks eaten commonly by the Indian would be found most unpalatable by white men; indeed of the 24 species existing in this part of the world there is only one, the stock-duck, that can be relied on as being always free from a fishy taste.

None of these tribes are cannibals. An isolated instance

of a man who eats human flesh may be found; but he is generally looked upon with horror and dread by the rest of his people. Still cannibalism is not altogether unknown among them; and instances may be adduced of wretches, who have actually exhumed and eaten human corpses.

For drink they are very fond of tea, and always delighted to get it when travelling, although I have never heard them ask for it in barter. I remember, on leaving a village in Jervis Inlet where my party had been sleeping, that the headman came to me and asked for a little tea for his mother, who, he said, had a bad pain in the face and was very ill. When they can obtain spirits, they will always get drunk; but I think they would rather be without them even when they are at work, travelling or otherwise. I have never yet been asked for spirits by any of a travelling party, but always for tea; and when I had not enough of that to give them, they used to fill up my kettle with water, reboil it, and drink the miserable decoction with the greatest relish. When they cannot get tobacco, the Indians will smoke a small leaf like that of the box-shrub. There is another leaf which they also use for this purpose: to prepare it they pluck a small bough, hold it over the fire for a few minutes, then strip the leaves off and rub them in their hands till fine enough to smoke.

I have previously had occasion to refer to the fashion among the Indians of carving the faces of animals upon the ends of the large beams which support the roofs of their permanent lodges. In addition, it is very usual to find representations of the same animals painted over the front of the lodge. These crests, which are commonly adopted by all the tribes, consist of the whale, porpoise, eagle, raven, wolf, and frog, &c. In connexion with them are some curious and interesting traits of the domestic and social life of the Indians. The relationship between persons of the same crest is considered to be nearer than that of the same tribe; mem-

S

bers of the same tribe may, and do, marry—but those of the same crest are not, I believe, under any circumstances allowed to do so. A Whale, therefore, may not marry a Whale, nor a Frog a Frog. The child again always takes the crest of the mother; so that if the mother be a Wolf, all her children will be Wolves. As a rule also, descent is traced from the mother, not from the father.

At their feasts they never invite any of the same crest as themselves: feasts are given generally for the cementing of friendship or allaying of strife, and it is supposed that people of the same crest cannot quarrel; but I fear this supposition is not always supported by fact. Mr. Duncan, who has considerable knowledge of their social habits, says that the Indian will never kill the animal which he has adopted for his crest, or which belongs to him as his birthright. If he sees another do it he will hide his face in shame, and afterwards demand compensation for the act. The offence is not killing the animal, but doing so before one whose crest it is. They display these crests in other ways besides those I have mentioned, viz., by carving or painting them on their paddles or canoes, by the arrangement of the buttons on their blankets, or by large figures in front of their houses or their tombs. They have another whimsical custom in connexion with these insignia: whenever or wherever an Indian chooses to exhibit his crest, all individuals bearing the same family-figure are bound to do honour to it by casting property before it, in quantities proportionate to the rank and wealth of the giver. A mischievous or poor Indian, therefore, desiring to profit by this social custom, paints his crest upon his forehead, and looks out for an opportunity of meeting a wealthy person of the same family-crest as himself. Upon his approach he advances to meet him, and when near enough displays his crest to the unsuspecting victim; and, however disgusted the latter may be, he has no choice but to make the customary offering of property of some sort or other. In this, as in

many other respects, the Indians are so strangely superstitious
as to allow themselves to be imposed upon by their more astute
and unscrupulous brethren. It is common enough for an
Indian living by his wits to circulate a report, some weeks
before the commencement of the fish or berry season, that
he has had a dream of a large crop of berries, or influx
of salmon to some particular spot, which he will disclose for
a certain present. He will then go through various ceremonies, such, for instance, as walking about at night in lonely
places ; taking care that it shall be publicly known that
he is " working on the hearts of the fish " to be abundant
during the coming season. His supposed influence over the
weather and the inclination of the fish are so readily credited,
that he will in all probability command large prices for his pretended information and intercession. A canoe's crew will often
give a third of their first haul to the " fish-priest " to propitiate
him, and ensure good luck for the rest of the season. The
prophet of course takes care to send them to a place where
fish are generally found in abundance ; and, even should they
be unsuccessful, it is easy for him to assert that they have
done something to offend the Spirits. The habits of the fish
themselves, perhaps, tend to the prevalence of such superstitious fancies ; as they will often quit particular places
altogether for a season, or for several years. Old women,
also, often obtain much influence from the profession of
second-sight and the power of foretelling births, deaths,
marriages, famines, &c. Dreams are generally used as their
machinery for these purposes. They also claim more than
the gift of prophecy, and insist that they can prevent people
they dislike from sharing in the success of the others, and in
many ways influence their lives. It is not uncommon to see
these old witches communicating their dreams to the tribe ;
men and women standing by with open mouths, and impressed
wonder-stricken faces. I take it these poor old creatures
often adopt this profession in the hope of lengthening their

lives; for the Indians are very cruel to the aged, and when they become useless and burdensome to them will often kill them outright or leave them on some small desert island to starve. Thus the poor old creatures will go on gathering clams and berries as long as they can stand, or making themselves useful in some such way, knowing well that their lives are not worth much when they cease to work.

The most influential men in a tribe are the medicine-men. Their initiation into the mysteries of their calling is one of the most disgusting ceremonies imaginable. At a certain season, the Indian who is selected for the office retires into the woods for several days, and fasts, holding intercourse, it is supposed, with the spirits who are to teach him the healing art. He then suddenly reappears in the village, and, in a sort of religious frenzy, attacks the first person he meets and bites a piece out of his arm or shoulder. He will then rush at a dog, and tear him limb from limb, running about with a leg or some part of the animal all bleeding in his hand, and tearing it with his teeth. This mad fit lasts some time, usually during the whole day of his reappearance. At its close he crawls into his tent, or falling down exhausted is carried there by those who are watching him. A series of ceremonials obervances and long incantations follows, lasting for two or three days, and he then assumes the functions and privileges of his office. I have seen three or four medicine-men made at a time among the Indians near Victoria, while twenty or thirty others stood, with loaded muskets, keeping guard all round the place to prevent them doing any mischief. Although a clever medicine-man becomes of great importance in his tribe, his post is no sinecure either before or after his initiation. If he should be seen by any one while he is communing with the spirits in the woods, he is killed or commits suicide; while if he fails in the cure of any man he is liable to be put to death, on the assumption that he did not wish to cure his patient. This penalty is not always inflicted; but, if he fails in his first attempt, the life of a medicine-man is not, as a rule, worth much. The people who are bitten by these maniacs when they come in from the woods consider themselves highly favoured.

The ceremony of curing or trying to cure a sick person is very curious. I give the following description of such a process upon an old woman—a Tyee—in Shoalwater Bay.

" She had been sick some time of liver-complaint, and finding her symptoms grow more exaggerated she sent for a medicine-man to ' mamoke' (work) spells to drive away the ' memmelose' or dead people, who, she said, came to her every night.

" Towards night the doctor came, bringing with him his own and another family to assist in the ceremony. After they had eaten supper, the centre of the lodge was cleaned, and fresh sand strewed upon it. A bright fire of dry wood was then kindled, and a brilliant light kept up by occasionally throwing oil upon it. I considered this to be a species of incense offered, as the same light could have been produced, if desired, by a quantity of pitch-knots, which were lying in the corner. The patient, well wrapped in blankets, was laid on her back, with her head a little elevated and her hands crossed on her breast. The doctor knelt at her feet, and commenced singing a refrain, the subject of which was an address to the dead, asking them why they had come to take his friend and mother, and begging them to go away and leave her. The rest of the people then sang the chorus in a low, mournful chant, keeping time by knocking on the roof with long wands they held. The burden of the chorus was to beg the dead to leave them. As the performance proceeded, the doctor got more and more excited, singing loudly and violently, with great gesticulation, and occasionally making passes with his hand over the face and person of the patient, similar to those made by mesmeric manipulators; a constant accompaniment being kept up by the others with their low chant and beating with their sticks. The patient soon fell asleep, and the performance ceased. She slept a short time, and woke refreshed. This was repeated several times during the night, and kept up for three days; but it was found that the patient grew no better, and another doctor was sent for, who soon came with his family of three or four persons, the first doctor remaining, as the more persons they have to sing the better.

" 'Old John,' as the last doctor was usually called, had no sooner partaken of food than he sat down at the feet of the patient, covering himself completely with his blanket. He remained in this position three or four hours, without moving or speaking. He was communing with the 'To-man-na-was,' or familiar spirit.

" When he was ready, he commenced singing in a loud and harsh manner, making most vehement gesticulations. He then knelt on the patient's body, pressing his clenched fists into her sides and breast till it seemed to me the woman must be killed. Every few seconds he would scoop his hands together as if he had caught something, then turning towards the fire would blow through his fingers, as though he had something in them he wished to cast into the flames. The fire was kept stirred up, so as to have plenty of embers, on which, it appeared, he was trying to burn the evil spirit he was exorcising. There was no oil put on the fire this time, for the Indians told me they put on oil to light up their lodge, to let their dead friends see they had plenty, and were happy, and did not wish to go with them; but now all they wanted was to have the fire hot enough to burn the 'skokeen' or evil spirit the doctor was trying to expel. The pounding and singing were kept up the same as at the first performance. Old John sang to his 'To-man-na-was' to aid him;

then, addressing the supposed spirit, he by turns coaxed, cajoled, and threatened to induce him to depart. But all was of no avail, for in two days the woman died." *

At all the feasts the chiefs and heads of families give away and destroy a great deal of property; this raises them greatly in the estimation of their own and the people of other tribes summoned to the feast. Individuals and even tribes will sometimes travel 100 miles or more to be at the feasts of another tribe. The whole object of amassing wealth, indeed, seems to be for the gratification of afterwards destroying it in public. I was at a feast once where 800 blankets were said to have been destroyed by one man. I saw three sea-otter skins, for one of which 30 blankets had been offered and refused a few days previously, cut up into little bits about the size of two fingers, and distributed among the guests. In the interchange of presents the same crests never give to or receive from each other. I say, in the ' interchange :' for in making a present an Indian always has in view the return that will be made him. Indeed, should an Indian make you a present at a feast, and you omit to repay the compliment by presenting him with something equally valuable at the next feast, he will not hesitate to demand his gift back again. Mr. Duncan speaks thus of the *religious* feasts, and, among other customs, of the destruction of property on such occasions :—

" Their greatest luxury at such times is rice and molasses : their second dish of importance is berries and grease. Now and then I hear of a rum-feast being given, which is generally succeeded by quarrelling and sometimes murder. They are very particular about whom they invite to their feasts, and, on great occasions, men and women feast separately, the women always taking the precedence. Vocal music and dancing have great prominence in their proceedings. When a person

* ' Three Years in Shoalwater Bay,' by T. Swan.

is going to give a great feast, he sends, on the first day, the females of his household round the camp to invite all his female friends. The next day a party of men is sent round to call the male guests together. The other day, a party of eight or ten females, dressed in their best, with their faces newly painted, came into the Fort-yard, formed themselves into a semicircle; then the one in the centre, with a loud but clear and musical voice, delivered the invitation, declaring what should be given to the guests, and what they should enjoy. In this case the invitation was for three women in the Fort who are related to chiefs. On the following day a band of men came and delivered a similar message, inviting the captain in charge.

"These feasts are generally connected with the giving away of property. As an instance, I will relate the last occurrence of the kind. The person who sent the aforementioned invitations is a chief who has just completed building a house. After feasting, I heard he was to give away property to the amount of 480 blankets (worth as many pounds to him), of which 180 were his own property and the 300 were to be subscribed by his people. On the first day of the feast, as much as possible of the property to be given him was exhibited in the camp. Hundreds of yards of cotton were flapping in the breeze, hung from house to house, or on lines put up for the occasion. Furs, too, were nailed up on the fronts of houses. Those who were going to give away blankets or elk-skins managed to get a bearer for every one, and exhibited them by making the persons walk in single file to the house of the chief. On the next day the cotton which had been hung out was now brought on the beach, at a good distance from the chief's house, and then run out at full length, and a number of bearers, about three yards apart, bore it triumphantly away from the giver to the receiver. I suppose that about 600 to 800 yards were thus disposed of.

"After all the property the chief is to receive has thus

been openly handed to him, a day or two is taken up in apportioning it for fresh owners. When this done, all the chiefs and their families are called together, and each receives according to his or her portion. If, however, a chief's wife is not descended from a chief, she has no share in this distribution, nor is she ever invited to the same feasts with her husband. Thus do the chiefs and their people go on reducing themselves to poverty. In the case of the chiefs, however, this poverty lasts but a short time: they are soon replenished from the next giving away, but the people only grow rich again according to their industry. One cannot but pity them, while one laments their folly.

"All the pleasure these poor Indians seem to have in their property is in hoarding it up for such an occasion as I have described. They never think of appropriating what they gather to enhance their comforts, but are satisfied if they can make a display like this now and then; so that the man possessing but one blanket seems to be as well off as the one who possesses twenty; and thus it is that there is a vast amount of dead stock accumulated in the camp doomed never to be used, but only now and then to be transferred from hand to hand for the mere vanity of the thing.

"There is another way, however, in which property is disposed of even more foolishly. If a person be insulted, or meet with an accident, or in any way suffer an injury, real or supposed, either of mind or body, property must at once be sacrificed to avoid disgrace. A number of blankets, shirts, or cotton, according to the rank of the person, is torn into small pieces and carried off."

The numberless antics practised at these feasts would take far more space to describe than I can devote to them. I believe, however, there is some system in them, and that much which appears to us sheer folly has a meaning and a purpose to these poor creatures. Their sacred feasts are of several kinds, but the most common is that which takes

place at the commencement of each season, to invoke the aid
of the deity for fine weather, plenty of fish, &c. &c. A
glimpse of one of these is given by the Rev. Mr. Garrett (of
whom I shall have occasion to speak hereafter in connection with the missions to the Indians), in a letter to his
brother:—

" *Dec.* 16.—When crossing the bridge to the Indian School
to-day, I was astonished by a very loud noise proceeding from
one of the houses of the Songhies. Guided by the sound, I
entered the house to see what was going on. For a time, so
great was the din, I could make nothing of it. At length, by
force of inquiry, and pressing through the crowd to the front,
I witnessed the following scene. A space, about 40 feet by
20 feet, had been carefully swept; three large bright fires
were burning upon the earthen floor; round three sides of
this space a bench was fixed, upon which were packed, as
close as they could fit, a crowd of young women. I do not
think there were any men or boys among them, but there
being only the light of the fires, I could not see very distinctly.
Each of these individuals was armed with two sticks. In front
of them, extending all the way round the rectangular space,
was a breadth of white calico. Under this calico the row of
sticks exhibited themselves. Upon the ground, in the corner
on my right, was a young man provided with a good-sized box,
which he had fixed upon an angle and used as a drum. Also,
on the ground, still nearer to me, sat an old man and an old
woman; and flat upon the ground, apparently dead, lay a
female chief, with her head-reclining in the lap of the old
crone; while around me there stood a motley crowd of all
tribes, staring first at me and then at the *stage*. All this time
the choir upon the benches kept up a sort of mixture between
a howl and a wail, while they beat time upon the bench with
the forest of sticks with which they were armed; our friend
upon the ground making his wooden drum eloquent of noise.
It is utterly vain to attempt to give any description of the

terrible noise which was thus occasioned. This continuing for about twenty minutes, the female chief began to show signs of life; first, by a slight motion of the hands, then of the arms, then of the shoulders, and so on, until her whole frame became violently agitated; the din and the uproar increasing in intensity as her agitation increased. At length she shook herself into a sitting position, when, with hair dishevelled and glaring eyes, she formed a singularly repulsive spectacle. Her agitation increased, until there could have been no part of her body which did not shake—the storm and rattle of sticks and the howling unmeaning wail steadily keeping pace with her—when, suddenly, at a motion of her hand, there was an instantaneous silence. They watched her narrowly and her every motion was observed. Upon a signal they began again, and stopped as suddenly. At length she got upon her *hunkers,* and in that not very graceful position jumped about between the fires. Presently, as her inspiration increased, she raised herself and ultimately got herself erect. Having, then, by a series of very ungraceful motions, completed a journey round the fires, she came to a stand at the end of the rectangle next which the old man and woman were sitting. . . . This being done, such a clatter and rattle and yell were raised as nearly deafened me. . . . My time being now exhausted, I was obliged to leave this strange but interesting scene. . . .

"It was refreshing to breathe the sea-air again and gaze upon the light of day, after emerging from so unearthly a place. Pursuing my way, I met a man carrying two large boilers. I cross-examined him, and ascertained that the female chief, who was playing her part within among the women, would presently give an abundant feast of wild-fowl to all the men, and that he was bringing down the boilers to cook the same. He further stated that all the men were assembled in his house, awaiting the gift, and that, if I wished, he would gladly show me where they were. I accompanied him joyfully. I found a very large house, carefully swept, with several good fires burning brightly upon the earthen floor, and about fifty or sixty men assembled, in patient expectation of the birds. I inquired into the nature of the musical entertainment going on. They told me that was their ",Tamānoes," or sacred feast; that they always played and danced so during the latter half of the last month in the year; that they did so for two reasons—first, to make their hearts good for the coming year, and secondly, to bring plenty of *rain*, instead of *snow*; that if they did not do so, a great deal of *snow* would come, and they should be very much *afraid*."

At their grand feasts and ceremonies some of the chief men wear very curious masks and dresses—the former composed of the heads of animals decorated with feathers, and painted various colours. At Fort Rupert, "Whale," one of the Quawguult chiefs, showed me his masks, which he kept carefully locked up in a large box. One in particular was most extraordinary: it was a wooden head, large enough to take his own inside easily, and I think meant for an eagle; the mouth was very large, and could be opened by strings, which were carried through the top of the mask and down the back, so as to be worked by the wearer's hands. I have seen others with strings to make the wings flap, and to turn the head from side to side.

On all occasions of peace-making, whether it be feast or palaver, the chiefs cover their heads with eagles' down and scatter it about them and over the person with whom they are making peace. I have seen this done on several occasions and under different circumstances. With them, as with us, white always denotes peace. For example, the Indians, whom we employed on board as interpreters, always put white feathers in their caps when going among a strange tribe. Mr. Duncan also speaks of this occurring at their reception of him on two different occasions.

He says:—"Much to my sorrow, he (the chief) put on his

dancing-mask and robes. The leading singers stepped out, and soon all were engaged in a spirited chant. They kept excellent time by clapping their hands and beating a drum. (I found out afterwards that they had been singing my praises, and asking me to pity them and do them good.) The chief Kahdoonahah danced with all his might during the singing. He wore a cap which had a mask in front, set with mother-of-pearl and trimmed with porcupine-quills. The quills enabled him to hold a quantity of white birds' down on the top of his head, which he ejected while dancing by jerking his head forward; thus he soon appeared as if in a shower of snow. In the middle of the dance a man approached me with a handful of down and blew it over my head, thus symbolically uniting me in friendship with all the chiefs present and the tribes they severally represented."

On another occasion he says :—" The usual course was pursued. Kinsahdad dressed himself up in his robes, and then danced while the people sang and clapped their hands. During the performance I was nearly covered with white downy feathers. A man, after having feathered Kinsahdad's head, came and blew a handful over me. One great feature of the dance was that the performer should keep a cloud of feathers flying about his guest. It was done in this way : the dancer, after making a graceful approach, would commence a retreat, still keeping his face toward me, and, in perfect time with the song and clapping of hands, jerk his head forward at every step, and thus keep a quantity of feathers flying from his head-dress."

The reader will notice in these extracts, and in all that has been said about the Indian feasts, a curious distinction between the customs of the West and those of the East. Here it is always the men, and the chief men, who dance and take a part in all the antics, while in the East the women are the performers. I have never seen an Indian woman dance at a feast, and believe it is seldom if ever done. The young men sit round and look on with awe at what Easterns would regard as beneath the dignity of man. So with work: the woman of the West is a slave, performing the most menial offices, while the woman of the East lives a life of luxurious idleness.

On missions of peace also this down is, as I have said, made use of. One day in talking to Mr. Bamfield, the Indian agent on the West coast of Vancouver Island, who has resided among the Ohyat tribe several years, we were comparing many of the Indian customs with those of Europe, and he told me that on the occasion of a quarrel between the Ohyat and another tribe, a chief, who was one of the best speakers among them, was employed for several days as envoy, going frequently to the enemy's camp to negociate, and that his diplomacy averted war. During the whole time of the negociations the peace-maker wore eagles' down all over his head, so that he looked as if he had been powdered, and eagles' feathers in his cap, or secured to a band round his head. I remember Mr. Bamfield mentioning another occasion, on which they came to blows, as illustrative of the systematicmethod of their approach and attack. The Ohyats and Nootkas joined forces against the Clayoquots; and Mr. Bamfield accompanied them part of the way. When they approached the Clayoquot village they were to attack, they put into a sandy beach and landed: the chiefs then held a consultation with those who knew the place best, and having hit upon a young man who had a Clayoquot wife, told him to draw a plan of the place on the sand. He commenced by marking out the ground, then the houses; describing the partitions in them, how many men were in each, whether they were brave or cowardly: in fact, describing the place accurately. They then divided the work between the two tribes, and, standing back to back some little way apart, the chiefs told off each man to his duty. Everything, he said, was perfectly arranged. The attack was, however, not successful, as

INDIAN BURIAL-GROUND

Page 271

the Nootkas failed in their part and would not leave their canoes. The Ohyats took 18 heads, and lost about the same number. The cause of the war was that the Clayoquots had murdered a white man, and tried to put the blame on the others, among whom he was living.

As a rule, the Indians burn their dead, and then bury the ashes. The mode of depositing these remains differs even among members of the same tribes. Sometimes they are buried in the ground, sometimes in trees, in boxes or in canoes. There is, I think, no rule or rules observed in sepulture. I have seen more suspended among the branches of the trees than buried in the ground, but their mode of sepulture depends very much upon convenience and circumstances. More are laid on the ground than in it, for the Indians have, I believe, a decided objection to interment —whether from any idea of a resurrection or not, I cannot say. When buried on the ground, they are generally placed among the bushes on some small islet, and the top of the box is always covered with large stones. We used quite commonly to come across the bleached bones when putting up surveying-stations. It is very common for a man's property to be buried with him, or suspended over his grave. In the case of great men the latter course is, I think, chosen generally for the purpose of showing their wealth. I have seen the grave of a chief inland with a number of blankets cut in strips hanging over it, several pairs of trowsers, and two or three muskets. At Nanaimo there is a small hut built over the remains of the late chief. In the case of a chief it is also customary to paint or carve his crest on the box in which his bones lie, or to affix it on a large sign-board upon a pole or neighbouring tree. Mr. Duncan says that if the crest of the deceased happens to be an eagle or a raven, it is usual among the Northern Indians to carve it in the act of flying—the bird being affixed to the edge of the box with its wings spread, so that it appears to a passer-by as if just about to leave the coffin; and he (Mr. Duncan) very naturally asks whether this may come of any knowledge of a resurrection of the dead among the Indians.

They will not usually let strangers witness the burial of their dead. It was at one time not uncommon for Indians to desert for ever a lodge in which one of their family had died; but this rarely, if ever, happens now.

The rites of mourning are carried out strictly, but not until the corpse is buried. After this, at sunrise and sunset, they wail and sing dirges for the space of some thirty days.

I never witnessed a funeral myself; but I think that, except when the person to be buried is of some rank, there is very little ceremony.

At Fort Simpson it appears to be the regular custom to burn the dead, but this is departed from in some cases; for Mr. Duncan mentions witnessing a funeral there from the Fort Gallery. He says: "The deceased was a chief's daughter, who had died suddenly. Contrary to the custom of the Indians *here* (who always burn their dead), the chief begged permission to inter her remains in the Fort Garden, alongside her mother, who was buried a short time ago, and was the first Indian thus privileged. The corpse was placed in a rude box, and borne on the shoulders of four men. About twenty Indians, principally women, accompanied the old chief (whose heart seemed ready to burst) to the grave. A bitter wailing was kept up for three-quarters of an hour, during which time about seven or eight men, after a good deal of clamour (which strangely contrasted with the apparent grief of the mourners), fixed up a pole at the head of the grave, on which was suspended an Indian garment. At the head of the mother's grave several drinking-vessels were attached, as well as a garment.

It is certain that the Indians have some idea of a Superior Being; and this idea, no doubt, dates before the appearance of any priests among them. They believe, too, that thunder is

his voice. I remember on one occasion, when I was travelling in a canoe during a violent thunderstorm, that, at
each peal, all the rowers rested on their paddles, and said a
prayer, taught them, no doubt, by the Romish priests, and I
could not get them to paddle on till they had finished it.

After a storm on the coast, they always search for dead
whales, and seem to connect them in some way with thunder.
It is very difficult indeed to get at any of their traditions,
and still more difficult to distinguish between their own
standard doctrines and the teaching of the priests. One of
the settlers on the west coast of Vancouver Island, who has
been there for a number of years, told me that there was at
Ohyat a carving of two eagles with a dove in their centre
and two serpents in the rear, with a whale seemingly seeking
protection from the serpents. This carving representing
thunder, under its native name Tuturrh, was held in great
respect by them. An old half-breed once told me that one of
their legends was that crows were white once, but were made
black by a curse: what they had done to deserve this
punishment I could not ascertain.

The Indians appear generally to have some tradition about
the Flood. Mr. Duncan mentions that the Tsimsheans say that
all people perished in the water but a few. Amongst that few
there were no Tsimsheans; and now they are at a loss to tell
how they have reappeared as a race. In preaching at Obser-
vatory Inlet he referred to the Flood, and this led the chief
to tell him the following story. He said: "We have a tradition about the swelling of the water a long time ago. As you
are going up the river you will see the high mountain to the
top of which a few of our forefathers escaped when the waters
rose, and thus were saved. But many more were saved in
their canoes, and were drifted about and scattered in every
direction. The waters went down again; the canoes rested
on the land, and the people settled themselves in the various
spots whither they had been driven. Thus it is the Indians

T

are found spread all over the country; but they all understand the same songs and have the same customs, which
shows that they are one people."

Schoolcraft, the American writer, in his 'History of the
Indians,' narrates a similar tradition, which is found current
on the east side of the Rocky Mountains.

As their languages become more known, many other
legends and traditions will doubtless come to light; but I
must not conclude this notice of them without reference to
the most interesting yet known, viz., a belief in the Son of
God. "This [Observatory Inlet] being" (says Mr. Duncan)
" a noted place, the Indians have several legends connected
with the various objects about. I listened to some, and remarked that in most of them the *Son of the Chief above* occupies the place of benefactor or hero, and most-of the acts
ascribed to him are acts of mercy. It was he, they say, that
first brought the small fish to this inlet for them, which now
forms one of their principal articles of food."

As I have before said, the Roman Catholic priests have, so
far as regards forms and the observance of certain religious
customs, done a good deal among them. I remember one
Sunday in Port Harvey, Johnstone Strait, when we were
all standing on deck, on a bright sunny morning just before
church-time, looking at six or eight large canoes which
hung about the ship, they suddenly struck up a chant, which
they continued for about ten minutes, singing in beautiful
time, their voices sounding over the perfectly still water
and dying away among the trees with a sweet cadence that I
shall never forget. I have no idea what the words were, but
they told us they had been taught them by the priests. The
Roman Catholic priest, indeed, has little cause to complain
of his reception by the Indians. On the west coast, at a
place where the priest had been before, but had not time to
revisit them, he sent his shovel-hat in the canoe in his stead;
and upon its arrival the whole village turned out, shouting

"Le Prêtre! Le Prêtre!" and had prayers at once upon the spot. I have seen other Indians, on the priest's arrival among them, cease their fishing and other occupations, and hurry to meet him.

At Esquimalt all the Indians attend the Romish mission on Sunday morning, and at eight o'clock the whole village may be seen paddling across the harbour to the mission-house, singing at the top of their voices. Certainly the self-denying zeal and energy with which the priests labour among them merit all the success they meet with. To come upon them, as I have done, going from village to village alone among the natives, in a dirty little canoe, drenched to the skin, forces comparisons between them and the generality of the labourers of other creeds that are by no means flattering to the latter.

Perhaps the worst failing of the Red man, next to his love of fire-water, is his passion for gambling. Most of them will gamble away everything they have—houses, wives, property, all are staked upon the chances of their favourite games. If in passing their village at night you leave them sitting in a ring gambling, the chances are that, upon your return in the morning, you will find them at it still. I have only seen two games played by them, in both of which the object was to guess the spot where a small counter happened to be. In one of these games the counter was held in the player's hands, which he kept swinging backwards and forwards. Every now and then he would stop, and some one would guess in which hand he held the counter, winning of course if he guessed right. The calm intensity and apparent freedom from excitement, with which they watch the progress of this game is perfect, and you only know the intense anxiety they really feel by watching their faces and the twitching of their limbs. The other game consisted of two blankets spread out upon the ground, and covered with saw-dust about an inch thick. In this was placed the counter, a piece of bone or iron about the size of half-a-crown, and one of the players shuffled it about, the others in turn guessing where it was.   These games are usually played by ten or twelve men, who sit in a circle, with the property to be staked, if, as is usual, it consists of blankets or clothes, near them.   Chanting is very commonly kept up during the game, probably to allay the excitement.   I never saw women gamble.

The Indians are well known to be polygamists, but I believe that a plurality of wives is general only among the chiefs of tribes, the rest being commonly too poor to afford this luxury.   No other cause for any such abstinence on their part exists.   When Mr. Stain was the Colonial Chaplain at Victoria, the chief of the tribe residing there went to him for some medicine for his wife, who was ill.   He gave him something which cured her, and, to the astonishment of the chaplain and his family, a day or two afterwards the chief came to his house, leading his wife by the hand, and, in gratitude for her recovery, presented her to his benefactor.   On being remonstrated with, I believe, by the chaplain's wife, who objected, not at all unnaturally, to the nature of the offering, he said it was nothing, not worth mentioning in fact, as he could easily spare her, she being one of eleven !

I have said that intrigue with the wives of men of other tribes is one of the commonest causes of quarrel among the Indians.   This is not surprising, when it is considered, among other things, that marriage is entirely a buying and selling process, and the bargain is frequently made when the principals are children.   The man or his friends give so many blankets for the wife, while yet a child. If when she grows up she refuses to marry the man who has purchased her, she or her friends must return all the property paid for her ; if they cannot do this, she is obliged to go to the buyer.   There is generally a feast at the wedding of any one of importance in a tribe ; but this, I think,

INDIAN GIRL, SHOWING CONICAL FORM OF SKULL.

Page 277

depends entirely on the wealth of bride and bridegroom, much as in our own country.

In appearance the Indians of Vancouver Island have the common facial characteristics of low foreheads, high cheek-bones, aquiline noses, and large mouths. They all have their heads flattened more or less; some tribes, however, cultivating this peculiarity more than others. The process of flattening the head is effected while they are infants, and is very disgusting. I once made a woman uncover a baby's head, and its squashed elongated appearance nearly made me sick. By far the most flattened heads belong to the tribe of Quatsino Indians, living at the north-west end of the island. Those who have only seen the tribes of the east side of the island may be inclined to think the sketch of this girl exaggerated, but it was really drawn by measurement, and she was found to have 18 inches of solid flesh from her eyes to the top of her head. It does not appear that the process at all interferes with their intellectual capacities. Among some of the tribes pretty women may be seen: nearly all have good eyes and hair, but the state of filth in which they live generally neutralises any natural charms they may possess.

Half-breeds, as a rule, inherit, I am afraid, the vices of both races: I speak of the uneducated half-breed, to whose Indian abandonment to vice and utter want of self-control appears to be added that boldness and daring in evil which he inherits from his white parent.

The Indian's head is generally large, often so large as to be somewhat out of proportion to the rest of his frame. Men and women both part their hair in the middle, and wear it long, hanging over the shoulder. The hair is generally good, but so neglected that it looks, and is, very dirty. The custom of painting prevails among all Indians in North America. They paint the face in hideous designs of black and red (the only colours used), and the parting of the hair is also coloured red. I have seen them when travelling, and when I knew they had not washed for three weeks, take the greatest pains in colouring their faces, oiling their hair with fish-oil, and painting the parting. The northern males sometimes wear their hair cut short, or rolled up into a sort of ball on the top of the head ; but the southern tribes consider it a disgrace to have short hair. A Barclay Sound lad, whom we took on board the 'Hecate,' and who had been persuaded to have his hair cut, said he could not go back to his tribe until it had grown again.

The men very seldom have beards or moustaches, and are in the habit of pulling out any hair that appears on their faces. This beardlessness appertains to almost all the North American Indians, and I believe not to them only, as the natives of the Congo, who are very fine men, have no hair on their faces. The hair of their heads is almost always dark brown, though sometimes an Albino is seen with quite white hair. The strong feature in all their faces is their eyes. which are nearly always fine, and among the half-breeds very beautiful.

Their constant diet of dry fish, &c., has the curious effect of destroying the teeth, so that you hardly ever see an Indian over middle age with any visible, having worn them down level with the gums.

Some Indians, especially the tribes of Queen Charlotte Islands, carve very well, and much of their leisure time is spent in decorating their canoes and paddles, making dishes and spoons in wood or slate, bracelets and rings of metal. They make busts out of whales' teeth, that are in some cases very faithful likenesses. Like the Chinese, they imitate literally anything that is given them to do; so that if you give them a cracked gun-stock to copy, and do not warn them, they will in their manufacture repeat the blemish. Many of their slate-carvings are very good indeed, and their designs most curious.

One of their strangest prejudices, which appears to pervade

all tribes alike, is a dislike to telling their names—thus you never get a man's right name from himself; but they will tell each other's names without hesitation.

I have previously mentioned that slavery is universally practised among these tribes, and the subsequent extracts from Mr. Duncan's Journal will show with what horrid cruelty their captives are treated—indeed, it often happens that some crime is atoned for by a present of three or four slaves, who are butchered in cold blood.

I have also spoken of the intense hatred of them all for the "Boston men." * This hatred, although caused chiefly by the cruelty with which they are treated by them, is also owing in a great measure to the system adopted by the Americans, of moving them away from their own villages when their sites become settled by whites. The Indians often express dread lest we should adopt the same course, and have lately petitioned Governor Douglas on the subject.

Their phraseology abounds in highly figurative and flowery expressions. It is so little known, however, as yet, that anything like an accurate account is impossible. In illustration, I will, however, quote from Mr. Duncan's Journal an account given him by an Indian, of the first appearance of white men among his people, the Keethratlah Indians, near Fort Simpson. "One very old man," he writes, "with characteristic animation, related to me the tradition of the first appearance of the whites near this place. It was as follows:—'A large canoe of Indians were busy catching halibut in one of these channels. A thick mist enveloped them. Suddenly they heard a noise as if a large animal were striking through the water. Immediately they concluded that a monster from the deep was in pursuit of them. With all speed they hauled up their fishing-lines, seized the paddles, and strained every nerve to reach the shore. Still the

* Americans.

plunging noise came nearer. Every minute they expected to be ingulphed within the jaws of some huge creature. However, they reached the land, jumped on shore, and turned round in breathless anxiety to watch the approach of the monster. Soon a boat filled with strange-looking men emerged from the mist. The pulling of the oars had caused the strange noise. Though somewhat relieved of fear, the Indians stood spell-bound with amazement.

" 'The strangers landed, and beckoned the Indians to come to them and bring them some fish. One of them had over his shoulder what was supposed only to be a stick: presently he pointed it to a bird that was flying past—a violent poo went forth—down came the bird to the ground. The Indians died!—as they revived, they questioned each other as to their state whether any were dead, and what each had felt.

" 'The whites then made signs for a fire to be lighted; the Indians proceeded at once, according to their usual tedious practice, of rubbing two sticks together. The strangers laughed, and one of them, snatching up a handful of dry grass, struck a spark into a little powder placed under it. Instantly another poo!—and a blaze. The Indians died! After this the newcomers wanted some fish boiled: the Indians, therefore, put the fish and water into one of their square wooden buckets, and set some stones on the fire; intending, when they were hot, to cast them into the vessel, and thus boil the food. The whites were not satisfied with this way: one of them fetched a tin kettle out of the boat, put the fish and some water into it—and then, strange to say, set it on the fire. The Indians looked on with astonishment. However, the kettle did not consume; the water did not run into the fire. Then, again, the Indians died!

" 'When the fish was eaten, the strangers put a kettle of rice on the fire; the Indians looked at each other, and whispered *Akshahn, akshahn!* or, "Maggots, maggots!" The rice being

cooked, some molasses was produced and mixed with it.
The Indians stared and said, *Coutree um tsakah ahket,* or
"The grease of dead people."

"'The whites then tendered the rice and molasses to the
Indians; but they only shrank away in disgust. Seeing this,
to prove their integrity, they sat down and enjoyed it themselves. The sight stunned the Indians, and again they all
died. Some other similar wonders were worked, and the
profound stupor which the Indians felt each time to come
over them, they termed death.

"'The Indians' turn had now come to make the white
strangers die; they dressed their heads, and painted their
faces. A *Nok-nok* or wonder-working spirit possessed them:
they came slowly and solemnly, seated themselves before the
whites, then suddenly lifted up their heads and stared; their
reddened eyes had the desired effect—the whites died!'"

The "heart" is the word always used by them in speaking
of motive, disposition, or feelings. If a person is angry, they
say—"His heart is bad to them." If they wish to express
their kind feelings or intentions, they say—"Their heart is
very good towards you." And if the fish leave a place
where they are usually caught, or it is a bad season, they
say the fishes' hearts are bad.

All the Indians, both men and women, wear ornaments in
the ears, nose, and lips. These are made of shell or bone;
the commonest earrings worn by almost all, are bits of
a blue shell like the inside of an oyster, and called in
trade "kopose." Rings of the same material passed through
the cartilage of the nose are very common: the northern
tribes wear also very generally a small round shell, called
the "hai-qua," in appearance not unlike a piece of clay-
pipe stem one or two inches long, stuck into their lower
lips at an angle of 45° with the chin. Some also wear a
piece of bone inside the lower lip, making it project in a
horridly ugly way. Preparation for this, of course, has to be

commenced while the "patient" is young: they first bore a
hole in the hollow of the under lip, in which is put a piece of
silver the shape of a pen. After some time this is taken out
and an oval-shaped piece of wood inserted horizontally; after
a time this becomes too small, and a larger piece is inserted,
till, as a woman gets towards old age, she will have a piece
of wood three inches long and two inches wide in the lip.
Fortunately this custom is only practised among the northern
tribes, for it makes a woman the most hideous creature
imaginable. The lip-piece is concave on both sides, while the
edge is grooved so as to keep it in its place; this sometimes
answers the purpose of a spoon, and Mr. Duncan says he has
seen an old woman put her food on it for a few seconds while
it cooled, and then raising her lip, empty this semi-natural
platter into her mouth. This lip, he says, is considered a
mark of honour among these poor creatures: a woman's
rank among women—that is, as far as her word, opinion,
or advice is concerned—is settled according to the size
of her wooden lip; so that if a young woman dares to
quarrel with an old one, the latter will not remind her
of her youth, inexperience, and consequent unfitness to
dictate to age, but will reproach her with the inferior
size of her lip. Red is the colour most commonly used
in painting the face; but sometimes black is applied. I
have seen three or four canoes full of Haida Indians (from
Queen Charlotte Island), each canoe holding 16 or 18 people,
all black as my hat. The face is sometimes tatooed, but
not so commonly as on the eastern side of the continent.
For dress many now wear shirts and trowsers, purchased at
the stations of the Hudson Bay Company; but the normal
style is still a blanket brought round the body, and pinned
with a wooden skewer on the shoulder, or held by the hand.
On my first visit to this place, this was rather a picturesque
costume, as they mostly wore native blankets made of dogs'
hair, and stained various colours; but now they use English

blankets, and as they are always very dirty, the near effect is
not pleasant, though they still look picturesque at a distance.
Very small feet and well-made hands are common among
them ; as a rule, they all go bare-footed and bare-headed,
though, as I have before mentioned, when travelling they
wear mocassins. These are of no use, however, for keeping
out wet ; for, being made of plain deer-skin, they soon get
quite soft and sloppy. No doubt many of the diseases so
common among them are attributable to constant wet feet.
Sometimes they wear caps or tie handkerchiefs round their
heads, and in wet weather they frequently wear mushroom-
shaped hats made of the bark of the thuja, cut in narrow strips,
plaited much like Panama straw, and painted with various
devices. Their canoes are of all sizes, from frail things a man
can hardly find room to sit in, to boats large enough to hold
30 or 40 people with their equipment. They are all made of
single trees, although sometimes the very large ones have a
bow and stern tacked on. After they cut the tree down
they burn out the inside, and then finish it off and shape it
with axe and knife. The models of some are beautiful, their
shape and fashion varying according to the place they are
required for. Thus all the Indians inside the island and
northward of it have round and pointed sterns, while in the
Strait of Fuca and on west coast of the island they have
straight-up and down sterns, each being adapted to the
waters in which they are used. The birch-bark canoes, made
from the bark of Betula papyracea, and so celebrated in the
interior and east of the Rocky Mountains are unknown, or at
least unused, on the coast.

I must not omit to mention that most of the Indians
are good shots at a fixed object; but they never think
of firing at a bird on the wing. Nothing excites their
admiration more than to see birds shot flying; but I could
never get them to try it. No doubt a great reason for
this is their scanty supply of powder and shot; they are

always begging for these, and will barter almost anything for
them. Their mode of approaching wild-fowl is very curious
and characteristic: a man will take a small canoe and fill
the bows with branches of evergreens, so as completely to
conceal himself seated behind it. Through the middle of
this *hedge* he points his gun, letting the barrel rest along the
stem of the canoe. He then paddles the canoe very quietly
along in the direction of a number of birds sitting on the
water, taking care to keep the bows straight towards them:
the birds are very sharp, and will swim across the canoe
to ascertain if there is any deception; but as they all go
one way, the man is able to keep the canoe facing them,
and they fancy it is a floating bush. So careful are these
men of their powder, however, that they are not generally
content to get within shot of one bird, but will manœuvre
about till they can get two or three in a line. I have seen
them devote half a day to this, perhaps only firing once in
several hours.

For vermin they set traps with large stones, very like our
brick traps, except that they are open at both ends; this is
put in some place where the animal is in the habit of
passing, and falls on him as he runs under it.

To shoot deer, they usually ascertain the spot on some
stream where the animals go to drink; they then select the
first hollow tree within shot of the trail, and build up the
entrance to it with bushes so as to shelter themselves from
view. Towards evening or before dawn, they ensconce themselves in this tree, from whence they get a deliberate shot at
the unsuspecting animal as he passes.

The value of the following extracts from Mr. Duncan's
letters to the Church Missionary Society respecting these
Coast Indians is so great that, lengthy as they are, I will
make no excuse for giving them to the reader.

"Sometimes slaves have to be sacrificed to satiate the
vanity of their owners, or take away reproach. Only the

other day we were called upon to witness a terrible scene of
this kind.   An old chief, in cool blood, ordered a slave to be
dragged to the beach, murdered, and thrown into the water.
His orders were quickly obeyed.   The victim was a poor
woman.   Two or three reasons are assigned for this foul act :
one is, that it is to take away the disgrace attached to his
daughter, who has been suffering some time from a ball
wound in the arm.   Another report is, that he does not
expect his daughter to recover, so he has killed his slave in
order that she may prepare for the coming of his daughter
into the unseen world.   I think the former reason is the most
probable.

"I did not see the murder, but, immediately after, I saw
crowds of people running out of those houses near to where
the corpse was thrown, and forming themselves into groups
at a good distance away.   This I learnt was from fear of
what was to follow.   Presently two bands of furious wretches
appeared, each headed by a man in a state of nudity.   They
gave vent to the most unearthly sounds, and the two naked
men made themselves look as unearthly as possible, proceeding in a creeping kind of stoop, and stepping like two proud
horses, at the same time shooting forward each arm alter-
nately, which they held out at full length for a little time in
the most defiant manner.   Besides this, the continual jerking
their heads back, causing their long black hair to twist about,
added much to their savage appearance.

"For some time they pretended to be seeking the body,
and the instant they came where it lay they commenced
screaming and rushing round it like so many angry wolves.
Finally they seized it, dragged it out of the water, and laid
it on the beach, where I was told the naked men would commence tearing it to pieces with their teeth.   The two bands
of men immediately surrounded them, and so hid their horrid
work.   In a few minutes the crowd broke again into two,
when each of the naked cannibals appeared with half of the

body in his hands. Separating a few yards, they commenced,
amid horrid yells, their still more horrid feast. The sight
was too terrible to behold. I left the gallery with a depressed
heart. I may mention that the two bands of savages just
alluded to belong to that class which the whites term 'medicine men.' The superstitions connected with this fearful
system are deeply rooted here; and it is the admitting and
initiating of fresh pupils into these arts that employ numbers,
and excite and interest all, during the winter months. This
year I think there must have been eight or ten parties of
them, but each party seldom has more than one pupil at once.
In relating their proceedings I can give but a faint conception of the system as a whole, but still a little will serve to
show the dense darkness that rests on this place.

"I may mention that each party has some characteristics
peculiar to itself; but, in a more general sense, their divisions
are but three—viz., those who eat human bodies, the dog-
eaters, and those who have no custom of the kind.

"Early in the morning the pupils would be out on the
beach, or on the rocks, in a state of nudity. Each had a
place in front of his own tribe; nor did intense cold interfere
in the slightest degree. After the poor creature had crept
about, jerking his head and screaming for some time, a party
of men would rush out, and, after surrounding him, would
commence singing. The dog-eating party occasionally carried
a dead dog to their pupil, who forthwith commenced to tear
it in the most doglike manner. The party of attendants kept
up a low growling noise, or a whoop, which was seconded by
a screeching noise made from an instrument which they
believe to be the abode of a spirit. In a little time the
naked youth would start up again, and proceed a few more
yards in a crouching posture, with his arms pushed out behind
him, and tossing his flowing black hair. All the while he is
earnestly watched by the group about him, and when he
pleases to sit down they again surround him and commence

singing. This kind of thing goes on, with several little
additions, for some time. Before the prodigy finally retires,
he takes a run into every house belonging to his tribe, and is
followed by his train. When this is done, in some cases he
has a ramble on the tops of the same houses, during which
he is anxiously watched by his attendants, as if they expected
his flight. By-and-by he condescends to come down, and
they then follow him to his den, which is signified by a rope
made of red bark being hung over the doorway, so as to
prevent any person from ignorantly violating its precincts.
None are allowed to enter that house but those connected
with the art: all I know, therefore, of their further proceedings is, that they keep up a furious hammering, singing,
and screeching for hours during the day.

"Of all these parties, none are so much dreaded as the
cannibals. One morning I was called to witness a stir in the
camp which had been caused by this set. When I reached
the gallery I saw hundreds of Tsimsheeans sitting in their
canoes, which they had just pushed away from the beach.
I was told that the cannibal party were in search of a body
to devour, and if they failed to find a dead one, it was probable they would seize the first living one that came in their
way; so that all the people living near to the cannibals'
house had taken to their canoes to escape being torn to pieces.
It is the custom among these Indians to burn their dead;
but I suppose for these occasions they take care to deposit a
corpse somewhere, in order to satisfy these inhuman wretches.

"These, then, are some of the things and scenes which
occur in the day during the winter months, while the nights
are taken up with amusements—singing and dancing. Occasionally the medicine parties invite people to their several
houses, and exhibit tricks before them of various kinds. Some
of the actors appear as bears, while others wear masks, the
parts of which are moved by strings. The great feature in
their proceedings is to pretend to murder, and then to restore

to life, and so forth. The cannibal, on such occasions, is generally supplied with two, three, or four human bodies, which he tears to pieces before his audience. Several persons, either from bravado or as a charm, present their arms for him to bite. I have seen several whom he has thus bitten, and I hear two have died from the effects.

"One very dark night I was told that there was a moon to see on the beach. On going to see, there was an illuminated disc, with the figure of a man upon it. The water was then very low, and one of the conjuring parties had lit up this disc at the water's edge. They had made it of wax, with great exactness, and presently it was at the full. It was an imposing sight. Nothing could be seen around it; but the Indians suppose that the medicine party are then holding converse with the man in the moon. Indeed there is no wonder in the poor creatures being deluded, for the peculiar noises that were made, while all around was perfectly still, and the good imitation of the moon while all around was enveloped in darkness, seemed just calculated to create wild and superstitious notions. After a short time the moon waned away, and the conjuring party returned whooping to their house.

"Before any young persons can join these medicine parties they are supposed to go into the bush for some days, and be there alone, whence they receive their supernatural gifts. But I am inclined to believe that this is not strictly carried out, for it is also supposed that they are not visible when they come back: it therefore becomes an easy matter to conceal them in their houses for a short time, and then publish a lie. The end of all these proceedings is the giving away property; so the chiefs reap the benefit. No person need think of becoming "Allied" until he or his friends have amassed considerable property, and are disposed to beggar themselves.

"One Sunday I was startled by a peculiar noise proceeding

from the camp, and on going to see what was the cause, I observed a man, who, it seems, had finished his education as an "Allied," and was now going to give away his goods. He was proceeding to a distant part of the camp, and stepping all the way like a proud unmanageable horse. Behind him were about fifteen or twenty men, all holding on to a kind of rope, which went round his waist. They were pretending to keep him back, or hold him from taking his flight. Presently this party was joined by other two, upon a similar errand, and they now seemed to try which could make the greatest noise, or look the most unearthly. The three bands, after a good deal of manœuvring, proceeded, I think, to the same chief's house.

"I think it is generally supposed that these parties I have described are the doctors of the Red Indians, because their proceedings are called 'medicine work,' and they 'medicine men;' but I find that the medical profession is altogether a distinct business, and the doctors a distinct class. After investigation of the matter, I am led to conclude that these medical practitioners are, for the most part, those who have themselves been visited with some serious sickness, and have recovered; or else have been, at some time in their lives, exposed to great peril, but have escaped uninjured. For instance, if a man or woman is taken in a fit, and remains motionless for so long that they are concluded dead, should such a one ultimately recover, that is the person who is regarded as competent to deal with diseases: for it is believed, that, during the period of unconsciousness, supernatural power and skill was vouchsafed them; and also, by their recovering, it is concluded that they have successfully resisted the effects of bad medicine, or the evil workings of some malevolent being. Still I do not mean to say that all their doctors arise from these circumstances, but mostly so. I believe that any shrewd or eccentric man may, by fasting,

U

successfully prognosticating, or otherwise acting so as to excite the superstitious reverence of the people in his favour, secure a footing in this lucrative profession.

"Next, as to the means employed by the doctors to recover patients. For pains in the body they employ a bag of hot ashes, after first placing a damp cloth on the skin. If the patient is afflicted with a pain in the head, they strike him on the place with small branches of the spruce-tree. For wounds they have a salve, but they seldom use it except in bad cases: the most ordinary method is simply to place a quantity of gum over the lips of the wound to keep them closed. For most of the diseases which afflict them, they have some herb or decoction which they give as a counteractant.

"But the chief thing relied upon and resorted to, in case of failure of other means, is incantation. The instrument used is a rattle, generally in the shape of a bird or a frog, in the body of which a few small stones are placed.* This is whirled about the patient while a song is sung. Occasionally the doctor applies his ear, or his mouth, to the place where the pain or disorder chiefly rests. It is also very common, at this stage, to make incisions where the pain is felt, or to apply fire to the place by means of burning tinder made of dried wild flax. If relief follows these measures, the doctor asserts that he has extracted the foul substance that has done the mischief; which substance is supposed by them to be the bad or poisonous medicine some evil-disposed one had silently inserted into the invalid's body. At such an announcement made by the doctor, the patient, and the patient's friends, overjoyed at his success, liberally present him with such property as they have got. If, however, a relapse ensues, and the invalid dies, the doctor returns every particle of the property he has received. When no relief follows the first

* I have seen these rattles made of the bills of the horned puffin, three or four dozen being strung together.—AUTHOR.

trial, a more furious attack is made another time. If still
without effect, there is but little hope of the patient's
recovery.

"Another curious matter connected with these operations
is, that when the doctor has got pretty warm in his work, he
boldly asserts that he can see the soul of the patient, if it is
present. For this he shuts his eyes for some time, and then
pronounces his sentence. Either the soul is in its usual
place, which is a good sign; or it is out of its proper place,
and seems wanting to take its flight, which makes the
patient's case doubtful; or else it has flown away, in which
case there is no hope for the invalid's recovery. The bold
deceiver does not even hesitate to tell the people that the soul
is like a fly in shape, with a long curved proboscis.

" This people ascribe nearly all their bodily afflictions, and
most deaths, to the secret working of malevolent persons.
This being the case, when any person dies—if of any importance amongst them — and especially if suddenly, the
friends of the deceased fix upon some one as the cause, either
a slave, or a stranger just arrived in the camp, or, more probably still, a person with whom the deceased has lately
quarrelled. Whoever the victim is, however, whether man
or woman, nothing short of his or her life will satisfy the
bereaved persons. They believe in two ways an evil-disposed
person may effect his purpose. One is by placing some bad
medicine in the meat or drink of his victim, or, if sick, by
persuading the individual to drink a poisonous draught. The
other way is by magic, and this is by far the most common
method they suppose. In this case, they say that the deadly
substance is transmitted from the hand of the destroyer to
the body of his victim, without the latter having any per-
ception of the event.

" Such superstition as this is well calculated to produce
that distrust of each other which I find so prominent amongst
them; and also makes it somewhat dangerous for one to

assist them a little with real medicine. I hear that several white persons—some of whom are American missionaries—have been murdered for attempting this kindness, all because their medicine did not prevent death. There has not been a case of that sort among the Indians here yet; but I see that the same superstitions which have led other Indians to commit murder are deeply rooted here, so that it behoves one to be cautious. I have already given medicine and advice to some, which the Lord has been pleased to bless: so that they are beginning to gain confidence and appreciate my coming amongst them. My efforts in this way have as yet been nearly all confined to the Fort people; but as the Indian women in here are generally the most influential in the tribe to which they belong, in gaining their confidence a great blow is struck at the prejudices of the people outside.

"If one Indian is vexed with another, the most effectual way of showing his displeasure, next to killing him, is to say to him (what would be in English), *By and by, you will die.* Not unfrequently the poor victim thus marked becomes so terrified that the prediction is verified. When this is the case, the friends of the deceased say that they have no doubt about the cause, and therefore (if they are able to meet the contest which may ensue) the prognosticator, on the first opportunity, is shot for his passionate language.

"The young man named Clah, whom I have had to assist me in Tsimshean, only a little time before I came shot a woman, because by some silly expression she excited his belief that it was owing to her evil influence a piece of wood, which was being carried by some Indians, fell from their shoulders and seriously hurt one of them, a relative of his. Now I hear that this woman's son (although Clah has paid him 30 blankets) is watching his opportunity to revenge her death. Thus is the stream of murder fed from time to time.

"In the majority of cases, I think the sick receive a great deal of attention from their friends. I have always found one or two nurses to an invalid, if the case was at all bad; the sympathy of the nurses, too, seemed very great. It seemed to me, however, that they never thought of washing the sick, for nearly all who had been laid up for any length of time were literally immured in dirt. If any one suggested the propriety of a good wash, they would immediately say they had no soap, which amounted to asking one to supply it, yet scarcely any are without ample means of purchasing it if they would.

"When a person dies, except in the case of a slave, very great lamentation is made by surviving friends. Their mourning lasts for several days. A few days ago, I saw a poor woman in the bush, at some distance behind the camp. She was sitting with her face towards the stump of a tree, and continued her bitter wailing for a long time. This is the second instance I have seen of this kind. Occasionally, mourners may be seen going about the beach. Only lately I saw a woman coming away from a house of death. She proceeded along the beach to where another tribe is settled, and continued her woful cry all the way. Persons whom she passed took no notice whatever of her; it seemed nothing strange to them.

"Soon after death the corpse is conveyed away in a canoe to a distant part of the beach, and there burned to ashes. Mourners accompany it, and they make the air to ring with their piercing cries all the time the body is consuming. The ashes are collected and placed in a little house appointed to receive them.

"A slave, after death, is at once placed in a canoe and thrown into the harbour, without any sorrow being expressed. The Tsimsheeans, I find, believe in two states after death: the one good, and the other bad; the morally good are translated to the one, and the morally bad are doomed to the other. The locality of the former they think to be above, and that of the latter is somewhere beneath. The enjoyment of heaven and the privations of hell they understand to be carnal.

"They do not suppose the wicked to be destitute of food any more than they were here, but they are treated as slaves and are badly clothed.

"What is very strange, they imagine that as the various seasons leave them they advance to the abode of the wicked. For instance, when the fish get out of the reach of their nets, they suppose they are then becoming the prey of the wicked beneath.

"The idea they entertain of God is that He is a great chief. They call him by the same term as they do their chiefs, only adding the word for above—thus, 'shimanyet' is chief, and 'lakkah' above; and hence the name of God with them is Shimanyet Lakkah. They believe that the Supreme Being never dies; that he takes great notice of what is going on amongst men, and is frequently angry and punishes offenders. They do not know who is the author of the Universe, nor do they expect that God is the author of their own being. They have no fixed ideas about these things, I fully believe; still they frequently appeal to God in trouble: they ask for pity and deliverance. In great extremities of sickness they address God, saying it is not good for them to die.

"Sometimes, when calamities are prolonged or thicken, they get enraged against God, and vent their anger against Him, raising their eyes and hands in savage anger to Heaven, and stamping their feet on the ground. They will reiterate language which means 'You are a great slave!' This is their greatest term of reproach. By far the most prominent trait of character in this people is pride, yet many other of the corruptions of our fallen nature they exhibit in deplorable measure. Revenge with them, which is their only way of adjusting wrongs, is so dire and determined that many years and change of circumstances cannot extinguish it. Several instances have been known where it has burst forth in terrible vengeance more than twenty years after its birth, and simply because an opportunity to satisfy it never occurred before. But, as I said before, pride or conceit is the passion they most strikingly exhibit. It is astonishing what they will do or suffer in order to establish or maintain dignity. Yesterday a young man fell down, and cut himself a little with an axe. On arriving home, his father immediately announced his intention to destroy some property which was to save his son from any disgrace attached to the accident. When a few people or friends were collected to witness the brave act, the father would carry out his vow, with no small show of vanity. I hear that instances are numerous where persons who have been hoarding up property for ten, fifteen, or twenty years (at the same time almost starving themselves for want of clothing), have given it all away to make a show for a few hours, and to be thought of consequence."

I come now to the Indians of the interior, of whom, however, I regret to say, much less is known than of those upon the coast.

At and about the entrance of the Fraser River is the Kwantlun tribe: they live in villages which extend along the banks of the river as far as Langley. Next to these, and extending from Langley to Yale, are the Smess, Chillwayhook, Pallalts, and Teates—which latter are called by the upper tribes Sa-chin-ko. These all appear, from their similarity of language and customs, to be branches of the Kwantlun tribe, although, as usual, their dialects differ considerably. They have villages placed on the tributary streams as well as the main river. The Smess Indians occupy the Smess river and lake, and the Chillwayhooks the river and lake of that name. In the summer, however, they nearly all congregate on the banks of the Fraser River to fish. As every village seems to have an old long-standing feud with some of their neighbours—which what has been said of their revengeful spirit readily accounts for—constant bickerings and frequent murders signalise these annual gatherings. For these reasons, and to guard against the incursions of the coast-tribes for slaves, the permanent villages are all stockaded—a measure which, though more common here than on the coast, is sometimes resorted to there, as at Cape Mudge. It is a curious fact that, though living in a constant state of alarm, no Indians in this country ever keep watch at night. To be sure, they always have a number of barking curs about the lodges, but these are easily bought over by cunning foes, with food, &c., and thus their villages have no real protection against the night attacks which are sometimes made upon them. I have frequently suggested the propriety of keeping watch when in my travels we camped near strange villages, but never could get them to do it. I believe this to be from superstitious dread of spirits, as they are not the least afraid to be out at night looking for deer, fishing, or stealing.

Yale is the limit to the wanderings of the above-mentioned tribes, and at Spuzzum, a village six miles above the Cañon, a race very different both in habits and language is found. These are the Nicouta-much or Nicouta-meens, a branch of a widely-extended tribe. They, with their cognate septs, the At-naks or Shuswap-much, occupy the Fraser River from Spuzzum to the frontier of that part of the country called by the Hudson Bay Company New Caledonia, which is within a few miles of Fort Alexandria (about 330 miles from the river's mouth), making the extent of their wanderings about 250 miles.

From Thompson River other septs of this race—the Shuswaps, Skowtous, Okanagans, Spokans, Skoi-el-poi (of Colville), Pend'oreilles, and Cœurs d'Aleines—occupy the country as far as the Flathead Passes of the Rocky Mountains, where the Sae-lies or Flatheads form the eastern portion of the race. The Rocky Mountains on one hand, and an imaginary line running east and west 60 to 100 miles south of the parallel of 49° N. lat., may be said to define the tract occupied by these people between the Thompson River and the Flathead country.

Mr. A. C. Anderson, who has travelled a great deal in this country, estimates the number of Nicouta-meen and Shuswap-much Indians mustering annually on the Fraser at 6000 or 8000. He considers that in North-West America, generally, there is not more than one man to ten square miles, although this population is not by any means distributed evenly over the country, which would make it appear more dense in those parts best known. This estimate would give an Indian population of about 20,000, which I fancy is not far wrong.

Between the Rocky Mountains, the Upper Columbia and its tributary the Killuspehn or Pend'oreille, and watered by an intermediate stream called the Kootanais River, is an angular piece of country peopled by a small, isolated tribe, bearing the same name as the last-mentioned river, on the banks of which they principally live. This country of the Kootanais being very poor, they have to cross the Rocky Mountains for the buffalo, and when there they are constant'y attacked, murdered, or driven back by the Blackfeet. Thus they are constantly diminishing. Isolated, and speaking a language of their own, it is not easy to imagine their origin; but it appears probable that they once belonged to some more powerful southern tribe, from which they became cut off by the intervention of larger tribes. Mr. Anderson says they are brave and possess more than ordinary virtue. Their country is very difficult to get at, either by land or water, as the Kootanais River is too rapid for navigation, and only fordable or passable for horses in spring before the melting of the snow, and in the autumn when it is beginning to freeze again. In 1848 Mr. Anderson was travelling among these Indians, and he made his interpreter take a census, with the following results:—

	Men.	Lads.	Women and Children.	Total.
Upper Kootanais	35	18	113	166
Kootanais who visit Flathead country	44	39	183	266
Lower Kootanais or Arc Plattes ..	78	46	273	397
	157	103	569	829

The number of this tribe, however, is now probably reduced to about 500 or 600.

All the natives of the Upper Fraser are called by the Hudson Bay Company, and indeed generally, "Porteurs," or carriers, and as I have shown, when speaking of travelling in this country, they well deserve the name. It originated from their bearing a corresponding designation among their northern neighbours, the "Beaver" Indians. They (the Beavers) call themselves Ta-cully, or Tah-killy, signifying "wanderers on the deep." They form the western branch of the great Chipewyan tribe, a race whose wanderings extend from Fort Churchill on Hudson Bay, and thence far north coterminously with the Esquimaux of the coast.

In 1839 Mr. Anderson estimated the population of this northern district of British Columbia, then New Caledonia, as follows:—

	Men.	Women.	Children.	Total.
•At M'Leod's Lake	49	40	113	202
Chilcotin	224	132	244	600
Alexandria	292	223	232	747
Fort George	75	50	62	187
Connolly Lake..	28	30	87	135
Babine Lake	69	47	65	181
Fraser Lake	98	87	100	285
Stuart Lake	62	79	147	288
	897	688	1040	2625

Their number has probably been much decreased since

that time, though from the wildness of this region and the absence of white men they may have kept up their numbers much better than the tribes nearer the coast have done. There is a curious currency used by the Hudson Bay Company in trading with these natives, viz. Haiqua shell, which I have mentioned as being worn in the under-lip of the northern Coast Indians. This little shell is obtained off Nootka Sound. It is found clinging in clusters to the rocks in deep water, and is dragged up by the Indians with long poles and hooks. They (the Nootkas) sell them to the Company at Fort Rupert and other coast posts, and they are sent up to the interior to be used as money; the inland Indians having a great partiality for them, and using them in large strings, much in the same way, I fancy, as the Eastern North American Indians use the celebrated wampum-belts.

Almost all the tribes mentioned in the above census inhabit the country west of the Fraser River, or between it and the coast, and they all visit the coast more or less frequently, their journeys depending chiefly upon the supply of salmon, &c., in their own districts. The routes by which they go are as yet little known. Some have been explored lately, and one or two by earlier employés of the Hudson Bay and North-West Companies, including among their number Sir A. M'Kenzie. Of these, however, it will be remembered that I have spoken when describing the inlets along the coast, and discussing the probability of a practicable route being found from the sea to the upper part of British Columbia, from the head of some one or other of them. Some of the interior tribes spend half their year inland and half at the coast: for instance, the " Loquilt " Indians have their home in the winter on Lake Anderson and the surrounding district, whence they descend to the coast in Jervis Inlet in the summer; while the Chilcotin Indians spend much of their time at Bellhoula in the Bentinck Inlet.

The natives eastward of the Fraser, viz. the Skowtous,

Shuswap, Okanagan, &c., own numbers of horses, and are for the most part mounted. I have already, while narrating my travels in British Columbia, alluded to the feeling of respect which the traveller entertains generally towards mounted Indians. After being used to the dwarfed natives of the coast, whose limbs have assumed almost the shape of the canoe that is their constant home, it is startling to come among the fine athletic Indians of the interior, and to behold the skill and courage with which they manage their half-wild horses, and train themselves in the sports of peace for war. These tribes, as I have before said, are not addicted to slavery as a trade, which probably conduces much to their superior moral condition. Virtue is not, however, I fear, much more regarded as a principle and motive of action among these poor people than by the Indians of the coast, although their comparative seclusion and freedom from foreign influences preserve them from that utter abandonment of decency which is found near the white settlements. I remember discussing this question, when I was staying at Fort Kamloops, with an employé of the Company, who had been eight or ten years in the country; and he said he had only heard of one instance of an Indian woman expressing any other ground for chastity than the fear of some man, father or husband. In this solitary case, he said, upon the man assuring her that her deeds would never be known, she said, " There is One who knows everything;" and as she spoke she pointed to the sky. I think he said this girl was an Okanagan. Mr. Anderson, whom I have before quoted, asserts that these Indians are much more virtuous than those of the coast, but from the conversations I have had with various traders living among them, I am inclined to fear that any difference there may be, is, as I have said above, owing to force of circumstances rather than to any fixed principle.

As may readily be supposed, the tastes of these Indians for

hunting and riding tends to make them less industrious than the more sedentary Coast natives, and they are, I believe, less provident. Since the discovery of gold, especially, many have taken to gold-washing in the summer instead of laying by a winter stock, and the result has been that, during the severity of winter, they have died of starvation in great numbers. Their principal food is salmon, venison, bear, wild sheep, and berries, mosses, and lichens. The principal of these latter is the black lichen (*L. jubatus*), called by them Whyelkine, of which I have already spoken.

Far inland, and occasionally even in the neighbourhood of the coast, may still be seen the deer-skin dress, ornamented with beads and porcupine-quills, in which Indians are always represented in pictures; but shirts and trowsers are so easily obtained, and save so much trouble, that most of the men now wear them, while the women use blankets, generally white, though sometimes blue or red, and fastened in the same way.

They also make capes of bark, similar to their mats. These are generally trimmed with fur round the edge, and go over the head like a South American poncho. They only reach to the elbows, and are seldom worn except in wet weather. Like the Sea-shore Indians, they generally go bare-headed, although many may be seen wearing the blue cap with a leather peak, commonly used by mariners, and ornamented with some feathers or ribbons. Mocassins are much more generally worn than at the coast: these are sometimes very neatly ornamented with beads, but often they are mere pieces of deer-skin laced round the foot. Frequently, however, they ride about barefooted, holding the piece of cord, which serves both as stirrup-leather and stirrup, between the first and second toes. They occasionally wear leggings made of cloth, and very prettily ornamented with beads. Nearly all use the Spanish wooden saddle, which they make with much skill; and the bridle is a simple cord, often the

hair of the wild sheep, for it cannot be called wool, plaited.
The middle of this is passed through the horse's mouth,
and hitched round his lower jaw, and the ends brought up on
each side of his neck.

In their huts or lodges, which are similar to those of the
coast, they have the same mats of cypress or cedar bark.
Of their feasts and ceremonies I know little: their fashion of
exchanging presents, however, resembles that of the Coast
Indians. Their medicine-feasts are also much the same,
and, like the others, they all wear charm-bags round their
necks.

The medicine-bag charm ordinarily worn is small, but on
feasts and great occasions the chiefs and medicine-men wear
very large ones. As a rule, nothing can be done without the
aid of the medicine-men and their mummeries. The bag I
have spoken of is, I believe, generally made of the skin of
some animal, bird, or reptile, as the beaver, otter, polecat, or
weasel; eagle, magpie, or hawk; snake, or toad. Anything—
dry grass, leaves, &c.—is stuffed into it, and it is carefully
sewn up and ornamented.

Before a young man is admitted to be a man and a warrior,
he has to get his medicine, which he does, or is supposed to do,
by roaming about the woods, fasting and praying to the great
spirit to help him to medicine, much in the same way, though
to a less extent, as the medicine-men prepare themselves for
the higher mysteries. His medicine-animal is the first animal,
bird, or reptile he dreams of during this process; and, having
dreamt of it, he immediately kills one, and it becomes his
medicine for ever. His bag is or should be made of this
animal's skin; but there is much trickery in all these matters.

Among the principal of those medicine-tricks which I have
omitted to speak of is that of rain-making. In most of the
valleys in which the Indians live they suffer occasionally
from want of rain. It constantly pours on the hills around,
without a drop falling in the valleys. There is nothing for

which greater credit is got by a medicine-man than being a skilful rain-maker. Of course if the clouds do not gather or break at once, the rain-makers have only to go on with their ceremonies until they will. This they manage to do by persuading the others that the Great Spirit is offended; and when they see that rain is at hand, they redouble their energies, winding up, when it is on the point of falling, with some still more frenzied appeal to the Great Spirit, and sometimes, I have been told, shooting an arrow into the cloud to burst it, when it is evident the rain is on the point of descending in torrents. The Indians never appear to lose their faith in the operator's power, however long he may have kept them waiting; but as all the shrewder men of the tribe are or desire to be medicine-men, this is not much to be wondered at.

The children of all these tribes have their heads flattened, more or less, and the women carry them in the same curious little cradles slung at their backs : these are made, I believe, of the bark of cypress, and look like little canoes. The child lies at full length, and the sides of the cradle are sufficiently high to enable the mother to lace it in by a cord passed from side to side, a small block being put at one end as a pillow. When the mother is travelling she carries the cradle on her back in a nearly upright position, with the head just appearing above her shoulder; but if she is working, she suspends the infant from a pliant branch of a tree, or sticking a pole in the ground at a slight angle hangs the cradle, sometimes upright, sometimes horizontally, on the end of it. They move pole and cradle so as to keep it near them, and every now and then give it a swing, so that it rocks up and down. It is said that when children die they are often put in some lake or pool in their cradles and left to float about them, the natives regarding the water as sacred ever after; but I fancy this is more common on the east side of the mountains than the west.

Like the Coast Indians, they frequently bury their dead in trees, and whenever they are laid on the ground they always cover the lid of the coffin with stones. I have heard this custom attributed, as I have before said, to some instinctive feeling that the dead will rise again; but I am inclined to believe it is only done to protect them from the wild animals of the forest. I have seen some coffins also raised on posts, six or eight feet above the ground, when there were no trees to put them in. I do not think they are ever guilty of burying alive, though, as I have said of the Coast natives, they are very careless of and cruel to the old men and women when they get past work, and will often leave them to starve.

The dialects of the Indians of the interior are numerous as among those of the island and shore. When I was at Pavillon, on the Upper Fraser, a man who had been there many years, and who had travelled much among them, told me that between that place and Alexandria, a distance of some 120 miles, there were nine dialects spoken, and that these differed so much as to be almost distinct languages. It will be many years before much more than this is likely to be known of them. Indeed, it is probable, if not certain, if the white emigration continues and the colony progresses, that, before any opportunity of the kind comes, the tribes who use them will have almost, if not entirely, vanished from the face of the earth.

CHAPTER XII.

—•◦•—

Religious and Educational condition of the Colonies.

IN speaking of the religious and educational condition of these Colonies, I purpose to glance shortly at the position which the Church of England has already assumed in that distant land, dwelling next upon the missionary efforts of those who, in carrying the Christian religion to its Indian inhabitants, have undertaken labours, and striven successfully through difficulties of no ordinary character. Foremost among these, as the earliest Protestant missionary to our possessions in the North Pacific, and the successful introducer of education among the neglected Indian children of its shores, is that Mr. William Duncan whose name is already familiar to the reader of these pages. The journals and letters, published and unpublished, of this gentleman have been most kindly placed in my hands by the Secretary of the Church Missionary Society. And in the following account of the religious and educational condition of British Columbia and Vancouver Island, it will be found that I have used them largely.

Before 1857 no Protestant missionary had ever traversed the wilds of British Columbia, nor had any attempts been made to instruct the Indians. At Victoria the Hudson Bay Company had a chaplain stationed, but he was devoted entirely to the white settlers. I must except the exertions of the Roman Catholic priests. If the opinion of the Hudson Bay people of the interior is to be relied upon, they effected no real change in the condition of the natives. The sole

x

result of their residence among them was, that the Indians who
had been brought under their influence had imbibed some
notions of the Deity, almost as vague as their own traditions,
and a superstitious respect for the priests themselves, which
they showed by crossing themselves devoutly whenever they
met one. Occasionally, too, might be seen in their lodges,
pictures purporting to represent the roads to Heaven and to
Hell, in which there was no single suggestion of the danger
of vice and crime, but a great deal of the peril of Pro-
testantism. These coloured prints were certainly curious in
their way, and worth a passing notice. They were large, and
gave a pictorial history of the human race, from the time
when Adam and Eve wandered in the garden together,
down to the Reformation. Here the one broad road was split
into two, whose courses diverged more and more painfully.
By one way the Roman Catholic portion of the world were
seen trooping to bliss; the other ended in a steep bottomless
precipice over which the Protestants might be seen falling.
Upon the more sensible and advanced of the Indians,
teaching such as this had little effect. I remember the chief
of the Shuswap tribe, at Kamloops, pointing out to me such
an illustration hanging on his wall, and laughingly saying, in
a tone that showed quite plainly how little credence he
attached to it, " There are you and your people," putting his
finger as he spoke on the figures tumbling into the pit.

Of such kind was the only instruction that the Indians had
received prior to 1857. Its influence was illustrated in that
year at Victoria, where a Roman Catholic Bishop and several
priests had been resident for some time, and were known to
have exerted themselves among the Songhie Indians, who
reside there. A cross had been raised in their village, and
some of them had been baptized; but when these were called
before the bishop for confirmation, they refused to come unless
a greater present of blankets was made to them than had
been given at their baptism. The bishop was said to have

been very angry with the priests when this came to his knowledge: he having very possibly been deceived by them as to
the condition of the Indians.   I am informed that he had
a large heart painted upon canvas, through which he drew a
blanket, and represented it to the Indians as symbolical of
their condition.

Upon H.M.S. 'Satellite' being commissioned in 1856,
Captain Prevost offered to give a free passage to a missionary
if the Church Missionary Society would send one.   This
Society, which had been endowed by an anonymous benefactor
with the sum of 500*l.* to be devoted to such a purpose, offered
the work to Mr. Duncan, who had been trained at the
Highbury College, and who readily accepted it.   The
'Satellite' sailed in December, 1856, and reached Vancouver
Island in June, 1857, when Mr. Duncan, whose name is now
known and beloved by almost every Indian in the two
colonies, at once prepared to commence his labours.

After some question with the colonial authorities as to
where he should begin his work, considerable desire being
expressed on the Hudson Bay Company's part to place him
at Nanaimo, it was determined that he should go to Fort
Simpson on our northern boundary.   This spot had been
previously fixed upon by the Society at home for the scene of
Mr. Duncan's labours.   The Indians there were known to be
more free from the contagion of the white man, and were
assembled in larger numbers than at any other place on the
coast.   Another advantage possessed by this locality was that
at Simpson the trade of the fort brought a great number of
different tribes together.   Indeed the tribe of the Tsimsheeans, among whom Mr. Duncan's labours have been most
productive of good, had been attracted to Fort Simpson
from another spot on this account, and had since settled
there altogether.   ,

From June till October, 1857, Mr. Duncan found it
necessary to remain at Victoria, being unable to get a passage

to Fort Simpson, a distance of 800 miles, until the Hudson Bay Company's steamer should proceed thither. This interval, however, he employed most profitably in learning the language of the Indians among whom he was intending to reside (the Tsimsheeans), and otherwise in preparing for the work before him.

Upon his arrival at Simpson, Mr. Duncan was, in pursuance of orders to that effect given by the Governor, quartered in the Fort of the Hudson Bay Company, and one of the smaller houses was allotted to him, which was large enough for a school, as well as for his dwelling. In the Fort he found eighteen men assembled—one Scotch, one English, three ·Sandwich Islanders, and thirteen French Canadians, each having an Indian woman living with him. There were also seven children, and he was told there were some half-breed children scattered about the camp, who, if he pleased, might be received in the Fort for instruction.

On Sunday, the 11th October, he first performed Divine service in this the scene of his new and arduous labours, and on the 13th he opened school with but five half-breed boys belonging to the Fort as pupils, the eldest not five years old. Speaking of this he writes, " I am very glad for their sakes that they are so young. These I intend to teach in English. Their parents seem exceedingly delighted. I did think of taking a few half-breed children out of the camp, but I find they have been so long abandoned by their fathers that they have forgotten every word of English, and become so much like the Indians that I shall be obliged to deal with them as such."

A few days after, writing upon the same subject, he says, " To-day a chief called, whose principal anxiety was to ascertain whether I intended giving dollars to the Indians, to get them to send their children to school., I think I shamed him a little, at least I tried to do so, for entertaining such a selfish notion. I have a good many visitors, and all seem desirous of ingratiating themselves; some by referring me to numerous papers which they bring, obtained in general from the Company's officers. These papers, however, rarely say more for them than that they are influential men and great beggars. Other of my visitors, not blessed with papers, will tell me what good hearts they have, and how rich and influential they are." I may, in reference to this remark of Mr. Duncan, mention that the fashion of producing their testimonials to visitors is common among all the Indians. You rarely come across one of any importance in his tribe, but he produces three or four papers, carefully kept in a box, and smelling horribly; while every Indian who does anything for you expects a testimonial as well as payment for his services. Of course they do not know what is said of them; and I have had papers shown me that, had their contents been known to the bearer, he would have been by no means proud of exhibiting. Speaking also of their habit of begging, Mr. Duncan says:—" When they beg, which is generally the case, I mostly satisfy and always lessen their expectations by saying I have not come to trade. This opens a way to telling them what I have come to do for them; and in every case, as soon as my object is realised, I hear the oft-repeated 'Ahm, ahm' (Good, good), and their faces exhibit every expression of joy of which they are susceptible. I make a practice of telling all, that I shall expect their assistance in erecting a school-room outside the Fort as soon as I can talk their language a little better. Without exception they assent to my proposal; but whether they will be ready to act when the time comes, remains to be seen. I already see several difficulties in the way; their jealousies and feuds are not the least. It is a pity we cannot put their sincerity to the test at once, but I feel it would not be prudent to do so. The winter is at. hand, and their long and all-absorbing medicine-feasts come with it; besides, I do not yet feel possessor of so much of their tongue as such a work would require. However, I hope by the carrying out of what is already begun in the Fort, and what I intend yet to commence, under God's blessing, to keep alive at least, if not increase, the desire already awakened around me for instruction."

On many other occasions Mr. Duncan mentions the visits of chiefs and others while his school was going on, and of the seriousness of their looks when he and his pupils knelt in prayer, and the invariable "Ahm, ahm" which followed a spectacle so novel to them. But although this approval was manifested by so many individuals, it had little or no effect on the conduct of the mass; and the scenes of cruelty and horrible murder which he had, and even still has, to witness, would daunt the heart of a less brave and earnest man.

The first holiday which he gave his scholars, is thus described by him:—"This afternoon (December 9, 1857) I assembled my little boys for a breaking-up for a few days. They came clean and nicely dressed, with hearts ever so joyful. The father of each boy, and another visitor or two, were present. We sang several hymns, and I then gave each of them a present, and after a little drilling they marched away. Their fathers seemed highly gratified. I did not let the little fellows read or repeat catechism (both of which they can do a little), as they were so excited. Thus I feel," he continues, "as though something had been done these last two months. May God prosper the small beginning, and make it the earnest of a great future harvest."

Nor had Mr. Duncan confined himself to educational efforts. Already his influence for good was being felt by the Indians, and men of importance in their tribes had come to him for aid and advice.

"To-day," he writes, "a chief came who is suffering from a bad cough, and seems wasting away. He very anxiously desired relief; but it is of no use giving them any medicine

for such complaints, as their habits prevent any good effects
ensuing. I perceived he wanted to tell me something serious
by his countenance. Like a man about to take a long
journey, he seemed gasping for directions about the way.
Oh! how I longed to tell him my message, but could not.
I made him understand that I should soon be able to teach
them about God, that I had His book with me which I
should teach from, and my object was to make them good
and happy. . . . . His constant response was 'Ahm, ahm'
(Good, good). Upon another occasion the same man asked to
see 'Shimanyet Lak-kah Shahounak' (God's book). His
anxious gaze and sighs showed me how he longed to know
its contents, while I, too, longed to tell him. Again and
again I mentioned the name of our Saviour. I could do
little else."

Upon another occasion he writes:—"To-day the chief
officer came to me while I was busy with my Indian scholars,
and asked to speak to me privately. I went aside with him,
and he began telling me that an Indian woman, who is living
with one of the white men in the Fort, had been treating her
slave (a poor girl) very unmercifully while we were at Divine
service yesterday. He wished me to go and speak to the
woman, for he believed if she was not interfered with the
slave would be certain to lose her life. At first I objected,
on account of my inability to speak her language sufficiently;
but presently I thought I would go, for I could see that
although it was necessary to be done; the man who lives with
her dared not, for peace sake, and the captain dared not, for
conscience sake, undertake the duty: I accordingly went,
having first asked the counsel and blessing of God. I found
her washing clothes, and, although somewhat soured in expression, she greeted me with her usual recognition of respect. I
commenced telling her in English what I had come for, which
she quickly understood, and hung her head over the washing-
tub and remained motionless while I spoke. I used as kind

a tone as I could command, and when I had finished I wished
her good morning; to which she very solemnly responded.
This evening her husband has been at school, and from him I
learnt that she had been weeping nearly all the day.   Almost
immediately after school the woman, with tears in her eyes,
came to see me.   Her face told the sorrow that was awakened
within, and how bitterly she had been mourning.   One of the
men was with me at the time, so I desired him to go away,
for I saw she wished to unburthen her mind; but she prevented him from doing so, wishing to use him as an interpreter.
Then, with her eyes upon the ground and her heart sobbing
with grief, she commenced to unfold her feelings : the man
interpreted.   I then explained my mind a little more fully to
her, hoped she would amend, and then shook hands with her.
I need hardly say how her countenance brightened, and how
relieved she seemed when she went away.   This was the first
woman I ever reproved, and she a Red Indian, a heathen, and
of naturally a proud and haughty temper.   The result seemed
to astonish me.   Was it not of the Lord?   I thought how
much more like a Christian she had acted than many who
call themselves such would have done."   Such scenes show
how susceptible of improvement these people are.

Speaking of the first Christmas-Day that Mr. Duncan
passed at Fort Simpson, he writes :—"This day has passed
off much better than I expected.   In the morning we had
Divine service, when fifteen men and four boys were present
—the greatest number we have ever had.   After breakfast
(according to usual custom here) the men had each *a pint and
a half* of rum served out to them, and therefore I feel not a
little thankful that so many should have put aside the temptation and come to service.   From two sources I have had an
account of the wretched way in which Christmas Days have
been spent, and glad I am to have seen things so orderly and
quiet to-day.   Many have expressed their astonishment at
the great and sudden change; but to me it only appears yet

an outward change, such a one as man is able to effect in and
by himself. I am waiting and longing for that change which
only God can effect : when I see this, I will rejoice indeed."

With the commencement of the new year he began his
labours among the Indians outside the Fort :—" Though I was
not in a position to do them much good, still I thought I
would at least go and see them all, and endeavour to win a
little of their esteem and confidence."

" It would be impossible to give a full description," he says,
" of this my first general visit to the Indians in their houses,
for the scenes were too exciting and too crowded to admit of
it. I confess that cluster after cluster of these half-naked
and painted savages round their fires was to my unaccustomed
eyes very alarming ; but the reception I met with was truly
wonderful and encouraging. On entering a house I was
greeted by one, two, or three of the principal personages with
' Clah-hōw-yah,' which is the complimentary term used in the
trading jargon. This would be repeated several times ; then
a general movement and a squatting ensued, followed by a
breathless silence, during which every eye was fixed on me.
After a little time several would begin nodding and smiling,
at the same time in a low tone reiterating ' Ahm ahm-ah-ket
—ahm shimanyet ' (Good, good person, good chief). In
some houses they would not be content till I took the chief
place near the fire, and always placed a mat upon a box for
me to sit upon. My inquiries after the sick were always
followed by anxious glances and deep sighs : a kind of solemn
awe would spread itself at once. I found forty-seven sick,
and three in a state of lunacy."

It appears that the officer in charge here, some years before,
took an account of the Indians, and very soon after great
numbers were swept away by measles. Of course the Indians
attributed the calamity to their being numbered, and upon
this occasion Mr. Duncan found that they were not free from
certain superstitious fears: " still in many houses," he says,

"they told me of the difference they placed upon the motive of his visits and mine. Many were inclined to think that the very contrary would result from my visit." Poor creatures! when the horrors of illness to them, with no kind of relief, no hope, and often the most barbarous treatment by their doctors are considered, it is not surprising that they should have a superstitious dread of anything that appears likely to bring disease among them. I remember once seeing a man at a village in Cowitchen with his face frightfully scarred by fire, which they told me was applied to burn out the evil spirit that was making him ill.

More than once Mr. Duncan reverts to their desire for knowledge:—"There is one cheering feature connected with this people which my visit has prominently shown me, that is, they are *longing* for instruction. The presence of the whites and their own visits to the south have shaken their superstition and awakened inquiry; but that is all. There is a general belief amongst them that the whites do possess some grand secret about eternal things, and they are gasping to know it. This is the propitious moment. Oh that the people of God were awake to their responsibility, duty, and privilege!"   ·

Again, a little later, he says, " My Indian interpreter tries every day to lift up the veil a little higher to let me see his people. He assures me that the Indians are wanting to hear what is good, and are even becoming impatient. They have begun to think that the Fort people are monopolizing my time and attention in order to keep them in ignorance. An Indian, who is very much feared, wanted to see me teach a night or two since; but they would not let him stop in the Fort. On going away he said to the officer that he and his people wanted to learn to be good, but the Fort people stood in the way. The same man told my Indian the other day that when he was in his own house he always felt angry and wanted to murder somebody, but as soon as he came within the precincts of the Fort he felt quite good, which change he attributed to my being in the Fort. The secret of it is, he is mostly in the Fort-yard when I cross to or from breakfast, and I always give him a pleasant look and a kind word, and these produce what he attributes to magic."

In the autumn of 1858, Mr. Duncan commenced building his school-house outside the Fort, a work in which the Indians greatly assisted, providing plank and bark for the roof, to the value, he estimated, of at least five pounds.

"I had," he says, "to go to every house to receive their donations, which were presented with a great deal of ceremony and good feeling. Many took boards off their own roof to give me, and some even the pieces that formed part of their bed." And on November 12th, he writes in his journal :—" By Monday next, the 15th, I hope the plastering of the school-house will be dry enough for whitewashing, and then how glad I shall be that this troublesome work is over. I have had many unforeseen difficulties and vexations to contend with, but out of them all the Lord has carried me."

A few days before this he recounts his first night-visit to the Indian encampment.

"Last night was the first time I had ventured out in the camp during dark. It was to see a poor dying woman, sister to the late head chief. I had seen her three or four times before, but could do her no good ; still, as her friends had come to the Fort desiring aid, I accompanied them back. On arriving at the house, I found the sick woman laid before a large fire, round which some twenty Indians were squatted. After administering a little medicine, I began speaking to them a few words which the solemn scene suggested. I showed them our condition, and only remedy in Jesus our adorable Saviour, adding, too, upon what conditions we were saved by Him. They all understood what I said, and two of the women that sat close at the head of the sick person very earnestly reiterated to her my words, and questioned her if

she understood them. It was, I think, the most solemn scene
I have witnessed since I have been here. Before I went
away, one man said that she and her people did not know
about God, but they wanted to know, and learn to be good."

I cannot, perhaps, do better than to allow Mr. Duncan to
tell, in his own words, the progress of his teaching during the
winter of 1859.

" *November* 16.—I have, these last few days, been making
some special visits to inform the Indians what are my intentions and hopes with respect to commencing the school. In
a few houses I was also enabled to set forth the blessed truths
of the Gospel. In every house I was attentively listened to,
and greeted in their warmest way.

" The season in which the deep heathenism and darkness
of this people is manifested has just set in. My heart was
gladdened, however, to-day by the chiefs of our tribe coming
to my house to say that they had made up their minds to
abandon these sorceries, or medicine-work. Since then I
have heard of another tribe that has made the same resolution; and on a visit to an old chief yesterday afternoon, I
gathered from him that his tribe were meditating the same
thing. Thus I feel thankful to God that one heathenish
custom, and that one decidedly the most gross and deeply
rooted, is tottering, and ready to fall, since three tribes out
of the nine here have already declared against it. Whenever
I speak against this medicine-making, as it is called, I am
sure to be reminded of its long existence as a custom of great
importance among them.

" My class of Indians, resident in the Fort, which I have
been teaching of a night at my house from the black-board,
have begun reading in books to-night. The books are of my
own making, and I add a little each day. This measure I
have adopted more as a stimulant to the Indians outside than
anything else. When they see these little books, and hear
their own people read and explain them, I think that a good

effect will be produced. Very little things, I have already learnt, either done or said among this people, produce effects, either for good or evil, in commencing anything new amongst them.

"I am frequently reminded about the papers which the Romish priests have distributed among some Indians, whose place is about 150 miles away north of this. The papers were given to them while on a visit south, either at Victoria or some American port near.

"The Indians regard such gifts as charms, and wonder, or rather have wondered, why I did not treat them similarly. An Indian, lately from the south, told me yesterday that the priests informed him they intended soon to establish themselves here. This I regard as very probable, especially since the priests have heard I am here.

"*Nov.* 17.—The school is finished, and oh, how thankful I feel! We have washed the floor, and made all clean and tidy, both inside and around to-day. To-morrow the seats and desk will be done, and placed in the school, and on Friday I begin teaching.

"After prayer to-night for God's especial blessing, I feel greatly strengthened and comforted. I can look my work in the face without fear, nay, even with joy, and my plan for proceeding in the school is much more clear to me now than it has ever appeared before. I will endeavour to lean fully upon God, and so move on. He has shown me frequently what a thing of nought I am in myself. May He now show me what I can be and do while dealing with His strength and relying upon His wisdom.

"*Nov.* 18.—Fresh trials and fresh mercies to-day. A very severe storm awoke me early this morning. After breakfast, a man came running to inform me that the roof of the school-house was blown off. My heart quailed for a moment; but before I had time to get out and look for myself, the man returned, saying that the roof had not

gone, and not even the bark had stirred on one side. I
learnt, too, from whence emanated the untrue and unkind
report. Many wait for my halting, but the Lord disappoints
them. When I went to the school, I found that only a slight
damage had come to one side of the roof; but still the wind
continued to blow so fiercely, that I was afraid more damage
might ensue, and it was impossible to go up and mend, or
prevent the matter. I therefore knelt down in the school,
and poured out my cries to the Lord who holds the storm.
I entreated Him to disappoint His enemies, and support His
lonely and feeble servant. He heard my cry. Before an
hour had passed the wind had ceased. This afternoon willing
hearts came forward to assist me. One man gave me a plank,
mounted the roof to repair the breach, and wanted no remuneration. Several others also carried my seats and desk into
the school, and waited for no return.

"*Nov.* 19.—Through the mercy of God, I have begun school
to-day. It has been a strange day to me, but the Lord
helped me through. In the morning I plainly saw that a
superstitious fear was spreading powerfully among the Indians : crowds wanted to come to school, but who were to be
the first to venture? Here I reaped the fruit of my few
weeks' labour in the chief's house during last summer. The
little flock I had there eagerly enough rushed to the school
when they saw me coming, and one even gladly mounted the
platform and struck the steel for me, to call their more timid
companions to the place. I had arranged to have the children in the morning, and the adults in the afternoon; but I
now see reason to change that plan, and have all together, at
least for a while. My first start was with only fifteen children ; but, before we had finished, we mustered about seventy.
In the afternoon came about fifty adults, and fifty children.
I felt it very difficult to proceed with such a company, and
should have found it much more so, but for the few children
whom I had already had under training.

" Both morning and afternoon I finished with an address, previously prepared, in their own tongue; in which I endeavoured to show them my intention, their need and condition, and also the glorious message which I had come to make known, namely, salvation through Jesus Christ, the Son of God. They were very attentive, and I hope and pray the Lord will now begin His work amongst them, to the glory of His great name.

" *Nov.* 20.—This morning about one hundred children and forty adults came. Last night I spoke to the head chief about his little girl not coming to school. I had heard that she was kept away because it was intended that she should be initiated into the medicine-art this winter; not so much from the desire of her parents, but because the tribe, or at least part of it, demanded she should. I was told that my interposition would be acceptable. This morning I was glad to see that my visit was not without effect; both the chief and his little girl came neat and clean to school. He sat down and learnt with the others, and had occasionally something to say to the scholars.

" I am very thankful that I am able to say there is amongst the Indians a great stir of opinion against their heathenish winter-customs, and four of the tribes out of nine have, indeed, cut them off. Those tribes which still adhere to them are carrying them on exceedingly feebly; so much so, that I am assured by all whom I speak to about the matter, that what I now see is really nothing compared with what the system is when properly carried out. They tell me that they were afraid to cast the custom away all in one year, but would rather that part should do so this year, and the remainder next; so, according to this, I sincerely hope that this is the last winter any of these savage practices will be seen.

" *Nov.* 23.—Both yesterday and to-day we mustered about one hundred children, and from forty to fifty adults at school. Every day shows me more and more what a dense mass of

ignorance I have come into contact with. I have also now
to meet all the evil reports continually emanating from very
evil and superstitious persons. Some are watching, I believe,
for a calamity to arise and explode the work. Others are in
suspense, hoping we shall succeed, but feel afraid we cannot.
Some keep a scrutinizing eye over all our movements, and
when they feel satisfied we have no tricks to injure them, I
suppose they will countenance us. But we go on, and I am
glad to hear every day, in contrast with the incessant and
horrid drumming of the medicine-men, the sweet sound of
our steel, calling numbers to hear and learn the way of life.

"On leaving the school this morning, I spoke to a man
who is of considerable power and influence in the camp, as to
why he did not send his children to school, and come himself.
He replied that he was waiting till the Indians had done with
their foolishness and dancing, which time was not far distant,
then he would come. He both wanted himself and his
children to learn, but would not come yet, as it is not good,
he said, to mix his ways and mine together. He intended
soon to give up his, and then he would come to school. This
afternoon he just dropped in to school simply as a gazer: he
would join in nothing. Nevertheless, he heard a short address, which I gave in Tsimsheean, and which I hope will
not be lost to him. It was the first of the Gospel he ever
heard, for he was not here when I gave my addresses in the
summer.

"Nov. 25.—This morning about 140 children, and, in the
afternoon, about 120. Adults seldom vary from about fifty
each time. I am glad to see already an improvement in their
appearance, so far as cleanliness is concerned. I inspect
them daily. Some few have ventured to come with their
faces painted, but we have less of it daily. A good many,
too, have cast away their nose-rings, yet some come who have
very large ones in use still.

"I visited three sick persons to-day, and was able to speak

to two about our Saviour. One of them had been very
anxious to see me; and when I went, he said he had refused
to call in the medicine-men to operate upon him, and begged
very earnestly for me to give him a little of my medicine.
This is the first instance that has come under my notice, in
which the power of their medicine-men or women has been
slighted; for, as a whole, this people place implicit confidence
in these lying wonder-workers.

"Nov. 27.—Last night, after repeating the Lord's Prayer,
I read to my scholars a prayer which I have written and
translated. This is the first time they ever heard their
language arranged for such a purpose. They remained
serious. This morning we offered up this prayer in their own
tongue.

"Nov. 29.—After school-teaching was over this morning, a
chief remained behind; he had a serious difficulty. His
people, who had before decided to give up their medicine-
working, were beginning to repent of their decision. According
to the chief's statement, they professed themselves unable to
leave off what had been such a strong and universal custom
among them for ages. He heard my remarks, and then set
off, seemingly satisfied that I was right; and, I hope, in a
mind determined to hold on in its present improved course. I
had some talk with another chief to-day, on the same subject
of medicine-work. He and his people seem stedfast in their
purpose to cut the abominable system off; still, he says, he
feels very much ashamed when he comes into contact with
their chiefs who are carrying it on.

"I laboured to set before the same old man the way of
salvation, and he gave me serious attention, and looked eager
to learn. When speaking of prayer, he asked me how often
I prayed each day.

"To-night I visited two houses where there are sick. In
both I directed the inmates to Jesus as our only Saviour,
and I was much assisted and comforted.

Y

"*December* 1.—I was told to-day, by the manager of the Fort, that the head chief of the Indians is going to ask me to give up my school for about a month; his complaint being, that the children running past his house to and from school, tend to unsettle him and his party in working their mysteries. My mind is made up, and my answer ready, if such a request is made.

"After school this afternoon, a chief, who is a regular scholar, came to inquire whether I had promised to close the school during the medicine-season, as a report to that effect was afloat. I see now, that although I have been as careful as possible not to give unnecessary offence, yet a storm is in the horizon. I must prepare for fierce opposition, and that from the chief I had least expected to show it.

"I had a delightful round to-night. I was in nine houses. I found myself able to hold conversation and·give instruction in the Indian tongue with some freedom, in one house especially, which was a chief's. When I was seen going in, a number of his people followed me, and we soon formed a large group round the fire. I had some difficulty in commencing; but, when that was overcome, I felt quite at home in addressing them. I laid down our condition and remedy plainly before them, and exhorted them frequently to amend their ways; I was greatly delighted with the response they made. One man held both his hands out before him, and then gave them a sudden turn over, exclaiming, 'Thus it was going to be with the hearts of the Tsimsheeans soon.' The old chief, too, with his eyes upon the ground, listened very attentively, and after I had begged them to desist from some of their bad practices, such as prostitution and rum-drinking, he, very chief-like, reiterated to them something of what I said. I returned quite cheered at what I had seen and heard.

"*Dec.* 8.—I learnt, yesterday, that the head chief had been 'speaking bad,' as the Indians say, against me. He has been exhorting all to have nothing to do with the school; but, blessed be God, he is too late: his speech had but little effect. Indeed, I may say that none but a few of his own tribe took any notice of it: the mass of the Indians are disgusted with him for making it, because only a little time ago, when I had school in his house, he spoke so much in favour of me and my work, and his contradictory speech now, without any cause, has only rendered him contemptible.

"I visited at four houses to-night, and met with grateful looks and greetings everywhere.

"The Indians are exceedingly fond of the singing I am teaching them. I have got them to understand the difference between sacred and secular music, and they are particularly solemn when we sing hymns. They are often telling me how they long to be able to sing to God. I hear, too, that several Indians have begun to pray before they go to sleep. Oh! that the Lord would manifest Himself to them!

"*Dec.* 10.—It is still very cold, but 130 were present in school to-day.

"*Dec.* 13.—After school to-night, a medicine-man came to ask me for a little *English* medicine, as he felt himself sick. I brought him to my house in the Fort, and talked to him for some time about his ways. He excused himself as much as possible. I told him not to lie, but tell me truthfully if he believed what he had just said, when he frankly confessed he did not.

"*Dec.* 14.—I bless the Lord for His gracious care of me this day. As I went through part of the camp on my way to the school, this morning, I met a strong medicine-party full in the face; they seemed ashamed and confounded, but I quietly walked on. Their naked prodigy was carrying a dead dog, which he occasionally laid down and feasted upon. While a little boy was striking the steel for me at school, some of the party made their appearance near the school, I imagine, for all at once the boy began to be irregular and feeble in his strokes, and when I looked up at him I saw he was looking very much afraid. On inquiring the cause, he told me the medicine-folks were near; I told him to strike away, and I stood at the door of the school. Some few stragglers of the medicine-party were hovering about, but they did not dare to interfere with us. When all were assembled, and the striking ceased, my adult pupils commenced a great talk; I had seen, as they came in, there was something serious on their minds. After a little time, a chief came and told me that the Indians were 'talking bad' outside, by which I understood that the medicine-folks had been using more threats to stop us. However, I quickly stopped the consultation, and got them on at work; on leaving school I came into contact with the same medicine-party which I met on going to school. I almost hesitated about proceeding, but the Lord did not let me halt.

"The medicine-men were ashamed to meet me, and so took a short turn. They then became very much scattered. some hung behind, the charm seemed broken, and all seemed lost. On nearing the Fort, I met one of the most important men in the medicine-business, a chief, and father to one of the little boys that are being initiated. I spoke to him. He stopped, and I then told him how angry God is to see such wickedness as he and his party were carrying on; and also how grieved I was to see it. He spoke very kindly, and told me that if they did not make their medicine-men as they had always been used to do, then there would be none to stop or frustrate the designs of those bad men who made people sick, and therefore deaths would be more numerous from the effects of the evil workings of such bad men. I told him if they put away their wicked ways, then God would take care of them. He did not say much more, except assuring me it was the intention of all soon to do as I wished them, but at present the medicine-parties must go on. I learnt shortly afterwards, from the chief officer of the Fort, that this very man and another had just visited the Fort to tell him they would now be content if I would stay school for a fortnight, and, after that, they would all come to be taught; but if I did not comply they intended stopping me by force, for they had determined to shoot at my pupils as they came to the school. I had a long talk to two of the officers about the matter, giving them plainly to understand that I did not intend in the least degree to heed the threats of the Indians, but go on with my work I would, in spite of all. I told them that Satan had reigned long enough here; it was high time his rule was disturbed (as it is). I went, of course, to school as usual this afternoon; about 90 pupils were present. After we had done, a chief who was present began to address them, encouraging them to continue; after he had done, I began to speak on the matter to them. I was afraid I should not be able to convey my feelings to them in their own tongue, yet, thanks be to God, I was enabled to do so. The effect I desired, was produced: they all reassured me of their continuing, come what would.

"After school, as I had several calls to make to see the sick, I went out, and found plenty of grateful hearts to acknowledge my feeble endeavours for their good; I was in ten houses. Everywhere I hear intimations of the struggle that is now going on. Oh! that the Almighty arm would interpose, that this people may be delivered from the chains which have so long fettered them.

"*Dec.* 20.—This day has been a great day here. I have to thank heartily that all-seeing Father who has covered me and supported me to-day. The devil and wicked men leagued to overthrow me this day, but the Lord would not have it so. I am still alive.

"This morning the medicine-party who are carrying on their work near to the school, broke out with renewed fury, because, as they assert, the child of the head chief had just returned from above. The little boy that lights my fire came in great excitement to tell me that the head chief was not willing for me to have school to-day, and was anxious to know if I intended going; he seemed greatly amazed at my answer. On going to school, I observed a crowd of these wretched men in a house that I was approaching. When they turned to come out, they saw me coming, and immediately drew back until I had passed. As soon as I got into school, the wife of the head chief came to beg me to give up school for a little time : she was certainly very modest in her manner and request, but altogether unsuccessful. I spoke to her a little, and then she said (what I know to be false) that it was not she nor her husband that desired to go on with the medicine-work, for they often cried to see the state of things, but it was the tribe that urged them to do what they were doing. When she saw she could prevail nothing, not even so much as to prevent striking the steel, which they have a peculiar hatred for, she left me. I then went up the ladder and struck the steel myself, as I did not like to send a boy up; very soon about 80 pupils were in the school, and we went on as usual.

"This afternoon, a boy ran to strike the steel, and not many seconds elapsed before I saw the head chief approaching, and a whole gang of medicine-men after him, dressed up in their usual charms. The chief looked very angry, and bade the boy cease: I waited at the door until he came up. His first effort was to rid the school of the few pupils that had just come in; he shouted at the top of his voice, and bade them be off. I immediately accosted him, and demanded to know what he intended or expected to do; his gang stood about the door, and I think seven came in. I saw their point: it was to intimidate me by their strength and frightful appearance, and I perceived the chief, too, was somewhat under the influence of rum; but the Lord enabled me to stand calm, and without the slightest fear to address them with far more fluency, in their tongue, than I could have imagined possible—to tell them of their sin faithfully—to vindicate my conduct—to exhort them to leave their bad ways, and also to tell them they must not think to make me afraid. I told them that God was my master, and I must obey Him rather than them, and that the devil has taught their fathers what they were practising, and it was bad; but what I was teaching now was God's way, and it was good, and that all the Tsimsheeans knew.

"Our meeting lasted for more than an hour. I saw a great many people at a distance looking anxiously at our proceedings, the school-door being open, and we stood near it. Nearly all my pupils had fled in fear. The chief expressed himself very passionately, now and then breaking out into furious language, and showing off his savage nature by his gestures. Sometimes I pacified him by what I said, for a little time; but he soon broke out again with more violence. Towards the close of the scene, two of the confederates, vile-looking fellows, went and whispered something to him, upon which he got up from a seat he had just sat down upon, stamped his feet on the floor, raised his voice as high as he could, and exhibited all the rage, and defiance, and boldness that he could. This was all done, I knew to intimidate me, but, blessed be God, he did not succeed: finding his efforts unavailing, he went off, but not before he had been almost deserted by his gang. As he went away, he kept addressing those who had been witnesses; but none seemed to heed him or give any encouragement. After this I shut the door, and found 16 scholars presently around me, and we commenced work.

" We had not gone on long before the chief returned to the school; he gave a loud knock on the door with a stick. I went to open it, and my pupils began to squat about for shelter. When he came in I saw he was in rather a different mood, and he began to say that he was not a bad man to the white people, but that he had always borne a good character with them; this he could prove by papers containing his character, given him by the officers of the Fort. After this he despatched his wife in great haste to fetch me the papers; when they came, I read them, and then he soon left us again. It was now time to leave school, so we concluded by singing a hymn. All appeared solemn, and when they went away they wished me good night.

"The leading topics of the chief's angry clamour I may class as follows:—He requested four days' suspension of the school; he promised, that if I complied, he and his people would then come to school; but threatened, if my pupils continued to come on the following days, he would shoot at them;—lastly, he pleaded, that if the school went on during the time he specified, then some medicine-men, whom he expected on a visit shortly from a distant tribe, would shame, and perhaps kill him.

"Some of his sayings during his fits of rage were, that he understood how to kill people, occasionally drawing his hand across his throat to show me what he meant; that when he died he knew he should go down; he could not change; he could not be good; or, if I made him good, why then he supposed he should go to a different place from his fore-fathers: this he did not desire to do.

"On one occasion, while he was talking, he looked at two men, one of them a regular pupil of mine, and the other a medicine-man, and said 'I am a murderer, and so are you, and you' (pointing to each of these men), 'and what good is it for us to come to school?' Here I broke in, and, blessed be God, it gave me an opportunity of telling the three murderers that pardon was now offered to them if they would repent, and amend, and go to Jesus our Saviour. After school I took the opportunity of speaking again to the one who comes to the school, setting the mercy and love of God before him, and the terms upon which God will now pardon and save us. He seemed very solemn, and I hope the truth will sink into his heart.

" After this another chief came to my house, and spoke of the difficulties in the way of attending school now, and so offered me the use of his house for a school, where the children and others would not be afraid to come. I readily availed myself of his kindness, and I hope that good will arise out of the arrangement.

" Dec.·21.—I have had school to-day in the chief's house. About 100 scholars attended. A medicine-party from a distant tribe has arrived to-day, and caused great stir among the parties here. In one house to-night, where I dropped in, I found about fifteen quietly sitting over the fire, two or three of whom were interesting the rest by going over the reading-lesson of the day, which they had written on a slate I had lent them.

" Dec. 23.—School as usual in the chief's house, both yesterday and to-day.

" I am told that the head chief is still doing, or rather saying, all he can to hinder my work. Yesterday, at a feast of the medicine-parties, he gave a speech full of bitter feeling towards us. I hear, too, he is taunting the chief who has lent me his house. How all this will end I cannot tell, but I leave it with God.

" Dec. 24.—At the close of school-work this morning I gave my audience an address on the coming Christian festival, which has hitherto only been distinguishable to the Indians as a time of riot and drunkenness among the whites.

" While in school there was ' a frightful outburst of the medicine-parties, setting the whole of the camp round about in a kind of terror. A party were, with their naked prodigy, on the beach when I went out of the school, but on seeing me they immediately ran into a house until I got past.

" I hear that the chief of the medicine-party strangers who have arrived lately here has proposed to try the strength of my medicine, which means he will try how strong I can talk,

or whether I can resist his strong talk and his imaginary evil
influence.

" *Dec* 25: *Christmas-day*.—Yesterday I told my scholars to
bring their friends and relatives to school to-day, as I wanted
to tell them something new. I found a strong muster when
I arrived at the chief's house, and a long train of all ages
followed me in. We numbered over 200 souls. I felt the
occasion to be a very important one, and longed to turn it to
some good account. We did not read as usual, but I tried to
make them understand why we distinguished this day from
others. After this I questioned the children a little, and
then we sung two hymns, which we also translated. While
the hymns were being sung, I felt I must try to do something more, although the language seemed to defy me. I
never experienced such an inward burning to speak before,
and therefore I determined to try an extemporaneous address
in Tsimsheean. The Lord helped me : a great stillness prevailed, and, I think, a good deal of what I said was understood. I told them of our condition, the pity and love of God,
the death of the Son of God on our account, and the benefits
arising to us therefrom. I then exhorted them to leave their
sins, and pray to Jesus; warning them of the consequences if
they refused, and told them of the good which would follow
to them on obedience. On hearing me enumerate the sins
of which they are guilty, I saw some turn and look at each
other with those significant looks which betokened their
assent to what I said. I tried to impress upon them the
certain ruin which awaited them, did they proceed in their
present vices. Very remarkably, an illustration corroborating
what I said was before their eyes. A poor woman was taken
sick, not four yards from where I stood, and right before the
eyes of my audience. She was groaning under a frightful
affliction, the effect of her vices.

" *Dec.* 28.—School as usual in the chief's house; over 150
pupils on each occasion. One man came to-day to return

thanks to me for giving him a little medicine, which, he says, has been the means of his recovery from sickness. It is rather an interesting case to me, because this person is the first, so far as I know, who, being dangerously ill, has refused to call in the aid of the medicine-folks, from a conviction they could do him no good, but only told him lies. Having recovered without them, he is making a great talk about it.

" *Dec.* 29.—After school to-night I went to take a little medicine to a sick man, and found in his house a group of Indians of the tribe which have lately sent a party of medicine-men here to show themselves off. I therefore felt an increased desire to set forth the Gospel on this visit, that these poor creatures might go back and tell their people something of the glad tidings they had heard. Their village is about 80 to 100 miles away from here, I think. For some time I could not begin; however, I would not go away, but stood musing and praying, my heart burning, but full of misgiving. At last an opportunity was afforded me, and I began, and, by God's blessing, I was enabled to set the Gospel clearly and fully before them—that is, as to the first and essential great truths of it. While I was speaking, one or two would make remarks as to the truth and reasonableness of what I said. Several times one man exclaimed —' *Ahm malsh! ahm malsh!*' (Good news! good news). And another, when I had done, said, ' *Shimhow,*' which means ' It is true,' and it is equivalent, in their way of speaking, to ' Amen,' ' I believe.' They all seemed thankful for my visit, and I hope the Lord will bless it. I tried to enforce the duty of love and obedience to God, by alluding to the attachment and obedience they expected from their children. To this they agreed, and fully believed the Indians would not be long before they would be altogether changed."

It will be seen from the above that Mr. Duncan's work had much increased: feeling that he could not carry it on single-handed, he wrote home requesting very earnestly that a coadjutor might be sent to him. About this time a serious difficulty began to embarrass him, viz., what was to be done with the children who were being taught, when they passed from his hands. It was evident to him, and to the Indians themselves, that they and the well-disposed adults among them would be far too weak numerically to be able to carry out their new principles in their old camp. The necessity of transplanting them, therefore, was evident; although how such a number could be removed against the wish, probably, of many of their parents and the tribe generally, was a problem most difficult of solution.

In it, however, he was not without assistance from some of the Indians themselves. In his journal for June, 1859, he writes: "Had some talk with a chief, who entreated me to beg for another missionary, and to remove the well-disposed Indians and their children away to some good land about 30 miles from here, that they might thus escape the present scenes of wickedness." A few days later the same chief came again, knowing that Mr. Duncan was writing letters to Victoria, and again urged his request for another missionary, and for a separation to be made in the camp. He said, that the Indians were willing to give Mr. Duncan their children to teach and bring up as he wished, adding, however, that the grown people desired no change.

With the approach of autumn and the renewal of the medicine-orgies among the Indians, Mr. Duncan's difficulties recurred. What progress he made, his own words will best describe :—

"*August* 18, 1859.—This morning forty-three children and fourteen adults were at school. After the usual lessons, I gave them a short address, or rather tried to impress upon them the safety of God's people, and the insecurity of the wicked. The Lord enabled me to express myself with feeling earnestness, and disposed my hearers to attention and solemnity. Having a good deal of writing to do in the books which I

write for my pupils for. home lessons, I announced we would
have no school in tho afternoon of to-day. After dinner a
loud and unusual knock was given at the door. I opened it.
It was a chief, bringing me the broken lock of the school,
and the sad intelligence that Cushwaht (a notoriously bad
man), being drunk, had with an axe broken my door open,
entered the school, and smashed all the windows. The chief
then entered into a passionate explanation of the cause of
this deed, and assured me that Cushwaht stood alone in the
mischief; not another Indian would have dared or thought
of such a thing.

  "Very soon several other Indians came—some to bring me
the utensils of the school, and others to tender their sympathy.
Thus it has pleased the Lord to permit us to have another
check; but I trust and pray He will make it administer
good. This is the explanation. The Indian that did tho
mischief has a bad leg. He sent his wife this morning to
beg of —— a little salve for it, but she was unsuccessful.
—— refused to assist because of his bad conduct, he having,
only a few days ago, struck a woman who lives in the Fort
with a sword, and wounded her severely, and for no cause.
Being denied the salve, and under the influence of rum, he
went, Indian like, to revenge himself on what came readiest
of the white man's property, and that happened to be the
school. Here is the good providence of God in ordering that
I and my scholars were not to be in the building when the
wicked savage was to vent his rage upon it. Had we been
assembled, I tremble to think what might have been the consequences. The chief who came to my house to bring me
the lock, &c., entreated me not to go outside the Fort, as
the enraged villain might fire upon me; but I felt assured
that the Lord would protect me while in the path of duty.
On seeing me on the beach, several Indians came to speak
with me, to tender their sympathy, and express their anger
with the man. I remember an old man saying 'the whole

camp was crying, and many guns were ready and waiting for
the villain if he dared to appear.' I entreated them not to
shed his blood; said that it was very wrong indeed what he
had done, but that I was inclined to pity and forgive him.
One house I had to go to was the next but one to that occupied by Cushwaht. On approaching it, many thought, probably, I was going to see him. They looked very much
alarmed, expecting, no doubt, that firing would ensue. But on
seeing me enter the house where the sick person was, many
followed me, among whom was the wife of the mischievous
rascal. I never alluded to my own troubles or wrongs, but
applied myself to the case of the poor invalid, whose state
was indeed alarming.

"*September* 15.—Some sad work has occurred in the camp
this afternoon. A young man, an Indian, under the influence
of drink, irritated one of the chiefs, who was also partly
drunk. The chief immediately seized a pistol, and shot the
brother of the man who had offended him. Then commenced
a series of encounters, and two more were killed. The firing
is going on, and quite close to the school-house.

"*Sept.* 19.—Another very serious disturbance to-day. As
I went to the school-house, to see about repairing it, I observed that some of the Indians of one tribe were having a
rum-feast. On nearing the house of the man who broke the
school-windows (Cushwaht), I saw that his house was the
point of attraction, and, from what I heard, concluded that a
good many were already drunk within. I had nothing but
civility shown me, both in going and returning, although I
passed some that were drunk. I had only just got back to
the Fort, when a quarrel took place in Cushwaht's house,
and Cushwaht himself, as usual, the cause of it. It was not
long before firing ensued. Two women have been killed,
one of them Cushwaht's sister, and Cushwaht has been shot
in the hand. These murders and riots are all tending very
powerfully to awaken the minds of those who have been

under instruction, and to wean them more and more from this place of darkness. I find many flock around me now to speak of their trouble, and they listen with much more attention and seriousness to the Gospel message. I have been for some time desiring to speak to the cannibal chief. To-day the opportunity was afforded me, and I had some talk with him. This man heads the most degrading superstition this people have got; but he is a young man, and has a noble look. It will be a hard struggle if he ever sets himself to escape from the meshes of that horrid custom which he has taken upon himself to perpetuate; but I hope and pray God may give him light and strength for the conflict, and bring him, clothed and in his right mind, to the feet of Jesus. He met my proposals very kindly, and promised to come under my instruction when he returns from a place whither he is going to purchase food.

" *Sept.* 27.—By the good pleasure of our Heavenly Father we began school again to-day. About 50 children and 10 adults attended. The tide was so high that many had to come in canoes. It rained, too, all the day. I saw some of my little scholars, washed and with their best clothes on, waiting for me outside the Fort, hours before the time appointed for opening school, although it rained.

" *Sept.* 28.—I put Bibles into the hands of my first class to-day. What a blessed event, indeed, when it is remembered that the entrance of God's Word giveth light! We commenced with St. Matthew's Gospel.

" *October* 9th: *Lord's-day.*—Only between 40 and 50 souls present at school this morning. Many have gone away during last week to a place where they usually purchase large quantities of provisions. I was enabled, by the blessing of God, to introduce a happy change in our usual Sunday course. I handed ten of my pupils Bibles, and they read out simultaneously, several times over, the passage (Psalm cxlv.

18–20) from which I addressed them. We also translated it, clause by clause, several times over.

" *Oct.* 10.—A very solemn event has taken place this evening. I was informed, on coming out of the school this afternoon, that a young man, who has been a long time suffering in consumption (brought on by a severe cold), and whom I have visited several times, was dying; so, after a little reflection, some misgiving, and prayer, I started off to see him. I found him, as his wife had said, dying. Over 20 persons were about him : some were crying, and two, I am sorry to say, were partly intoxicated. I looked on for some time in silent sorrow. When I wished to speak, silence immediately ensued. I rebuked the noise and tumult, and directed the dying man to fix his heart on the Saviour Jesus, to forget the things about him, and spend his little remaining time in praying in his heart to God to save him. His reply was, ' O, yes, Sir ! O, yes, Sir !' and for some moments he would close his eyes, and seem absorbed in prayer. On one occasion he spoke of his heart being happy or resigned. I could not make out the exact expression, as there was some talking at the time, and the remark was in Tsimsheean.

" He begged me, with much earnestness, to continue to teach his little girl. He wanted her to be good. This little girl is about seven years old; her.name is Cathl. She has been very regular at school since I commenced, and has made nice progress.

" Much to my comfort, a young woman sat by his side who has been one of my most regular pupils. She is in the first class, and can read portions of the Bible. Her intelligence is remarkable, and I have observed her to be always very serious when listening to religious instruction. Thus, here was one sitting close to the dying man who could tell him, much more accurately than I, the few directions I desired to utter. What remarkable providence it seemed to me! With tears in her eyes she begged him to give his heart to God and to pray to Him. I longed to pray with him, and watched anxiously a long time for the opportunity. The opportunity came, and the strength came with it. I knelt down by his side. All was hushed, and I prayed from a full heart to the Lord our God to have mercy upon the poor soul about to come into His presence, for the sake of His dear Son Jesus. I feel sure that the Lord heard my prayer, and I can indulge a hope for this poor man's salvation. The whole of the circumstances seemed ordered of God for my commencing this solemn and important duty of prayer with dying Indians. In the case of this poor man, I can say I have felt my heart exceedingly rejoiced more than once, when I have left him, for what I had been permitted to see and hear. I know he understood the main and leading truths of the Gospel, and he frequently told me that he prayed much to God. During his sickness he never permitted the medicine-folks to operate upon him; and this of itself shows a wonderful change in the man. After I had prayed with him he gave me his hand, which I shook, and he bade me good-bye.

" Oct. 11.—The young man alluded to above died last night. He reassured the people around him of his safety, and he had a very solemn parting from his little girl."

This is only one instance of many in which Mr. Duncan found the hearts and intellects of the Indians open to his teaching. The labours of men of his class among the distant heathen are undervalued by the world, which refuses to credit the fact that savages, such as these Coast Indians undoubtedly are, can receive and retain impressions so utterly at variance with their nature and habits. But the following extracts from the journal of one of Mr. Duncan's Indian pupils at Fort Simpson—a lad aged 19—will be read with interest by those who believe that the aborigines of these colonies may assuredly be Christianised and civilised. From this curious document,

Z .

which was presented to me by Captain Prevost, R.N., I extract the following "passages from the Journal of Shooquanahts," written after ten months of occasional instruction by Mr. Duncan:—

"*Tuesday, April* 4, 1860.—If will die my father, then will very poor my heart 4 my brother all die; only one Shooquanahts save; and two my uncle save. I will try to make all things. I want to be good, and I want to much work hard. When we have done work, then will please, sir, Mr. Duncan, will you give me a little any thing when you come back.

"*April* 9.—Please, sir, I want to speak to you. I wish I had some powder for my gun. All done shot: all done for me. What for you want to shoot ducks? Because it is very sweet. Please, sir, Mr. Duncan, will you give me a little powder and little shot? If you will give me any powder, then I will be very happy. If I get some ducks, then I will give Mr. ——. Perhaps no want ducks, Mr. ——.

"*April* 10.—I could not sleep last night. I must work hard last night. I could not be lazy last night. No good lazy—very bad. We must learn to make all things. When we understand reading and writing, then it will very easy. Perhaps two years then we understand. If we no understand to read and to write, then he will very angry, Mr. Duncan. If we understand about good people, then we will very happy.

April 27 : *School, Fort Simpson.*—Shooquanahts not two hearts—no always one my heart. Some boys always two hearts. Only one Shooquanaht's—not two heart, no. If I steal any thing, then God will see. Bad people no care about Son of God. When will come troubled hearts, foolish people. Then he will very much cry. What good cry? Nothing. No care about our Saviour, always forget. By and by will understand about the Son of God.

April 29.—How many ducks you get yesterday? 5 ducks I shoot yesterday. Did you see many ducks yesterday?

Yes, very many; not far away, but near. To one man I give one duck yesterday, and one duck I eat yesterday. The name of that man is Nahs-lukolik. He want to work for you. If it rain to-morrow, then we cannot go to Sebassah. If it do not rain to-morrow, then we go to Sebassah.

"*8th May*, 1860.—The brother of Sebassah is not good, he understand to eat dead people: no good—very bad, that man. They understand make lie: no good, those men—very bad. Not a good place, Sebassah place: always want to steal some little things. They cannot rest; they love bad ways; they always like to make afraid the people.

"*14th May*, 1860.—The Shad-Zahu, by and by, will give rice at our place, and molasses; and all the brothers of Shad-Zahu will give rice at our place, and two sisters of Shad-Zahu will give rice at our place. My father wants to make two houses; when he has done making the houses, then he will call three chiefs, and all people will sit together in the house. My father then will give elk-skins to three chiefs, and to all men he will give elk-skin by and by. Perhaps two winters first will give little things, and by and by he will give more.

"*May* 16, 1860.—When you go way Victoria, sir, then he will speak to Mr. Compton, sir. Good will tell Mr. Compton, sir, to pity me when you go way Victoria, sir. Who take care me, sir, when you go way? who will give the soap for me, sir? who will give the tobacco for me when you go way Victoria, sir? who will give the medicine for me, sir, when you go way Victoria, sir? No, not any will pity me when you go way, sir. Good will speak, sir, Mr. Moffat will pity me when you go way Victoria, sir. Then will, please, sir, Mr. Duncan, will you give me a little medicine and little soap?—not now, sir; no, when you will go way Victoria, sir. Then good will pity me.

"*May* 17, 1860.—I do not understand some prayers—only few prayers I understand, not all; I understand, no. I wish to understand all prayers. When I understand all prayers, then I always prayer our Saviour Jesus Christ. I want to learn to prayer to Jesus Christ our Saviour, by and by. I understand all about our Saviour Christ; when I understand all what about our Saviour, then I will happy when I die. If I do not learn about our Saviour Jesus, then I will very troubled my heart when I die. It is good for us when we learn about our Saviour Jesus; I wish to understand to prayer our Saviour Jesus. When I understand about our Saviour, then I will very happy when I die."

In writing of the journal from which I have given the above extracts, Mr. Duncan explains: "Last winter, for the sake of exercising my first class in composition, I gave each of them a copy-book wherein to record their own thoughts in their own way, after school-hours. But neither the writers nor I ever expected them to be exhibited. I therefore was loth for Captain Prevost to take one away, because several entries in it require explanation, or they may give wrong impressions. For instance, on one occasion the boy asks, ' who will give him tobacco,' &c., during my absence. From this the reader might infer that I encouraged him to smoke, and supplied him with tobacco for that purpose. The fact is, that, because the boy worked so hard and pleased me so much, I made him one of my school-assistants, also school-cleaner, for which I paid him about two shillings a week—not in money, but in goods, which he exchanged for provisions. He, of course, chose the kind of goods for which there was then the readiest market."

I will now quit Mr. Duncan to speak of the progress of the Church which had in this year (1859) sprung up in other parts of the colony.

The only clergyman in the colony previous to this was the Rev. E. Cudge, Chaplain to the Hudson Bay Company, who had been established at Victoria for four or five years.

Early in the year 1859 four Wesleyan missionaries arrived

from Canada and commenced their labours. The head of this mission was Dr. Evans, a most zealous man and able preacher. He settled himself at Victoria, where he has since built a pretty church, which is very well filled. His staff were soon disposed of—one going to Nanaimo, another to New Westminster, and the third to Fort Hope. These men, zealous and active, have been working hard in their districts; but their mission, like that of our own Church, has been more to the whites than the Indians.

A missionary of the Church of England, under the auspices of the Colonial Church and School Society, had arrived previous to this (on Christmas Day, 1858), and established himself at what was then the capital of British Columbia, New Langley or Derby. In the course of the year the Society for the Propagation of the Gospel despatched three missionaries, and the Special Fund endowed by Miss Burdett Coutts sent two. In addition to this a bishop had been appointed (Dr. Hills), who, however, was detained in England raising further subscriptions for the mission. Besides these, two other missionaries—I am not sure of what denomination—arrived about this time. Thus in 1859 eleven missionaries of different denominations betook themselves to their duties in various places—some at and around Victoria, others on the Fraser River.

On the 5th of January, 1860, the Bishop reached Esquimalt and commenced an organization of his forces, which were soon augmented by the arrival of five other clergymen. An iron church, which had been sent from England, was erected. The expense of its construction was, as may be imagined, very large, and the edifice was not free from debt when I left the island.

Among the most pressing needs of the colony were good schools for either sex: to this the Bishop's attention was immediately directed, and the Rev. C. T. Woods and his wife, the Rev. O. Glover, and the Misses Penrice, left England in the summer of 1860 for the purpose of establishing them.

On the arrival of this staff, a school for boys and a ladies' college were immediately organised; and so earnest and zealous were the labours of their promoters, that in the winter of that year there were 41 boys and 21 girls in attendance. The difficulties in the way of starting these schools cannot be appreciated by those who have not lived among such a mixture of peoples as is found in newly-settled countries, each representative of his race clinging with peculiar tenacity to its prejudices. The fact of Mr. Glover, the second master of the school, being distinguished at home as a Hebrew scholar, was, I believe, of no little importance in this way; for the Jews, of whom there are several in Vancouver Island, all sent their sons, delighted at the chance of their acquiring Hebrew. The great want of the ladies' school for a long time was a piano, and I do not know whether it has been since supplied.

The limited state of the funds of the British Columbian Mission proved a serious hindrance to its successful progress. Most people in the colony had an idea that Miss Coutts had undertaken the whole expense of the mission, church and school building, &c.; whereas her bounty, noble as it was, was confined to two objects, viz., a provision of 600l. a-year for the bishop, and 400l. a-year towards the archdeaconries. After his appointment the Bishop worked hard to raise money in England, and succeeded in obtaining 11,000l. But this sum did no more than pay the initiatory expenses, and the whole of it was exhausted before 1861 in the payment of outfits and passages for clergy, in grants, and in land investments.* The annual fund of the mission the bishop estimates at 1500l., which suffices merely for the support of the clergy and teachers. The clergy of St. John's, Vic-

* Bishop of Columbia's Speech at Victoria, January, 1861.

toria, the iron church spoken of, and Trinity, New Westminster
—a church built by subscription—were not included in this
sum, as they were supposed to be supported by their congre-
gations. The financial state of the latter I do not know;
but up to the time I left (September 1861), St. John's was
still in debt, and its rector had not received any salary at all.
Those clergy who were sent out by societies have their
incomes temporarily secured to them to the extent of 1700l.
a-year, making the support of clergy and teachers in the
colony amount altogether to about 4000l. In a speech on
the subject, delivered at Victoria in January, 1861, the
Bishop proposed that the organisation of a parish primarily
should include a rector, churchwarden, church committee, and
vestry—the last consisting of pewholders. Ultimately he
hoped to have a complete diocesan organisation under one of
the various titles of Convention, Synod, Assembly, or Council.
Pending the formation of this, he proposed that there should
be, as in other colonies, a Church Society, supported by subscriptions and church collections gathered from all parts of
the diocese, for the support of ministers, building of churches,
parsonages, and schools, the aid of widows and orphans of
clergy, and other objects, and regulated by a committee
chosen by subscribers. But perhaps of all the Bishop's cares
and difficulties none pressed more hardly upon him than the
question what to do with and for the Indians.

The Songhies, near Victoria, were still living the most
debased lives imaginable, while the many Indians who visited
Victoria from the North—and their number increased yearly
—could scarcely fail to imbibe their habits. Under these
circumstances, it was but too clear that Mr. Duncan's work,
far away among the Tsimsheeans at Fort Simpson, was likely
to be counteracted by the bad lessons which his former pupils
would learn upon their visits to the South. In the hope,
therefore, of providing a remedy for this state of things, Mr.
Duncan was induced to go to Victoria to consult with the

Governor and Bishop as to the steps that should be taken for the Indians' safety.

Mr. Duncan remained at Victoria during the summer, organising the plans decided upon, and continuing his ministrations among such of his old friends, the Tsimsheean Indians, who happened to be there. By them and the Indians generally the most implicit confidence was placed in his good faith and motives. It was very strange to notice among these—the fiercest of the Coast-tribes—the childlike affection which they displayed towards him, and the thorough trust they expressed in his integrity. Speaking of them himself, he says: "My duties have kept me from noon till night among the Indians. They so appreciate my exertions for their temporal welfare, that many have come to receive religious instruction who would otherwise have stayed away. The Indians are continually coming to me with their troubles, and seem very grateful for my assistance. I also succeeded in getting several into good places as servants."

In June, when the Governor returned from British Columbia, he at once acceded to the plans submitted to him for the benefit of the Indian population, and took the necessary steps to carry them into action. At a public meeting 60l. was collected for the erection of a school-house. The Governor himself made this sum up to 100l., and the building was immediately commenced.

. On the 8th August Mr. Tugwell, who had been sent by the Church Missionary Society to join Mr. Duncan, arrived, and it was determined that they should both go at once to Fort Simpson in order that Mr. Duncan might introduce his companion to his duties there, and then return to Victoria for the winter to superintend the new schools. They accordingly left Victoria on the 13th, and reached Simpson on the 21st August. While there, to his great delight, news reached him that the Rev. A. C. Garret and Mr. Mallandaine had volunteered to take charge of the Indian schools at Victoria, and that his return for that purpose was not therefore necessary. These gentlemen at once assumed their self-imposed duties, and in a short time brought the schools into a highly flourishing condition. The difficulties which beset their path were of course many and great. The example set in the Indian huts but too often paralysed the school-teaching, while the attendance of the children was necessarily often interrupted. They were very quick and ready at receiving instruction, however; and those visitors who attended the public examination in December, 1860, were with reason amazed at the progress made. The following is Mr. Garret's account of this examination :—

" *Dec.* 22.—Our examination came off to-day. There were 157 Indian scholars in the room when the Governor arrived. We had the Governor, the Bishop, the Colonial Secretary, Chief Justice of British Columbia, and many other influential laymen, with all the clergy here who could attend, and Mr. Knipe, who arrived yesterday, among the number. We began by singing. Then Mr. Mallandaine, the catechist, examined them in reading the diagrams, and showed that they knew the English names for the various objects, and could spell and pronounce them. This, for three months' work, was considered very excellent by the Governor and all the visitors. After this the most advanced class, who have been somewhat longer at school, read in their *books*, and satisfied the suspicions of the Chief Justice of British Columbia by reading *backwards*, thus showing they were not crammed like parrots, but that they thoroughly understood what they had learned. This being over, the copies were produced, which elicited universal admiration. One especially, the production of a fine young man, who has received but *one month's* schooling in his life, fairly astonished the strangers. I send it to you as a curiosity. I then examined the various tribes (there were three present, Songhies, Haidas, and Tsimshecans) in the Chinook catechism, which I

have composed; and showed that they knew the history of
the Creation, the Fall, Cain and Abel, and the Flood—in
the Old Testament; and also that they knew about Jesus
Christ, whose Son He is, and what He did on earth, why He
died, how long He was dead, where He is now, what we must
do to be saved, &c."

Before leaving Victoria, Mr. Duncan had been informed
that the arrival of Mr. and Mrs. Tugwell at Fort Simpson
must necessarily interfere with his previous position there.
The three could not expect from the Hudson Bay Company
the favours that had been granted to him. It was necessary, therefore, that he should vacate the quarters which
he had hitherto occupied in the Fort, and that a dwelling-
house should be built outside its stockade.

"Thus the time is come," he writes, "when mission-
buildings are to figure among the poor Indians on this
dreary coast. And thankful am I to say that I believe
matters are fully ripe for such a step. Of course we must
expect many annoyances in thus putting ourselves entirely
into the hands of the Indians, but I do not anticipate any
great danger to either our persons or property. The great
question before us is, where shall we build? You will have
seen from my journal that many of the Indians are strongly
desiring to return to their old villages situated in a lovely
channel about 15 miles from here, and are anxiously
waiting for me to lead the way. On my visit to the Keeth-
rahîlah Indians last spring, I saw these spots, and, in my
journal accompanying this, I have written a short description
of them. They are called Met-lah-kah. Therefore the choice
of a site for our mission premises rests, I think, between the
neighbourhood of Fort Simpson and Met-lah-kah. I will
compare the two places, and I think you will agree with me
that the latter place is decidedly to be preferred. The only
advantage of Fort Simpson is a negative one—that is, by
remaining here we shall avoid the trouble of a move. But

the disadvantages are great. The influence of the Fort, and
the immoralities allowed on board the Company's ships which
come here, greatly oppose the influence of the mission.
More than all, the physical character of the country in the
neighbourhood of the Fort is exceedingly bad, and, to my
mind, condemns the place at once. One effect the missions
must have upon the Indians will be to make them desire
social improvemement. How necessary, therefore, it is that
the mission be established where social improvement is possible! But at Fort Simpson it is *not* possible. First as to
beach-room. This is essential to the comfort and welfare of
these Coast Indians, who have so many canoes to take care
of. But the whole of the beach at Fort Simpson is now more
than conveniently occupied. And then as to land about this
place, it is all in such a state that it could not be made available for gardens without immense labour, and a calling for
appliances which the Indians do not possess.

" Met-lah-kah, however, not only possesses these two essen-
tials to improving the Indians socially, viz., plenty of beach-
room and plots of land suitable for gardens, but its channel is
always smooth and abounds with salmon and shell-fish, while
its beauty stands in *great* contrast to the dreary country
around." Mr. Duncan states, further, that the Company,
aware of the desire of the natives to return there, had sent
people to try to find an eligible spot nearer Simpson, and says
one of them who went as far as Nutlahkah, not only failed in
finding any other suitable spot, but declared he did not believe there was such another in that part of the country.

" It may be asked," he continues, " why did not the Company establish their Fort there? This is easily explained.
Twenty-five years ago, when Fort Simpson was built, the
Company had *sailing* ships employed up the coast, and the
passage to the old Tsimsheean village being rather narrow,
they preferred this, as the entrance to the harbour is wider;
but to steamers, the way into Met-lah-kah presents no diffi-

culty.   The Indians were induced to leave their ancient
home for the sake of trading with the Fort ; there is now no
necessity for their remaining near it·for that purpose; other
facilities for trading are opening up; a schooner, not the
Company's, is at this moment in the harbour, doing a famous
trade with the Indians : indeed, I may say, that the importance of Fort Simpson as a central trading-port is gone ; very
few Indians from other places come here now, as they used
to do, and fewer will continue to do so ;—everything seems
propitious and prepared for a move to be made for the social
welfare of these poor tribes, and surely it is worthy of this
Mission to be the leader in such a praiseworthy undertaking."

I have given this extract in full, as it concerns more than
the mere selection of the spot for the Mission, important as
that is : it shows the change which is gradually coming over
those parts of the country uninfluenced by the discovery of
gold.* This consists mainly in the far greater freedom
that will be given to the Indians for trading purposes, and
which will enable them now to live where they please, since
trade will follow them to their homes, and they will always
find a market there for anything they have to sell.

The proposal for the re-settlement of the Indians at Met-
lah-kah has met with the Governor's entire approval, and I
believe steps are being taken for its execution.

After remaining a year at Fort Simpson, Mr. Tugwell's
health became so seriously affected that he was obliged to
resign his labours and retire to Victoria.   Mr. Duncan, therefore, is again left to labour single-handed.   The plan which
they had purposed carrying out, had they been permitted,
was, that Mr. Duncan should remain at Simpson, while Mr.
Tugwell went to Met-lah-kah, built a house there, and drew
the Indians round him as they left Simpson.   This purpose, however, Mr. Tugwell's illness has frustrated; nor

---

* Since writing this I believe, however, that gold has been discovered near
Fort Simpson.

can it be carried out until some one is found to take his place. There can be little doubt but some earnest worker will volunteer his services for the purpose, but the qualifications necessary for the task, both physical and moral, are many and great. Strong as Mr. Duncan is, his labours have told severely upon his constitution. In the spring of last year he suffered from repeated attacks of exhaustion, and was compelled to go to Victoria for change of air and rest. The character of man required, indeed, to share his labours, cannot be described better than in his own words :—" We want more men, but they must be men of a peculiar stamp, simple and hearty, hardy and daring,—men who are able and willing to endure rough work."

Before finally quitting the subject of Indians, I will record one of those little incidents which offer good evidence of moral improvement, and cheer the Missionary's labours. Writing in August, 1860, Mr. Duncan, says " I will give one instance in proof of my statement just made, that many Indians have begun to pray. One night when I was en-camping out, after a weary day, the supper and the little instruction being over, my crew of Indians, excepting one old man, quickly spread their mats near the fire, and laid down to sleep in pairs, each sharing his fellow's blanket. The one old man sat near the fire, smoking his pipe. I crept into my little tent, but after some time I came out again to see that all was right. The old man was just making his bed, a thin bark-mat on the ground ; a little box of grease and a few dry salmon for his pillow ; a shirt on and a blanket round him ; another bark-mat over (head and all) was to form his bed in the open air during a cold dark night in April. When everything was adjusted, he put his pipe down and offered up in his own tongue this simple little prayer : 'Be merciful to me, Jesus ;' then he drew up his feet, and was soon lost to view."

Though I have spoken of the difficulties of the Bishop's

work with regard to money, schools, &c., I have said
nothing of the disheartening moral condition of the mass of
the civilized population of these colonies. By far the larger
portion of the colonists are miners, who, though as yet their
conduct since they arrived in British territory has been very
praiseworthy, had previously been living for years in California, where the "Almighty Dollar" is the only object of
worship. Apart from this, the very nature of a miner's life
tends to ungodliness: he is perpetually roving about, in the
morning rich, at sunset poor; to-day a gentleman—in the
American sense of the term—to-morrow a labourer. For
a few years some perhaps work with the notion of returning as rich men to their native land; but during that time
the many fluctuations of the struggle, and the hard, wild life
they lead, so unfit them for domestic existence, that, if they are
fortunate enough to have made money and leave the country,
they probably spend it all in the first large town they come
to; or, reaching home, tire of it in a few months, and return
to the life which has become second nature to them. These
miners, as I have before said, are by no means always uneducated; many men of good parentage and education are to
be found among them, and this very fact renders the inculca-
tion of religion more difficult than it otherwise would be. I
am not, of course, speaking of those who, beginning as poor
men, steadily work their way to competence or wealth, bene-
fiting themselves, those around them, and the country of
their adoption, but of those who, so soon as they have made
two or three thousand dollars, instead of enlarging their
works, or laying the money by, rush to San Francisco, spend
it like fools, and return beggared.

In the few books that have been written about these
colonies, various remarks have been made on the society of
Victoria. It would ill become me to pass over without a
word that society in which I have spent four as happy years
as any of my life, from which I have always met with the

greatest kindness, and in which it will give me real pleasure
again to mix if fate should send me to Victoria. That my
opinion is shared by most of the members of my profession,
any impartial witness of the social proceedings of the last
five years will allow; and if most of the ladies of Victoria
have not joined that profession, matrimonially at least, it has
been from no want of invitation on the part of its members.

I must not omit to mention the African Negroes, several
hundreds of whom left California when British Columbia
sprung into life.   It is well known to all who have lived
among Northern Americans that they treat free negroes
infinitely worse than an Englishman would treat a dog.   In
California neither coloured men nor Chinese are allowed the
benefit of the laws, such as they are, and their evidence is
not taken in the courts, so that a black man may be
murdered in the midst of a hundred other blacks, and if there
is no white man to impeach the murderer, redress cannot be
obtained.   This feeling was not lessened in the hearts of the
Americans at Victoria when they found this hated race, that
they had illused in every way, enjoying precisely the same
privileges as themselves.   The consequence was that on one
occasion there was a pitched battle in the theatre between
blacks and whites, in which, I believe, the former came off
victorious.   Then the whites objected to the blacks being
allowed to go to the same church with them, and actually
appealed to the Bishop to prevent it.   The Bishop was firm
in his refusal to do anything of the kind, but I believe many
stayed away from church in consequence.   One of the dis-
senting ministers from Canada was obliged to leave the
country for giving the same refusal.   The whites all deserted
his church and went to another who was anti-black, and
the negroes were unable to support their champion.   As
a rule these free negroes are a very quiet people, a little
given perhaps to over familiarity when any opening for it is
afforded, very fond of dignity, always styling each other Mr.,

and addicted to an imposing costume, in the way of black coats, gold studs and watch-chains, &c.; but they are a far more steady, sober and thrifty set than the whites by whom they are so much despised.

The Chinese are also very quiet and harmless. They make fair cooks and servants, and where they take to digging are generally content to work claims discarded by the regular miners; they do not do much good to the colony, however, as they eat little and drink less, and spend little or no money in the country.

I have before said that one or two churches have been built since the Bishop's arrival. More are, I understand, being erected, and the mission has spread by this time as far as Cariboo, which it was the Bishop's intention to visit this summer. For any further particulars, however, I refer the reader to the Report of the Columbia Mission, where all the details connected with this most important work will be found recorded.

CHAPTER XIIL

—◦◦—

Routes to British Columbia — Agricultural Resources of British Columbia and
Vancouver Island—Natural History — Land System — Roads, Climate, &c.

In this chapter I propose to treat of the resources of Her
Majesty's dominions in the Pacific, comprising, as the reader
already knows, the country between the 49° and 54° 40'
north latitude and the Rocky Mountains and Pacific Ocean,
with the islands of the coast comprised in those limits. In
doing so, I shall speak of the general condition of the country
and its probable future ; offering, at the same time, an account of the various routes by which emigrants may reach it,
with the approximate cost of each. I shall also have occasion
to speak of the routes that may hereafter be opened up to the
great gold-fields of the Pacific. In so doing I shall not hesitate to avail myself of the information afforded by Parliamentary papers, the labours of others, and the press;
selecting from these and more private sources such facts and
suggestions as my own experience of the country may lead
me to approve.

The claims of the Hudson Bay Company to the possession
of the territory they have so long held by grants from the
Crown, renewed from time to time through a couple of centuries, have been so fully discussed in and out of Parliament
that it is needless for me now to enter upon this subject. I
think, however, that those who blame the Company's rule
do not sufficiently consider the vast difficulties with which
these traders have had to contend. Living, as their assailants
do, under the protection of British law, they are little capable
of appreciating the absolute necessity of many apparently
cruel acts, which however were directly traceable to the

2 A

instinct of self-preservation. I do not mean for a moment
to deny that there were acts of cruelty committed by the
Hudson Bay people, which even this consideration could
not justify; but I do maintain that a handful of white men,
hundreds of miles away from the protection of their own flag,
surrounded by a population, among whom were many both
fierce and treacherous, should not, in common justice, be
judged by the rules which apply to a more civilised state of
existence. One of the main charges against the officers of
the Hudson Bay Company in what was then New Caledonia
is, that while their lease of the country specified that offences
above a certain degree should be tried by the Courts of
Canada, they, instead of sending criminals there, executed a
species of retaliatory justice themselves. But it was simply
ridiculous to expect any such slow and awkward machinery
for the repression or punishment of crime to be used. As it
was, the Company, under that instinct of self-preservation I
have before put forward in their defence, appointed the best
men they had to the charge of their posts, and left them to
hold their own and maintain law and order among the Indians
as best they could. No one who has travelled much among
the natives of British Columbia can fail to be convinced that
one result of the Company's rule has been that the white
man is respected by them everywhere. Even the missionaries
—who complain of the little that has been done during these
many years for the spiritual welfare of the Indian tribes—
must admit that but for their familiarity with the traders,
and the opinion they have thereby gained of the honesty and
justice of the Englishman generally, their reception would
be very different to what it now is.

Again; the abuse which has been showered upon the long
and undisturbed monopoly of the trade of these regions
enjoyed by the Hudson Bay Company would have been
more deserved had their possession of them been valued or
envied by others. As it was, the country was unheeded by

emigrants, neglected by the Government, and but for the Company's tenure of it, might have fallen into the hands of Russia, France, the United States, or any other nation that cared to take it.

The time has undoubtedly come when their pretensions to its longer possession should be rightly unheeded. But I think it should have been resumed by the English Government with · thanks for the Company's care of it, rather than with vague distrust and suspicion of their past occupation. I for one feel convinced that I should have found it impossible to travel about British Columbia with the ease and freedom from danger which I felt, but for the influence of the Hudson Bay Company exerted in my favour. The name of Mr. Douglas, as I have more than once said, proved to be a talisman, wherever it was mentioned, that secured me respect and help. The reports of Captain Palliser show also that the success of his three years' exploration in the Rocky Mountains was owing, in no small degree, to the influence and assistance rendered him by the Company. The following extract from one of his despatches will, I think, serve to illustrate this sufficiently. One of a deputation of Indians who waited upon him, an old chief, spoke thus:—

"I do not ask for presents, although I am poor and my people are hungry. But I know that you have come straight from the great country, and we know that no man from *that country ever came to us and lied.* I want you to declare to us truthfully what the great Queen of your country intends to do to us when she takes the country from the Fur Company's people. All around I see the smoke of the white men to arise. The Longknives (Americans) are trading with our neighbours for their land, and they are cheating and deceiving them."

Who but the officers and men of this much-abused Company could have inspired this spokesman of the Indian people with the trust in the word of an Englishman which is here expressed?

. Again; any one who knows the condition of the Indians in British Columbia, and will take the trouble to compare it with that of the tribes in American territory, must come to the conclusion that some salutary influences—wanting there —have been at work among them. Scarcely a paper reaches Victoria from Oregon or Washington states that does not contain an account of some brutal murder of whites by the Indians, or some retaliatory deed of blood by the troops of the United States. So confirmed, indeed, has their enmity become, that what is little short of a policy of extermination is being pursued towards the Aborigines.

But in British Columbia troops have not once been called upon to oppose the Indians; and men of every class, from the Bishop on his visitation to the friendless miner, travel among them in confidence and unmolested.

While, therefore, quite prepared to admit that in their government of the country the Hudson Bay Company have been guilty of sins both of commission and omission, I cannot, in common justice, forbear from stating the good they have actually accomplished in British Columbia.

With respect to the routes to British Columbia, there are at present five open:—

1st. By the Royal West India mail-steamers to Aspinwall, across the Isthmus of Panama, and thence by American packets to San Francisco and Victoria.

2nd. By the Cunard steamers to New York, and thence by American steamer to Aspinwall; the rest of this route being by the same conveyance as the last.

3rd. Round Cape Horn, or through Magellan Straits, and thence direct to Victoria by the same ship all the way.

4th. Across the American continent, from Lake Superior or St. Paul's to Red River, and thence over the Rocky

Mountains. Or, perhaps, it would be better to say across the continent in British territory, as there are several ways by which this may be done. And—

5th. Across the continent in American territory to California, and thence by steamer to Victoria; or by land to Portland, in Oregon, and from there by steamer to Victoria.

By the first of these routes the total expense of the journey may be estimated at 90*l.* for first class, proportionately less of course for second and third; the time occupied, if there are no delays on the way, being under six weeks. Adopting this route, the traveller may embark at Southampton on the 1st or 16th of any month, and proceed direct to St. Thomas, a passage of 12 or 14 days. At St. Thomas he takes an intercolonial steamer, and in four to six days reaches Aspinwall, the port on this side of the Isthmus of Panama. Crossing the Isthmus by rail, in 3½ hours Panama is reached. Here the great drawback to this route is often experienced in the fact that there is no certainty of finding a Pacific steamer ready to sail, and that very often the traveller has to stop at Panama a week or ten days before one starts. This delay, of course, adds considerably to the expense of the journey, to say nothing of Panama being a most unhealthy place to stay in. Arrangements, however, are said to be making to remedy this inconvenience.

The passage to San Francisco occupies 14 or 15 days, and on the way the steamer calls at Acapulco for coal. Arrived at San Francisco a further delay takes place, and it is sometimes a week or ten days before the steamer for Victoria leaves. Some arrangement has, I believe, lately been entered into, however, which has made the line between San Francisco and Victoria more regular.

By the second route the latter half of the journey is the same as the first, the difference being that the traveller starts by the Cunard steamer from Liverpool for New York.

At New York the traveller may have to stay a few days,

but this is better than waiting at Panama, and then he goes
to Aspinwall in a regular line of American packets: the
great advantage of this line being that it is connected with
the Pacific Mail Company's steamers to San Francisco, and
therefore there is no chance of being—unless, indeed, the
Atlantic packet brings more passengers than the Pacific one
can carry away—kept eight or ten days on the Isthmus.

The third route is, by the old way, round Cape Horn, or
through the Straits of Magellan. The drawback to this is
the length of the sea-voyage, which may be said to average
five months, although it has been done in four. The
Hudson Bay barque, 'Princess Royal,' has for years made
a yearly trip out and home, leaving England in the
autumn, reaching Victoria in January or February, and
returning home again by the end of June. She still bears
the palm for quick passages. Captain Trivett, who has commanded her for years, says his great object always is to
get out well to westward after passing Cape Horn, not caring
if he have to go somewhat to southward in doing so, by
which he finds he gains greatly on those who fear getting too
far westward, and hug the coast rather than stretch far out.
His quickest passages have been 118 days out and 110 days
home; his average of five passages out 133 days. This route
is by far the cheapest yet open, and indeed may be said to
be the only one within the reach of the poorer class of
emigrants. The cost varies considerably, but will get cheaper
as passengers become more numerous. The Hudson Bay
Company's charge has always been 70l. for first class and
30l. for second class. Their charges for freight also have
always been high also, but vessels are constantly advertised
to sail by first-rate firms; and a line of clipper ships of 1200
tons is announced to carry passengers at more moderate rates.

The fourth way lies across our own part of the continent.
This route must be for some time virtually impassable. The
fate of those emigrants who, deluded by the misrepresenta-

tions of the bubble British Columbian Overland Transit Company, started to make a supposed easy journey from St. Paul's across the Rocky Mountains, must still be fresh in the recollection of my readers. The inducements held out by the so-called Company, calculated as they undoubtedly were to deceive the public generally, could impose upon no one who had any practical experience of the country. For instance, one of their statements was, that above 1000 carts travelled annually along the line they proposed to follow. The impression conveyed by this is that these carts crossed the Rocky Mountains into British Columbia by the route proposed to be taken by the Company; whereas the truth is, that they simply trade to the Red River and the Saskatchewan country, and no further. That a waggon-road will some day be carried over the passes of the Rocky Mountains that lie beyond the Red River settlement, and between that point and British Columbia, I have no doubt. It may be, indeed, that before very long the whistle of the locomotive will be heard among them. But that as yet they are impassable for waggons, and that they present great, and at times almost insurmountable, difficulty to all save the experienced unincumbered traveller, the following quotations from the reports of Captains Palliser and Blakiston and Dr. Hector will, I think, be found to contain conclusive proof.

It will assist the reader in forming a judgment upon this matter if I first give, from the report of Captain Blakiston, an account of the passes of the Rocky Mountains by which British Columbia may be reached. "In anticipation," writes Captain Blakiston, "of the establishment of a continuous route through British North America, it is proper here to refer to the passes of the Rocky Mountains north of latitude 49°, or, in other words, in British territory. There are many points at which the chain of these mountains can be traversed; but omitting for the present that known as ' Peel's River Pass,' within the Arctic circle, and that from Fraser Lake to Pelly

Banks, at the head-waters of the Youkon in latitude 62°, as
well as one from Dease's House to Stickeen, and others only
known to the hardy fur-traders of the far north, we come to
three : one of which crosses from the Findlay branch of the
Peace River to Babine River, the northern boundary of the
province of Columbia ; while the other two, at the very head-
waters of Peace River, in latitude 55° north, connect with
Fraser River at its most northern bend, one of which was
described, as long ago as 1793, by that intrepid traveller, Sir
Alexander Mackenzie. The connection with these being,
however, by water, and rather far north on the east side, I
shall pass on to enumerate the known passes more to the
southward, and which may be called the passes to British
Columbia. In commencing with the North, they stand
thus :—

	Latitude.
" 1. Cowdung Lake Portage, or Leather Pass	54 0 N.
2. Boat Encampment on original Athabasca portage	53 0
3. Howse's Pass	51 45
4. Kicking-Horse Pass	51 25
5. Vermilion Pass	51 10
6. Kananaskis, or Emigrant Pass	50 40
7. Crow's-nest Pass	49 40
8. Kootonay Pass	49 25

" The first of these connects the head-waters of Athabasca
River with the great fork of the Fraser, and has never been
used except as a portage between these two rivers.

" 2. The second is that which, until the last few years, was
used regularly by the Hudson Bay Company for the conveyance of a few furs, as well as despatches and servants, from
the east side to the Pacific, by the way of the Columbia
River, and which, from the 'Boat Encampment,' is navigable
for small craft; but this, like the first, has not been used in
connection with any land-route on the west side.

" 3. The third was probably first used by either Thompson
or Howse (author of the Cree grammar), who, following up

the north branch of the Saskatchewan, crossed the watershed
of the mountains to the north fork of the Columbia, and
thence to its source, the Columbia Lakes, where, striking the
Kootonay River, he followed it down to the south of 49°
north.

"4. The 'Kicking-Horse Pass,' so named by Dr. Hector,
crosses the watershed from near the head-waters of the Bow
River to those of the Kootonay, and may be reached by
following up either the north or south branches of the Saskatchewan by land.

"5. While another (see Parliamentary Papers, June 1859),
the 'Vermilion Pass,' likewise traversed and laid down by Dr.
Hector during the summer of 1858, occurs also on Bow River
so near the last-named one, that it is unfortunate that the
western edge of the mountains was not reached, as it would
then have proved whether these passes can be of value in
connection with a continuous route across the country.*

"6. The next pass which enters the mountains in common
with the fifth on Bow River, has been named the 'Kananaskis
Pass' (see Parliamentary Papers, June 1859), and was laid
down by latitude and longitude observations during the
summer of 1858 by Captain Palliser. This also leads to the
Kootonay River, passing near the Columbia Lakes. It is
generally supposed that this pass was only discovered last
year, but a description of it is to be found in 'An Overland
Journey Round the World,' by Sir George Simpson, who,
together with a party of emigrants, 50 in number, under the
late Mr. James Sinclair, passed through, but not with carts,
as had been stated,† to the lower part of the Columbia in
1841, besides which it has been used by other travellers.
If we are to consider its western extremity to the south of
the Columbia Lakes, it is a long and indirect route, but as

---

* See *post*, extract from Dr. Hector's report of this.
† See Evidence before the Select Committee, 'Hudson Bay Question.'

yet it has only been used for following the valley of the Kootonay, and thence into American territory.   In the event of the country west of the Columbia Lakes proving suitable for a land-road, this, as well as the previous three, would prove available for crossing from the Saskatchewan north of latitude 51°.

"For 100 geographical miles of the mountains south of Bow River no pass is at dresent known to exist until we come to the Mocowans, or Belly River, a tributary of the Saskatchewan, on the branches of which four passes enter the mountains—the 'Crow-nest,' the 'Kootonay,' the 'Boundary,' and the 'Flathead.'

"7. Of the first of these, we know only that its eastern entrance is on the river of the same name, and that it emerges in the vicinity of the Steeples, or Mount Deception, while neither of the two last are entirely in British territory—hence the name of 'Boundary Pass' for that which has its culminating point north of 49°.

"8. The 'Kootonay Pass,' is the most southern, and, of those yet known, by far the shortest in British territory.

"These passes, of which the altitudes are known, do not differ greatly; and I refrain from commenting on their relative merits, because before any particular one can be selected for the construction of a road, the easiest land-route from Hope and the western bend of the Fraser River should be ascertained, which, considering the distance, would be no very great undertaking.   In conclusion, I would only remark, that at present *no pass in British territory is practicable for wheeled-carriages.*" *

It should be remembered that Captain Blakiston wrote this before an overland route was thought of.   But he has since told me, that during his explorations he came upon

* 'Blue Book,' June, 1860, p. 61.

the remains of the waggons of Mr. Sinclair's party upon this side of the mountains, the idea of transporting them farther having been abandoned at that spot.

Dr. Hector, the geologist accompanying Captain Palliser's expedition, upon reaching the Rocky Mountain house, in the most northerly of the passes enumerated above, writes of it thus : "The mountain-house is at a distance of not less than 100 miles from the main chain of the Rocky Mountains, which are nevertheless distinctly seen from it as a chain of snow-clad peaks. The principal chain is, however, screened by a nearer range, distant about 45 miles. . . . . . I made an attempt to reach this near range, *but failed in forcing a road through the dense pine-wood with which the whole country is covered.*" *

Of the Kananaskis Pass, the sixth of the above list, Captain Palliser writes thus: "On the 18th of August I started to seek for the new pass across the Rocky Mountains, proceeding up the north side of the Saskatchewan or Bow River, passing the mouth of the Kananaskis River; five miles higher up we crossed the Bow River, and entered a ravine. We fell upon Kananaskis River, and travelled up in a south-westerly direction, and the following day reached the Kananaskis Prairie, known to the Indians as the place 'where Kananaskis was stunned but not killed.' On the 21st we passed two lakes about two miles long and one wide. We continued our course, winding through this gorge in the mountains among cliffs of a tremendous height, yet our onward progress was not impeded by obstacles of any consequence; the only difficulty we experienced was occasioned by quantities of fallen timber caused by fires. . . . . . On the 22nd August we reached the height of land between the waters of Kananaskis River and a new river, a tributary of the Kootonay River. Our height above Bow Fort was now

* Letter to Captain Palliser, June, 8, 1858 ; 'Blue Book,' p. 26.

1885 feet, or 5985 feet above the sea. Next morning we
commenced our descent, and for the first time were obliged
to get off and walk, *leading our horses down a precipitous slope
of 960 feet over loose angular fragments of rock*. This portion
of our route continued for several days through dense masses
of fallen timber, destroyed by fire, where our progress was
very slow—NOT owing to any difficulty of the mountains, but
on account of the fallen timber, which we had first to climb
over and then to chop through to enable our horses to step
or jump over it. We continued at this work from daybreak
till night, and even by moonlight, and reached the Columbia
Portage on the 27th of August.

"On September the 6th I started to recross these mountains by the Kootonay Pass (the eighth upon the above list).
This is frequently used, but not the general pass of the
Kootonay Indians, who have a preferable one in American
territory.

"On the 7th of September we passed the height of land—a
formidable ascent, where we had to walk and lead the horses
for two hours. This is the height of land which constitutes
the watershed. We encamped for the night in a small
prairie after making a considerable descent.

"On the 8th of September our course continued through
woods and swamps, for about 15 miles, till we reached another
ascent. This was also a severe ascent, though not so formidable as that of the day previous; we reached its summit
about four o'clock through a severe snow-storm (this in September), the snow falling so fast as to make me very appre-
hensive of losing the track. We descended that evening,
and camped on the eastern side, and next day arrived at the
eastern extremity of the pass. I regret that I cannot give
the altitudes of this pass, as our barometer was broken by
one of the horses. It is, however, far from being so favourable as the more northern, by which I entered on Kananaskis
River, which has but one obstacle, in the height of land, to

overcome, and where the whole line is free from swamps and marshes." *

Dr. Hector, accompanying the same expedition, in speaking of the Vermilion Pass (the fifth upon the list), says of it : "On the 20th I crossed Bow River without swimming the horses or unloading the packs, and, after six hours' march *through thick woods,* reached the height of land the same afternoon. The ascent to the watershed from the Saskatchewan is hardly perceptible to the traveller who is prepared for a tremendous climb, by which to reach the dividing ridge of the Rocky Mountains; and no labour would be required, *except that of hewing timber,* to construct an easy road for carts, by which it might be attained."

Of the Beaver, or Kicking-Horse Pass (fourth upon our list), he says : "The bottom of the valley (that of the Koutanay River) is occupied by so much morass, that we were obliged to keep along the slope, although the fallen timber rendered it very tedious work, and severe for our poor horses, that now had their legs covered with cuts and bruises. . . . . On the 31st of August we struck the valley of the Kicking-Horse River, travelling as fast as we could get our jaded horses to go and as I could bear the motion [he had been badly kicked by a horse]. On the 2nd Sept. we reached the height of land. In doing so we ascended 2021 feet. Unlike the Vermilion River, the Kicking-Horse River, although rapid, descends more by a succession of falls than by a gradual slope. Just before we attained the height of land, *we ascended more than* 1000 *feet in about a mile,* down which the stream leaps in a succession of cascades." †

I cannot do better than conclude the consideration of this question of an overland passage to British Columbia with the following extract from the Report of Captain Palliser to the Secretary of State for the Colonies, in 1859 :—

* Letter to Captain Palliser, June 8, 1858; 'Blue Book,' p. 33.
† Letter of Dr. Hector, p. 38.

" In answer to the third query contained in your Lordship's letter, viz., 'What means of access exist for British
immigrants to reach this settlement?' I think there are no
means to be recommended save those viâ the United States.
The direct route from England viâ York Factory (Hudson's
Bay), and also that from Canada viâ Lake Superior, are
too tedious, difficult, and expensive for the generality of
settlers. The manner in which natural obstacles have isolated the country from all other British possessions in the
East is a matter of considerable weight; indeed it is *the*
obstacle of the country, and one, I fear, almost beyond the
remedies of art. The egress and ingress to the settlement
from the east is obviously by the Red River valley and
through the States."

Further on the same subject Captain Blakiston writes : " In
answer to the fourth query contained in your Lordship's
letter, viz., 'Whether, judging from the explorations you
have already made, the country presents such facilities for the
construction of a railway as would at some period, though
possibly a remote one, encourage Her Majesty's Government
in the belief that such an undertaking, between the Atlantic
and Pacific Oceans, could ever be accomplished?' I have no
hesitation in saying that no obstacles exist to the construction of a railway from Red River to the eastern base of the
Rocky Mountains; and probably the best route would be
found in the neighbourhood of the south branch of the Saskatchewan. An amount of capital very small in proportion
to the territory to be crossed would be sufficient to accomplish
the undertaking so far; but the continuation of a railway
across the Rocky Mountains would doubtless require a considerable outlay.

" In my letter to Her Majesty's Government, dated 7th
Oct., 1858, I have referred to two passes examined by myself
and Mr. Sullivan, my secretary, both of which I found practicable for horses right across the chain of the Rocky Moun-

tains to the Columbia River, and that a small outlay would render the more northern one practicable for carts, and even waggons.

" On the return of Dr. Hector from his branch expedition, I found he had also crossed the mountains as far as the valley of the Columbia River, by the Vermilion Pass, which leaves the valley of the Bow River nearer to its source than the pass I had myself traversed. In that pass he had observed a peculiarity which distinguishes it from the others we had examined, viz., the absence of any abrupt step at the commencement of the descent to the west, both ascent and descent being gradual. This, combined with the low altitude * of the greatest elevation passed over, led him to report very favourably upon the facilities of this pass for the clearing of a waggon-road ; and even that the project of a railroad by this route across the Rocky Mountains might be reasonably entertained."

Before taking leave of this subject, I think it but right to correct another impression which appears likely to mislead the public. This is, that the quantity of buffalo on the route proposed to be taken by the bubble Overland Transit Company is so great as to render it impossible for a man with a gun in his hand to starve. Now, although enormous herds of buffaloes may be met with—indeed Captain Palliser writes of them, " The whole region as far as the eye could reach was covered with buffaloes in bands varying from hundreds to thousands "—yet it is quite possible for the traveller to die of slow starvation and exhaustion without seeing one. Dr. Rae, the eminent Arctic traveller, informed me that he spent three weeks in these plains with a party of gentlemen, and that during that time they saw nothing larger than a beaver, and only shot two martens !

Again we have seen that Dr. Hector was glad to travel

* Kananaskis Pass.

21 out of 24 hours for want of food; and in a letter of Captain Palliser, written in the midsummer of 1858, he says: "On my arrival at the Bow Fort, I found my hunters waiting for me. They had been out in every direction, but could not fall in with buffalo. They had also found elk and deer very scarce." In the same letter we also find him writing: "Owing to the absence of buffalo during the winter, my hunters, as well as those belonging to the Fort, have had to go to great distances in order to get meat, which they obtained in such small quantities, that the Hudson Bay Company's officer in charge of this post was obliged to scatter the men, with their families, all over the plains in search of food. Even Dr. Hector and Mr. Sullivan were obliged to leave this post and go to Forts Pitt and Edmonton in order to lessen the consumption of meat, of which the supply there was quite inadequate. Fortunately, however, the winter has been an unusually mild one, otherwise the consequences might have been very serious indeed."

Speaking of the mountains on the west side, Captain Palliser also remarks: "The fact is, the knowledge the Indians possess of the mountains is very small; and even among those said to 'know the mountains,' their knowledge is very limited indeed. This is easily accounted for by the *scarcity of the game*, which offers no inducement for the Indians to go there."

Dr. Hector also writes: "While traversing this valley, since coming on the Kootanie River, we have had no trail to follow, and it did not seem to have been frequented by Indians for years. This makes the absence of game all the more extraordinary. The only animal which seemed to occur at all was the panther. The Indians saw one; and in the evening we heard them calling, as they skirted round our camp, attracted by the smell."

To this testimony of others, I may add my own experience. I have travelled 600 miles in British Columbia without seeing

anything larger than grouse, or having the chance of more
than half-a-dozen shots at them. I have also had occasion
to speak of death by starvation among the Indians. This
has been by no means uncommon of late, since they have
neglected the culture of their land for the more alluring
search after gold. If, then, the native of these plains finds it
impossible to support life upon the wild animals frequenting
it, what chance, under similar circumstances, could the artisan
or the peasant, fresh from the loom or plough, be expected to
have ?

The last of the routes which I have to consider is that
across the continent in American territory. A way between
New York and San Francisco has been for some time open,
and so regular and speedy is the transmission of mails by it,
that the American postal subsidy has been taken away from
the Panama Steam Company, and given to the Overland.
The traveller by this route proceeds by rail to St. Louis
on the border of Illinois and Missouri. Thence by stage
across Missouri to St. Joseph, by the Missouri River to
Omaha city, and from there across Nebraska and Utah to
the Great Salt Lake city. From Utah the route passes
southward of the Humboldt Mountains to Carson city and
into California. A telegraph now runs along the whole of
this line, while a stage-coach goes three times and the pony-
express twice a week—the latter making the journey in
about seventeen days. The whole distance from New York
to San Francisco is about 3000 miles, of which 900 are
travelled over by rail.

From San Francisco the traveller can reach his destination
by land through California and Oregon to Portland, and
thence by steamer to Victoria : or viâ the Columbia River to
Walla-Walla and thence through Okanagan across to the
Thompson River, and so direct to the mines. This route
across the continent is considered pretty safe, and I know a

lady who crossed by it; but the mails are sometimes waylaid
by Indians, and the passengers murdered or ill-treated.

Before treating of the mineral resources of British Columbia.
I will endeavour to describe its physical aspect. The coast
of British Columbia is fringed with dense forest, sometimes growing on low ground, but generally covering mountain-ridges of all shapes, which terminate in numbers of
irregular peaks shooting up in every possible form and in
heights varying from 1000 to 10,000 feet. All these ridges
and peaks have the same general appearance, being composed
of trappean or granitic rocks and covered with pine-trees to
the height of 3000 or 4000 feet, and sometimes higher. Here
and there the constant fires caused by the carelessness of
the Indians have stripped the branches from all the trees
on a hill-side, leaving nothing but scorched trunks standing
on the blackened rock; while in other places they appear
stripped in the same way from top to bottom of a mountain,
the whiteness of the trunk, however, forbidding the notion
of fire. The reason of this phenomenon, which was of frequent
occurrence in the inlets, caused us much speculation. The
conclusion arrived at was, that it was caused by a slide of
frozen snow from the mountain's summit. These mountain-
ridges are divided at intervals all along the coast by the long
inlets of which I have before spoken.

Behind all these minor ranges and inland of the heads of
the inlets, the Cascade Range runs nearly parallel with the
coast, and at a distance of 60 to 100 miles from it, forming
a barrier but too effectual to shut out intruders into the
Eldorado that lies beyond it. The highest peak of this range
is Mount Baker, situated in latitude 48° 44' N. and consequently upon American territory. Its height is 10,700 feet,
and it forms a prominent feature in the view from any part
of the Strait of Fuca or Gulf of Georgia. Though, as I have
mentioned when describing the inlets of the coast, there is

usually a valley, sometimes of considerable extent, at the head of these sea-arms, the Cascade Mountains, as far as explorations have yet been carried, appear always to bar approach to the country beyond. Sometimes they recede from the coast so much that it is possible to steam 40 or 50 miles inland; but in time the mountains are sure to be found closing in and barring farther progress. The valley of the Fraser River forms the single exception to this rule. Here the river has certainly mastered the rocks, and, attacking them from the rear, cut itself a devious way to the sea. But it has done no more, the rocks so closing in upon its course that, as in the cañons I have described, there is hardly footing left for a goat along the high precipitous banks.

These coast-mountains have as yet been imperfectly examined, and little therefore is known of their geological formation or mineral resources. Dr. Wood, who, it will be remembered, accompanied me on my excursion inland from Jervis Inlet, says of those we passed on that occasion, " On the right side of the upper arm of Jervis Inlet the mountains, against whose sides the sea washes, give indications of being composed of porphyritic granite; the granite rocks generally are deeply imbued with copper oxides; their veins of white quartz are frequently seen intersecting the granite. The rocks forming the sides of the second inlet, some six or eight miles distant, are more rugged and precipitous, and consist generally of a strongly micaceous quartzose granite. A mountain-stream which we crossed, presented in the granite and trap boulders, which formed its bed, singularly rich specimens of iron pyrites without any observable indications of other metals. Upon another mountainous stream which we crossed, I saw the largest boulder of quartz (transported) I ever witnessed; it must have been four or five tons' weight, and was deeply stained on one side with oxides of iron." During this journey, I perceived indications of nothing but

2 B 2

trap and granite, with here and there thin veins of quartz.
Indeed, I may say, that all the inlets surveyed by the
'Plumper' presented the same geological characteristics.
Texbada Island, which lies off the entrance of Jervis Inlet, is,
however, an exception: nearly the whole of the northern end
being limestone, mostly blue, but some white and comparatively soft; the blue being very hard. I found a few small
outcrops of limestone in the entrance of Jervis Inlet afterwards, but they were only thin veins, round which the
igneous rock had hardened. Clay-slate frequently occurs in
the inlets, but usually in very small outcrops. I have remarked its occurrence also in the cañons of the Fraser River,
and Lieut. Palmer, R.E. when in the same range (Cascade)
on the Harrison-Lilloett route, says, "From the cursory
view I was enabled to take of the general geological character
of the country, trappean rocks appear to prevail, consisting
principally of greenstone, dense clay-slate (here and there
presenting a laminated structure), and compact hornblende.
The exposed surfaces of the rocks are generally covered
with felspar, and are occasionally stained red with iron,
forming an agreeable contrast in the landscape. Quartz-
veins permeate the clay-slate in many places, of an average
thickness of one to twelve inches; the formation, in fact,
would suggest the high probability of metalliferous deposits.
The mountains rise bold, rugged, and abrupt, with occasional
benches on their sides, on which are found quantities of worn
rounded boulders, principally of coarse-grained granite, occasionally porphyritic. The granite contains golden-coloured
and black mica in large quantities. The crystals of felspar
in the porphyritic granite are very numerous, but small.
The soil appears in many places to have been formed by the
decomposition of granite, it being light and sandy and containing much mica.

"Below the soil is very generally found a white compact

mass, very hard and approaching to a conglomerate, containing pebbles of every description in a matrix of decomposed clay-slate. Lime seems wanting even in the conglomerate, and I saw no traces of limestone or sandstone all along the route, though I understand there is plenty of the former at Pavillon.* "

Along the coast, between Jervis Inlet and Desolation Sound, the appearance of the rocks changes somewhat, and quartz and slate predominate.

Speaking of Desolation Sound, Mr. Downie says, "This is the first time I have seen pure veins of sulphuret of iron, which looks very much like silver. . . . I came across a number of seams of the same kind; it lies in quartz, the same as gold. I have no idea that the gold is confined to the Fraser River alone; and if it can only be found from the seaboard, or on the rivers at the head of some of these inlets, the country will soon be prospected." At the head of the same inlet, he says, "I have seen more black sand here in half a day than I did in California in nine years; it looks clear and bright, as if it came from quartz." † Seeing it was out of the question to proceed farther, we put back, and came down along shore, breaking and trying the rocks, finding much iron pyrites and sulphuret of iron, but no gold.

In Knight's Inlet I have mentioned plumbago as having been found; and on Queen Charlotte's Island (which may be regarded, in common with the rest of these islands, as chips off the coast), gold-bearing quartz and coal.

Of the geological features of the interior little is yet known. Wherever I have been, the same trappean rocks predominate as on the coast, except at and around Pavillon, 220 miles up the Fraser, where limestone occurs in large quantities. In the Cariboo district Mr. Nind, the Gold

* 'Blue Book,' part iii. p. 48, and ' Geographical Journal,' 1861, p. 231.
† It is in this black sand that the loose gold is usually found.

Commissioner, says he has observed "masses of quartz;" and when travelling near the Antler Creek, in the valley of which some of the richest diggings occur, he says, "The streams I passed were very numerous; and where it was possible, from the falling in of the ice and snow, to observe their beds, I noticed the same characteristics of large quartz boulders and a kind of slate-rock, covered with red gravel, said to bear a close resemblance to the rich auriferous beds of the streams of the southern mines of California.

Of the Semilkameen district, in the southern part of the colony, Lieutenant Palmer, R.E., in his Report quoted before, writes:—"The geological character of the several districts (Fort Hope and Fort Colville) is throughout very uniform, the rocks belonging principally to the igneous and metamorphic series. The bulk of Manson Mountain * appears to be granite, tipped with slate; here and there presenting particles of white indurated clay, found, on examination, to contain fragments of white quartz.

"This formation may be said to consist of granite, with its felspar decomposed and reduced to a state of indurated clay; it extends to the dividing ridge of the Cascades, and partly into the valley of the Tulameen. In the latter valley may be seen vast masses of white quartz; in all probability the exposed face of the rock, which, with granite, constitutes a large portion of the district, extending into the Semilkameen valley.

"On approaching the summit of the Tulameen range, the quartz partially disappears, and is replaced by a species of variegated sandstone, in which traces of iron occur. To what extent the sandstone prevailed I had no opportunity of judging, the weather being snowy while I was there, and the rocks, as a rule, imbedded in peaty turf.

* A mountain a few miles north of Fort Hope.

"As we leave the Tulameen Mountains, and descend into the valley below, indurated clay appears to predominate to a considerable extent. This clay varies in character as we approach the Vermilion Forks; a portion I noticed near that point being a white silicate of alumina mixed with sand. On one specimen which I picked up were the fossil remains of the leaves of the hemlock.

"Further down, in the Semilkameen valley, the clay acquires a slaty texture, and becomes stained with iron, to a greater or less extent. Blue clay also exists, only, however, in small quantities.

"The mountains bordering the Semilkameen consist chiefly of granite, greenstone, and quartz, capped with blue and brown clay-slate. The beds of both the Tulameen and Semilkameen are covered with boulders of granite, of every description and colour; of greenstone and of trap, and vary in form and size.

"Boulders of the same character prevail on the river-bottoms, to a greater or less extent. Like that of most of the other explored parts of British Columbia, the geological character of this region appears to indicate the high probability of auriferous deposits. In the lower portion of the Semilkameen, and near the 'Big Bend,' gold was discovered shortly after I passed through, by some of the men attached to the United States Boundary Commission. Report pronounced the discovery a valuable one, as much as 40 dollars to the hand being taken out in three hours, without proper mining-tools; but I cannot speak positively as to the truth of this statement, neither could I discover whether the place spoken of was in British or American possessions. Probability would suggest the former. Beyond Osoyoos Lake* I did not deem it necessary to pay much attention to the geological

* A lake in the Okanagan River, which falls just on the boundary line.

character of the country, the route lying almost entirely in American possessions. Suffice it to say that but few features of interest presented themselves, and that in no place did I see any sign of stratified rocks."

The only part of the country which can be said to have been geologically surveyed, is the neighbourhood of the Harrison Lake and the portage which lies between Port Douglas and Lilloett. In the summer of 1860, Dr. Forbes, of H.M.S. 'Topaze,' undertook this service; and his Report contains, among other things, much valuable information as to the existence of silver there. Of the Harrison Lake, he says: "At the mouth of the stream (on the east side of the lake) and extending on both sides along the shore of the lake, were water-worn boulders of granitic and quartzose rocks; gneiss, with garnets; mica-schist, with garnets; pieces of good roofing-slate, together with masses of a pure white quartz, containing excellent indications of metal. The mountain, the top of which is somewhat rounded in its outline, having a flat surface to the westward, and a remarkable pinnacle or finger-like rock at its immediate base, is composed of trap; having resting upon it, and tilted at a high angle, micaceous, talcose, and horn-blendic schists, all highly charged with iron, the oxidation of which has produced disintegration of these rocks. At a point 500 yards from the mouth of the stream, on its proper right bank, a mass of trachytic rock has been erupted, shattering the surrounding rocks, itself much shaken and shattered; great masses, dislodged by weather and other causes, having slipped and rolled to the bottom of the ravine.

"In this rock, of volcanic origin, was found a mass of quartz, of a beautiful white colour, containing good indications of silver and copper; which indications proved true, for, on assaying a specimen by the reducing process, a globule of each of these metals showed itself. The mass or vein of quartz dips northerly, beneath the overlying

trachytic rocks.   It is wedge-shaped, the thickness increasing
with the depth.   From it, in all directions, radiate veins of
quartz; which, guarded on each side by a fissile rock, of a
French-grey colour, permeate the mass of trachyte in all
directions.   Those only which run north and south are metalliferous; the east and west veins, or cross courses, are barren.
. . . . I proceeded to examine the veins, *seriatim*, as they
radiated from the great central mass.   Rising in a north-
westerly direction is a quartz-vein, running through or along
with the fissile rock above alluded to, containing ores of
silver; and to the right, having the same north-west and
south-east direction, about 200 yards above the 'mother
vein,' a quartz-vein shows itself in the broken precipitous
face of the continuing trachytic rock.   It runs between two
great bands of French-grey coloured rock, separated from it
by masses of partially decomposed pyrites; which besides, in
a band about three inches in thickness, accompanies the
quartz-vein throughout its course.

"Besides these masses and bands of iron pyrites, masses of
a dark-green chlorite rock occur; and nodules containing
sulphuret of silver are clearly discernible, both in the vein
itself and the rock through which it passes.

"Following the ravine, and at the same time ascending, I
found, at an elevation of about 600 or 700 feet, another
quartz-vein, of the same character, dipping in the same direction, and belonging to the same system; and, from the numerous angular fragments of quartz and quartzose rocks everywhere scattered about, I believe there are numerous other
veins, which I had not time to look for or explore.   I worked
into the quartz-matrix and its ramifying veins, and satisfied
myself of the existence of silver at this spot, which, however,
will require somewhat extensive mining-operations to procure
in paying quantities.   The geological character of this locality affords a good type of the general formation of the whole

eastern side of the lake, and may here be briefly described
as a region of primary, metamorphic, and volcanic rocks,
crossed and recrossed by trappean dykes and veins, and
seams of metalliferous quartz and quartzose rocks. The
primary and igneous rocks, which form the central axis of
the mountain-range, have on their flanks transverse ridges
and spurs of trappean rock, bedded and jointed; resting on
which, at various angles, lie the metamorphic schistose rocks,
which, again broken through, disturbed, and shattered by
successive intrusions of volcanic rock, have in many instances
undergone a second metamorphosis, and show an amorphous,
crystalline structure, accompanied by segregation of metal
into the permeating veins."[*]

Speaking of the country that lies farther up the lake, he
says: " The great mass of *débris* in all the slips was composed
of plutonic, trappean, and quartz rocks; all of them full of
beautiful groups and strings of crystals of iron pyrites, both
massive and in cubes, and all possessing good indications of
the proximity of valuable mineral."

Of the road between Douglas and Lilloett, he observes:
" The argentiferous rock is of a pale-blue colour, with masses
and strings of quartz running through it. Sulphuret of silver,
argentiferous pyrites, and some specks of gold, were to be
seen along with iron pyrites in cubes and masses. The vein
runs through trap, which, when in contact with the vein, is
of a trachytic character. Great volcanic disturbances have
taken place, numerous faults existing in the trappean range,
which runs in parallel ridges north and south, slips and slides
having taken place in the planes of bedding; and the bluff
in which this metalliferous rock is found appears to be the
result of a great slip from the boundary range of the valley
on its eastern side." Of the whole way to the Hot Springs

---

[*] ' Blue Book,' part iv. p. 33.

on the Douglas road, 23 miles from Port Douglas, he says:
"The geological formation is trap of various characters in
reference to its crystallization and bedding; in some cases
both these characteristics very perfect, in others less so.
Metamorphic rock, altered and disturbed by its intrusion,
permeating quartzose veins, in some cases metalliferous, in
others not so, run through the whole formation. Near the
Hot Springs an erupted granite-rock, having a highly crystalline trap on both flanks, occurs, which extending eastward
has relation to the granitic rock developed in the argentiferous
formation at Fort Hope, if indeed it be not the same.

"Trap rises in lofty precipices on the western side of the
river (Lilloett River), and continues on the east, resting on a
rocky range of white-coloured stone, which, on examination,
proved to be a silicious rock, containing a few indications of
copper. The formation on the western side of the river indicates that these veins (quartz) pass along a ravine which dips
to the river-bed, under which they pass to rise again. The
most promising vein is a quartzose mass, 6 feet in thickness,
bedded in and running along with a silicious rock, having
masses and fragments of talcose schist in the immediate
vicinity. The quartz contained strings of sulphuret of silver,
and is, I believe, the outcrop of a valuable mine." *

Summing up these indications, Dr. Forbes remarks: "The
elevation of all these ranges is due to the action of volcanic
forces, causing, in the first place, in this north-west and
south-east line, a slow and gradual upheaval of the primary
and igneous rocks composing the crust of the earth. Then,
as these forces increased in intensity, upheavals and disturbances of the mountain masses occurred, both generally
and locally, until the geographical features of the country
assumed their present aspect, viz. great mountain-chains,

* 'Blue Book,' part iv. p. 39.

running north-west and south-east, having, at right-angles to their axis of elevation, trappean rocks running east and west in transverse spurs and ridges. Resting on these spurs, tilted by them at various angles, are detached and broken masses of metamorphic rock of various kinds, such as clay-slate, micaceous, hornblendic, talcose, and chlorite schists, all permeated by dykes and veins of erupted rock, which, in many instances, have changed the metamorphic rocks at the points of contact into amorphous semi-crystalline masses."

I have before mentioned the discovery of coal at other places than Nanaimo, where it is now worked. All the north end of Vancouver Island, indeed, contains coal-measures, and some quantity has been taken out a little way to the northward of Fort Rupert. The specimens we had on board when we were there were considered quite equal to Nanaimo coal, and the Indians brought some from the mainland opposite, which was also very good. In 1859, coal was found in Coal Harbour, Burrard Inlet, and we took six bags from the outcrop there, upon the quality of which the engineer reported very favourably. It is no exaggeration, indeed, to say that coal exists all along the shores of both colonies; and, when any of the inlets become of sufficient importance to make the work remunerative, there is no doubt it will be found in working position and sufficient quantities. At Nanaimo the seams have lately been tested by bores with the most satisfactory result; and, quite lately, it has been found close to the water's edge on one of the islands 40 or 50 miles north of that place. In the beginning of last year, Mr. Nicol, the manager of the coal-mines at Nanaimo writes: " We have got the coal in a bore nearly 5 feet thick. I have now fully proved 1,000,000 tons. A shaft 50 or 52 fathoms deep will reach the coal; dip, 1 in 7; a very good working seam. I have no doubt there is another seam underlying this one, of an inexhaustible extent. I have got the outcrop inland, and, from dip to strike, I am sure it is about 30 fathoms below; so that by continuing the same shaft, if necessary, another larger seam containing millions will be arrived at; but the first seam will last my life, even with very large works. With about 5000*l.* or 8000*l.* I could get along well, and start a business doing from 60,000 to 100,000 tons a year. The price is 25*s.* to 28*s.* alongside the ship."

It will give a better idea of the comparative cheapness of this coal if I say that at San Francisco the Nanaimo coal sells from 12 to 15 dollars (2*l.* 8*s.* to 3*l.*), while the cheapest good English coal cost, when I was there, 20 dollars, or 4*l.* a ton, and it had been worth more than that. At Panama the U. S. frigate 'Saranac.' had to lay in some coal, and paid 35 dollars (7*l.*) a ton for it. I happened to be in San Francisco later, when the same vessel came there to be docked. The coal was taken out to lighten the ship, and it was so bad and dusty that it was not considered worth taking on board again.

Mr. Bauermann, the geologist of the Boundary Expedition, says of the Nanaimo coal: "Two seams of coal, averaging 6 or 8 feet each in thickness, occur in these beds, and are extensively worked for the supply of the steamers running between Victoria and Fraser River. The coal is a soft black lignite, of a dull earthy fracture, interspersed with small lenticular bands of bright crystalline coal, and resembles some of the duller varieties of coal produced in the South Derbyshire and other central coalfields in England.

"In some places it exhibits the peculiar jointed structure, causing it to split into long prisms, observable in the brown coal of Bohemia. For economic purposes these beds are very valuable. The coal burns freely, and yields a light pulverescent ash, giving a very small amount of slag and clinker." [*]

* 'Geological Society's Journal, 1860,' p. 201.

These beds were first brought to notice in 1850 by the Indians bringing some coal to one of the Hudson Bay Company's agents. This was found on Newcastle Island, in the harbour, and they said they had seen the same on the mainland. It proved to come from the outcrop of the Douglas seam, which was afterwards found to cross the harbour to the island mentioned, where some of the best coal is now taken out. Since its discovery it has been worked by a Company known as the Nanaimo Coal Company, which, however, was really under the management of the Hudson Bay Company's officials. Quite recently, however, a new Company has been formed, who have purchased good-will, stock and fixtures. It is to be hoped that better fortune will attend this enterprise. Strange enough, whatever else than furs the Hudson Bay Company meddle with appears almost invariably to prove a failure. They mismanaged affairs at Nanaimo, certainly. Good and expensive machinery was sent and fixed, but sufficient capital to work it was not forthcoming; so that the managers were impeded at the outset and, not enabled to develop the resources of the place.

The greatest objection to the Nanaimo coal is its dust and dirt. It burns well, however, and H.M.S. 'Satellite' was able to get better steam with it than with any other coal. We used it constantly in the 'Plumper' for four years without having any other reason of complaint than the dirt arising from it. One of the originators of the new Company which has taken these mines assures me that one valuable quality of this coal is its adaptability for making gas. At San Francisco and in Oregon it is preferred for this purpose to any other coal, on account of its being so highly bituminous. It may be remarked, that the deeper the workings at Nanaimo are carried the better the quality of the coal becomes.

The natural resources of British Columbia, however, independently of its mineral wealth, are such as to make it well worthy of the consideration of agricultural settlers.

After the Cascade Range is passed, or from Lytton upwards, the country assumes an entirely different aspect from that of the coast. The dense pine-forests cease, and the land becomes open, clear, and in the spring and summer time covered with bunch-grass, which affords excellent grazing for cattle. Although this country may rightly be called open, that word should not be understood in the sense in which an Australian settler, for instance, would accept it. There are no enormous prairies here, as there, without a hill or wood to break the monotony of the scene far as the eye can reach. It is rather what the Californians term "rolling country," broken up into pleasant valleys and sheltered by mountain-ridges of various height. These hills are usually well clothed with timber, but with little, if any, undergrowth. The valleys are generally clear of wood, except along the banks of the streams which traverse them, on which there is ordinarily a sufficiency of willow, alder, &c., to form a shade for cattle. The timber upon the hills is very light, compared with its growth upon the coast; indeed, there is nothing more than the settler requires for building, fuel, and fencing. Several farms are now established in different parts of the country. I have mentioned one at Pavillon in the account of my journey there, and since there have been greater facilities for obtaining land many others have, I believe, been started. Mr. McLean, who was in charge of Fort Kamloops, when I visited it, has since left the Company's service, and cultivates a farm near the Chapeau River. He has been many years in the country, and at Kamloops carried on considerable farming operations on behalf of the Company. Governor Douglas, speaking of this district, over which I travelled in 1859, viz. that of the Thompson, Buonaparte, and Chapeau rivers, says:—

"The district comprehended within those limits is exceedingly beautiful and picturesque, being composed of a succession of hills and valleys, lakes and rivers, exhibiting to the traveller accustomed to the endless forests of the coast districts the unusual and grateful spectacle of miles of green hills crowning slopes and level meadows, almost without a bush or tree to obstruct the view, and even to the very hill-tops producing an abundant growth of grass. It is of great value as a grazing district,—a circumstance which appears to be thoroughly understood and appreciated by the country packers, who are in the habit of leaving their mules and horses here when the regular work of packing goods to the mines is suspended for the winter. The animals, even at that season are said to improve in condition, though left to seek their own food and to roam at large over the country: a fact which speaks volumes in favour of the climate and of the natural pastures. It has certainly never been my good fortune to visit a country more pleasing to the eye, or possessing a more healthy and agreeable climate, or a greater extent of fine pasture-land; and there is no doubt that, with a smaller amount of labour and outlay than in almost any other colony, the energetic settler may soon surround himself with all the elements of affluence and comfort. Notwithstanding these advantages, such have hitherto been the difficulties of access that the course of regular settlement has hardly yet commenced.

"A good deal of mining-stock has been brought in for sale, but, with the exception of eight or ten persons, there are no farmers in the district. One of those, Mr. McLean, a native of Scotland, and lately of the Hudson Bay Company's service, has recently settled in a beautiful spot near the débouche of the Hat River, and is rapidly bringing his land into cultivation. He has a great number of horses and cattle of the finest American breeds; and, from the appearance of the crops, there is every prospect that his labour and outlay will be well rewarded. He is full of courage, and as confident as deserving of success. He entertains no doubt whatever of the capabilities of the soil, which he thinks will, under proper management, produce any kind of grain or root crops. The only evil he apprehends is the want of rain, and the consequent droughts of summer, which has induced him to bring a supply of water from a neighbouring stream, by which he can at pleasure irrigate the whole of his fields."

Again ; Mr. Douglas, in speaking of the farm at Pavillon, which I mentioned in my account of that place, says :—

"I received an equally favourable report from Mr. Reynolds, who commenced a farm at Pavillon in 1859, and has consequently had the benefit of two years' experience. His last crop (1860), besides a profusion of garden vegetables, consisted of oats, barley, turnips, and potatoes, and the produce was most abundant. The land under potatoes yielded 375 bushels to the acre. The turnip-crop was no less prolific ; one of the roots weighed 26 lbs., and swedes of 15 lbs. and 16 lbs. were commonly met with.* He could not give the yield of oats and barley, the greater part having been sold in the sheaf for the mule-trains passing to and from the mines ; but the crop, as was manifest from the weight and length of the straw, which attained a height of fully four feet, was remarkably good. He generally allows his cattle to run at large, and they do not require to be housed or fed in winter. The cold is never severe ; the greatest depth of snow in 1859 was 12 inches, and the following winter it did not exceed 6. Ploughing commences about the middle of March. The summers are generally dry, and Mr. Reynolds is of opinion that irrigation will be found an indispensable application in the process of husbandry in this district. In the dry summer of 1859 he kept water almost constantly running through his fields, but applied it only twice during the summer of 1860, when the moisture of the atmosphere proved otherwise sufficient for the crops." †

* Roots of this weight, and even heavier, are quite common in California and Oregon.

† 'Blue Book,' part iv. pp. 54, 55.

Although the irrigation spoken of as necessary may appear a great drawback, it is not so really; for so numerous are the streams all over the country, and in such a variety of directions do they run, that very little care will enable a man so to lay out his fields that he may always have plenty of water at his command. The Governor remarked this. "The numerous streams," he says, "which permeate the valleys of this district afford admirable facilities for inexpensive irrigation. So bountiful, indeed, has Nature been in this respect, that it is hardly an exaggeration to say that there is a watercourse or rivulet for every moderate-sized farm that will be opened in the district." *

I think it will be found, however, that, as civilization advances, as the hill-tops are denuded of trees, and the soil of the valleys is broken up, artificial irrigation will not be so necessary as it now is. Experience elsewhere shows that the climate changes as a country becomes settled; and already this is felt in other parts of this colony. Last year the rain fell in the summer time much more abundantly than it had been known to do before; while the winter, in which hitherto all the rain had fallen, was drier. I think that Victoria has seen the last of the regular wet and dry seasons that used to set in, and that henceforth there will be rain throughout the year as in England. The rain also becomes much less partial as settlement progresses. A few years ago we used to have rain at Victoria when not a drop fell at Esquimalt, three miles off; and I have seen it rain hard on shore on one side of the harbour, when there was none falling on the other. This, however, seldom happens now.

The country lying south-east of the district we have been considering, is perhaps even richer and more open. I have never visited it myself; but every one whom I have heard speak of it called it the best agricultural district in the colony. It is

* 'Blue Book,' part iv. pp. 54, 55.

usually called the Semilkameen country, from the river of that name which runs through it; and it extends from the Nicola River and head-waters of the Thompson, at the Shuswap Lake, down by the Okanagan Lake and River to the boundary line. This region has lately been opened up by a trail cut from Fort Hope through a gorge in the Cascade range of hills, which at that point are called Manson Mountains; and thence descending upon the Semilkameen and Okanagan Rivers. Beneficial as this trail will be to that district, like most of the mountain-trails of the country, it will only be available from four to six months of the year from the depth of snow in the gorge through which it passes.

In September, 1859, Lieutenant Palmer, R.E., was sent to examine this trail and, the country adjoining it; and although he reports very favourably on the soil and general capabilities of it, he thinks the difficulty of obtaining provisions, &c., will deter settlers for some time. Of the soil he says: "The grass is generally of a good quality, the prickly-pear and ground-cactus, the sore enemy to the moccassined traveller, being the surest indication of an approach to an inferior quality. Timber is for the most part scarce, but coppices appear at the sharp bends of the river tolerably well wooded, and abounding in an underbush of willow and wild cherry, while near the base of the mountains it exists in quantities easily procurable, and more than sufficient for the requirements of any settlers who might at some time populate the district. The soil is somewhat sandy and light, but free from stones, and generally pronounced excellent for grazing and farming; and though the drought in summer is great, and irrigation necessary, many large portions are already well watered by streams from the mountains, whose fall is so rapid as greatly to facilitate such further irrigation as might be required. In corroboration of my expressed opinion relative to the yielding properties of the soil, I may mention that in spots through which, perchance,

some small rivulet or spring wound its way to the river, wild
vegetation was most luxuriant, and grass, some blades of
which I measured out of curiosity, as much as nine feet high,
well rounded and firm, and a quarter of an inch in diameter
at its lower end. The river throughout its course is confined
to a natural bed, the banks being steep enough to prevent
inundation during the freshets (a favourable omen for agriculture), and its margin is generally fringed with a considerable growth of wood of different kinds." *

In concluding his report he says: "The present unde-
veloped state of British Columbia, and the absence of any
good roads of communication with the interior, would probably render futile the attempt to settle the Semilkameen
and other valleys in the vicinity of the 49th parallel. Extensive crops, it is true, might probably be raised, but the immi-
grant would have to depend for other necessaries of life either
on such few as might from time to time find their way into
the country from Washington territory, or on such as might,
during four months in the year, be obtained from Fort Hope
and other points on the Fraser River, and either of which
could not be obtained but at prices too exorbitant for the
pocket of the poor man. It would seem, therefore, that the
Buonaparte and Thompson River valleys are the natural
starting-points for civilization and settlement. Starting from
these points, civilization would gradually creep forward and
extend finally to the valleys of the frontier." †

While quite agreeing with Lieutenant Palmer that the
Buonaparte and Thompson valleys have at present the advantage of the Semilkameen, I think he overestimates some of
the difficulties of settling the latter. The great advantage
possessed by the former is in the fact of their lying on the
road to the richest diggings now worked in the country
(Cariboo). This, of course, enables the farmer to find a near

* 'Blue Book,' part iii. p. 85.   † Ibid.

and convenient market for his produce; as, for instance, in one
of the reports from which 1 have quoted, Mr. Reynolds, a
farmer there, is said to have sold all or nearly all his oats and
barley in the sheaf to the mule-trains trading to the mines.
Just now the Semilkameen country, in which very rich
diggings were discovered, has been deserted for the superior
attractions of Cariboo; but a lucky find, which is likely to
occur at any time, will bring the miners hurrying back again,
to the profit, of course, of the settlers farming there.   In
proof of the probability of this occurring, it may be mentioned
that in May 1861, Mr. Cox (the Gold Commissioner at Rock
Creek) reports: "We prospected nine streams, all tributaries
of the lake (Okanagan), and found gold in each, averaging
from thirty to ninety cents a pan."   He then mentions other
good prospects which have not been made public, "as it would
only lead to bad results just at present.   The miners in this
(Rock Creek) neighbourhood would be easily coaxed off, and
the mines now in preparatory condition for being worked,
abandoned; improvements going on in buildings or farms
would be checked; town lots would be almost unsaleable; in
fact, the expected revenue receipt would be seriously interfered
with." *

As to the necessaries and even the luxuries of life, there is
no doubt that the settlers in the Semilkameen districts could
command them cheaper and more readily than those upon the
Upper Fraser, obtaining them as they might across the boundary from Walla-Walla and Colville upon the Columbia River.
I have before mentioned that this fact of the Americans carrying on a trade across the frontier was a great cause of complaint to the British merchants, who, having to take their
goods up the Fraser River, found themselves undersold by
their more fortunate rivals.   To remedy this, in December
1860, an order was issued prohibiting the transmission of

* 'Blue Book,' part iv. p. 50.

goods across the frontier except at a high rate of duty, and
then only "pending the completion of the communications in
British Columbia." This prohibitory proclamation was issued
because when the Governor visited New Westminster in
October 1860, "there was much depression in business circles,
and a marked decrease of trade; . . . . a casualty generally attributed by business men to the growing overland
trade with the possessions of the United States in Oregon and
Washington territory, which now supply, on the southern
frontier of the colony, a large proportion of the bulky articles,
such as provisions and bread-stuffs, consumed in the eastern
districts of British Columbia." * This clearly shows that
the southern districts of the colony can be more easily supplied than any others: while, for agricultural purposes, the
advantages of climate there will be a consideration of great
weight.

In the northern part of the colony, from Alexandria
upwards, although the soil, wherever it has been tried by the
Hudson Bay Company's people, has been found good, the
country is too cold and liable to frost, in the early summer,
to offer the attractions as a producing district possessed by
the country farther south.

Mr. McLean, however, who lived many years at Alexandria, told me that he had known a bushel of wheat
planted there yield forty bushels; but this was considerably
more than an average produce. Of the Upper posts, Mr.
Manson, who was seven years at Fort St. James, told me the
soil is good, but the crops, except barley, are almost always
nipped by frost. During the whole of his residence there,
they only got two crops of potatoes. At Fraser Fort, which
is in nearly the same latitude as Fort James, but considerably to the westward of it, vegetation thrives much better,
and barley, peas, turnips, and potatoes, almost always yield

* 'Blue Book,' part iii. p. 22.

good crops. The country southward of Fraser Fort and down
to the Chilcotin River, I was told by Mr. McLean, as well as
by a settler whom I met at Pavillon, contained very good
farming-land, but on most of it there are two or three feet of
snow every winter: so that these regions will not yet vie with
those before spoken of; for at Pavillon, in the northern part of
the Thompson River district, Mr. Reynolds, as I have before
mentioned, said they had only twelve inches of snow in the
winter of 1859-60, and only six inches in 1860-61. Moreover, in the north the cattle must always be stall-fed in
winter.

Of the banks of the Lower Fraser, between the mouth
of the river and Fort Hope, the Governor writes: " The
banks of this river are almost everywhere covered with
woods.   Varieties of pine, and firs of prodigious size, and
large poplar-trees, predominate. The vine and soft maple,
the wild apple-tree, the white and black thorn, and deciduous
bushes in great variety, form the massive undergrowth. The
vegetation is luxuriant, almost beyond conception, and at this
season of the year presents a peculiarly beautiful appearance.
The eye never tires of ranging over the varied shades of the
fresh green foliage, mingling with the clustering white flowers
of the wild apple-tree, now in full blossom and filling the air
with delicious fragrance. As our boat, gliding swiftly over
the surface of the smooth waters, occasionally swept beneath
the overhanging boughs that form a canopy of leaves impervious to the sun's scorching rays, the effect was enchanting."

Although I have said that the country seaward of the
Cascade Range is, as a whole, unfit for agricultural purposes,
there are some spots of very fine land near the coast quite sufficient to produce all that will for a long time be required by
the population there. I have before spoken of the Lilloett
meadows at Port Pemberton, and of the valley of the
Squawmisht, at the head of Howe Sound, as containing much
valuable land. At the mouth of the Fraser, also, there is

an extensive plain which is covered in summer with most luxuriant hay, and which, although now flooded when the water is high, might, I think, easily be reclaimed. The hay from this plain has already become a source of considerable profit to some settlers, who cut and send it to Victoria.

Five miles above New Westminster, on the banks of the Pitt River, are also found extensive clear plains called the Pitt meadows. These will no doubt soon be cultivated for the supply of New Westminster, their only drawback being that many parts are liable to overflow. In 1860 the Governor visited Pitt Lake, from which the river of that name flows, and, speaking of these meadows, he says: "The banks of the Pitt River are exceedingly beautiful: extensive meadows sweep gracefully from the very edge of the river towards the distant line of forest and mountain. The rich alluvial soil produces a thick growth of grass, interspersed with the Michaelmas daisy, the wild rose, and scattered groups of willows. This fine district contains an area of 20,000 acres of good arable land, requiring no clearing from timber, and ready for the immediate operations of the plough. Many parts of it are, however, exposed to overflow through the periodical inundations of the Fraser, which commence about the first week in June, and generally subside before the middle of July. Owing to this circumstance, the Pitt meadows are not adapted for raising wheat or other cereals which require the entire season to mature; but it may be turned to good account in growing hay and every kind of root crop, and may also be used extensively for pasturing cattle, and for the purposes of dairy." *

In addition to these localities, there is a considerable quantity of clear land around, and opposite to, the deserted city of Derby. Land may now be obtained in British Columbia under the enactments of the new pre-emption

* 'Blue Book,' part iv. p. 8.

system readily, and at a very low rate, in those parts of the
country yet unsurveyed; which include indeed all but that
immediately surrounding the settlements. An intending
settler has merely to fix upon the site of his farm, and give
such a description of its locality, boundaries, &c., as he is
able to the nearest magistrate, paying at the same time a fee
of 8s. for its registration. These regulations extend, however,
to 160 acres only. A settler desiring to pre-empt a larger
quantity than that, must pay down an instalment of 2s. 1d.
per acre. This payment entitles him to possession of the
land until it is surveyed by the Government, when the full
value at which it may be assessed—which cannot, however,
exceed 4s. 2d. an acre—becomes payable. To prevent speculators holding large tracts of country, and thus keeping out
bonâ fide settlers, land held under the pre-emption system
cannot be legally sold, mortgaged, or leased, unless the pre-
emptor can prove to the magistrate that he has made permanent improvements on the land to the value of 10s. an
acre. As this land-system is of great importance to the
intending settler, the latest proclamations upon the subject
are given in full in the Appendix.

· On Vancouver Island, although the quantity of agricultural land is very small in comparison with that in British
Columbia, there are many lovely spots for farms; and the
soil, wherever it has been tried, is very fertile. To name all
the clear spots on the island would take too much space, and
would be of no advantage to the settler unacquainted with
the country. I will, therefore, merely speak of the larger
tracts which have been examined, and of the system by
which these, or any portions of them, may be occupied.

The districts of Soke and Metchosin, at the south-east
extreme of the island, contain a large quantity of good land,
much of which is still unsettled. Of the capabilities of this
tract, I cannot do better than quote the evidence of the late
Colonel Grant, who was one of the first immigrants to Van-

couver, and whose farm was in this district. He says that
he found the soil produce abundantly, when cultivated,
any crops that can be grown in Scotland or England.
After describing Soke Harbour, he continues:—"Along the
eastern shore there is little or no available land.   Following the shore of the harbour, we come to no available
land until half-way to the Indian village, which is situated
at the bend above-mentioned; round it are a few hundred
acres of available woodland.   At this point the Soke River
discharges itself, which takes its course in two lakes, one
about 12 miles in a direct line to the north, and the other
about 25 miles up.   There are a few patches of open meadow-
land near the mouth of the river, on which the Indians grow
considerable quantities of potatoes.   Small canoes can go up
the river to a distance of three miles; there is a little level
land along it at intervals for that distance, consisting of a
rich alluvial soil, covered with a magnificent growth of timber.
This land, however, where it exists at all, merely extends
for a few yards back from the river, and beyond the whole
country is utterly unavailable.   From the mouth of the river
all along the west coast of the harbour, the land is rich and
level; and, though at present covered with woodland, may,
doubtless, some day be brought into cultivation.   Near the
entrance of the harbour, and running from it across a
peninsula to the Straits, is a small prairie of 315 acres.
The soil in the prairie is a rich, black vegetable mould from
three to four feet deep, with a stiff clay subsoil, resting on
sandstone, and the surrounding woodland also consists of very
rich soil."

Colonel Grant then proceeds to state that " five square
miles, of which 330 acres in all are open land, and the
remainder tolerably level woodland, will certainly comprise
the whole available land in the district." In this estimate,
however, there is no doubt that he is a good deal under
the mark.

Immediately round Victoria, and in the Saanitch district, on the peninsula spoken of before, is much good land; but this is now all or nearly all settled and under cultivation. The Cowitchen Valley, which I mentioned in my journal as comprising a very large quantity of available land, was surveyed in 1860, and in the surveyor's report will be found the following remarks :—" I am firmly persuaded that under a common judicious system of farming, as good returns can be obtained from these lands as in any part of the continent of America. The climate, it may be noted, is one especially adapted for the pursuits of agriculture, not being subject to the heats and droughts of California, or to the colds of the other British American provinces and the eastern United States. The loamy soils everywhere possessing a depth of two or three feet, and containing a large proportion of the calcareous principle, are especially eligible for fruit-culture; and the oak-plains around the Somenos and Quamichan lakes,* with a sandy clay subsoil, are exceedingly well adapted for fruit or garden purposes. Among the native fruits the blackberry, mulberry, raspberry, strawberry, gooseberry, currant, and high bush-cranberry, would require little pains or culture to produce luxuriantly. The varieties of plants are very numerous; a few only were noted growing on the plains or meadow lands, among which are the following:—Wild pea, wild beans, ground-nut, clover, field-strawberry, wild oat, cut grass, wild timothy, reed meadow-grass, long spear-grass, sweet grass, high ostrich-fern, cowslip, crowfoot, winter cress, partridge-berry, wild sunflower, marigold, wild lettuce, nettles, wild Angelica, wild lily, broad-leafed rush, and reed-bush. The ferns attain a height of six or eight feet, and the grasses all have a vigorous growth.

"The following are some of the trees or shrubs:—Oak, red or swamp maple, alder, trailing arbutus, bois de flèche,

* In the Cowitchen Valley.

crab-apple, hazel-nut, red alder, willow, balsam-poplar, pitch-juice, and various other species; balsam-fir, cedar, barberry, wild red cherry, wild blackberry, yellow plum, choke-cherry, black and red raspberry, swamp-rose, bearberry, red elder, mooseberry, snowberry, blueberry, bilberry, whortleberry, cranberry, red and white mulberry.

"The whole area surveyed is 57,658 acres, of which 45,000 acres of plain and prairie land may be set down as superior agricultural lands, the remaining portion being woodland, either open or thick."

Though I have not perfect confidence in all the details of the gentleman who was charged with this survey, and who was not one of the regular staff, the general outline may be trusted; and I have given the above extracts to show generally how rich the country is wherever it is free from the heavy timber. The luxuriance of the growth of wild fruits and flowers exceeds that of any country I have ever been in. I do not, of course, mean to compare it with the rank vegetation of the tropics, but I assert that it is more naturally fertile than any region I have ever visited.

Above the Cowitchen Valley come the Somenos Valley and the Nanaimo district. In each of these there is much good land.

Mr. Pearce, the assistant-colonial surveyor, who examined and reported on these districts, divides the land around Nanaimo into four divisions—the Mountain, Cranberry, and Cedar districts, and the Delta plains—estimating them to contain together 43,450 acres. He says of the second of these:—"The soil is sandy, but covered with the most luxuriant vegetation, fern, wild fruit-bushes, and trees, among which it may be noted the crab-apple and cherry are everywhere found. The woods are, for the most part, open, and free from bush and fallen timber, and present quite a tropical appearance. The principal timber is cedar, pine, maple, and poplar, all of which grow to gigantic size, the pines rising to

100 feet without a branch, and having many distinct and
separate tops; the branches of the cedar grow to the very
ground.   Some of these trees measure 27 feet in circumference, and are perfectly sound.   The maple and poplar-
trees are very tall and straight, and average 10 feet in
circumference."   Of the Cedar district, which contains 11,000
acres, he says:—"Nearly the whole of this is available for
cultivation.   The soil is very fertile, and of a good depth,
with a clay subsoil, and abounds in springs of beautiful water,
especially along the coast, which are probably caused by the
drainage from the lakes in the interior.   The south-eastern
part is also filled with large lakes, though the land generally
is poor and rocky around them, but the pine, cedar, and
maple timber, is all of the finest kind.   The lakes are perfectly full of trout, and the surrounding country abounds with
all kind of game before mentioned; i. e., elk, deer, bear,
grouse, partridge, wildfowl, crane, and pigeon."   Of the
Delta plains, which contain about 1000 acres, he says:—
"The southern portion consists of rich vegetable soil, of a
great depth, with a subsoil of muddy clay or loam, the deposit
of ages; the north portion is apparently subject at long intervals to floods, but is, nevertheless, admirably suited for a
stock or grazing farm, or rather farms, bearing a long rich
grass, which the Indians annually cut and sell to the settlers
at Colville town (Nanaimo)."

Of the Komoux, Salmon River, and other clear places
farther north on the island, I have spoken in the description
of my visits to them.   According to Mr. Pemberton, the
colonial surveyor, there must be a good deal more clear land
at Komoux, Courtenay River, than we saw, as he estimates it
at 30 square miles.

At Fort Rupert, which is the most northern spot on the
island where cultivation has been attempted, the produce of
vegetables and flowers in the garden is yearly most luxuriant.
Nor is this strange, when it is remembered that the northern-

most point of the island is only in the same latitude as the
Thompson River district.

I have given in a previous chapter some extracts from the
Journal of Mr. Moffat, the only white man who has visited
the interior of the island at the north end. In his summary
he says:—

"The timber in the interior of the island is very fine; in
fact the banks of both sides of the Nimpkish River, from the
first lake almost to the Nootka Inlet, are lined with splendid
red pines,* large and long enough for the spars of the largest
men-of-war. The water-communication is also a great consideration. Spars could be squared, rolled into the water, and
floated down without difficulty to any depôt, such as the
anchorage at Illeece, or even Beaver Cove.

"The various berries of the country grow in great abundance, with the exception of the small dark berry resembling
a beaver-shot; I am unacquainted with the name. It is
plentiful down south and at Comoux. Salmon of various
kinds, of splendid quality, are found in abundance on the
coast, as well as halibut and other sea-fish.

"Rock-oysters of large size I procured to the north of
Nootka, some 50 miles, but saw few other shell-fish, except
the large sea-mussel and the barnacle. Crabs and sea-egg
were plentiful, also the sea-cucumber, and the various species
of star-fish and sea-anemones.

"The zoology is the same as other parts of Vancouver
Island, except that the purple marmot is occasionally found
at Koskimo, but not the common grey marmot. The white
land-otters, which have at various times been forwarded from
here, were killed near Kioquettuck.

"The depth of the Nimpkish Lake I have since sounded,
and got no bottom at seventy-five fathoms from the stern of a
canoe, her bow being aground ashore."

* Probably Red Fir (*Abies Douglasii*).

Mr. Moffat also mentions having discovered at the Nimpkish Lake " a tree resembling a walnut, with a trunk about
4½ feet in circumference, and emitting a fine perfume."
So rapid has been the commercial progress of the colony
since the discovery of gold to the present time, and so
necessarily fluctuating are all the tariffs of a country whose
population doubles or trebles in a month or two, and then
in a few months dwindles nearly to a cipher, that it is
impossible to give anything like a satisfactory account of its
commerce.   The principal trade is with San Francisco, and
from the custom-house books we can learn the tonnage
which has arrived at, and cleared from, California during the
past year.   From these we find a decrease in the trade of
1861 from that of 1860, which is owing, doubtless, to the
increasing trade with England and the eastern states of
America, and to the large stock left on hand from the pre-
ceding year.   But of the export of gold we are unable to get
any just estimate, on account of so large a proportion of it
having been exported by private individuals, of which the
Custom-house at Victoria takes no cognizance.   We find
from the colonial returns in January, 1862, that the number
of vessels, including steamers, that arrived at San Francisco
was 46 ; the tonnage, 29,597 tons; the total exports, not
including gold, 48,905 dollars.   Fifteen vessels, all steamers,
left the colony in ballast, and consequently all the exports of
the colony were carried in 31 vessels.   The ports at which
they loaded, the tonnage, and the value, were as follows :—

	Vessels.	Tonnage.	Exports.
			Dollars.
Soke	2	576	6,500
Nanaimo	15	4252	34,124
Victoria	14	6533	8,381

This shows that Nanaimo exceeds Victoria in exports four-
fold, which is reasonable enough, when it is remembered that

all the coal exported from that port is known, while the gold
sent from the other is not ascertainable. The comparison
above-mentioned of the years 1860 and 1861 shows a decrease
of 11 vessels and 14,291 tons arriving at San Francisco, and
that the falling off in the number of vessels cleared for Victoria
is greater than in the number entered. In 1860, 116 vessels.
with a total tonnage of 62,998 tons, cleared for British
Columbia and Vancouver Island. In 1861 there were only
84 vessels carrying 43,675 tons; showing a decrease of 32
vessels and 19,323 tons. If we did not know that more gold
has been found in that than in any previous year, this would
appear alarming; but the fact being that the supply of gold
is increasing, it must be attributed to the overstocked markets
of 1860. This, indeed, I know was the case, for merchants at
Victoria, well aware that good news from the upper country
might at any time bring a rush of immigration, laid in a large
supply of such stores as would not perish, so as to be ready
in case of emergency.

The statistics of the treasure (coin) sent up from California
show only two shipments: in January, 24,000 dollars, in
September, 3500 dollars. This is doubtless true as regards
the custom-house books, but that much more must have
come in some way is certain from the amount of dust
which was bought for cash in Victoria. Wells, Fargo, and
Company, of whom I have before spoken, are stated to have
sent down 1,339,895 dollars (279,145*l.*) in gold-dust during
the year 1861, and another Company (Macdonald and Co.) to
have shipped between June and December 296,895 dollars
(62,269*l.* 15*s.* 10*d.*), making a total of 1,636,790 dollars
(342,414*l.* 11*s.* 8*d.*), of which a large part is said to have been
paid for in Victoria.

In the interior of the country the prices are never steady;
not only do they rise and fall with summer and winter, but
any delays on the route, the non-arrival of a pack-train when
it is expected, or the influx of 100 or 200 men, will always
run the prices up for a few days at least. The whole ten-

dency, however, is doubtless towards cheapening the supplies as the communications become more complete and less liable to interruption from bad roads, &c. I have mentioned that the winter before I went up the country, *i. e.*, 1858-59, bacon was selling at "Bigbar," 100 miles below Cariboo, at 1½ dollars (6*s.*) per lb., and flour at 75 cents (3*s.*).

I now give the prices current in the summer of 1860. In September, 1860, the prices at Alexandria, 100 miles South of Cariboo, were—*

		£.	*s.*	*d.*
Flour	per lb.	0	1	2
Beans	,,	0	1	3
Bacon	,,	0	3	1
Sugar	,,	0	3	1½
Rice	,,	0	1	3
Tea	,,	0	6	0
Coffee	,,	0	3	1
Lard	,,	0	3	1½
Candles	,,	0	5	0
Soap	,,	0	2	0
Salt	,,	0	2	0
Pepper (ground)	,,	0	4	0
Yeast-powder	per tin	0	4	0
Butter	per lb.	0	6	0
Rope	,,	0	3	1½
Tobacco	,,	0	8	0
Potatoes	,,	0	1	0
Steel shovels	each	1	4	0
Picks	,,	1	0	0
Sluice forks	,,	1	8	0
Axes (Collins')	,,	1	4	0
Nails	per lb.	0	2	0
Quicksilver	,,	0	12	0
Overshirts	each	0	10	0
Undershirts	,,	0	9	0
Canvas trousers	per pair	0	10	0
Kentucky tweed trousers	,,	0	12	0
Corduroy (common)	,,	1	0	0
Boots	,,	1*l.* 12*s.* to 2*l.* 8*s.*		
Shoes (common)	,,	0	14	0
Drilling	per yard	0	1	3
Duck	,,	0	3	4
Oregon blankets	per pair	2	0	0

* 'Blue Book,' part iv. p. 43.

In September of the same year they were—

		£.	s.	d.
Bacon	per lb.	0	3	0
Sugar	„	0	3	0
Flour	„	4	1	2
Beans	„	0	1	4
Tea	„	0	6	4
Coffee (green)	„	0	2	8
Lard	„		3s. to 3s. 6d.	
Candles	„	0	5	2
Soap	„	0	2	0
Pepper (ground)	„	0	4	2
Yeast-powder	per tin	0	4	2
Butter	per lb.	0	6	4
Rope	per fathom	0	3	0
Tobacco (common)	per lb.	0	8	4
Potatoes	„	0	1	0
Onions	„	0	2	0
Grey shirts	each	0	10	6
Undershirts	„	0	7	0
Canvas trousers	per pair	0	10	6
Common corduroy trousers	„	1	1	0
Boots (mining)	„		1l. 13s. to 2l. 2s.	
Shoes (common)	„	0	15	0
Drilling	per yard	0	1	3
Duck	„	0	3	4
Oregon blankets	per pair	2	2	0
Shovels (steel)	each	1	5	0
Collins' picks	„	1	1	0
Sluice-forks	„	1	9	0
Axes	„	1	13	0
Quicksilver	per lb.	0	12	6
Nails	„	0	2	0
Powder	„	0	8	0
Lead	„	0	4	0

In January, 1861, we have the prices at Hope—

Flour	per barrel	1l. 8s. to 1l. 12s.
Bacon	per lb.	10d. to 11½d.
Beans	„	2½d. to 4d.
Sugar	„	5d. to 1s. 0½d.
Coffee	„	1s. to 1s. 2d.
Tea	„	2s. to 4s.
Butter	„	1s. 2½d. to 2s. 7d.
Lard	„	10d. to 1s. 3d.
Rice	„	4d. to 4½d.
Candles	„	1s. 8d. to 2s. 1d.

In the Semilkameen district at same date—

		s.	d.
Flour .. .. per lb.	1	4¼
Bacon .. .. ,,	1	10
Lard .. .. ,,	2	0
Sugar .. .. ,,	1	3
Tea.. .. .. ,,	5	0
Coffee .. .. ,,	2	0

At that time the rates of freight were very low, in consequence of excessive competition; only 3*l.* per ton being charged from Victoria to Yale, while in the spring of 1860 10*l.* per ton was charged. Mr. Sanders, the Assistant Gold Commissioner at Yale, says:—"The miner and labouring man can live comfortably there on 3*s.* a day. Charge of restaurants is 2*l.* a week. Rate of wages 10*l.* per month and keep." *

He estimates the probable yield of the road-toll between Yale and Lytton for the year at—

	£.	s.	d.
5000 mules, 300 lbs. each, or 1500 tons ..	3000	0	0
400 tons by boats..	800	0	0
750 tons carried by Indians	1500	0	0
	£5300	0	0

According to the list kept by him during the past season (1860), 2723 mules were packed to the interior from that town (Yale). The revenue of the district of Yale for 1860 was—

	£.	s.	d.
Mining licences	267	0	0
Mining receipts (general)	201	6	2
Tolls and ferries..	238	17	5
Sales of lands	272	0	0
Fines and Fees	96	14	0
Spirit licences	320	0	0
Tracking licences	141	0	0
	£1536	17	7

Since that time, however, some new roads have been

* 'Blue Book,' part iv. p. 48.

completed and several begun, and each mile of these makes things cheaper. Writing at the same time, the Governor says: " The works we propose to execute this year are as follows :—

	Miles.
Cart-road from Pemberton to Cayoosh, length about	36
„ from Hope to Semilkameen	74
Improvement of the navigation of the Semilkameen River ..	60
Horse-road from Boston Bar to Lytton	30
„ from Lytton to Alexandria	150
„ from Cayoosh to junction with Lytton Road ..	30

In Progress.

Road from New Westminster to Langley	15
„ from New Westminster to Burrard Inlet	9
„ from New Westminster to boundary line at Semiahmoo	14
„ from Spuzzum to Boston Bar (nearly finished)	20

For these purposes he says the colony can find 25,000*l.*, and asks for a loan of 50,000*l.**

If the routes which are now being tried between Bute Inlet and Bentinck Arm to Cariboo succeed, it will make a considerable change in the commercial position of the towns on the Fraser, and very probably some difference to Victoria. For Bute Inlet the traffic will still go in by the strait of Fuca and past Victoria, but if Bentinck Arm becomes a thoroughfare, vessels bound thither will do much better to keep outside the Vancouver Island rather than go up the inner channels, for the entrance to Bentinck Arm is 70 miles north of the north end of the island. It will be a considerable advantage to these routes if they are able to avail themselves of inland water-carriage, as it is always so much cheaper than land-carriage. I have mentioned in proof of this that on the Lilloett River in the winter of 1858-59, the Indians were taking goods up the river in their canoes for 5 cents (2½*d.*) per lb., while the packers on the trail were charging 15 cents (7½*d.*).

* 'Blue Book,' part iv. p. 44.

Mr. Nind, the magistrate of the Cariboo district, tells me that the Fraser River between Alexandria and Fort George is navigable for steamers, and by the latest accounts a steamer is being placed on the river there. If the Stuart or West Road Rivers are found to be navigable also, it will shorten the coast routes both in time and expense immensely, and still more if the Bellhoula River is navigable for any distance from the coast.

In speaking of the resources of these colonies, the immense supply of fish of all kinds must not be omitted. The quantity of salmon is almost beyond description; but it will give some idea of it to say that a Hudson Bay Company's officer, who lived many years on the Columbia, told me that on a sudden falling of the water such numbers were left on the banks as to cause the river to stink for miles. The usual way of catching this fish is by spearing from the canoe; in salt-water the Indians do this as they paddle about the harbours, or, if it be at the mouth of a river, drive stakes in to keep the fish back, and then spear them while they are trying to get through. In the rivers a net is fixed into a frame; the fish run into this and are speared, or, when the water is still, are taken out with a small scoop-net fastened on the end of a pole. They use spindles of the Thuja plicata as corks for the upper part of these nets, and weight the lower part with stones. "The rope of the net is made of Salix or Thuja, and the cord of Apocymene piscatorium (A. hypericifolium ?), a gigantic species peculiar to this country, whose fibre affords a great quantity of flax." * I have frequently watched this proceeding. Mr. David Douglas, the botanist, gives such a capital description of the way these nets are fitted, in his journal, that I cannot do better than transcribe it literally:—

"The quantity of salmon (Salmo scoulieri?—Richardson)

* Douglas, 'Botanical Magazine,' p. 90.

taken in the Columbia, he says, is almost incredible; and the Indians resort in great numbers to the best fishing-spots, often travelling several hundred miles for this purpose. The salmon are captured in the following manner :—Before the water rises, small channels are made among the rocks and stones, dividing the stream into branches, over which is erected a platform or stage on which a person can stand; these are made to be raised or let down as the water falls or rises. A scoop-net which is fastened round a hoop, and held by a pole 12 or 15 feet long, is then dropped into the channel, which it exactly fits ; and the current of the water carrying it down, the poor fish swims into it without being aware, when the individual who watches the net instantly draws it, and flings the fish on shore. The handle of the net is secured by a rope to the platform, lest the force of the current should drive it out of the fisher's hands. The hoop is made of *Acer circuiatum,* the net of the bark of an *Apocymene,* which is very durable and tough, and the pole of pine-wood." He gives also the size of some fish, and an average weight rather higher than I should give; but he speaks of the Columbia River, where, perhaps, the fish are larger. He says they generally weigh 15 to 25 lbs. He measured two: one was 3 ft. 5 in. long, and 10 inches broad at the thickest part, weighing 35 lbs.; the other 3ft. 4 in., and 9 inches broad, weighing a little less. Both were purchased for 2 inches of tobacco (about half an ounce) value two-pence. In England they would have cost 3*l.* or 4*l.*

The mention I have before made of salmon being used as manure at Fort Rupert will also give an idea of their quantity. Since the influx of whites into the country, the Indians ask a much higher price for their fish than they used; but when I first went there, in 1849, I remember the largest salmon bought on board weighed 50 lbs., and the price it fetched was two sticks of tobacco !

The sturgeon also is caught in very large numbers, and of

great size in some parts, the mouth of the Fraser particularly. Mr. Douglas, the botanist, mentions one caught by one of my companions, which measured 12 feet 9 inches from the snout to the tip of the tail, and 7 feet round the thickest part, while its weight exceeded 500 pounds.*

Hallibut also reach an immense size, and are caught in great numbers everywhere; but, as I have said, particularly off the entrance of the Strait of Fuca.

The herring literally swarm over the harbours in myriads; nothing can give a better idea of the number of these fish than the way they are caught. A dozen or so of sharp nails or spikes are driven into a flat piece of wood 16 or 18 feet long, and 2 or 3 inches broad, making an instrument like a rake; an Indian sits in the bows of his canoe, and dipping this down perpendicularly under water sweeps it along towards the after end of the canoe, pinning some six or eight fish on the nails each sweep he makes; every time he brings it up, he turns the nails points downwards, and gives the rake a tap on the gunwale, which knocks the fish off into the bottom of the canoe. In this way a man will often half fill his canoe in an hour or so.

There is much more game on Vancouver Island than in British Columbia; when travelling in the latter, the absence of animal life has always appeared to me remarkable, while on the former it is generally abundant. On Vancouver Island, when I went from Alberni to Nanaimo, I shot a wapiti and two deer, without going out of my way, and might have shot three or four more wapiti, if we had stopped to do so. This, it must be remembered, however, was in a part of the island before untrodden by man; and a settler must not expect to meet deer straying about his fields, or he will be grievously disappointed. In Columbia, on the other hand, there are large numbers of mountain-sheep, which are

* Douglas, 'Memoir,' p. 91.

unknown on the island. This animal is only found on the mountains whose summits are covered with perpetual snow. I only saw one while I was in the country, and that was when in the snow crossing from Jervis Inlet to Howe Sound; instead of wool it has a short thick coarse hair, and from this circumstance is called by the Company's servants *mouton gris*. I have never tasted it, but Mr. David Douglas says "the flesh is fine, quite equal to that of the domestic sheep." He adds, "the horns of the male, weighing sometimes 18 to 24 lbs., are dingy white, and form a sort of volute; those of the female bend back, curving outwards toward the point." I think Mr. Douglas is wrong as to the colour of the horns. I have seen many of them among the Indians, by whom they are made into spoons, and they are far more generally black than dingy white.

The great set-off that Vancouver Island has against the gold of British Columbia, is her timber; for though timber abounds in British Columbia, we came upon no place there where such fine spars were to be found, and with such facilities for shipping as at Barclay Sound and the neighbourhood of Fort Rupert.

The following is the list of trees found at Barclay Sound, as given by the woodsmen employed there by the Mill Company already spoken of. I give first the local names, the scientific being appended, so far as they are known, by Dr. Lindley :—

> Yellow Fir, or Douglas Pine, sometimes misnamed Oregon Pine—Abies Douglasii.
> White Fir—probably Abies alba.
> Spruce Fir—probably Abies nigra.
> Balsam Fir—Abies balsamea.
> Willow Fir—Salix rostrata.
> White Pine—Pinus monticola.
> Yellow Pine.
> Cedar—Possibly Juniperus occidentalis.
> Alder—Probably Alnus viridis.
> Dogwood—Cornus alba.
> Yew—Taxus baccata.

Crab-apple—Pyrus rivularis.
Maple (two kinds)—Acer macrophyllum and probably Acer rubrum.
Hemlock—Abies Canadiensis.
Cotton Wood—Populus balsamifera, or Populus monilifera.
Aspen —Populus tremuloides.
Arbutus—Arbutus procera.
Yellow Cypress—Thuja gigantea.

Foremost among them all stands the Douglas fir (Abies Douglasii), named after its discoverer, David Douglas, the botanist. As timber for spars or plank, this tree is un-equalled. It grows to the height of 200 to 300 feet, and usually as straight as an arrow. This wood has been planted in several places in England, and should become one of the common trees of this country. The value of this wood for spars has been tested and reported on by the engineer of the French dockyard at Cherbourg, whose report was greatly in its favour. As plank, it is equally fine. Dr. Lindley tells me he has had two planks, about 20 feet long each, which have been in his house in a room where there is constantly a fire, since 1827, and that neither of them has warped or shrunk the least since they were first placed there.

The following extract relating to the Douglas fir is from the ' Gardeners' Chronicle ' :—" We now know that this most beautiful tree, the Douglas fir, is unsurpassable in the qualities which render timber most valuable. It is clean-grained, strong, elastic, light, and acquires large dimensions in ungenial climates. It thrives everywhere in the United Kingdom, except the extreme north, and is therefore of all trees that which most deserves the attention of planters for profit. To which we may add that no evergreen surpasses it as an ornament of scenery.

" Little or nothing was known of the Douglas fir until it was brought into notice by the Horticultural Society, which received its seeds from the hardy collector whose name it bears, and distributed some thousands of young plants among its Fellows. As this happened about five-and-thirty years ago, there must already be an abundance of good specimens in the country. The purpose of this notice is to increase them to the utmost, by inducing landed proprietors to substitute the Douglas fir for the very inferior spruce.

"The Douglas fir makes its first appearance on the mountains of Northern Mexico, in the country near the Real del Monte mines. Thence it follows northwards the western slope of the Rocky Mountains, at least as high as the now celebrated but savage Caribœuf, or Cariboo gold-field, in British Columbia. Douglas, the collector, who crossed the Rocky Mountains a little to the south, through the ' Committee's Punchbowl Pass,' reported that it formed vast forests there on the lower ranges, and struggled upwards till it became mere scrub. We ourselves had, till lately, bark of the tree from those desolate regions fully six inches thick.

A spar of this fir, more than 200 feet high, has been erected in the Royal Botanic Gardens at Kew; and sections, cut at intervals of 15 feet, of a tree 309 feet long, were sent to this country for the International Exhibition. A horizontal section of another tree having been sent for the same purpose, a careful examination of it was made to ascertain its age and rate of growth. The result of this examination, which has appeared in the 'Gardeners' Chronicle,' will be found interesting.

"The diameter is 6 feet, viz., 34 inches on one side, 38 on the other. Its rate of growth on the 34-inch side has been as follows:—

				Years.
" The first 2 inches across were made in ..	..	..	7
The second	,,	,,	.. .. ..	9
The third	,,	,,	.. .. ..	12
The fourth	,,	,,	.. .. ..	19
The fifth	,,	,,	.. .. ..	17
The sixth	,,	,,	.. .. ..	23
The seventh	,,	,,	.. .. ..	16
The eighth	,,	,,	.. .. ..	17
		Carried forward	.. .. ..	120

						Years.
Brought forward			..	..	..	120
The ninth	,,	,,	..	..	..	14
The tenth	,,	,,	..	..	..	18
The eleventh	,,	,,	..	..	..	24
The twelfth	,,	,,	..	..	..	21
The thirteenth	,,	,,	..	..	..	24
The fourteenth	,,	,,	..	..	..	24
The fifteenth	,,	,,	..	..	..	31
The sixteenth	,,	,,	..	..	..	36
The seventeenth	,,	,,	..	..	..	42

Or 34 inches in semidiameter in 354

"It is as well to remark that this British Columbian fir, although three centuries and a-half old, and although for the last forty-two years it increased little more than 1-10th of an inch in diameter yearly, *is perfectly sound to the heart.* Foresters will understand the importance of this fact."

Mr. Sproat, the Barclay Sound Mill Company's agent at Victoria, says of this wood:—" The bark of the tree is very like that of the Canadian hemlock. At its base, and for some distance up, the bark is often a foot thick; the sap is always thinner in proportion as the bark is thick, and *vice versâ.* The sappiest trees are those that grow in the sunshine. The wood varies in colour; a yellowish colour predominates, though a good many are reddish. The colour appears to depend much on the age and situation of the tree, on its greater or less exposure to the sun."

The cone of this tree can never be mistaken, as on the outside of each scale is a sort of claw, with three fingers to it, distinguishing it plainly from all other fir-cones.

The white fir (Abies alba) is poor, compared with the Douglas, though the trees are often a considerable size.

The white pine (Pinus monticola) makes very good plank for building purposes.

The yellow cypress (Thuja gigantea), which abounds more in the north than the south of the colony, is a very useful wood, light, tough, and elastic; it makes the best plank for boat-building that I have ever seen. Its leaf differs from that of the other and common cypress (Thuja occidentalis), in being convex on both sides.

For ornamental purposes the bird's-eye maple (Acer macrophyllum), dogwood (Cornus alba), cedar (Juniperus occidentalis), and arbutus (Arb. procera), are all valuable.

The maple and cedar are very plentiful, and the latter grows to a great size.

The fertility of the soil wherever it has been tested is, as I have before said, great; and the quantity of wild fruits and flowers which abound everywhere is very remarkable. In all swampy places cranberries of two or three sorts grow so plentifully that a flourishing trade is driven with them at San Francisco. Wild strawberries and raspberries, sallal, barberries, black and blue berries, salmon-berries, currants, and gooseberries abound. In the summer, when we were away surveying, the Indians brought such quantities of these alongside that the whole ship's company were usually surfeited before the season was over.

There are also several kinds of bulbous roots, the commonest is the camass (Scilla esculenta), of which the Indians eat a great deal; it has a slight onion flavour, but is sweet.

I need not attempt a detailed account of the plants and shrubs of the colonies. Mr. David Douglas has described many; and a fuller account may be expected from Dr. D. Lyall, who has been attached to the Boundary party, and with them examined the country from the coast to the summit of the Rocky Mountains.

I may mention, however, that hops grow remarkably well, and that a species of tobacco and tea are to be found in Columbia. The former of these was first collected by Mr. Douglas, who says, "Among the most interesting of the plants which I gathered last year (1825) is a species of tobacco, the Nicotiana pulverulenta of Reush, correctly surmised by Nuttall to grow on this side of the Rocky Mountains; though whether this country, or the Rocky Mountains themselves, or the banks of the Missouri, be its original habitat, I am quite unable to say. I am inclined to think, however, that it is indigenous to the mountains, where the hunters say that it grows plentifully. The Nicotiana is never sown by the Indians near the villages, lest it should be pulled and used before it comes to perfect maturity. They select for its cultivation an open place in the wood, where they burn a dead tree or stump, and, strewing the ashes over the ground, plant the tobacco there. They say the wood-ashes invariably make it grow large." * I have smoked this at Fort Kamloops, and liked the flavour—which was similar to that of mild tobacco—very much.

The wild tea-leaf resembles that of China tea. I have never tasted it, but Mr. Pemberton says, " its flavour is not bad and effect exhilarating." He adds, " Some years ago the Hudson Bay Company imported a cargo, but it was stopped at the Custom-house and thrown overboard to avoid the duty." †

I have been favoured by my friend Dr. Wood, of H.M.S. 'Hecate,' with the following remarks upon the natural history of the two colonies. I have much gratification in being able, by Dr. Wood's friendly compliance with my request, to lay before the reader information so trustworthy and valuable.

" In the following remarks I do not assume to give more than a cursory sketch of those sections of the natural history of British Columbia and Vancouver Island which are of most interest to the general reader. Separated by a few miles of ocean, the Fauna and Flora of both colonies are the same—insular position and a less extensive area, however, causing one to be sparse in many things which her larger neighbour possesses in profusion, while again the ocean-washed shores of the western

* Journal of Mr. David Douglas.   † Pemberton, p. 20.

side of Vancouver Island are rich in resources which British Columbia possesses less abundantly. As I am personally better acquainted with Vancouver Island, and as less is known of it than of British Columbia, I will in a great measure confine my remarks to the former, asking the reader to remember, however, that, unless the contrary is indicated when speaking of either colony, I include both.

" I pass over the First and Second Orders of Mammals (the first embracing the peculiar province of the Ethnologist ; the second, or monkey-like animals, not being represented in these colonies), and commence with the Carnivora, the first and second families of which are also sparingly represented. Among them are

" BEARS.—The Black Bear, *Ursus Americanus*, is often seen, and falls easily to the gun of the sportsman. Unless when wounded, it never attacks man. This bear is chiefly a vegetable feeder. The flesh is coarse, but good ; and the skin, which is of little marketable value, makes a good rug.

" The Grizzly, *Ursus horribilis*, is not found on the Island : it is sometimes shot in British Columbia, but its chief home is the Rocky Mountains. It is wisest to leave him unmolested.

" The Racoon, *Ursus lotor*, is a harmless animal, easily tamed. It feeds mostly on wild fruits and, it is said, small birds. It is very numerous in some parts of the coast.

" MARTENS.—The yellow-breasted or Pine Marten, *Mustela martes*, and one of a whole colour, are very numerous. Their skins are in great request, and are collected in large numbers by the fur-traders. A good one is worth from 6s. to 8s. The Common Mink, *Putorius vison*, is also found in great numbers. The Skunk is also frequently seen.

" OTTERS.—The Land Otter, *Mustela lutra*, is frequently shot by the Indians. The skin is of little value. The Sea Otter, *Enhydra marina*, is found throughout the north-west coast of Vancouver. The skin is much sought after, being an extremely valuable fur. The skin of a full-sized one, undressed, and measuring 6 feet, commands the price of thirty blankets—12*l.* to 14*l.* They are sent to England, and, when dressed, forwarded to China, where the finest sometimes fetch 100 dols. (American) apiece.

" WOLVES.—Two species of wolf are known to the settlers, and are commonly spoken of as the Red and Black Wolf. They do not much frequent the settled districts except in winter, when they are very destructive to sheep unless watched. They are cowardly, and I have not heard of their ever attacking men.

"Foxes.—There are two varieties of this animal, the 'Red' and 'Silver Fox.' The latter is found in British Columbia, not upon the Island.

" The American Panther or Puma, *Felis concolor*, is often shot upon Vancouver Island. They are destructive to sheep, and more particularly to pigs and poultry. When followed, they often take refuge in a tree, from whence they are easily shot by a common fowling-piece. Dogs will also attack them. They are quite harmless to men.

" Seals.—One variety of Seal frequents the mouth of the Fraser River, British Columbia, where it may constantly be seen by visitors in summer, seated on a log of wood drifting downwards with the current. Another is found on the sea-coasts of Vancouver Island, and is shot in some numbers by the Indians, who sell their skins to the fur-traders.

" The Squirrel, *Sciurus* (*Cuv.*), is very numerous throughout the pine forests, feeding on the cones of the various fir or pine trees. They are shot in great numbers for the table, and are excellent eating. There are two or three varieties, smaller and otherwise characteristically different from the English species. Ground squirrels are also found.

" The Marmot, *Arctomys monax*, is kept by the settlers sometimes as a domestic pet. It is said that rats never stay in a house in which a marmot is a resident.

" The European Rat is very common on the Island in settled districts, as much a pest as it is at home. Both rats and mice indigenous to the Island and British Columbia exist, but they do not require separate mention.

" The Beaver, *Castor Canadiensis*, is found on the Island, and also in British Columbia. Very few are now trapped for the sake of their skins. They are sometimes shot by Europeans for the sake of their flesh, which is palatable. The tail, which is extremely fat, is considered a delicacy, and somewhat resembles the fat of the turtle. A few years ago 780 beaver-skins were traded in a twelvemonth at one establishment of the Hudson Bay Company on Vancouver Island. The Beaver, as also other fur-bearing animals, is said to be increasing in numbers since the partial settlement of the western shores of North America, from the fact of its being less molested, owing to the employment of the 'trapper' in other pursuits.

"I have not seen a specimen of either a Hare or Rabbit obtained from Vancouver Island. Several varieties of both exist on the neighbouring continent and throughout British Columbia. They differ much, however, from the English varieties, both in habits and appearance.

"The Canadian Stag or Wapiti, and the Elk, *Cervus Canadiensis*, exist in numbers; they sometimes equal the horse in stature, and I have known them shot, weighing, when dressed, 600 lbs. The horns are very handsome. The Black-tailed Deer—the Fallow Deer of the Pacific, *Cervus Columbianus*—are found throughout both colonies, and are very numerous on the small islets, to which they swim, I believe, to escape the wolves. They become, in certain localities, very fat towards autumn, but, though excellent, want the flavour of English venison; from 60 to 80 lbs. is an ordinary weight. The district of Cariboo in British Columbia, now so noticeable for its produce of gold, is so called from a large deer which frequents its pasturage—probably the Rangifer caribou of Audubon. The 'Mountain Goat' and the 'Mountain Sheep' are found in the mountains of British Columbia. I am not aware of their existence on Vancouver Island.

"The American Buffalo, *Bos Americanus*—has lately found its way, it is said, through the Rocky Mountains to the upper plains of the Columbia.

"CETACEA.—With this order of mammals I am little acquainted. Whales, 'Black-fish,' and Porpoises are common off the coast of Vancouver and the inland sea separating it from British Columbia. Considerable ingenuity is shown by the Indians in the capture of the whale. A seal-skin, prepared so as to be air-tight, is attached to a harpoon, the head of which, with a short rope made from cedar-bark, can be detached from the staff. With this attached to him, the whale is not long before he makes his appearance above water, when he is killed by spears, great numbers taking part in his destruction. The flesh is much esteemed by the natives as food.

"BIRDS OF PREY, *Raptores*.—A frequent object met with on the coast-shores of both colonies is the White-headed Erne or Great Fish Eagle, *Falco leucocephalus*. Couples of these birds are frequently seen sailing majestically in air, descending occasionally in graceful circles to their abode in some tall pine-tree where their nest is placed. Another common object is the American Osprey or Fish Hawk, *Pandion Carolinensis*. The Har rier and the Sharp-shinned Hawk, with several others, are also constantly met with. The 'Great Snow Owl,' *Nyctea nivea*, and the Pigmy Owl, *Glaucydium gnoma*—not so large as an English blackbird—are also found, with several others.

"SCANSORES.—In this order occur the Cuckoos. I have not seen a specimen on the island or in British Columbia, but their note has been heard by myself and others. The Woodpeckers are numerous: thus, I may name *Picus Harrisii; Sphyrapicus ruber*, or Red-breasted Woodpecker; *Colaptis Mexicanus*, or Red-shafted.

"INSESSORES.—I have collected three varieties of Humming-birds on Vancouver Island. These beautiful little creatures make their appearance early in spring, even before the snow has left the plains, buzzing their way from bush to bush in restless search of some half-opened blossom. The Indian boys snare them in numbers, and, fastening a dozen or more to a stick by one foot, bring them off alive to the ships for sale. A Night Hawk—known among settlers as the Mosquito Hawk—breeds upon the island, and makes its appearance on summer evenings. A common object along the sea-coast and the mouths of rivers is the Belted Kingfisher, *Ceryle alcyon*—a much larger, but not so handsome a bird as the English Kingfisher. The Flycatchers have several representatives. The Singing Birds are few. Amongst the Swallows may be named the Violet-green Swallow, *Hirundo thalassina*. Wrens, Creepers, Nut-hatches, Titmice, Shore Larks, Finches, the Red Crossbill, *Curvirostra Americana*, the Snow Bunting, Sparrows, the Red-winged Blackbird. Among the crows may be named the American Raven, the Fish Crow, the Common Crow. Jays, *Cyanura stelleri*.

"RASORES.—Pigeons and Doves are represented in both colonies. A more numerous family exist in the Grouse: the Dusky Grouse, *Petras obscurus;* the Blue Grouse of settlers; the Ruffed Grouse, *Bonasa umbellus;* and the Willow Grouse, *Lagopus albus*, are found on Vancouver Island in immense numbers, and also in British Columbia, which has several other varieties,—the Sage Cock, the Sharp-tailed Grouse, the Prairie Hen, and Ptarmigan: all of these are excellent eating, but are too easily shot to afford much amusement to an English sportsman. The Blue and the Ruffed Grouse roost on trees during the day, when not sunning themselves on some hillock or prostrate trunk of a tree, where their 'drum' is loudly heard. The Blue Grouse reaches the weight of 4½ lbs.; it may often be seen perched on the topmost branch of some tall pine-tree, from

2 E

whence he refuses to move for repeated charges from an ordinary fowling-piece, and is only to be brought down by a rifle. As the country becomes cleared, their habits will probably change, and Vancouver Island will be as noticeable for good sport as Scotland.

"GRALLATORES.—The Great Blue Heron or Crane, *Ardea herodias*, is frequently seen and shot. In the sub-order *Grallæ* may be enumerated Golden Plover; Kill-deer; King Plover; the Surf Bird, *Aphriza virgata*; Bachman's Oyster-catcher, *Hæmatopus niger*, and Turnstone; Wilson's Snipe, or English Snipe; Grey Snipe; Jack Snipe; Sandpipers; and Sanderlings.

"NATATORES.—Swans are often shot on the lakes of Vancouver Island and British Columbia; and on the approach of winter myriads of Geese arrive: among these may be named the Snow Goose, *Anser hyperboreus*; the White-fronted Goose, *Anser gambelii*; the Canada Goose, *Bernicla Canadiensis*; the Brant Goose. The Canada Goose is often shot 17 lbs. in weight. The Ducks are innumerable. Amongst them are found the Mallard, *Anas boschas*; Black Duck, *Anas obscura*; Pintail, *Dafila acuta*; Green-winged Teal, *Nettion Carolinensis*; the Shoveller, or Spoonbill, *Spatula clypeata*; American Widgeon, *Mareca Americana*; the Summer Duck, *Aix sponsa*; the Scaup Duck, *Fulix marila*; Canvas-back, *Aythya vallisneria*; the Golden Eye, *Bucephala Americana*, and *albeota* or Buffle-head; the Harlequin Duck, *Histrionicus torquatus* Amongst the Sea Ducks are the Velvet Duck, *Melanetta velvetina*; the Surf Duck, *Pelionetta perspicillata*; the Scoter, *Oidemia Americana*. Among the Fishing Ducks is the Goosander, *Mergus Americanus*; the Red-breasted Merganser, *Mergus serrator*; the Hooded Merganser, *Lophodytes cucullatus*; and I believe a fourth which is not named. In the sub-order *Gaviæ*, I may mention the Sooty Albatross, *Diomedia fuliginosa*; and two or three Petrels. Among the Gulls, the Glaucous-winged Gull, *Larus glaucescens*; the Herring Gull, *Larus argentatus*; the Western Gull, *Larus occidentalis*. Among the Cormorants, the Violet-green Cormorant, *Graculus violaceus*, is extremely common. In the family of Divers are the great Northern Diver, *Colymbus glacialis*; the Black-throated, *Colymbus arcticus*; the Pacific, *Colymbus Pacificus*; and the Red-throated, *Colymbus septentrionalis*. The tufted Puffin, *Mormon cirrhata*; the Horn-billed Guillemot, *Cerorhina monocerata*, are numerous on the sea-coasts of Vancouver and its adjacent islands, and the sea around them is often literally alive with the Sea Dove or Dovekie.

" The Reptilia do not require an extended notice. Several varieties of Snakes are met with, but they are not, I believe, venomous. Lizards and Frogs are numerous. The Bull-frog in summer is rather a nuisance by his loud croakings. The Indians are partial to snakes as an article of diet; immediately they are caught they are skinned and eaten by them, as a stick of celery is eaten by a schoolboy, and with as little cooking.

" Fishes.—The fish of Vancouver Island and British Columbia require a more extended experience than mine to do justice to them. I cannot, however, but think that, among the domestic resources of both colonies, few can equal their value. The seas and large inlets, the bays and rivers, are literally alive with fish. Salmon, Cod, Halibut, Sturgeon, Herring, Trout, Smelt, Sea Perch, Hake, Sardines, Anchovy, Flat Fish, Dog Fish (highly useful for oil), and the Houlakan, so called by the Indians; the latter, the size of a herring, makes its appearance with un-erring regularity in various parts of the coast for a few days only, and is taken in shoals; it is so fat on its arrival as to defy ordinary cooking, melting by the heat; it is pressed for oil by the natives, who trade with it in British Columbia with the inland tribes, and is also dried, in which state, lighted at one end, it makes a capital torch, and is constantly used as such by the Indians. The oil has been used medicinally in place of cod-liver oil, and I have seen the happiest effects from its administration. So numerous are the Salmon, that rivers become offensive from the putrid bodies of those who have failed to make their way up the ' falls ' of the various rivers. Tons' weight of Halibut may be caught in a day. The shores are thickly covered with Acorn-shells, Limpets, Muscles, Clams, &c. Crabs of many varieties are found everywhere, some edible, and of large size. The Shrimp is a constant visitor in the dredge, and Prawns are extensively caught in the neighbourhood of Victoria, Vancouver Island. Every pool is lined with brilliant Sea Anemones; and nearly throughout the year is the sea lightened with Medusæ.

" Flora.—In the magnificent work of Sir W. J. Hooker, 'Flora Boreali Americana,' may be found an epitome of the botany of these colonies. I will confine my observations, there-fore, to an enumeration of the Natural Orders, which contain most of the Flora of interest to the settler.

" Order 1. *Nymphæaceæ*, Water-lilies.
"   „   2. *Ranunculaceæ*, Crowfoots.
"   „   5. *Cruciferæ*, Cressworts.

2 E 2

" Order 7. *Berberidaceæ*, Berberryworts. The ' Oregon Grape' of the settlers is a small shrub very common in the woods: it bears a yellow flower, and produces a cluster of berries of a deep blue colour, of a pleasant acid, astringent taste. The root yields one of the best known yellow dyes.

" Order 8. *Violaceæ*, Violetworts.

" ,, 16. *Ceraceæ*, Maples. The Maple grows to a large size, and is extensively found; it produces by the changing hues of its foliage a handsome object in the somewhat monotonous landscape of the colonies: its wood is very inferior.

" Order 17. *Geraniaceæ*, Cranesbills.

" ,, 21. *Rhamnaceæ*, Rhamnads.

" ,, 22. *Fabaceæ*, Leguminous Plants. Representatives of their order are extensively found. The Blue Lupine, Purple Clover, and several varieties of Vetch are everywhere growing wild as large and strong as any I have seen cultivated in other places.

" Order 23. *Rosaceæ*, Roseworts. Species of this order are also very numerous: in the spring every plain is covered with the Wild Rose and Sweet Brier: in the sub-order are Wild Apples, the Mountain Ash (scarce), the Service Tree, Bird Cherry or Cluster Cherry.

" Order 28. *Grossulariaceæ*, Currantworts. Wherever the ground is clear abound Currant and Gooseberry bushes of endless varieties; the Flowering Currant, Ribes sanguinea, is a beautiful object in the 'bush.'

" Order 30. *Apiaceæ*, Umbellifers, the Conium.

" ,, 32. *Cornaceæ*, Cornels. The Dogwood tree is very common, and makes a handsome object for the shrubbery. In this order is the 'La Broue' plant of the Canadian voyageurs: it bears a small red berry which is dried and stored for use. Mixed in small portions with a little water it is after standing *whisked* up with branches; it gradually expands and becomes converted into a substance resembling 'trifle,' which is eaten with sugar sifted over it.

" Order 33. *Caprifoliaceæ*, Caprifoils. Two varieties of Elder tree very common.

" Order 38. *Campanulaceæ*, Bellworts. The Campanula.

" ,, 39. *Ericaceæ*, Heathworts. In a Sub-order are the Cranberries. These shrubs abound everywhere, and yield a most delicious berry; there are many varieties—from one, the Oxycoccus palustris, I have known of 100 barrels being collected,

the produce of one season. The berries do not require putting
down, keeping remarkably well simply immersed in water. The
Gualtheria shallon, the 'Salal' of the Indians, is a common
shrub: it bears a handsome blossom and a bunch of large deep
purple berries, much used by the natives, who make it into cakes
which they dry in the sun for winter use; it is also used in the
households of settlers for pies and puddings, but is not equal to
the Cranberries.

" Order 41. *Gentianaceæ*, Gentianworts.

"   ,, 56. *Urticaceæ*, Nettleworts. A wild Nettle, the
Urtica cannabina, is used by the Indians to make hemp; it is
extremely strong, and is manufactured by them into twine, rope,
and nets.

" Order 57. *Corylaceæ*, Mastworts. The Oak is abundant in
the southern part of Vancouver Island; there is none in British
Columbia, I am told by Mr. Anderson, of the Hudson Bay
Company, except a few small specimens on the eastern borders of
the Rapids above Fort Yale. The Hazel Nut is common in
British Columbia.

" Order 58. *Saliaceæ*, Willowworts. Willows grow on all low
and swampy places; the 'Cotton Wood' Poplar and the Aspen
tree.

" Order 59. *Betulaceæ*, Birchworts. The common Birch is of
small size to the southward; in the northern parts of British
Columbia it is known as the 'Canoe Birch,' is abundant and
of large size, and is hard and durable (Mr. Anderson). The
common Alder grows to a large size, and is a useful wood for
turners.

" Order 61. *Pinaceæ*, Conifers. In this Order are found Yew
trees, Juniper bush, the Scotch Fir, Spruce Fir, the Douglas Pine;
the White Pine of commerce, *Pinus Weymouthii*; Canada Pine,
Balsam Pine, the 'Red Cedar,' and the 'Yellow Cedar.' The
most remarkable point in the forest-trees of both colonies is the
profusion of trees of this order, and the immense height and size
they attain. The Douglas Pine can be obtained anywhere 200 ft.
in length, and I have seen trees that would square 45 in. for 90 ft.
This pine makes the best spars for ships. The 'White Pine,' I
am told by those preparing it, is equal to that of the Eastern
States of America. From the bark of the 'Red' and Yellow
Cedar, articles of wearing apparel, ropes, &c., are made: the
plank of the latter tree yields a close-grained beautiful wood;
specimens of it made into boxes have been sent to the International Exhibition.

" Order 68. *Liliaceæ*, Lilyworts. The *Camassia esculenta*, the Camass of the Indians, is very common: the bulbs, being placed in shallow pits, are covered with a thick layer of dried grass damped with water, a thin layer of earth is placed above it, and a fire made over the pit. A gradual process of steaming goes on, perhaps for several days: the bulbs when removed are found mellowed, their colour changed to a light brown, and they contain a large portion of saccharine matter. They are then dried and stored for winter food.

" Order 73. *Graminaceæ*, Grasses. Varieties of nearly every grass which grows in England, and many which do not, are found in these Colonies: the Wild Oat is as vigorous a plant here as the one cultivated at home. I have seen ' Timothy Grass ' grown on the Island 8 ft. in height.

" I pass over the Ferns, Mosses, Lichens, the Fungi, and Sea-weeds, with the brief remark that they abound everywhere, the first in quantities somewhat troublesome to the agriculturist.

" CHARLES BIGLAND WOOD.

" *H.M.S. ' Hecate,' Victoria, Vancouver Island,*
" *July,* 1862."

It would be useless for general purposes to give a mass of statistics with regard to the climate of British Columbia and Vancouver Island. In a country embracing so many hundred miles of latitude there is of course great difference of temperature. The climate of Vancouver Island may be said generally to be about the same as that of the south of England. During the last winter, 1861-2, it has been unusually severe. In the four winters that I passed at Esquimalt Harbour we had a great deal of rain, very little snow, while the ice on the ponds bore skaters for about a fortnight each year, the thermometer being hardly ever below 25° Fahr. The south part of British Columbia is, perhaps, a little colder. This winter the Lower Fraser has been frozen over so as entirely to impede navigation; but I believe this has never been known before, and it certainly has only occurred once since 1856. Steamers were able to go to Langley every winter I was in the country, and were only prevented ascending to Fort Hope by the shallowness of the stream. It will also be remembered that I ascended the river to Fort Yale in February, 1859, without being seriously impeded by ice.

The fall of snow even during the late extraordinarily severe winter appears to have been very partial. The thermometer at Westminster stood at 8°, 10°, and 12° below zero, and 17° or 18° at Forts Hope and Yale. The deep snow at these latter places, however, made them less cold than at Lilloett, where there was only an inch or two of snow, and where the cold is described as having been intensely severe.

Further north, at Cariboo, the winter of 1860-1 was even more severely felt. On the night of the 1st of December the mercury of the thermometer congealed, and on the 25th and 26th of January it is said to have stiffened before sun-down, with the sun shining full upon it. Two thermometers at William Lake are reported in the Victoria papers to have burst from the effects of the cold, and many instances of severe frost-bites, &c., are given. In judging of the severity of the season from the reports of the miners, however, it must be remembered that their clothing and habitations would ill fit them to endure with patience the hardships of an ordinary winter even in England.

In a recent book on British Columbia one of the many objections urged against the country is said to arise from the danger of Indian aggression upon the colonists. I cannot conclude these remarks without giving this assertion an emphatic contradiction. My own experience—as the reader will have gathered—has led me to form an exactly opposite opinion of the temper and disposition of the Indians; and lest it should be thought that my official position gave me when tra-velling *alone* among them a protection which would be wanting to the ordinary colonist, I give the following quotation upon the subject from the letter of a young English clergyman whom I have lately had the pleasure of meeting. I withhold his name only because his letter was not intended for that public use which I venture to make of it. I should add that the writer had never visited an English colony until he went to British Columbia four years ago :—

"My experience leads me to say, what I find most persons confirm, that, so far as safety is concerned, there is far less risk in travelling in British Columbia than in many parts of England. Nothing can exceed the order of the country, and the marked absence of serious crime either on the part of the whites or Indians."

This was written after a journey of more than 500 miles in the interior, alone or with some fellow-clergymen. Those who desire further evidence of the kindly disposition of the Indians will find it abundantly in the extracts of the Bishop's Journal, published by the Columbian Missionary Society.

I have more than once spoken of Esquimalt as being admirably adapted for a naval station and dockyard. I wish to add that, important as this is for our squadron in the Pacific, I think it would be still more so for the squadron in the Chinese waters. Our ships there, which are sometimes almost disabled by sickness, could reach the healthy climate of Vancouver in six weeks, and might, if required, be relieved by vessels from the Pacific squadron. In 1859 the 'Tribune' and 'Pylades' were ordered across from China ; they arrived at Esquimalt with crews greatly debilitated, and all hands a good deal below par. They remained about a year there, and left, I believe, with the crews of both ships in perfect health. I may also mention that the healthy appearance of our crew was a subject of general remark to all ships arriving on the station.

The climate is said to be unfavourable for people who have previously been subject to rheumatism. The officers and men of the 'Plumper,' however, who lived constantly in camp, and were much exposed, never suffered seriously from this complaint.

In concluding this rough summary of the resources of the colonies, let me repeat, that in our North American possessions we have, independently of its mineral wealth, a country of immense extent and natural beauty, of—so far as it has been tested—invariable fertility, and with a climate closely resembling our own. Against these advantages, however, it must be remembered that all that is required to develop and utilise the many natural advantages of the colonies has yet to be done, and that for many years to come stout hearts and strong hands will find abundant occupation in accomplishing this work. He who is not possessed of these requisites of a bush-life is as unfit for British Columbia as for any other colony. But the man whose heart does not fail him at the prospect of hard living and harder work, will find there welcome and plenty awaiting him.

CHAPTER XIV.

Mineral wealth of British Columbia, Summary of — Conclusion.

I HAVE left myself but small space or time to speak of that which is undoubtedly the mainspring of British Columbia— its immense and apparently inexhaustible yield of gold. At starting, however, a few remarks upon the various methods of working mining-claims at the gold-fields may be found of interest to the general reader.

As a rule, picking up gold is a mere delusive figure of speech. It has to be dug and worked for hardly, with primitive appliances often; sometimes with all the resources of modern mechanism. Before attempting to describe shortly the various processes of extracting the precious mineral, I may say that they all require the aid of water and, with rare exceptions, quicksilver. It is the abundant natural supply of water that gives British Columbia so great an advantage over California. The country is, as I have before said, and as a glance at the map will show, intersected in every direc-tion by streams and rivers, while lakes of various size abound, the majority of which may be easily adapted to the purposes of mining. The very height of the hills also, which may be in other respects a disadvantage, proves in this case of use to the miner who can divert to his purpose the torrents which course down their sides. In California the want of water has been much felt, and the methods resorted to for meeting it illustrate as much as anything else in that marvellous country the enterprise and spirit of the American settler. In Grass Valley, Nevada county, one of the richest quartz districts in California, which I visited in 1860, and where 40 steam-mills were then at work, every drop of water used had to be brought by " flumes," from a distance of more than 40 miles !

Quicksilver has as yet always been found to exist in gold countries. California is abundantly supplied. It has been discovered in several places in Columbia; but as yet it has been found cheaper to procure it from California than to work it there.

In 1860 I made the tour of some of the richest diggings in California, with the view of seeing the various appliances in use there. In describing these various methods of gold working, I shall have to speak of several not yet in use in Columbia; some of them, indeed, being but newly introduced into California.

The first task of the miner attracted to a new gold country or district, by the report of its wealth, is " prospecting." For this purpose every miner, however light his equipment may otherwise be, carries with him a " pan " and a small quantity of quicksilver; the latter to be used only where the gold is very fine. Very little experience enables a miner to detect that " colour " of the earth which indicates the presence of the metallic sand in which gold is found. Wherever, as he travels through the new country, he sees this, he stops at once to wash a pan of dirt, and thus test its value. Although many diggings are found away from the bank of a stream, the river-sides are the places where gold is generally first looked for and worked. In saying this, of course I except the gold in quartz, of which I shall have to speak hereafter. The spots first searched are generally those upon the bank of a river where the deposit consists of a thick, stiff mud or clay, with stones. In some cases this is covered with sand, so that the surface has to be removed before the " pay dust " is revealed. All these workings on river-banks are called " bars," and are usually named after the prospecter, or from some incident connected with their discovery.

When the Prospecter comes to dirt which looks as if it
would pay, he unslings his pan from his back, and proceeds to
test it. This he effects by filling his pan with the earth, then
squatting on the edge of the stream, he takes it by the rim,
dipping it in the water, and giving it a kind of rotary motion
stirring and kneading the contents occasionally until the whole
is completely moistened. The larger stones are then thrown
out, the edge of the pan canted upwards, and a continual
flow of water made to pass through it until, the lighter portion
of its contents being washed away, nothing but a few pebbles
and specks of black metallic sand are left, among which the
gold, if there is any, will be found. The rotary movement,
by which the heavier pebbles and bits of gold are kept in the
centre of the pan, and the lighter earth allowed to pass over
its edge, requires considerable practice, and an unskilful prospecter will perhaps pass by a place as not being worth
working that an experienced hand will recognise as very
rich. The specific gravity of the black sand being nearly
equal to that of the gold, while wet they cannot be at once
separated, and the nuggets, if any, being taken out, the pan
is laid in the sun or by a fire to dry. When dry the lighter
particles of sand are blown away; or if the gold is very fine
it is amalgamated with quicksilver. The miners know by
practice how much gold in a pan will constitute a rich
digging, and they usually express the value of the earth as
"5," "10," or "15 cent dirt," meaning that each pan so washed
will yield so much in money. Panning, it may be remarked,
never gives the full value of the dirt, as may be imagined
from the roughness of the process. If the gold should be
in flakes, a good deal is likely to be lost in the process, as it
will not then sink readily to the bottom of the pan, and is
more likely to be washed away with the sand. In panning,
as well as, indeed, in all the other primitive processes of
washing gold, the superior specific gravity of this metal over
others, except platinum, is the basis of operations; all depend-

ing upon its settling at the bottom of whatever vessel may
chance to be used.

The "pan" is hardly ever used except for prospecting, so
that the "rocker" or "cradle" may be described as the
most primitive appliance used in gold-washing.   In the
winter of 1859, when I first went up the Fraser, the rocker
was the general machine—the use of sluices not having then
begun.   It was used in California as early as 1848, being
formed rudely of logs, or the trunk of a tree.   And yet,
ungainly as they were, they commanded, before · saw-mills
were established in the country, enormous prices.

The rocker, then, consists of a box 3½ to 4 feet long, about
2 feet wide, and 1½ deep.   The top and one end of this box
are open, and at the lower end the sides slope gradually
until they reach the bottom.   At its head is attached a
closely-jointed box with a sheet-iron bottom, pierced with
holes sufficiently large to allow pebbles to pass through.
This machine is provided with rockers like a child's cradle,
while within cleets are placed to arrest the gold in its passage.
One of the miners then, the cradle being placed by the
water's edge, feeds it with earth, while another rocks and
supplies it with water.   The dirt to be washed is thrown into
the upper iron box, and a continual stream of water being
poured in, it is disintegrated, the gold and pebbles passing
down to the bottom, where the water is allowed to carry the
stones away, and the cleets arrest the precious metal.

When the gold is very fine I have seen a piece of cloth
laid along the bottom box, covered with quicksilver to arrest
the gold.   When a party of miners work with rockers, they
divide the labour of rocking, carrying water, if necessary, and
digging equally among themselves.   The rocker is the only
apparatus that can be at all successfully worked single-
handed; and rough as it appears and really is, I have seen
men make 30 to 50 dollars a day with it, while far greater

sums have been known to be realized by it. In these
remarks I have assumed that my readers generally are aware
that quicksilver arrests whatever gold passes over it, and,
forming an amalgam with it, retains it until it is retorted
from it. In washing gold, quicksilver has to be used always,
except where the mineral is found very large and coarse.
Even then the earth is generally made to pass over some
quicksilver before it escapes altogether, in order to preserve
the finer particles. I may here mention that in a "sluice"
of ordinary size 40 or 50 lbs. of quicksilver are used daily;
in a rocker perhaps 8 or 10 lbs. Of course the same quicksilver can be used over and over again when the gold has
been retorted from it.

The first improvement on the "Rocker" was by the use of
a machine called the "Long Tom." This, though common
enough in California, I never saw used in British Columbia.
It consists of a shallow trough, from 10 to 20 feet long, and
16 inches to 2 feet wide. One end is slightly turned up, shod
with iron, and perforated like the sieve of a rocker. The
trough is placed at an incline, sieve-end downwards. A stream
of water is turned into the upper end of the Tom, and several
hands supply it with earth, which finds its way to the sieve,
carrying along with it the gold, which it washes or disintegrates
in its passage. Immediately beneath the sieve a box is placed,
in which are nailed cleets, or as they are more generally termed
"Riffles," which catch the gold as in the rocker. When the
gold is fine another box containing quicksilver is placed at
the end of the riffle, to catch the gold which passes it.

A man always attends at the end to clear away the "Tailings," or earth discharged from the machine, and also to stir
up the earth in the Tom, and keep the sieve clear of stones,
an iron rake being used for the purpose. By the use of the
"Long Tom," rather than the cradle, a great saving is
effected; the work being performed in a much more thorough

manner. It is estimated in California that the Tom will wash ten times as much earth as a cradle, employing the same number of hands.

The next important method is "Sluicing." This is by far the most commonly used both in British Columbia and California, employing, I suppose, one-half the mining population of both countries.

Sluicing is, moreover, an operation which can be carried on on any scale, from two or three men upon a river bar, to a rich company washing away an entire hill by the "Hydraulic" process. Whatever may be the scale of the operations, however, "sluicing" is necessarily connected with a system of "flumes," or wooden aqueducts of greater or less extent, either running along the back of a river-bar, and supplying the sluices at it, or cobwebbing and intersecting the whole country as in California. I have seen flumes on the Shady Creek Canal there, conveying an enormous stream of water across a deep ravine at the height of 100 to 200 feet.

"Sluice-boxes" are of various sizes, but generally from 2 to 3 feet long, by about the same width. These are fitted closely together at the ends, so as to form a continuous strongly-built trough of the required length, from 15 or 20 to several thousand feet, their make and strength depending entirely upon the work they have to do. I will here describe sluicing upon a moderate scale, as I found it in practice at Hill's Bar upon the Fraser during my visit there in 1858.

This bar was taken up in claims early in 1858, its size being then about 1½ mile, although it has since been much extended, the richness of the soil proving, I believe, greater as it is ascended. In this place, then, a flume was put up, carrying the water from a stream which descended the mountain at its southern end along the whole length of the bar, and behind those claims which were being worked. From this flume each miner led a sluice down towards the river; his sluice being placed at such an angle that the water would run through it with sufficient force to carry the earth, but not, of course, the gold with it. Its strength, indeed, is so regulated as to allow time for the riffles and quicksilver to catch the gold as it passes. The supply of water from the flume to each sluice is regulated by a gate in the side of the flume, which is raised for so much per inch. The price paid for water of course varies greatly with the cost of timber, engineering difficulties of making the flume, &c. It is ordinarily established by the miners, who meet and agree to pay any individual or company who may undertake the work a certain rateable rental for the water. Their construction, indeed, is one of the most profitable of colonial speculations. The flume I am now speaking of cost 7000 or 8000 dollars, and each miner paid a dollar an inch for water daily. Since that time it has become much cheaper, and the usual price is about 25 cents (1s.) an inch, the width of the gate being 1 foot. The sluice-boxes here were very slight, about inch-plank, as the dirt which had to pass through them was not large. In the bottom of each box was a grating, made of strips of plank nailed crosswise to each other, but not attached to the box like the riffles. In the interstices of these gratings quicksilver is spread to catch the fine gold, the coarse being caught by the grating itself. The sluice is placed on tressels or legs, so as to raise it to the height convenient for shovelling the earth in; the water is then let on, and several men feed the sluice with earth from either side, while one or two with iron rakes stir it up or pull out any large stones which might break the gratings.

Such is the working of ordinary sluices; but sluicing is also inseparable from the grandest of all mining operations—viz., "Hydraulic Mining." Hydraulic mining, as I witnessed it at Timbuctoo in California, is certainly a marvellous operation. A hill of moderate size, 200 to 300 feet high, may often be found to contain gold throughout its formation, but too thinly to repay cradle-washing, or even hand-sluicing, and not lying

in any veins or streaks which could be worked by tunnelling
or ground-sluicing.

A series of sluice-boxes are therefore constructed and put
together, as described above; but in this case, instead of
being of light timber, they are made of the stoutest board
that can possibly be got, backed by cross-pieces, &c., so as to
be of sufficient strength to allow the passage of any amount
of earth and stones forced through them by a flood of water.
The boxes are also made shorter and wider, being generally
about 14 inches long by 3 to 4 feet wide—the bottoms,
instead of the gratings spoken of above, being lined with
wooden blocks like wood-pavement, for resisting the friction
of the *débris* passing over it, the interstices being filled with
quicksilver to catch the fine gold. The sluice, thus prepared,
is firmly placed in a slanting position near the foot of the
hill intended to be attacked.

To shovel a mass of several million tons of earth into these
sluices would prove a tedious and profitless operation. In its
stead, therefore, hydraulic mining is called into play, by
which the labour of many men is performed by water, and
the hill worn down to the base by its agency. The operation
consists of simply throwing an immense stream of water upon
the side of the hill with hose and pipe, as a fire-engine plays
upon a burning building. The water is led through gutta-
percha or canvas hoses, 4 to 6 inches in diameter, and is
thrown from a considerable height above the scene of operations. It is consequently hurled with such force as to eat into
the hill-side as if it were sugar. At the spot where I saw this
working in operation to the greatest advantage they were
using four horses, which they estimated as equal to the power
of a hundred men with pick and shovel. There is more
knowledge and skill required in this work than would at
first sight be supposed necessary. The purpose of the man,
who directs the hose is to undermine the surface as well as
wash away the face of the hill. He therefore directs the

2 F

water at a likely spot until indications of a "cave-in" become apparent. Notice being given, the neighbourhood is deserted. The earth far above cracks, and down comes all the face of the precipice with the noise of an avalanche. By this means a hill several hundred feet higher than the water could reach may easily be washed away.

The greatest difficulty connected with hydraulic work is to get a sufficient fall for the water—a considerable pressure being, of course, necessary. At Timbuctoo, for instance, a large river flowed close by, but its waters at that point were quite useless from being too low; the consequence was, that a flume had to be led several miles, from a part of the river higher up, so as to gain the force required. Supplying water for this and similar mining purposes has, therefore, proved a very successful speculation in California. I am not able to give the exact length of the longest flumes constructed there, but I know that it has in some cases been found necessary to bring water from the Sierra Nevada, and to tap streams that have their rise there. It is not at all uncommon to bring it from a distance of 50 miles, and in some cases it has been conveyed as far again.

The expense of this is, of course, enormous, and it is in the ready supply of water at various levels, that the work of mining in British Columbia will be found so much more easy than in California. So scarce is it there, indeed, that it sometimes has been found cheaper to pack the earth on mules and carry it to the river-side than to bring the water to the gold-fields.

The difficulty of obtaining water in the early days of gold-digging in California gave rise to a very curious method of extracting the mineral, which, I believe, was only practised by the Mexicans. Two men would collect a heap of earth from some place containing grain-gold, and pound it as fine as possible. It was then placed in a large cloth, like a sheet, and winnowed—the breeze carrying away the dust, while the heavier gold fell back into the cloth. Bellows were sometimes used for this purpose also.

While upon this subject, I will take the opportunity of describing the most common appliance for raising water from a river for the use of a sluice on its bank. The machinery used is known as the "flutter-wheel," and the traveller in a mining country will see them erected in every conceivable manner and place. It is the same in principle and very similar in appearance to our common "undershot-wheel," consisting of a large wheel 20 to 30 feet in diameter, turned by the force of the current. The paddles are fitted with buckets made to fill themselves with water as they pass under the wheel, which they empty as they turn over into a trough placed convenient for the purpose and leading to the sluice. In a river with a rapid current, like the Fraser, they can be made to supply almost any quantity of water.

There is a kind of intermediate process between that which I have just described and tunnelling or "koyote-ing," partaking in a measure of both. This is called "ground-sluicing," and is quite distinct from "sluicing." The reader will better understand this process if I speak of "koyote-ing," and "ground-sluicing" together, the latter having become a substitute for the former.

As the miners in California began to gain experience in gold-seeking, they found that at a certain distance beneath the surface of the earth a layer of rock existed, on which the gold, by its superior specific gravity, had gradually settled. Experience soon taught the miner to discard the upper earth, which was comparatively valueless, and to seek for gold in the cracks or "pockets" of this bed-rock, or in the layer of earth or clay covering it. The depth of this rock is very various; sometimes it crops out at the surface, while at other times it is found 150 to 200 feet down. Where it is very deep, recourse must be had to regular shaft-sinking and tunnelling, as in a coal or copper mine; but when the rock is only 20 or 30 feet beneath the surface, tunnelling on a very small scale, known as "koyote-ing," from its fancied resemblance to the burrowing of the small wild-dog common to British Columbia and California, is adopted. These little tunnels are made to save the expense of shovelling off the 20 or 30 feet of earth that cover the "pay dirt" on the bed-rock, and their extraordinary number gives a very strange appearance to those parts of the country which have been thoroughly "koyote-ed." I have seen a hill completely honeycombed with these burrows, carried through and through it, and interlacing in every possible direction. So rich is their formation, however, that after they have been deserted by the koyote-ers they are still found worth working. I remember looking at one in the Yuba county in California which appeared so completely riddled that the pressure of a child's foot would have brought it down. Upon my expressing my conviction that anyhow that seemed worked out, a miner standing by at once corrected me. "Worked out, sir ?" he said—" not a bit of it ! If you come in six months, you'll not see any hill there at all, sir. A company are going to bring the water to play upon it in a few days." "Will it pay well, do you suppose ?". "All pays about here, sir," was the quick reply; "they'll take a hundred dollars each a-day."

The Koyote tunnels are only made sufficiently high for the workman to sit upright in them. They are generally carried through somewhat stiffish clay, and are propped and supported with wooden posts, but, as may be imagined in the case of such small apertures extending for so great a length as some of them do, they are very unsafe. Not unfrequently they "cave in" without the slightest warning. Sometimes, too, the earth settles down upon the bed-rock so slowly and silently, that the poor victims are buried alive unknown to their companions without.

The danger of this work and its inefficiency for extracting

the gold, much of which was lost in these dark holes, gave rise, as the agency of water became more appreciated, to " ground-sluicing." This consists in directing a heavy stream of water upon the bank which is to be removed, and, with the aid of pick and shovel, washing the natural surface away and bringing the " pay-streak " next the bed-rock into view.

Before proceeding to the subject of quartz-crushing, it will be well perhaps to give the reader some further idea of the great extent of those mining operations which, begun by a few adventurers, have become a regularly organised system, carried on by wealthy and powerful companies. As a striking monument of their courage and the extent of their resources, I would instance the fact of their having diverted large rivers from their channels so as to lay their beds dry for mining purposes. This has been done at nearly every bend or shallow in the numerous streams of California, and will doubtless be imitated in Columbia ere long. The largest of these operations that I ever saw was near Auburn, a large town in Placer county, on the American river.

Sometimes the water can be brought in a strongly-built flume from above, and carried by a long box over the old bed of the river ; at other times a regular canal has to be made and dams constructed upon a very large scale. The result is that the bed of the river is laid dry, when its every crevice and pocket is carefully searched for the gold which the water has generally brought down from the bases of the hills and the bars higher up the stream. These operations are frequently so extensive as to occupy several successive seasons before the whole is worked, and to employ hundreds of labourers besides the individuals composing the company, who usually in such an enterprise number fifty or sixty. Sometimes the premature approach of the rainy season, and consequent freshets, carry away the whole of the works in a night. These works occasionally yield immense returns, and it is not unfrequently found, on renewing them after the rainy season, that fresh deposits of gold have taken place, almost equal in value to the first. On the other hand, no amount of judgment can select with any degree of certainty a favourable spot for "jamming" or turning a river, and, after months of hard labour, the bed when laid bare may prove entirely destitute of gold deposits. The long space of still water below a series of rapids will sometimes be found in one spot to contain pounds of gold, while in another the workers who have selected that portion of the river above the rapids will find themselves in the paying place.

All gold operations, indeed, depend very much upon chance for success. No one can ever calculate with any degree of certainty on the run of the "lode" underground, or in the "pay streak" near the surface. Thus it is ever a lottery. As an instance of this on a large scale, I remember when I was at Grass Valley, "Nevada county," going to see the working at the "Black Bridge" tunnel there. The first shaft for this tunnel was sunk five years before my visit, and up to that time nothing had been taken, though it had been constantly worked and was nearly 20,000 feet long. It was commenced in 1855 by a company, who sunk a shaft nearly 250 feet, to strike, as they hoped and expected, a lode from the opposite side of the valley. The original company consisted of five men, and in the course of the five years some of them gave up and others joined, part of them working at other diggings to get money for provisions, tools, &c., to keep their firm going. At length, just before my visit, all the original projectors, and about three sets of others who had joined at different periods, gave the enterprise up as hopeless after carrying it, as I have said, nearly four miles. A new company then took possession of it and summoned the miners of the valley to a consultation. The meeting decided that they had not gone deep enough, and the shaft was accordingly sunk 50 feet lower, when the gold was at once struck. I tried to ascertain what had been expended upon this tunnel, but it

had passed through so many hands that it was impossible even
to estimate it. The gentleman who showed me over it, and
who was an Englishman and the principal man of Grass
Valley (Mr. Attwood), said it would cost the new company
12,000 or 14,000 dollars (3000*l.*) before they took out anything
that would repay them. The recklessness with which money
is risked and the apparent unconcern with which a man loses
a large fortune, and the millionaire of to-day becomes a hired
labourer to-morrow, is one of the most striking characteristics
of the American in these Western states. It is owing in a
great degree to the mere accident which gold-working is.
The effect of this upon society is of course most injurious.
The poor miner, hobbling along the street of San Francisco
or Sacramento trying to borrow—for there are no beggars in
California—money enough to take him back to the mines
from which ague or rheumatism have driven him a few months
before, knows that a lucky hit may enable him in a very short
time to take the place of the gentleman who passes by him
in his carriage, and whose capital is very probably floating
about in schemes, the failure of which will as rapidly reduce
him to the streets, or send him back again to the mines as a
labourer. The spirit, too, with which these changes of fortune
are borne is wonderful. I travelled once in California with a
man who was on his way to the mines to commence work as
a labourer for the third time. He told me his story readily :
it was simple enough. He had twice made what he thought
would enrich him for life, and twice it had gone in unlucky
speculations. An Englishman under these circumstances
would probably have been greatly depressed : not so my
fellow-traveller. He talked away through the journey cheer-
fully, describing the country as we passed through it, speaking
of the past without anything like regret, and calmly hopeful
for the future.

    To return to the gold-working, however. I have described
the various processes of extracting it from the earth or the

rock-surface. I come now lastly to the more arduous work of collecting it from the rock itself, known as quartz-crushing. Some very rich specimens of quartz have been found in British Columbia, near Lowhee Creek, Cariboo, and in other places. But while the surface-diggings continue to yield such rich returns and transport is so dear, it can scarcely be expected that quartz-crushing, which requires the use of ponderous machinery, will be commenced. The richest quartz district in California is Grass Valley, in Nevada county, which place, as I have before observed, I visited in 1860. In this valley there are forty steam-mills at work, drawing the earth from tunnels, crushing quartz, &c. The average value of the quartz there is 60 or 70 dollars a ton, though it sometimes runs as high as 200 dollars per ton. The Helvetia mill, which is one of the best, crushes on an average 30 tons daily, making therefore nearly 2000 dollars (400l.). The quartz is picked or blasted out in the usual way, and then conveyed on mules or by tramway to the mill, where it is broken by hand into pieces about the size of an egg.

The machinery is placed under a large shed or wooden building of some kind. It consists of a series of heavy stampers, made of iron, or wood shod with iron, the lower ends of which fit into boxes in which the quartz is placed. The stampers are moved by cogs connected with a revolving wheel, which lifts them and lets them fall into the boxes. The Helvetia mill works thirty-four of these stampers. The stamping-boxes are supplied with water by a hose or pipe on one side, while at the other side is a hole through which the quartz, as it is crushed, passes out in the form of a thick white fluid. As it comes out it is received upon a framework, placed at such an angle that it passes slowly over it: on this frame are several quicksilver riffles, which catch and amalgamate the gold as it glides along. Beyond this again is another frame, over which is spread a blanket, which arrests any fine particles which escape the quicksilver. Even with all this care there is considerable waste, and the "tailings" or refuse is generally worth a second washing. No way has yet been found of obviating this waste.

There is a more primitive method of quartz-crushing called the "rastra," or drag, which, though it will only crush about a ton a day, does its work more perfectly than the stampers. For this purpose a circular trough is made, and paved at the bottom. In the centre of this an upright post is fixed, with a spindle fitted into a frame at the top, so that it can be turned round. Through the lower part of this a horizontal pole is passed, one end of which plumbs the edge of the trough, while the other projects some way beyond it. To the short end a couple of heavy stones are attached; a mule or horse being harnessed to the other. The quartz is then put into the trough, being first broken up small, and ground by the friction of the stones, which are dragged round by the mule. A small stream of water is kept constantly flowing into the trough, and quicksilver is sprinkled in at intervals to amalgamate with the gold. After a certain time the water is turned off, the entire pavement of the trough taken up, and the amalgam carefully collected and retorted. Of course these are worked chiefly by parties who do not possess sufficient capital to construct steam-mills.

With respect to the existence of the precious mineral in North America, the theory which Sir Roderick Murchison maintains is that the matrix will be found extending the whole way along the slopes of the chain of mountains lying between the Rocky Mountains and the Coast Ridge. This theory is borne out by the discoveries in Rock Creek and Cariboo, which lie in the line attributed to it. All the river bars or "placers," as surface-diggings are called, which have been worked as yet are undeniably the alluvial deposits brought down by the streams on whose banks they are found. And nearly all these rivers take their rise in the chain of mountains spoken of, which form an almost unbroken line

between Rock Creek and Cariboo. The Cariboo Lake and
some of the rich Cariboo diggings, as Keithley's Creek,
Cottonwood River, &c., are on the west side of this ridge;
while Antler Creek, Cañon Creek, and others lie on the east,
showing that the gold is common to both slopes. This has
probably tended to make the Fraser River bars much richer
than they otherwise would have been, as all the small streams
which rise on the eastern side of these mountains also run
into the Fraser, which comes up from the southward behind
them, till, as I have before shown, it is turned southward by
the height of the land between it and the Peace River.

The few adventurers who have crossed this barrier to the
Peace River report all the appearances of an extremely rich
auriferous region there; and Mr. Nind tells me that it is
generally believed at Cariboo that the richest diggings will
be found in that direction. This fact undoubtedly confirms
Sir R. Murchison's theory, as the Peace River Valley stretches
northward in the same direction till it meets the Finlay River
in lat. 56½° N.

It would be simply waste of space to quote the accounts
of the richness of the gold-fields of British Columbia, given at
intervals in the journals of the day. New and more startling
discoveries are being so constantly made, that the marvels of
one day are always likely to be eclipsed by the still more
extraordinary reports of the next. We have also yet to receive the accounts of this summer's work at the gold-fields. I
will give, however, from the *Times* of February 6, 1862, the
estimate which its correspondent forms of the approximate
gross yield of gold for 1861 :—

"It is impossible to give a return of the 'yield' of gold
produced by British Columbia in the aggregate with certainty.
I shall merely attempt an approximation of the gross yield
from the best *data* within my reach.

"It is generally conceded that, including Chinese, there
were 5000 men engaged in gold-digging this year. The

various Government returns of Customs' duties and of interior tolls on roads charged on the passage of merchandise collected, justify this assumption, while the miners' licences issued tend to corroborate it. The mining population in the Cariboo country, including within this division the Forks of Quesnelle River (50 miles below) is put down on general testimony (of miners, travellers, other residents, and Government returns) at 1500 men. To work out the earnings of this aggregate of 5000 miners, I adopt a statement of names and amounts, made up from miners' information, of 79 men who together took out in Cariboo 926,680 dollars. The general opinion of the miners is, that (in addition to the 'lucky ones' who made ' big strikes,' and which I limit to the above number of 79) every man who had a claim or a share in a claim made from 1000 to 2000 dollars. Of these there were at the least 400, and taking their earnings at a medium or average between the two sums mentioned—say at 1500 dollars to each—they would produce 600,000 dollars. There remain 1021 men to be accounted for. Putting their earnings at 7 dollars a day each, which is the lowest rate of wages paid for hired labour in the Cariboo mines, and assigning only 107 working days as the period of their mining operations during the season, to make allowance for its shortness by reason of the distance from the different points of departure and of bad weather, they would have taken out 764,729 dollars. These several sums added would make the yield of Cariboo and Quesnelle 2,291,409 dollars to 1500 men for the season, by far the greater portion, or nearly all, in fact, being from Cariboo; although the north fork of Quesnelle is also very productive and so rich as to induce its being worked by fluming this winter by about 100 miners, who have remained for the purpose.

" The remaining 3500 of the mining population who worked on Thompson's River, the Fraser, from Fort George downwards ; Bridge River, Semilkameen, and Okanagan (very few),

Rock Creek, and all other localities throughout the country, I shall divide into two classes: the first to consist of 1500, who made 10 dollars a-day for—say 180 days (Sundays thrown off), and which would give 2,700,000 dollars for their joint earnings; the second and last class of 2000 men, who were not so lucky, I shall assume to have made only 5 dollars each a-day for the same period, and which would give 1,800,000 dollars as the fruit of their united labour.

"The three last categories, which number 4521 men, include the many miners who in Cariboo were making 20 to 50 dollars a-day each, as well as those who, in various other localities, were making from 15 dollars to 100 dollars a-day occasionally, so I think my estimate, although not accurate, is reasonable and moderate. The Government people think I have rather understated the earnings of the miners in these three classes of 4521 men; and the Governor himself, who takes an absorbing interest in the affairs of this portion of his government, and to whose ready courtesy I am indebted for some of the information given in this letter, as well as for much formerly communicated in my correspondence, thinks my estimate is a very safe one.

"But I must finish this long letter with a recapitulation, for I dread the inroads I have made upon your space:—

	Dollars.
79 miners took out an aggregate of..	926,680
400 ditto, claim owners, took out	600,000
1021 ditto, at 7 dollars a-day, in 107 days..	764,729
Total yield (nearly all) from Cariboo ..	2,291,409

	Dollars.	
1500 miners who worked in other places for 180 days, at 10 dollars per diem	2,700,000	
2000 ditto, at 5 dollars	1,800,000	
		4,500,000
5000 miners—gross yield for 1861		6,791,409

"This does not include the native Indians, as I have no means of estimating their earnings. They are beginning to

' dig,' in imitation of the white men, in some parts, and will eventually increase the yield of gold, as the desire for wealth grows upon them. As a proof of their aptitude and success in this, to them, new field of labour, I may mention that the Bishop of Columbia found a gang of them ' washing' on Bridge River last summer, and that he had the day's earnings of one Indian weighed when he ceased his labours, and found it to contain one ounce of gold. His Lordship purchased it of him, paying him 16 dollars 50 cents, the current issue, and carried it away as a *souvenir*."

The return of the assays of Cariboo gold, given by the same gentleman, are also of permanent interest, as showing the value of the dust. The highest assayed by Messrs. Marchand and Co., from whom the return is obtained, from Davis Creek, was 718 fine, value per ounce 18 doll. 97·64 c., or about 3*l*. 19*s*. The lowest, which came from Williams Creek, was 810 fine, value per ounce 16 doll. 74·12 c. (about 3*l*. 9*s*. 7*d*.). The average value of all Cariboo dust is 854 fine, value per ounce 17 doll. 65·37 c. (3*l*. 13*s*. 6*d*.).

In conclusion, I have merely to add, that I remained with the ' Hecate' at San Francisco until she was repaired, when, on the 21st October, 1861, I left that place in the United States mail steamer ' Orizaba,' and on the 27th November arrived " home."

APPENDIX.

———◆◇◆———

EXPLORATIONS IN JERVIS INLET AND DESOLATION SOUND, BRITISH COLUMBIA.

———————

Mr. WILLIAM DOWNIE to Governor JAMES DOUGLAS.

SIR,   Victoria, Vancouver Island, March 19th, 1859.

    I have the honour to inform your Excellency of my return to Victoria, after a sojourn of sixteen weeks in British Columbia.

    I have been for the last month in Desolation Sound. The snow and rain set in so as to make it impossible to start over the mountains from the head of Jervis Inlet to the Upper Fraser River for some time.

    I then thought it would be as well to visit the Klahous country, as I had heard a great deal about it.

    We started from the head of Jervis Inlet on the 22nd of February for Desolation Sound, in a small canoe with four Indians, pick, pan, shovel, and rocker; came down the west entrance of Jervis Inlet, which is much better than the eastern. From Scotch-Fir Point, up the coast, it is shallow, and rocks and reefs running out a good distance from the shore.

    It was most refreshing to come down on the gulf, where the land had all the appearance of spring, and after being so long up the inlet. No snow on any of the islands along the coast except Tarada. Savary Island has all the appearance of a farm under cultivation, from the abundance of grass on it : large patches of farming land make it look very enticing, but the water is scarce for farming purposes ; yet there are excellent pastures for stock all the year round. The mainland opposite this island changes in appearance with regard to the rock formation : quartz and slate along the shore up to Sarah Point.

    We arrived safe in Desolation Sound, which does certainly look somewhat desolate in a snow-storm ; but I am well pleased with the prospect of this section.

    This is the first time I have seen pure veins of sulphuret of iron, which looks very much like silver. The first I saw of it was a small square piece in the possession of an Indian : I offered him some tobacco for it, but he would not part with it, even if I gave him its weight in gold. I came across a number of seams of the same kind. It lies in the quartz, the same as gold. I have no idea that the gold is confined to Fraser River alone ; and if it can only be found from the seaboard or on the rivers, at the head of some of these inlets, the country will soon be prospected.

Bute Inlet (Homathco), that runs so much farther north than this inlet, has a large river emptying into it from the north-west. This river looks most favourable for gold, and I should much like to have prospected it ; but the Indians would not go, as they were afraid of the Euclitus tribes, but the principal reason was that the canoe was small, and we were not altogether prepared to give it a fair trial. It was snowing most of the time, and rather discouraging.

Camped near the Klahous Indians' village : they paid me a visit, as a matter of course, and I gave them each a small piece of tobacco. They seemed well pleased; but would have a look at our mining tools, and canoe, and blankets, and general appearance. When they had satisfied themselves on these points, they told my Indians I was not a Tyee—meaning a chief, a person of consequence (this was the unkindest cut of all). My Indians told them I was a Tyee ; but it was of no use. They said a Tyee would have a large canoe and plenty of blankets, whereas there was nothing of the kind visible ; only picks, pans, and an old rocker, and what was the use of that among Indians ?

I did not feel disposed to find fault with the poor Klahous Indians for judging from outward appearance, and, upon the whole, I got along with them very well. We got a few potatoes from them, so there must be something else besides rocks in Desolation Sound.

We went up to the head of the inlet, where the " Deserted Village " is on the map, but there were no Indians there. It looked as much like a deserted village as it did when it was named by Vancouver. About two miles above this the river comes in from the north-east. The sand washing out of the river has formed a large flat at the head of the inlet, in some places dry at low-water. We had some difficulty in getting the canoe into the river, which is also shallow, being filled up with sand from the continued wash from the mountains.

We went up the river about five miles. The Indians told me it would take five days to go to the head of it. Judging from the way a canoe goes up such rivers, the distance would be about sixty miles, which must be a long distance above the Quamish, and would not be far from the Lillooet. The Indians have gone this route to the head of Bridge River (Hoystier), which it may prove to be the best route to try. It is very evident there is a pass in the Coast Range here that will make it preferable to Jervis Inlet or Howe Sound. If a route can be got through, it will lead direct to Bridge River.

I have seen more black sand here in half a day than I did in California in nine years ; it looks clear and bright, as if it came from quartz.

Seeing that it was out of the question to proceed farther, we put back and came down along shore, breaking and trying the rocks, but did not discover any gold : lots of iron pyrites or sulphuret of iron.

The land on each side of the river is low, and must be overflowed in many places in spring ; but for all that, if a trail can be found through, it will not be difficult to make a road along the banks of the river.

In coming down we passed through what on the map is called the Island

" Redonda." This is a fine passage, and shortens the distance about ten miles in going to Klahous Inlet.

The distance from Klahous Inlet to Homathco Inlet (Bute Inlet on the chart) is about thirty miles; but I could not get the Indians to go in the small canoe.

The Indians told me that the colour of the water in the large river that comes in at the head of Homathco from the north-west was the same as Fraser River; and thus when I proceed thither I should be in or near the range of Queen Charlotte Islands, where I should get gold.

We had a hard passage to Nanaimo; but arrived all right, paid off the Indians, and heard from Captain Stuart that he had forwarded supplies to Jervis Inlet by order of your Excellency, so that I was all ready for a start again to Desolation Sound, if I could obtain a small decked-boat.

Fort St. James, Stuart Lake, New Caledonia,
Sir,   10th October, 1859.

I beg to make the following report of my trip to Queen Charlotte Islands, and my journey thence by Fort Simpson to the interior of British Columbia.

Having left Victoria on the 27th July, with twenty-seven practical miners, with stores, &c., for three months, we arrived in Gold Harbour, Queen Charlotte Islands, safely, on the 6th August, and immediately set about prospecting.

We examined the spot where a large quantity of gold was formerly taken out, and discovered a few specks of it in the small quartz-seams that run through the slate; two of the party blasting the rock, while others prospected round the harbour.

I then proceeded in a canoe to Douglas Inlet, which runs in south of Gold Harbour, hoping to find traces of the Gold Harbour lead, but without success. The nature of the rock is trap or hornblende, with a few poor seams of quartz straggling over the surface. Granite was found at the head of this inlet, but not a speck of gold. Next day we went up an inlet to the north of Gold Harbour, and here a white rock showed itself on the spur of a mountain.

After a difficult ascent we found it to be nothing but weather-beaten, sun-dried granite, instead of quartz. Farther up the inlet we saw a little black slate and some talcose rock, but nothing that looked like gold. On our return, we found that the men engaged in blasting the rock had given it up; the few surface specks being all the gold that could he found.

The large amount of gold that was formerly found with so little difficulty existed in what is called an offshot or blow. The question then arises how did the gold get here. Some of our party were of opinion that a gold lead exists close at hand, but it can only be put down to one of the extraordinary freaks of nature so often found in a mineral country.

The offshoots in question are not uncommon, as I have often seen them in California. On such a discovery being made, hundreds of miners would take claims in all directions near it, and test the ground in every way; but nothing farther could be found, except in the one spot, about 70 feet in length, running south-east and north-west: on being worked about 15 feet it gave out. Before work commenced I have blown the sand off a vein of pure gold.

I now proposed to test the island farther, and started for the Skidegate Channel. At a village of the Crosswer Indians, where we were windbound, the appearances were more favourable. Talcose slate, quartz, and red earth were seen. We tried to discover gold, but without success. Sulphuret of iron was found in abundance, and we discovered traces of previous prospectings. The Indians understand the search for gold well, and detect it in the rocks quicker even than I can.

The coast from the Casswer Indian village to Skidegate Channel is wilder than any I have ever before travelled; and we did not care to hunt for gold in such a place. Five Indians were drowned here to-day while fishing.

At the Skidegate Channel we found black slate and quartz prevailing; farther north granite appears, and then sandstone and conglomerate ; and as we were now in a coal country, it was of no use to look for gold.

We saw coal here, but I cannot speak as to its quality, not being a judge of it. The formation is similar to that of Nanaimo. From this we returned to Gold Harbour, where a party which had remained behind to prospect inland had met with no better success than ourselves. We then consulted what was the best thing to do. I did not wish to return to Victoria, as your Excellency had desired me to explore some of the inlets on the mainland; and I left Gold Harbour with a party of fourteen men for Fort Simpson, where we arrived in eight days. The north-west coast of Queen Charlotte Islands is a low sand and gravel flat, having no resemblance to a gold country.

I left Fort Simpson for the Skeena River on the 31st August. From Fort Simpson to Fort Essington is about 40 miles. The salt water here is of a light-blue colour, like the mouth of Fraser River, and runs inland about 30 miles. The coarse-grained quartz of Fort Simpson is no longer seen here, and granite appears; and the banks of the river are low, and covered with small hard wood and cotton-trees, with some good-sized white oaks, the first I have seen west of Fraser River.

Vessels drawing upwards of 4 feet of water cannot go more than 20 miles up the Skeena River; and it is very unlike the deep inlets to the southward. At our camp here some Indians visited us, and told us that they were honest; but next morning the absence of my coat rather negatived their statement. Next day we found the river shoal for loaded canoes, as it had fallen much. At our next camp I went up a small river called Scenatoys, and the Indians showed me some crystallized quartz, and to my surprise a small piece with gold in it, being the first I had seen in this part. The Indian took me to a granite slide, whence, as he asserted, the piece of quartz had come. I found some thin crusts of fine quartz, but no gold. From the river Scenatoys to Fort Essington, at the mouth of the Skeena River, is 75 miles. A little below the Scenatoys an Indian trail leads to Fort Simpson, through a low pass; and the distance is not great.

From this, 10 miles farther up, was a river called the Toes. On the south side hence is an Indian trail to the Kitloops on the Salmon River, the south branch of Salmon, which river is called Kittama.

By this time we were fairly over the Coast Range, and the mountains ahead of us did not look very high ; the current here was very strong, and much labour was required to get our canoe along, and we had to pull her up by a rope from the shore.

Gold is found here, a few specks to the pan, and the whole country looks auriferous, with fine bars and flats with clay on the bars ; the mountains look red, and slate and quartz were seen.

The next camp was at the village of Kitalaska, and I started in a light canoe ahead of my party, as our canoe, by all accounts, could not proceed much farther, and I then determined to penetrate to Fort Fraser. The Indian who was with me told me that a large stream, called the Kitchumsala, comes in from the north ; the land on it is good, and well adapted for farming, and that the Indians grow plenty of potatoes. To the south is a small stream called the Chimkoatsh, on the south of which is the Plumbago Mountain, of which I had some in my hand, as clear as polished silver, and runs in veins of quartz.

Near to this, on a tree, are the words " Pioneer, H.B.C.," and nearly overgrown with bark. The Indian told me it was cut by Mr. John Work, a long time ago.

From this to the village of Kitcoonsa the land improves, the mountains recede from the river, and fine flats run away 4 or 5 miles back to their bases, where the smoke is seen rising from the huts of the Indians engaged in drying berries for the winter. These Indians were very kind to us, and wished me to build a house there, and live with them.

Above the village of Kitcoonsa the prospect of gold is not so good as below. As the season was so advanced I was not able to prospect the hills, which look so well, and unless the Government takes it in hand, it will be a long while before the mineral resources of this part of British Columbia can be known. This is the best-looking mineral country I have seen in British Columbia.

From here to the village of Kitsagatala the river is rocky and dangerous, and our canoe was split from stem to stern.

At Kitsagatala we entered a most extensive *coal* country, the seams being in sight, and cut through by the river, and running up the banks on both sides, varying in thickness from 3 to 35 feet.

The veins are larger on the east side, and are covered with soft sandstone, which gives easily to the pick ; on the west side quartz lines the seams, which are smaller. The veins dip into the bank for a mile along the river, and could easily be worked by tunnels on the face, or by sinking shafts from behind on the flats, as they run into soft earth.

I have seen no coal like this in all my travels in British Columbia and Vancouver Island.

We experienced some danger from Indians here, but by a small present

2 G 2

of tobacco, and by a determined and unconcerned aspect, I succeeded in avoiding the danger of a collision with them. We could go no farther in the canoe than Kittamarks or the Forks of the Skeena River, and we had been twenty days from Fort Simpson, though the journey could have been done in a third of that time.

On the 21st September I left Kittamarks with two white men and two Indians, and started over a fine trail through a beautiful country for Fort Fraser. We crossed over an Indian suspension-bridge, and entered some first-rate land, our course being about east; we completed about 12 miles to-day. Next day it rained hard, but we succeeded in doing 12 miles again, passing through as fine a farming country as one could wish to see. To the south-east a large open space appeared, and I have since learnt that a chain of lakes runs away here, being the proper way to Fort Fraser; but as I always follow my Indian guides implicitly, I did so on this occasion. The third day the weather was fine, but the trail not so good; it ran along the side of a mountain, but below the trail was good and grass abundant. My Indians started after a goat up the mountain, but were quickly driven back by three bears. The fourth day we crossed what is called the Rocky Pass, which may be avoided by keeping the bottom. To the north a chain of mountains were seen covered with snow, distant about 30 miles, where the Hudson Bay Company have a post called Bears' Fort; to the south is the Indian village Kispyaths; along the bottom runs the Skeena, past the village of Allagasomeda, and farther up the village of Kithathratts, on the same river.

On the fifth day we encountered some dangerous-looking Indians, but got away from them. We passed through a fine country, with cotton-trees and good soil.

We now arrived at the village of Naas-Glee where the Skeena River rises. We were again on the river which we had left five days ago, having travelled 55 miles, when we might have come by the river. We had great difficulty with the Indians here, and it was fortunate that I knew the name of the chief, as otherwise they would have seized all our property; as it was, they surrounded us, and were most importunate: one wanted my coat, another my gun, a third took my cap from my head, and I really thought that they would murder us. These Indians are the worst I have seen in all my travels. Naas-Glee is a great fishing-station, and all the worst characters congregate there to lead an indolent life. Thousands of salmon were being dried at this village.

We hardly knew what to do, as they told us that it was ten days to Fort Fraser, and if we returned they would have robbed us of everything. I therefore determined to go on, if the chief Norra would accompany me, and on giving him some presents he consented to do so. The river from Naas-Glee downwards is very rapid, but as the banks are low and flat a waggon-road or railroad could easily be made.

The land around Naas-Glee is excellent, and wild hay and long grass abound. Potatoes are not grown here, owing to the thieving of the Indians.

There is no heavy pine timber hereabouts, and the canoes are made of cotton-wood.

Above Naas-Glee the river was very rapid, and it required all our energy to get along, as we had but a small quantity of dried salmon to last us ten days. Ten miles above Naas-Glee is an old Indian village, called Whatatt; here the shoal-water ends, and we enter the Babine Lake. Going through a fine country, we accomplished 20 miles this day, the lake being broad and deep. Next morning, to my surprise, I found a canoe at our camp, with Frenchmen and Indians, in charge of Mr. Savin Hamilton, an officer in the service of the Hudson Bay Company, from Fort St. James, Stuart Lake, New Caledonia, whither we were bound. He was on his way to Naas-Glee to purchase fish, and advised me to return with him there, and then to accompany him to Stuart Lake; but as I had seen enough of Naas-Glee I declined his offer, with thanks. Mr. Hamilton expressed his surprise that we had managed to get away from Naas-Glee, as we were the first white men who had come through this route; and even he found much difficulty with the Indians there. Having persuaded Narra, the chief, to let us have his canoe, we bid farewell to Mr. Hamilton, and proceeded on our journey.

It was fortunate that we sent back our two Indians, as otherwise we should have suffered from want of food, and as it was we reached Stuart Lake only with great difficulty. We made a fine run to-day before a fair wind to Fort Killamoures, which post is only kept up in the winter. Our course from Naas-Glee to this place was south-east, and the distance about 50 miles. The land is good the whole way, with long grass on the benches near the fort, which is a very lonely place. It is a great pity to see this beautiful country, so well adapted to the wants of man, lying waste, when so many Englishmen and Scotsmen would be glad to come here and till the soil. Babine Lake is deep, and in some places 5 or 6 miles wide, with islands and points of land to afford shelter from storms. From Fort Killamoures to the head of Babine is about 40 miles, direction south-south-east. From the head down about 20 miles it runs east and west. We arrived at the head of Babine on the seventh day after leaving Naas-Glee. We had seen no Indians, nor snow, and had made a favourable journey.

The district we had passed was well adapted for farming. Some of the land is rocky, but on the whole it is a fine country.

At the head of Babine Lake there is a good site for a town, and a harbour could be made, as a stream flows in which would supply the town with water. This is what I call the head-water of the Skeena River. The lake is navigable for steamers, and 100 miles in length.

From this to Stuart Lake there is a portage over a good trail, through the finest grove of cotton-wood I have ever seen. The ground was thickly strewed with yellow leaves, giving the scene quite an autumnal appearance, and presenting a picture far different to what we expected in this part of British Columbia.

Six miles from Babine we came to a small lake where were some Indians fishing for herrings. On our approach they appeared undecided whether to run or remain. I asked them for some food, and they soon provided us with some fish, which refreshed us much, and having paid for our repast, we started again. From this a small stream runs a distance of 4 miles to Stuart Lake.

Arrived at Stuart Lake, we found no means of crossing, no Indians to direct us, and no food to sustain us, nor had we any shot to enable us to kill ducks. We camped here three nights without food, sleeping the greater part of the time to stifle our hunger. The only thing that supported us was the great idea of the enterprise in which we were engaged, having been the first to explore the route from the Pacific to Fraser River.

One of our party found an old canoe split to pieces; this was rigged on a raft of logs, as well as circumstances would admit.

I returned to the Indians above mentioned, and purchased a few herrings, and walked back to our camp with difficulty, and found my limbs giving way. Next morning we started on our frail raft, expecting every moment to go down; we were obliged to sit perfectly still, as the least movement would have upset us. A slight breeze sprung up, and a small sea washed over us, and we had to run for a lee shore, where kind Providence sent an Indian to succour us. He welcomed us with a "Bonjour," invited us to his lodge, and gave us most excellent salmon-trout from the lake. We had at last reached this spot, with thankful hearts for our preservation through so many dangers. We stayed a night with this good Indian, and next day gave him a blanket to take us to the Fort. We abandoned our old canoe without regret, and proceeded towards our destination. The Indians all along this were very kind to us. About half-way across Stuart Lake we obtained a small prospect of gold. On the north side of the lake, for about 20 miles, the ground is rocky; but south, towards the Fort, the land is good, and will produce anything.

We reached Fort St. James on the 9th October, and were received by Mr. Peter Ogden with that kindness and hospitality which I have always found at the Hudson Bay Company's ports.

The Fort is very much exposed to all winds, and I found it colder than anywhere on the journey.

Stuart Lake is 50 miles long. The portage to Babine 10 miles; Babine Lake 100 miles; from Naas-Glee to Fort Simpson 250 miles, and 200 miles from Fort Simpson to Gold Harbour, Queen Charlotte Islands.

The names of the two men who accompanied me were William Manning an Englishman, and Frank Chotean a French Canadian. It is possible that I shall prospect the Fraser a little farther this fall.

LIST OF TREES AND SHRUBS OF ECONOMIC VALUE, FOUND IN VANCOUVER ISLAND.

(Extracted from Dr. Forbes's Prize Essay on Vancouver Island.)

POPULAR NAMES.	SCIENTIFIC NAMES.
The Douglas Pine or Oregon Red Pine	Abies Douglasii.
Spruce Fir	„ Menziesii.
Yellow Fir	„ grandis.
Balsam Fir	
Hemlock Spruce	Abies Canadiensis.
Wild Cherry	Cerasus mollis.
White Pine or Weymouth Pine ..	Pinus strobus.
Yellow Pine	Pinus ponderosa.
Cedar—the Oregon Cedar	Thuja gigantea.
Yellow Cypress	Cupressus Metkatenses.
Arbor Vitæ	Thuja plicata.
Yew	Taxus brevifolia.
The Oak	Quercus Garryana.
The white, or broad-leaved Maple ..	Acer macrophyllum.
Vine ditto ..	Acer circinatum.
The Oregon Alder	Alnus Oregona.
Oregon Dogwood	Cornus Nuttallii.
Arbutus	Arbutus Menziesii.
American Aspen	Populus tremuloides.
Oregon Crab Apple	
The Willow	Pyrus rivularis.
Cottonwood	Salix Scouleriana.

SHRUBBERY UNDERGROWTH.

The Hazel	Corylus Americana.
Red Cornel, or Willow	Cornus Drummondii.
Holly-leaved Barberry or Oregon grape	Berberis aquifolium.
Mock Orange or Seringa	Philadelphus macropetalus.
Red, white, and black Raspberry ..	Rubus Nutkanus, leucodermis.
Three kinds of Gooseberry	Ribes divaricatum, niveum, and sanguineum.
Serviceberry	Amelanchier Canadiensis.
Elder	Sambucus glauca.
Sallat Berry	Gaultheria shallon.
Huckleberry, or Blœberry	Vaccinium ovatum, ovalifolium,
Blackberry (Rubus)	and parvifolium.
Snowberry	Symphoricarpus racemosus.
Salmonberry	Rubus spectabilis.
Oregon Buckthorn	Frangula Purshiana.
Honeysuckle	Lonicera occidentalis.

POPULAR NAMES.	SCIENTIFIC NAMES.
Ivy	Hedera.
Hawthorn	Cratœgus Coccinea?
Fly Blossom, or Bearberry ..	Lonicera involucrata.
Wild Rose	Rosa fraxinifolia.

GRASSES, LEGUMINOUS PLANTS, &c. &c.

White Clover	Trifolium repens.
Reed Meadow-grass	Glyceria aquatica.
Bent Spear-grass	Poa pratensis?
Sweet Grass	Festuca pratensis.
Wild Timothy, or Herd's Grass ..	Phleum pratense.
Wild Oat	Stipa avenacea?
Broad-leaved Rush	Juncus.
Cowslip	Primula veris, vel Douglasii.

BRITISH COLUMBIA.

LAND PROCLAMATIONS

By his Excellency JAMES DOUGLAS, Companion of the Most Honourable Order of the Bath, Governor and Commander-in-Chief of British Columbia.

No. I. Dated 14th Feb. 1859.

WHEREAS it is expedient to publish for general information the method to be pursued with respect to the alienation and possession of agricultural lands, and of lands proposed for the sites of towns in British Columbia, and with reference also to the places for levying shipping and customs duties, and for establishing a capital and port of entry in the said Colony:

Now, therefore, I, JAMES DOUGLAS, Governor of the said Colony, do proclaim and declare as follows, viz. :—

1. All the lands in British Columbia, and all the mines and minerals therein, belong to the Crown in fee.

2. The price of lands not being intended for the sites of towns, and not being reputed to be mineral lands, shall be ten shillings per acre, payable one-half in cash at the time of the sale, and the other half at the end of two years from such sale. Provided that under special circumstances some other price or some other terms of payment may, from time to time, be specially announced for particular localities.

3. It shall also be competent to the Executive at any time to reserve such portions of the unoccupied Crown lands, and for such purposes, as the Executive shall deem advisable.

4. Except as aforesaid, all the land in British Columbia will be exposed in lots for sale, by public competition, at the upset price above mentioned, as soon as the same shall have been surveyed and made ready for sale.

Due notice will be given of all such sales. Notice at the same time will be given of the upset price and terms of payment, when they vary from those above stated, and also of the rights reserved (if any) for public convenience.

5. All lands which shall remain unsold at any such auction may be sold by private contract at the upset price, and on the terms and conditions herein mentioned, on application to the Chief Commissioner of Lands and Works.

6. Unless otherwise specially notified at the time of sale, all such sales of Crown land shall be subject to such public rights of way as may at any time after such sale, and to such private rights of way, and of leading or using water for animals, and for mining and engineering purposes, as may at the time of such sale be specified by the Chief Commissioners of Lands and Works.

7. Unless otherwise specially announced at the time of sale, the conveyance of the land shall include all trees and all mines and minerals within and under the same, except mines of gold and silver.

8. When any "Ditch Privilege" shall be granted, there shall be included (unless excluded by express words) the right to lop, dress, or fell any trees standing on unoccupied Crown lands, which in the opinion of the proprietors of the ditch might, by their accidental fall or otherwise, endanger the safety of the ditch or any part thereof.

No. II. Dated 4th Jan. 1860.

1. FROM and after the date hereof, British subjects and aliens who shall take the oath of allegiance to Her Majesty and her successors, may acquire unoccupied and unreserved and unsurveyed Crown land in British Columbia (not being the site of an existent or proposed town, or auriferous land available for mining purposes, or an Indian reserve or settlement), in fee simple, under the following conditions:—

2. The person desiring to acquire any particular plot of land of the character aforesaid shall enter into possession thereof and record his claim to any quantity not exceeding 160 acres thereof, with the magistrate residing nearest thereto, paying to the said magistrate the sum of 8s. for recording such claim. Such piece of land shall be of a rectangular form, and the shortest side of the rectangle shall be at least two-thirds of the longest side. The claimant shall give the best possible description thereof to the magistrate with whom his claim is recorded, together with a rough plan thereof, and identify the plot in question by placing at the corners of the land four posts, and by stating in his description any other landmarks on the said 160 acres which he may consider of a noticeable character.

3. Whenever the Government survey shall extend to the land claimed, the claimant who has recorded his claim as aforesaid, or his heirs, or in case of the grant of certificate of improvement hereinafter mentioned, the assigns of such claimant shall, if he or they shall have been in continuous occupation of the same land from the date of the record aforesaid, be entitled to purchase the land so pre-empted at such rate as may for the time being be

fixed by the Government of British Columbia, not exceeding the sum of 10s. per acre.

4. No interest in any plot of land acquired as aforesaid shall, before payment of the purchase-money, be capable of passing to a purchaser unless the vendor shall have obtained a certificate from the nearest magistrate that he has made permanent improvements on the said plot to the value of 10s. per acre.

5. Upon payment of the purchase-money, a conveyance of the land purchased shall be executed in favour of the purchaser, reserving the precious minerals, with a right to enter and work the same in favour of the Crown, its assigns and licencees.

6. Priority of title shall be obtained by the person first in occupation, who shall first record his claim in manner aforesaid.

7. Any person authorized to acquire land under the provisions of this Proclamation may purchase, in addition to the land pre-empted, in manner aforesaid, any number of acres not otherwise appropriated, at such rate as may be fixed by the Government, at the time when such land shall come to be surveyed, not to exceed 10s. per acre; 5s. to be paid down, and the residue at the time of survey.

8. In the event of the Crown, its assigns or licencees, availing itself, or themselves, of the reservation mentioned in clause 5, a reasonable compensation for the waste and damage done shall be paid by the person entering and working to the person whose land shall be wasted or damaged as aforesaid; and in case of dispute, the same shall be settled by a jury of six men to be summoned by the nearest magistrate.

9. Whenever any person shall permanently cease to occupy land pre-empted as aforesaid, the magistrate resident nearest to the land in question may in a summary way, on being satisfied of such permanent cessation, cancel the claim of the person so permanently ceasing to occupy the same, and record the claim thereto of any other person satisfying the requisitions aforesaid.

10. The decision of the magistrate may be appealed by either party to the decision of the Judge of the Supreme Court of Civil Justice of British Columbia.

11. Any person desirous of appealing in manner aforesaid may be required, before such appeal be heard, to find such security as may be hereafter pointed out by the rules or orders hereinafter directed to be published.

12. The procedure before the magistrate and judge respectively shall be according to such rules and orders as shall be published by such judge, with the approbation of the Governor for the time being of British Columbia.

13. Whenever a person in occupation at the time of record aforesaid shall have recorded as aforesaid, and he, his heirs, or assigns, shall have continued in permanent occupation of land pre-empted, or of land purchased as aforesaid, he or they may, save as hereinafter mentioned, bring ejectment or trespass against any intruder upon the land so pre-empted or purchased, to the same extent as if he or they were seized of the legal estate in possession in the land so pre-empted or purchased.

14. Nothing herein contained shall be construed as giving a right to any claimant to exclude free miners from searching for any of the precious minerals or working the same upon the conditions aforesaid.

15. The Government shall, notwithstanding any claim, record, or conveyance aforesaid, be entitled to enter and take such portion of the land pre-empted or purchased as may be required for roads or other public purposes.

16. Water privileges and the right of carrying water for mining purposes may, notwithstanding any claim recorded, purchase, or conveyance aforesaid, be claimed and taken upon, under, or over the said land so pre-empted or purchased as aforesaid, by free miners requiring the same, and obtaining a grant or licence from the Gold Commissioner, and paying a compensation for waste or damage to the person whose land may be wasted or damaged by such water privilege or carriage of water, to be ascertained in case of dispute in manner aforesaid.

17. In case any dispute shall arise between persons with regard to any land so acquired as aforesaid, any one of the parties in difference may (before ejectment or action of trespass brought) refer the question in difference to the nearest magistrate, who is hereby authorized to proceed in a summary way to restore the possession of any land in dispute to the person whom he may deem entitled to the same, and to abate all intrusions, and award and levy such costs and damages as he may think fit.

No. III.   Dated 20th Jan. 1860.

WHEREAS by virtue of an Act of Parliament made and passed in the 21st and 22nd years of the reign of Her most gracious Majesty the Queen, and by a Commission under the Great Seal of the United Kingdom of Great Britain and Ireland, in conformity therewith, I, JAMES DOUGLAS, Governor of the Colony of British Columbia, have been authorized by Proclamation, issued under the Public Seal of the said Colony, to make laws, institutions, and ordinances for the peace, order, and good government of the same.

And whereas it is expedient that town lots, suburban lots, and surveyed agricultural lands in British Columbia, which have been or which hereafter may be offered for sale at public auction, and remain unsold, should be sold by private contract.

Now, therefore, I, JAMES DOUGLAS, Governor of British Columbia, by virtue of the authority aforesaid, do proclaim, order, and enact as follows :—

The Chief Commissioner of Lands and Works for the time being for British Columbia, and all magistrates, Gold Commissioners, and Assistant Gold Commissioners, by the said Chief Commissioner authorized in writing in that behalf, may sell by private contract any of the lots and lands hereinafter mentioned, at the prices and on the terms hereinafter respectively stated, viz :—

(a.) Town and suburban lots which have been or hereafter may be offered for sale at public auction, and remain unsold, at the upset price, and on the terms at and on which the same were offered for sale at such auction.

(b.) Agricultural lands surveyed by the Government Surveyor which may or shall have been offered for sale at public auction, and remain unsold at 10s. per acre, payable one-half in cash at the time of sale, and the other half at the expiration of two years from such sale.

And the purchaser of any agricultural land aforesaid shall purchase, subject to such rights of way and water as may be hereafter declared by some writing under the hand of the Chief Commissioner of Lands and Works aforesaid.

No. IV. *Dated 19th Jan.* 1861.

WHEREAS, under and by virtue of an Act of Parliament made and passed in the session of Parliament held in the 21st and 22nd years of the reign of Her Majesty Queen Victoria, intituled ' An Act to provide for the government of British Columbia,' and by a commission under the Great Seal of the United Kingdom of Great Britain and Ireland, I, JAMES DOUGLAS, have been appointed Governor of the said Colony, and have been authorized by Proclamation under the Public Seal of the said Colony to make laws, institutions, and ordinances for the peace, order, and good government of the same.

And whereas, by a Proclamation issued under the Public Seal of the said Colony, on the 4th day of January, 1860, the price of unsurveyed land acquired by purchase or pre-emption under the provisions of the said Proclamation, was stated to be at such rate as might for the time being be fixed by the Government of British Columbia, not exceeding the sum of 10s. per acre.

And whereas, by a Proclamation issued under the Public Seal of the said Colony, on the 20th day of January, 1860, the price of agricultural land, surveyed by the Government Surveyor, which may or shall have been offered for sale at public auction and remain unsold, was fixed at 10s. per acre, payable one-half in cash at the time of sale, and the other half at the expiration of two years from the time of sale.

And whereas I have been empowered by Her Majesty's Government to lower the price of country lands in British Columbia, in all cases, to the sum of 4s. 2d. per acre.

Now, therefore, I do hereby declare, proclaim, and enact as follows :—

I. So much of the said Proclamation of the 20th day of January, 1860, as fixed the price of surveyed agricultural land at 10s. per acre is hereby repealed.

II. The price of all unsurveyed country land in British Columbia, whether acquired by pre-emption or purchase under the Proclamation dated the 4th day of January, 1860, shall be 4s. 2d. per acre.

III. The upset price of all country lands in British Columbia exposed for sale at public auction shall be 4s. 2d. per acre.

IV. This Proclamation may be cited for all purposes as the 'Country Land Act, 1861.'

> Issued under the Public Seal of the said Colony at Victoria, Vancouver Island; the 19th day of January, in the year of our Lord 1861, and in the 24th year of Her Majesty's reign, by me,
>
> JAMES DOUGLAS.
>
> By command of his Excellency,
>
> WILLIAM A. G. YOUNG,
> Acting Colonial Secretary.

A Proclamation, dated May 18, 1861, has also been issued, conferring certain remissions in the purchase-money of country lands purchased for actual settlement by retired military and naval officers.

VANCOUVER ISLAND.

LAND PROCLAMATIONS

By his Excellency JAMES DOUGLAS, C.B., &c. &c.

I.

WHEREAS I have been empowered by Her Majesty's Government to fix the upset price of country land within the colony of Vancouver Island and its dependencies at 4s. 2d. per acre.

And whereas I have been authorized as aforesaid to take such steps as may tend to promote the settlement of country land in the said colony.

And whereas it is expedient to make public the method by which *bona fide* settlers may acquire the same land.

Be it therefore known unto all men:

All country land to be sold at 4s. 2d. per acre.

I. That the upset price of all country land in Vancouver Island shall be from henceforth 4s. 2d. per acre.

British subjects may enter upon and occupy land, not being otherwise reserved, in certain quantities and in certain districts.

II. That from and after the date hereof, male British subjects, and aliens who shall take the oath of allegiance before the Chief Justice of Vancouver Island, above the age of eighteen years, may pre-empt unsold Crown lands in the districts of Victoria, Esquimalt, Metchosen, the Highlands, Sooke, North and South Saanich, Salt Spring Island, Sallas Island, and Chemanis (not being an Indian reserve or settlement), of the area and under the conditions following:

A single man, 150 acres.

A married man, whose wife is resident in the colony, 200 acres.

For each of his children under the age of eighteen years, resident in the said colony, an additional 10 acres.

Pre-emptor, before recording his claim, to take the oath of allegiance if a British subject who has become subject to some other nation.

III. All British subjects, who shall be desirous of pre-empting, and who may, at the time of record, have taken the oath of allegiance to, or become the subject or citizen of any foreign Sovereign, state, or nation, shall, as a condition precedent to recording their claims, take the oath of allegiance in manner aforesaid.

Pre-emptor to record his claim immediately on occupation.   Fee.

IV. Immediately after occupation, the pre-emptor shall record his claim at the office of the Surveyor-General at Victoria; paying for such record the sum of eight shillings and four pence.

Regulating the form of claims.

V. The land selected, if unsurveyed, shall be of a rectangular form, and the shortest side of said rectangle shall be two-fifths the length of the longest side; and the boundaries of such land shall also run as nearly as possible by the cardinal points of the compass.

VI. Where the land sought to be acquired is unsurveyed, and in whole or part bounded by rocks, mountains, lakes, swamps, the margin of a river, or the sea-coast, or other natural boundaries, then such natural boundaries may be adopted as the boundaries of the land selected.

VII. The claimant shall, if the land is unsurveyed, give the best possible description thereof in writing to the Surveyor-General at the time of record, with a map thereof, and shall identify the land, by placing a post at each corner, and by stating in his description any other landmarks which may be of a noticeable character.

Mode of recording claims in surveyed lands.

VIII. If the land, however, be surveyed, the claimant shall give the description aforesaid by identification with the landmarks laid down by the Government Survey.

Payment.

IX. The claimant shall, if the land be unsurveyed, pay into the Land Office at Victoria the sum of four shillings and two pence per acre for the same as soon as the land is included within the Government Survey; if the land be surveyed, he shall pay into the said Land Office the sum of four shillings and two pence per acre by three instalments, viz.: One shilling and one penny per acre within one year from the day of record; one shilling and one penny per acre within two years from the said day of record, and two shillings within three years from the said day; and any default in any of the payments aforesaid shall cause a forfeiture of the pre-emption claim, and of the instalments (if any) paid up.

Certificate of improvement to be granted after two years' occupation and 10s. per acre improvement.

X. When the pre-emptor, his heirs or devisees, shall prove to the Surveyor-General, by the satisfactory evidence of third parties, that he has, or they have, continued in permanent occupation of the claim for two years from the date of record, and has or have made permanent improvements thereon to the value of ten shillings per acre, the said Surveyor-General shall issue to him or them a certificate of improvement, in the form marked A in the schedule hereto.

Holder of certificate of improvement may sell, lease, or mortgage.

XI. Upon the grant of the certificate of improvement aforesaid, the person to whom the same is issued may, subject to any unpaid instalments, sell, mortgage, or lease the land in respect of which such certificate has been issued; but until the entirety of the purchase-money of the said land has been paid, no sale, mortgage, or lease of the said land shall be valid unless a certificate of improvement as aforesaid has been issued in respect thereof.

Conveyance of surveyed lands.

XII. Upon payment of the entirety of the purchase-money, a conveyance of the land shall be executed in favour of the pre-emptor, reserving to the Crown the right to take back so much thereof as may be required for roads or other public purposes, and reserving also the precious minerals, with a right to enter and work the same in favour of the Crown, its assigns and licencees.

Conveyance of pre-empted claim in unsurveyed lands.

XIII. If the land is not then included in the Government Survey, the conveyance shall, with the reservations aforesaid, be executed as soon as possible after the same is so included; and the pre-emptor shall, upon survey, be entitled to take any quantity of unpre-empted land, at the price of four shillings and two pence per acre, which may be laid off into the sections in which his pre-empted land is situate; or, if unwilling so to do, he shall forfeit so much of the pre-empted land as lies in those sections which he is unwilling to purchase.

Priorities.

XIV. Priority of title shall be obtained by the person who, being in actual occupation, shall first record his claim in manner aforesaid.

Forfeiture by cessation of occupation.

XV. Whenever any person shall cease to occupy land pre-empted as aforesaid for the space of two months, the Surveyor-General may, in a summary way, on being satisfied of such permanent cessation, cancel the claim of the person so ceasing to occupy the same, and record *de novo* the claim of any other person satisfying the requisitions aforesaid; and in the event of any person feeling aggrieved thereat, his remedy shall be personally against the person so recording.

Compensation for waste or injury.

XVI. In the event of the Crown, its assigns or licencees, availing itself or themselves of the reservation to enter and work the precious minerals as aforesaid, a reasonable compensation for the waste and damage done shall be paid by the person entering and working to the person whose land shall be wasted or damaged as aforesaid; and in case of any dispute, a jury of six men, to be summoned by the Surveyor-General, shall settle the same.

XVII. Nothing in the conditions hereinbefore contained, or in any title to be derived hereunder, shall be construed as giving a right to any claimant to exclude licencees of the Crown from searching for any of the precious minerals in any unenclosed land on the conditions aforesaid.

Saving of water privileges for mining purposes.

XVIII. Water privileges, and the right of carrying water for mining purposes, may, notwithstanding any claim recorded, certificate of improvement, or conveyance aforesaid, be claimed and taken upon, under, or over the land so pre-empted by miners requiring the same, and obtaining a grant or licence from the Surveyor-General in that behalf, and paying a compensation for waste or damage to the person whose land may be wasted or damaged by such water privilege or carrying of water, to be ascertained, in case of dispute, by a jury of six men in manner aforesaid.

Arbitration.

XIX. In case any dispute shall arise between persons with regard to any land acquired as aforesaid, any one of the parties in difference may (before ejectment or action of trespass brought) refer the question in difference to the Surveyor-General, who is hereby authorised to proceed in a summary way to restore the possession of any land in dispute to the person whom he may deem entitled to the same; and to abate all intrusions and award and levy such costs and damages as he may think fit, and for all or any of the purposes aforesaid to call in to his assistance the civil authorities or any process of law.

Given under my hand, &c.

JAMES DOUGLAS.

II.

WHEREAS I have been empowered by Her Majesty's Government to take such steps as may tend to promote the settlement of country land in the said colony.

And whereas it is expedient to extend the time during which a person may cease to occupy land pre-empted under the provisions of a Proclamation given under my hand and the public seal of this colony, and dated the 19th day of February, 1861.

Now therefore, be it known unto all men that any person having pre-empted land under the provisions of the said Proclamation may, if he shall have been continuously in occupation of the same for the space of (8) eight calendar months next previously to his leaving, leave the same for any period not exceeding (6) six calendar months, provided that within (21) twenty-one days from the date of his leaving the same he shall fill in a memorandum in the book kept for that purpose in the Land Office at Victoria, with the particulars and in the manner therein contained.

Given under my hand and the public seal, &c.

JAMES DOUGLAS.

INDEX.

2 H

LONDON : PRINTED BY W. CLOWES AND SONS, STAMFORD STREET,
AND CHARING CROSS.

LaVergne, TN USA
27 September 2009
159152LV00003B/40/A